Structuralist Poetics

Structuralist Poetics

Structuralism, Linguistics and the Study of Literature

Jonathan Culler

Brasenose College,
Oxford

ROUTLEDGE & KEGAN PAUL
London

First published in 1975
by Routledge & Kegan Paul Ltd
Broadway House, 68-74 Carter Lane,
London EC4V 5EL
Set in 10/11pt Monotype Times New Roman
and printed in Great Britain by
W & J Mackay Limited, Chatham
© Jonathan Culler 1975
ISBN 0 7100 7964 8 (c)
ISBN 0 7100 7965 6 (p)

Contents

Preface

What is literary criticism for? What is its task and what is its value? As the number of interpretive studies increases to the point where reading what has been written on any major author becomes an unmanageable labour, such questions force themselves more insistently upon anyone concerned with the study of literature, if only because he must decide how to allocate his time. Why should he read and write criticism?

In one sense, of course, the answer is obvious: in the process of literary education criticism is both an end and a means, the natural culmination of study of an author and the instrument of literary training. But if the role criticism has been called upon to play in the educational system serves to explain the quantity of critical writings it does little to justify the activity itself. Nor does the traditional humanistic defence of literary education – that we do not learn about literature and how to read it but about the world and how to interpret it – make out much of a case for criticism as an independent mode of knowledge.

If there is a crisis in literary criticism it is no doubt because few of the many who write about literature have the desire or arguments to defend their activity. And for this the prevailing critical climate in England and America bears some responsibility. The historical scholarship which was once the dominant mode of criticism could at least, whatever its other faults, be defended as an attempt to bring supplementary and inaccessible information to bear on the text and thus to assist understanding. But the orthodoxy bequeathed by the 'New Criticism', which focuses on 'the text itself', which prizes that encounter and the resulting interpretations, is more difficult to defend. An intrinsic or immanent criticism, which in principle if not in practice requires only the text of a poem and the *Oxford English Dictionary*, offers but a more thorough and perceptive version of what every reader does for himself. Citing no special knowledge which it deems to be crucial and from which it might derive its authority, interpretive criticism seems best defended as a pedagogic tool which offers examples of intelligence for the encouragement of others. But one needs only a few such examples.

What then are we to say of criticism? What more can it do? My claim in this book is that in trying to revitalize criticism and free it from an exclusively interpretive role, in developing a programme which would justify it as a mode of knowledge and enable us to defend it with fewer reservations, we might do well to look to the work of French structuralists. Not that their criticism is itself a model which could or should be directly imported and reverently imitated, but that through a reading of their works one may derive a sense of criticism as a coherent discipline and of the goals at which it might aim. An encounter with their works, that is to say, may enable us to see what criticism might do, even when the works themselves fail to satisfy.

The type of literary study which structuralism helps one to envisage would not be primarily interpretive; it would not offer a method which, when applied to literary works, produced new and hitherto unexpected meanings. Rather than a criticism which discovers or assigns meanings, it would be a poetics which strives to define the conditions of meaning. Granting new attention to the activity of reading, it would attempt to specify how we go about making sense of texts, what are the interpretive operations on which literature itself, as an institution, is based. Just as the speaker of a language has assimilated a complex grammar which enables him to read a series of sounds or letters as a sentence with a meaning, so the reader of literature has acquired, through his encounters with literary works, implicit mastery of various semiotic conventions which enable him to read series of sentences as poems or novels endowed with shape and meaning. The study of literature, as opposed to the perusal and discussion of individual works, would become an attempt to understand the conventions which make literature possible. The major purpose of this book is to show how such a poetics emerges from structuralism, to indicate what it has already achieved, and to sketch what it might become.

My work on this topic began when, as a research student at Oxford, I undertook a doctoral dissertation on 'Structuralism: The Development of Linguistic Models and their Application to Literary Studies'. I wanted to investigate the theoretical foundations of contemporary French criticism and to determine what sort of criticism it might be fruitful to attempt. Although this book is an expanded, reorganized and rewritten version of that thesis, it still bears the traces of its dual purpose, which led to a number of choices that may require explanation. First of all, there is so much work in literary criticism which might be called 'structuralist' that to have attempted a comprehensive survey would have led to a very large and unfocused book. If one were to organize this body of criticism and direct it towards a future it seemed more important to designate and analyse a centre than to map a boundary. Since structuralism's debt to linguistics had been repeatedly emphasized and since large claims had been made in France and elsewhere about the importance of linguistic methods in literary studies, this problem was taken as the central theme. The result is an account of structuralism based, at least in the first instance, on possible relationships between literary and linguistic studies.

The first part of the book considers the scope and the limitations of linguistic methods and reviews the various ways in which structuralists have attempted to apply linguistic models to the study of literature. It discusses what linguistics can and cannot do and tries to show that the relative successes and failures of various structuralist approaches are closely dependent on their interpretations of the linguistic model.

I have not tried in this section to write a history of the influence of linguistics. It is no doubt significant that Roland Barthes's linguistic 'initiation' took place in Alexandria in 1950 through the good offices of A. J. Greimas and that he read Viggo Brøndal before he read Saussure, but the reconstruction of detailed intellectual biographies would have distracted attention from the question of how linguistic models can reorganize literary criticism and what is their validity. However, my concentration on structuralism prevents this book from serving as a full account of the uses of linguistics in literary studies, for though I believe my conclusions to be generalizable, I have not tried to consider the proposals about the use of linguistics that have been made outside of structuralist circles.

The second part of the book turns to what I take to be the best use of linguistics: as a model which suggests how a poetics should be organized. After sketching a notion of literary competence and tracing various types of convention and modes of naturalization, I try to indicate how a structuralist poetics would approach or has approached the lyric and the novel. Those readers who are interested only in the positive contributions of structuralism might wish to skip chapters 2 to 5 and to concentrate on this section.

It is here that my own orientation has its most obvious effects. Although the discussion will make clear which works of criticism I find most valuable, I have not analysed or evaluated them one by one

but used them as sources to draw upon in my discussion of literary problems. Moreover, although I hope I am not guilty of failing to understand structuralists on their own terms, I have often disagreed with those terms and have organized my discussions accordingly. To anyone who objects to my placing critical works in a perspective which their authors might reject, I can only say that I have done so in an attempt to increase their value rather than to denigrate them and that, in any case, the kind of restructuring or reinterpretation in which I am engaged is amply justified by the theories propounded by the works that I may distort.

Finally, I have not attempted to distinguish systematically in this section between what structuralists themselves have proposed, what considering literature in a structuralist perspective has led me to think, and what in the work of critics from other traditions would help to advance a structuralist poetics. Since my concern is both with what has been and with what might be, such blurring of boundaries has seemed to me justified, and I would argue only that this kind of reorganization is itself the work of structuralist poetics. As Heidegger says,

> Je grösser das Denkwerk eines Denkers ist, das sich keineswegs
> mit dem Umfang und der Anzahl seiner Schriften deckt,
> um so reicher ist das in diesem Denkwerk Ungedachte,
> d.h. jenes, was erst und allein durch dieses Denkwerk als das
> Noch-nicht-Gedachte heraufkommt.

> (The greater the thought of an author – which has nothing
> to do with the extent and number of his writings – the richer
> is the Unthought of his intellectual work: that is to say,
> what emerges first and only through his thought as
> Not-yet-thought.)

It is very much to its credit that structuralism makes it possible to see new virtues in other criticism and to organize it in new ways.

Much of the material in this book has been used in lectures on structuralism and semiology given in the Department of Linguistics, Cambridge University. I am grateful to J. L. M. Trim, Director of the Department, for inviting me to lecture on these problems and to my listeners who, by their objections, comments or questions, helped me to clarify and revise. I should also like to thank Monsieur J. Bosquet of the Ecole normale supérieure, Dr Roger Fowler of the University of East Anglia, Professor John Holloway of Cambridge University, Professor Frank Kermode of University College, London, Dr David Robey of Oxford University and the organizers of the Gregynog

conference on contemporary criticism, for inviting me to discuss these
matters with interested audiences. I am much indebted to all those
who have read and commented on portions of the manuscript at
various stages: Jean-Marie Benoist, Professor A. Dwight Culler,
Professor Alison Fairlie, Dr Veronica Forrest-Thomson, Alan
Jackson, Professor Frank Kermode, Colin MacCabe, Dr Philip
Pettit, and Dr John Rutherford. I am especially grateful to the
examiners of my Oxford D.Phil. thesis, Professor John Weightman
and Dr Richard Sayce, for their pertinent criticisms and suggestions
and to Professor Stephen Ullmann, who generously agreed to super-
vise research on what must have seemed a rather questionable topic
and who has been a constant source of information, advice and
friendship.

Selwyn College, Cambridge
June 1973

Acknowledgments

Fragments of chapter 1 first appeared in *Structuralism: An Introduction*, ed. David Robey (Oxford University Press, 1973). An earlier version of portions of chapter 3 was published in *Language and Style* 5:1 (winter 1971). A version of chapter 4 appeared in *Centrum* 1:1 (1973). A version of chapter 10 appeared in *New Literary History* 4:3 (spring 1973). I am grateful to the editors and publishers for permission to reprint.

Ezra Pound's 'Papyrus' and 'In a Station of the Metro' are taken from Ezra Pound, *Personae*, Copyright 1926 by Ezra Pound. Reprinted by permission of New Directions Publishing Corporation, New York. Reprinted from the *Collected Shorter Poems* by permission of Faber & Faber. Tristan Tzara's 'Si les mots n'étaient que signes' is reprinted by permission of Fata Morgana.

All translations are my own. Full information concerning all references included in the text will be found in the bibliography.

PART ONE

Structuralism and Linguistic Models

CHAPTER 1

The Linguistic Foundation

Tout dit dans l'infini quelque chose à quelqu'un.*
HUGO

One cannot define structuralism by examining how the word has been used; that would lead only to despair. It may be, of course, that the term has outlived its usefulness. To call oneself a structuralist was always a polemical gesture, a way of attracting attention and associating oneself with others whose work was of moment, and to study such gestures with the seriousness and attention of scholarship would prove only that the common features of everything that has been called 'structuralist' are extremely common indeed. This is the conclusion one draws, for example, from Jean Piaget's *Le Structuralisme*, which shows that mathematics, logic, physics, biology and all the social sciences have long been concerned with structure and thus were practising 'structuralism' before the coming of Lévi-Strauss. But this use of the term leaves unexplained one important fact: why, in this case, did French structuralism seem new and exciting? Even if it be put down as just another Paris fashion, that alone argues some striking and differentiating qualities and provides *prima facie* reasons for assuming that there is something, somewhere, distinctively structuralist. So rather than reject the term as hopelessly vague one should determine what meaning it must be given if it is to play a role in coherent discourse, as the name of a particular intellectual movement centred around the work of a few major figures, among whom the chief, in the field of literary studies, is Roland Barthes.

Barthes himself once defined structuralism, 'in its most specialized and consequently most relevant version', as a mode of analysis of cultural artefacts which originates in the methods of contemporary linguistics ('Science versus literature', p. 897). This view can be

* Everything in the infinite says something to someone.

supported both from structuralist texts, such as Lévi-Strauss's pioneering article, 'L'analyse structurale en linguistique et en anthropologie',[1] which argued that by following the linguist's example the anthropologist might reproduce in his own discipline the 'phonological revolution', and from the work of structuralism's most serious and able opponents. To attack structuralism, Paul Ricoeur claims, one must focus discussion on its linguistic foundations (*Le Conflit des interprétations*, p. 80). Linguistics is not simply a stimulus and source of inspiration but a methodological model which unifies the otherwise diverse projects of structuralists. Signification, writes Barthes, has been my essential preoccupation; 'I have been engaged in a series of structural analyses which all aim at defining a number of non-linguistic "languages" ' (*Essais critiques*, p. 155). The continuity of his work comes from the attempt to analyse various practices as languages.

Moreover, and this is not the least of its virtues, this definition poses several obvious questions: why should the methods of contemporary linguistics be relevant to the analysis of other social and cultural phenomena? what methods are relevant? what are the effects of using linguistics as a model? what kind of results does it permit one to attain? To discuss structuralism one must define both the promise and the limitations of this use of linguistics – especially the latter, for, as Barthes says, the desire to ascertain the limits of the linguistic model is not a form of prudence but a recognition of 'le lieu central de la recherche'. Despite its centrality, however, structuralists have offered no satisfactory account of the uses of linguistics, and that is one of the needs which this work attempts to fulfil.

The notion that linguistics might be useful in studying other cultural phenomena is based on two fundamental insights: first, that social and cultural phenomena are not simply material objects or events but objects or events with meaning, and hence signs; and second, that they do not have essences but are defined by a network of relations, both internal and external. Stress may fall on one or the other of these propositions – it would be in these terms, for example, that one might try to distinguish semiology and structuralism – but in fact the two are inseparable, for in studying signs one must investigate the system of relations that enables meaning to be produced and, reciprocally, one can only determine what are the pertinent relations among items by considering them as signs.

Structuralism is thus based, in the first instance, on the realization that if human actions or productions have a meaning there must be an underlying system of distinctions and conventions which makes this meaning possible. Confronted with a marriage ceremony or a game of football, for example, an observer from a culture where these did not exist could present an objective description of the actions which took place, but he would be unable to grasp their meaning and so would not be treating them as social or cultural phenomena. The actions are meaningful only with respect to a set of institutional conventions. Wherever there are two posts one can kick a ball between them but one can score a goal only within a certain institutionalized framework. As Lévi-Strauss says in his 'Introduction à l'oeuvre de Marcel Mauss', 'particular actions of individuals are never symbolic in themselves; they are the elements out of which is constructed a symbolic system, which must be collective' (p. xvi). The cultural meaning of any particular act or object is determined by a whole system of constitutive rules: rules which do not regulate behaviour so much as create the possibility of particular forms of behaviour. The rules of English enable sequences of sound to have meaning; they make it possible to utter grammatical or ungrammatical sentences. And analogously, various social rules make it possible to marry, to score a goal, to write a poem, to be impolite. It is in this sense that a culture is composed of a set of symbolic systems.

When one takes as object of study not physical phenomena, but artefacts or events with meaning, the defining qualities of the phenomena become the features which distinguish them one from another and enable them to bear meaning within the symbolic system from which they derive. The object is itself structured and is defined by its place in the structure of the system, whence the tendency to speak of 'structuralism'.

But why should linguistics, the study of one particular and rather distinctive system, be thought to provide methods for investigating any symbolic system? Ferdinand de Saussure considered this problem when he came to postulate a science of 'semiology', a general science of signs, which did not yet exist but whose place, as he said, was assured in advance. If one considers rites and customs as signs they will appear in a new light, and linguistics, he argued, should be the source of illumination, 'le patron général de toute sémiologie'. In the case of non-linguistic signs there is always a danger that their meanings will seem natural; one must view them with a certain detachment to see that their meanings are in fact the products of a culture, the result of shared assumptions and conventions. But in the case of linguistic signs the conventional or 'arbitrary' basis is obvious, and therefore by taking linguistics as a model one may avoid the familiar mistake of assuming that signs which appear natural to those who use them have an intrinsic meaning and require no explanation. Linguistics, designed to study the system of rules underlying speech, will by its very nature compel the analyst to attend to the conventional basis of the phenomena he is studying (*Cours de linguistique générale*, pp. 33–5 and 100–1).

It would not be wrong to suggest that structuralism and semiology are identical. The existence of the two terms is in part due to historical accident, as if each discipline had first drawn certain concepts and methods from structural linguistics, thereby becoming a mode of structural analysis, and only then had realized that it had become or was fast becoming a branch of that semiology which Saussure had envisaged. Thus, Lévi-Strauss, fifteen years after his article on structural analysis in linguistics and anthropology had established his brand of structuralism, took the occasion of his elevation to a chair at the Collège de France to define anthropology as 'the bona-fide occupant of the domain of semiology' and to pay homage to Saussure's anticipation of his conclusions (*Leçon inaugurale*, pp. 14–15). Since I am not writing a history of structuralism, such shifts in terminology are of little moment, and since I am concerned with the function and efficacy of linguistic models there is no need to distinguish between the headings under which they might have been adopted. If, then, I choose to speak of 'structuralism' rather than 'semiology' it is not because I am distinguishing one theory from another so much as because 'structuralism' designates the work of a restricted group of French theorists and practitioners whereas 'semiology' might refer to any work which studies signs.

To claim that cultural systems may with profit be treated as 'languages' is to suggest that one will understand them better if one discusses them in terms provided by linguistics and analyses them according to procedures used by linguists. In fact, the range of concepts and methods which structuralists have found useful is fairly restricted and only some half-dozen linguists could qualify as seminal influences. The first, of course, is Ferdinand de Saussure, who waded into the heterogeneous mass of linguistic phenomena and, recognizing that progress would be possible only if one isolated a suitable object for study, distinguished between speech acts (*la parole*) and the system of a language (*la langue*). The latter is the proper object of linguistics. Following Saussure's example and concentrating on the system which underlies speech sounds, members of the Prague linguistic circle – particularly Jakobson and Trubetzkoy – effected what Lévi-Strauss called the 'phonological revolution' and provided what was to later structuralists the clearest model of linguistic method. Distinguishing between the study of actual speech sounds (phonetics) and the investigation of those aspects of sound that are functional in a particular language (phonology), Trubetzkoy argued that 'phonology should investigate which phonic differences are linked, in the language under consideration, with differences of meaning, how these differentiating elements or *marks* are related to one another, and according to what rules they combine to form words and phrases' (*Principes de phonologie*, pp. 11–12). Phonology was important for structuralists because it showed the systematic nature of the most familiar phenomena, distinguished between the system and its realization and concentrated not on the substantive characteristics of individual phenomena but on abstract differential features which could be defined in relational terms.

Hjelmslev and the Copenhagen school emphasized even more strongly the formal nature of linguistic systems: in principle the description of a language need make reference neither to the phonic nor graphic substance in which its elements may be realized. But Hjelmslev's influence may have been due more to his insistence that his 'glossematics' provided a theoretical framework which all humanistic disciplines should adopt if they wished to become scientific. '*A priori* it would seem to be a generally valid thesis that for every *process* there is a corresponding *system*, by which the process can be analysed and described by means of a limited number of premises' (*Prolegomena to a Theory of Language*, p. 9). This thesis became one of the axioms of structuralist method.

Emile Benveniste was another influential figure. Although his *Problèmes de linguistique générale* was not published until 1966, the articles which it contains were already known as incisive discussions of a wide range of linguistic topics. Not only did he provide structuralists with lucid accounts of the sign and of levels and relations in linguistics; his analyses of a number of sub-systems – personal pronouns and verb tenses – were directly adopted by structuralists in their discussions of literature.

Finally, one should say a word about Noam Chomsky. Although a few structuralists have in their later work adopted some of his terms, generative grammar plays no role in the development of structuralism. What it does offer, and what gives it its importance in this discussion, is a methodological statement of exemplary clarity. That is to say, Chomsky's theory of language enables us to see what structural linguists were actually doing, what their practice implied, and how their accounts of their discipline were misleading or insufficient. Although within linguistics itself the differences between Chomsky's approach and that of his predecessors are extremely important, at the level of generality which concerns those looking to linguistics for models to apply elsewhere, Chomsky's work can be taken as an explicit statement of the programme implicit in linguistics as a discipline but not hitherto adequately or coherently expressed. References to Chomsky in the following discussion are not therefore meant to indicate points on which he influenced structuralists but only to clarify basic concepts and analytical procedures which comprise the 'linguistic model' that structuralists have adopted.

Langue, parole

The basic distinction on which modern linguistics rests, and which is equally crucial to the structuralist enterprise in other fields, is Saussure's isolation of *langue* from *parole*. The former is a system, an institution, a set of interpersonal rules and norms, while the latter comprises the actual manifestations of the system in speech and writing. It is, of course, easy to confuse the system with its manifestations, to think of English as the set of English utterances. But to learn English is not to memorize a set of utterances; it is to master a system of rules and norms which make it possible to produce and understand utterances. To know English is to have assimilated the system of the language. And the linguist's task is not to study utterances for their own sake; they are of interest to him only in so far as they provide evidence about the nature of the underlying system, the English language.

Within linguistics itself there are disagreements about what precisely belongs to *langue* and what to *parole*: whether, for example, an account of the linguistic system should specify the acoustic and articulatory features that distinguish one phoneme from another (/p/ is 'voiceless' and /b/ 'voiced'), or whether such features as 'voiced' and 'voiceless' should be thought of as the manifestations in *parole* of what, in *la langue* itself, is a purely formal and abstract distinction. Such debates need not concern the structuralist, except in so far as they indicate that structure can be defined at various levels of abstraction.[2] What does concern him is a pair of distinctions which the differentiation of *langue* from *parole* is designed to cover: between rule and behaviour and between the functional and the non-functional.

The distinction between rule and behaviour is crucial to any study concerned with the production or communication of meaning. In investigating physical events one may formulate laws which are nothing other than direct summaries of behaviour, but in the case of social and cultural phenomena the rule is always at some distance from actual behaviour and that gap is a space of potential meaning. The instituting of the simplest rule, such as 'members of this club will not step on cracks in the pavement', may in some cases determine behaviour but indubitably determines meaning: the placing of one's feet on the pavement, which formerly had no meaning, now signifies either compliance with or deviation from the rule and hence an attitude towards the club and its authority. In social and cultural systems behaviour may deviate frequently and considerably from the norm without impugning the existence of the norm. Many promises are in fact broken, but there still exists a rule in the system of moral concepts that promises should be kept; though of course if one never kept any promises doubts might arise as to whether one understood the institution of promising and had assimilated its rules.

In linguistics the distinction between rule and behaviour is most conveniently expressed by Chomsky's terms *competence* and *performance*, which are related, respectively, to *langue* and *parole*. Actual behaviour is not a direct reflection of competence for a variety of reasons. The English language is not exhausted by its manifestations. It contains potential sentences which have never been uttered but to which it would assign meaning and grammatical structure; someone who has learned English possesses, in his ability to understand sentences that he will never encounter, a competence that outstrips his performance. Moreover, performance may deviate from competence: one may, either accidentally as one's thought changes or deliberately for special effects, utter sentences whose ungrammaticality one would recognize if they were played back. Competence is reflected in the judgment passed on the utterance or in the fact that the rule violated is partly responsible for the effect achieved.

The description of *langue* or competence is the explicit representation, by a system of rules or norms, of the implicit knowledge possessed by those who successfully operate within the system. They need not be aware of these rules and indeed in most cases will not be, for true mastery or competence generally involves an intuitive grasp of the rules which permits action or understanding without explicit reflection. But this does not make the rules any less real: mastery implies systematic ability. The experienced forester cannot explain how he distinguishes, from a distance, different species of trees, but in so far as it is not haphazard guessing his ability could in principle be defined as a programme employing a restricted number of functional variables.

Though the rules of *la langue* may be unconscious they have empirical correlates: in the case of language they are manifested in the speaker's ability to understand utterances, to recognize grammatically well-formed or deviant sentences, to detect ambiguity, to perceive meaning relations among sentences, etc. The linguist attempts to construct a system of rules that would account for this knowledge by formally reproducing it. Thus – and this is the important point – utterances themselves offer the linguist little that he can use. That a number of given sentences were uttered is of no significance. He needs to know, in addition, what they mean to speakers of the language, whether they are well formed, whether they are ambiguous and if so in what ways, what changes would alter their meaning or render them ungrammatical. The competence that the linguist investigates is not behaviour itself so much as knowledge which bears upon that behaviour. If other disciplines are to proceed in an analogous way they must identify a set of facts to be explained – isolate, that is to say, some aspects of the knowledge in question – and then determine what rules or conventions must be postulated to account for them.

The second fundamental criterion involved in the distinction between *langue* and *parole* is the opposition between the functional and the non-functional. If speakers of different ages, sexes and regions utter the sentence *The cat is on the mat*, the actual physical sounds produced will vary considerably, but those variations will be non-functional within the linguistic system of English in that they do not alter the sentence. The utterances, however different in sound, are free variations of a single English sentence. If, however, one speaker alters the sound in a particular way and says *The hat is on the mat*, the difference between /k/ and /h/ is functional in that it produces a different sentence with a different meaning. An account of the phonological system of a language must specify what distinctions are functional in that they are used in the language to differentiate signs.

This aspect of the distinction between *langue* and *parole* is relevant to any discipline concerned with the social use of material objects, for in such cases one must distinguish between the material objects themselves and the system of functional distinctive features which determine class membership and make meaning possible. Trubetzkoy cites the ethnological study of clothing as a project analogous to the description of a phonological system (*Principes de phonologie*, p. 19). Many of the features of physical garments which would be of considerable importance to the wearer are of no interest to the ethnologist, who is concerned only with those features that carry a social significance. Length of skirts might be an important differential feature in the fashion system of a culture while the material from which they were made was not. The contrast between bright and dark colours might carry a general social meaning while the difference between dark blue and brown did not. The ethnologist, isolating those distinctions by which garments become signs, is attempting to reconstruct the system of features and norms which members of that society have assimilated.

Relations

In separating the functional from the non-functional in order to reconstruct the underlying system, one is interested not so much in the properties of individual objects or actions as in the differences between them which the system employs and endows with significance. Whence comes the second fundamental principle of linguistics: that *la langue* is a system of relations and oppositions whose elements must be defined in formal, differential terms. For Lévi-Strauss one of the most important lessons of the 'phonological revolution' was its refusal to treat terms as independent entities and its concentration on relations among terms (*Anthropologie structurale*, p. 40). Saussure had been even more categorical: 'dans la langue il n'y a que des différences *sans termes positifs*' (*Cours*, p. 166). Units are not positive entities but the nodes of a series of differences, just as a mathematical point has no content but is defined by its relations to other points.

Thus, for Saussure the identity of two instances of a linguistic unit (two utterances of the same phoneme or morpheme) was not an identity of substance but of form only. This is one of his most important and influential principles, though it is also among the hardest to grasp. By way of illustration he notes that we feel the 8.25 p.m. Geneva-to-Paris Express to be the same train each day, though the locomotive, coaches, and personnel may be different. This is because the 8.25 train is not a substance but a form, defined by its relations to other trains. It remains the 8.25 even though it leave twenty minutes late, so long as its difference from the 7.25 and the 9.25 is preserved. Although we may be unable to conceive of the train except in its physical manifestations, its identity as a social and psychological fact is independent of those manifestations (ibid., p. 151). Similarly, to take a case from the system of writing, one may write the letter *t* in numerous ways so long as one preserves its differential value. There is no positive substance which defines it; the principal requirement is that it be kept distinct from the other letters with which it might be confused, such as *l, f, b, i, k*.

The notion of relational identity is crucial to the semiotic or structural analysis of all kinds of social and cultural phenomena, because in formulating the rules of the system one must identify the units on which the rules operate and thus must discover when two objects or actions count as instances of the same unit. It is crucial also because it constitutes a break with the notion of historical or evolutionary identity. The locomotive and coaches which on a particular day make up the 8.25 Geneva-to-Paris Express might have a few hours earlier formed the 4.50 Berne-Geneva Express, but that historical and material identity is not pertinent to the system of trains: the 8.25 has the same place in the system whatever the historical provenance of its components. In the case of language one may say with Saussure that, when trying to reconstruct the underlying system, the relevant relations are those which are functional in the system as it operates at a given time. The relations between individual units and their historical antecedents are irrelevant in that they do not define the units as elements of the system. The *synchronic* study of language is an attempt to reconstruct the system as a functional whole, to determine, shall we say, what is involved in knowing English at any given time; whereas the *diachronic* study of language is an attempt to trace the historical evolution of its elements through various stages. The two must be kept separate lest the diachronic point of view falsify one's synchronic description. For example, historically the French noun *pas* (step) and the negative adverb *pas* derive from a single source, but that relationship has no function in modern French, where they are distinct words that behave in different ways. To try to incorporate the historical identity into one's grammar would be to falsify the relational identity and hence the value that each of the words has in the language as now spoken. Language is a system of interrelated items and the value and identity of these items is defined by their place in the system rather than by their history.

If language is a system of relations, what are these relations? Consider the word *bed*. The identity of its various phonetic manifestations depends, first of all, on the difference between its phonological structure and those of *bread, bled, bend, abed, deb*. Moreover, the phonemes which compose it are themselves sets of differential features: the vowel may be uttered in various ways so long as it is distinguished from that of *bad, bud, bid, bade*; and the consonants must be differentiated from those of *bet, beg, bell, fed, led, red, wed*, etc. At another level, *bed* is defined by its relations to other words: those which contrast with it, in that they could replace it in various contexts (*table, chair, floor, ground*, etc.), and those with which it can combine in a sequence (*the, a, soft, is, low, occupied*, etc.). Finally, it is related to higher-level constituents: it can serve as the head of a noun phrase, as the subject or object of a sentence.

These relations are of two sorts. As Benveniste says, 'the relations between elements of the same level are *distributional*; those between elements of different levels are *integrative*' (*Problèmes de linguistique générale*, p. 124). The latter provide the most important criteria for defining linguistic units. Phonological distinctive features are identified by their ability to create and differentiate phonemes, which are the units immediately above them in the scale. Phonemes are recognized by virtue of their role as constituents of morphemes; and morphemes are distinguished according to their ability to enter and complete higher-level grammatical constructions. Benveniste is therefore led to define the form of a unit as its composition in terms of lower-level constituents and the *sens* or meaning of a unit as its capacity to integrate a unit of a higher level. The sentence is the maximal unit, whose form is its constituent structure. The 'meaning' of those constituents is the contribution they make to the sentence – their role as its constituents – and their form in turn is their own constituent structure. Although there is no reason to suppose that other systems will correspond to language in the number and nature of their levels, structural analysis does assume that it will be possible to break down larger units into their constituents until one eventually reaches a level of minimal functional distinctions. Certainly the notion that units of one level are to be recognized by their integrative capacity and that this capacity is their *sens* has an intuitive validity in literary criticism, where the meaning of a detail is its contribution to a larger pattern.

In order to make explicit the integrative capacity of an element one must define its relations with other items of the same level. These distributional relations are of two kinds. *Syntagmatic* relations bear on the possibility of combination: two items may be in a relation of reciprocal or non-reciprocal implication, compatibility or incompatibility. *Paradigmatic* relations, which determine the possibility of substitution, are especially important in the analysis of a system. The meaning of an item depends on the differences between it and other items which might have filled the same slot in a given sequence. To use Saussure's example, although in speech the French *mouton* and the English *sheep* may be used with the same signification (*There's a sheep* being synonymous with *Voilà un mouton*), the words have different values in their respective linguistic systems in that *sheep* contrasts with *mutton* while *mouton* is not defined by a corresponding contrast. The analysis of any system will require one to specify paradigmatic relations (functional contrasts) and syntagmatic relations (possibilities of combination).

Despite the importance of relations in the analysis of a linguistic system a certain scepticism is in order concerning the frequent claim, first made by Saussure, that language is a system in which 'tout se tient': in which everything is inextricably related to everything else. Hjelmslev admits that 'the famous maxim, according to which everything in the system of a language is related, has often been applied in too rigid, mechanical and absolute a fashion' (*Essais linguistiques*, p. 114). But it is an absolute maxim; and, as Oswald Ducrot observes, so absolute an affirmation of the systematic character of language may conceal a despair at being unable to discover the system ('Le structuralisme en linguistique', p. 59). When structuralists like Lévi-Strauss, attracted by the rigour of Saussure's principle, propose as an elementary methodological requirement that a structural analysis reveal a system of 'elements such that modification of any one entails modification of all the others', they are setting their sights on a goal seldom achieved in linguistics itself.[3] If the word *mutton* were dropped from English certain local modifications would ensue: the value of *sheep* would change radically; *beef, pork, veal,* etc. would become slightly more anomalous with the disappearance of one member of their paradigm class; sentences like *The sheep is too hot to eat* would become ambiguous, given the new value of *sheep*; but vast areas of the language would not be affected in discernible ways. The example of linguistics need not lead one to expect the complete solidarity of every system. Relations are important for what they can explain: meaningful contrasts and permitted or forbidden combinations.

Indeed, the relations that are most important in structural analysis are the simplest: binary oppositions. Whatever else the linguistic model may have done, it has undoubtedly encouraged structuralists to think in binary terms, to look for functional oppositions in whatever material they are studying.

Contrasts, of course, may be either discrete or continuous: if I mutter that I bought a big fish in the market you may be uncertain whether I said *fish* or *dish* but you know it was one or the other and not something in between; I may, however, lengthen the vowel of *big* on a continuous scale in order to stress the size of my acquisition. The place of continuous phenomena in linguistics has been a much-disputed question, but the tendency has been to relegate them to a minor place if not to exclude them from *la langue* altogether. 'If we find continuous-scale contrasts in the vicinity of what we are sure is language', observes Hockett, 'we exclude them from language.'[4] Whatever the rights of the linguistic case, for the semiologist or structuralist concerned with the social use of material phenomena the reduction of the continuous to the discrete is a methodological step of the first importance. Interpretation is always carried out in discrete terms: the vowel of *big* either has been lengthened in a significant way or it has not; width is a continuous phenomenon, but if a suit is fashionable because of the width of its lapels then it is because a discrete distinction between the wide and the narrow bears significance. Time is infinitely subdividable, but to tell the time is to give it a discrete interpretation. Moreover, the psychological reality of discrete categories seems incontestable: although everyone knows that the spectrum of colours is a continuum, within a culture people tend to regard individual colours as natural classes.

When reducing the continuous to the discrete, one calls upon binary oppositions as the elementary devices for establishing distinctive classes. Phonological analysis, which for many structuralists served as the model of linguistics itself, was based on a reduction of the sound continuum to distinctive features, each of which 'involves a choice between two terms of an opposition that displays a specific differential property, diverging from the properties of all other oppositions.' Defending the binary principle, Jakobson and Halle argue that it is methodologically preferable in that it can express any of the relations that could be handled in other terms and leads to a simplification of both framework and description; but they also suggest that binary oppositions are inherent in languages, both as the first operations that a child learns to perform and as the most 'natural' and economical code (*Fundamentals of Language*, pp. 4 and 47–9). Structuralists have generally followed Jakobson and taken the binary opposition as a fundamental operation of the human mind basic to the production of meaning: 'this elementary logic which is the smallest common denominator of all thought.'[5] But whether it is a principle of language itself or only an optimal analytical device makes little difference. Its methodological primacy would alone indicate its place as a fundamental operation of human thought and thus of human semiotic systems. The structuralist might simply accept Householder's conclusion that there is little reason to oppose a wholly binary analysis, provided that some provision can be made for distinguishing natural privative oppositions from purely theoretical constructs (*Linguistic Speculations*, p. 167).

The advantage of binarism, but also its principal danger, lies in the fact that it permits one to classify anything. Given two items one can always find some respect in which they differ and hence place them in a relation of binary opposition. Lévi-Strauss observes that one of the major problems that arise in using binary oppositions is that the simplification achieved by setting two items in opposition to one another results in complications on another plane because the distinctive features on which various oppositions turn will be qualitatively very different. If one opposes A to B and X to Y, the two cases become similar because each involves the presence and absence of a given feature, but this similarity is deceptive in that the features in question may be of very different kinds. It is possible, however, Lévi-Strauss continues, 'that rather than a methodological difficulty we have here a limit inherent in the nature of certain intellectual operations, whose weakness as well as whose strength is that they can be logical while remaining firmly rooted in the qualitative' (*La Pensée sauvage*, p. 89).

Certainly the strength and weakness are inseparable. Binary oppositions can be used to order the most heterogeneous elements, and this is precisely why binarism is so pervasive in literature: when two things are set in opposition to one another the reader is forced to explore qualitative similarities and differences, to make a connection so as to derive meaning from the disjunction. But the very flexibility and power of binarism depends on the fact that what it organizes are qualitative distinctions, and if those distinctions are irrelevant to the matter in hand, then binary oppositions can be very misleading, precisely because they present factitious organization. The moral is quite simple: one must resist the temptation to use binary oppositions merely to devise elegant structures. If A is opposed to B and X is opposed to Y then one could, in seeking further unification, set these oppositions together in a four-term homology and say that A is to B as X is to Y (in that the relation is one of opposition in both cases). But the formal symmetry of such homologies does not guarantee that they are in any way pertinent: if A were 'black' and B 'white', X 'male' and Y 'female' then the homology of A:B:X:Y might be wholly factitious and irrelevant to whatever system one was studying. The homology itself is, in binary logic, a possible extrapolation from the pair of oppositions but its value cannot be divorced from that of the qualitative oppositional features which it puts into relation. The relevant structures are those which enable elements to function as signs.

Signs

If, as Saussure and others have claimed, linguistic methods and concepts can be used in analysing other systems of signs, an obvious preliminary question is what constitutes a sign and whether different kinds of signs must not in fact be studied in different ways. Various typologies of signs have been proposed, the most elaborate by C. S. Peirce, but among the many and delicate categories three fundamental classes stand out as requiring different approaches: the icon, the index, and the sign proper. All signs consist of a *signifiant* and a *signifié*, which are, roughly speaking, form and meaning; but the relations between *signifiant* and *signifié* are different in these three types of signs. The icon involves actual resemblance between *signifiant* and *signifié*: a portrait signifies the person of whom it is a portrait not by arbitrary convention only but by resemblance. In an index the relation between the two is causal: smoke means fire in so far as fire is its cause; clouds mean rain if they are the sort of clouds that produce rain. In the sign proper as Saussure understood it the relationship between signifier and signified is arbitrary or conventional: *arbre* means 'tree' not by natural resemblance or causal connection but by virtue of a law.

Icons differ markedly from other signs. Although they have some cultural and conventional basis – some primitive peoples, it is said, do not recognize themselves or others in photographs and hence would not read them as icons – this is difficult to establish or define. Study of the way in which a drawing of a horse represents a horse is perhaps more properly the concern of a philosophical theory of representation than of a linguistically based semiology.

Indices are, from the semiologist's point of view, more worrying. If he places them within his domain he risks taking all human knowledge for his province, for all the sciences which attempt to establish causal relations among phenomena could be seen as studies of indices. Medicine, for example, tries among other things to relate diseases to symptoms and thus investigates symptoms as indices. Meteorology studies and reconstructs a system in order to relate atmospheric conditions to their causes and consequences and thus to read them as signs. Economics investigates the system of forces which produce surface phenomena that become, in turn, indices of economic conditions and trends. A whole range of disciplines attempts to decipher the natural or the human world; the methods of these disciplines are different and there is no reason to think that they would gain substantially by being brought under the banner of an imperialistic semiology.

On the other hand, one cannot exclude indices entirely from the domain of structural or semiological analysis, for in the first place any index may become a conventional sign. Slanted eyes are an index of Oriental extraction in that the relation is causal, but as soon as this connection is made by a society an actor may use this index as a conventional sign. Indeed, most motivated signs, where there is a connection between signifier and signified, may be thought of as indices that have been conventionalized by a society. In one sense a Rolls-Royce is an index of wealth in that one must be wealthy to purchase one, but it has been made a conventional sign of wealth by social usage. Its meaning is mythic as well as causal.[6] Second, within domains of particular sciences the meanings of indices change with the configurations of knowledge. Medical symptoms are read differently from one period to the next and there are changes in what is recognized as a symptom. It thus becomes possible for the semiologist or structuralist to study the 'regard médical' of various periods: the conventions which determine the scientific discourse of a period and permit indices to be read.[7] The semiologist is interested not in the indices themselves nor in the 'real' causal relation between index and meaning but in the reading of indices within a system of conventions, whether it be that of a science, of a popular culture, or of literature.

This principle has important implications. In his inaugural lecture at the Collège de France Lévi-Strauss declared that anthropology was a branch of semiology in that the phenomena it studies are signs: a stone axe, 'for the observer capable of understanding its use, stands for the different tool which another society would employ for the same purpose' (*Leçon inaugurale*, p. 16). This is somewhat suspect.

If the axe is related to a steel saw or to a gun it may become the index of a certain cultural level (the tribe in question have no metal technology) and the anthropologist may interpret it as such, but he is not involved in semiological investigation. If he wished to study the axe as sign he would be obliged to consider its meaning for members of the tribe. Alternatively, he could investigate how anthropologists read indices of this sort (what conventions govern anthropological discourse). In the latter two cases he would be working from the judgments and interpretations of natives or anthropologists and attempting to reconstruct the system or competence underlying these judgments, but in the former case he is placing the axe in a causal chain and treating it as an index only.

If the semiologist studies indices he will embroil himself in the investigation of causal relationships which are the province of a host of distinct sciences. His own domain is, as Saussure insisted, that of conventional signs, where there is no intrinsic or 'natural' reason why a particular *signifiant* and *signifié* should be linked. In the absence of intrinsic one-to-one connections, he cannot attempt to explain individual signs in piecemeal fashion but must account for them by revealing the internally coherent system from which they derive. There is no inevitable connection between the phonological sequence *relate* and the concept associated with it, but within the morphological system of English *relate* is to *relation* as *dictate* to *dictation*, *narrate* to *narration*, etc. Precisely because the individual signs are un-motivated, the linguist must attempt to reconstruct the system, which alone provides motivation.

The sign is the union of a *signifiant* and a *signifié*, both of which are forms rather than substances. The *signifiant* is quite easily defined as a form which has a meaning: not phonic or graphic substance itself but those relational features, functional in the system in question, by which it becomes a component of the sign. But the *signifié* is more elusive. The problem is not 'what is meaning?' – if it were, one could not, in any case, stay for an answer. The difficulty is one that arises because linguists have different ways of talking about *signifiés*. In speaking of the sign they may use formulae like Saussure's – 'the combination of a concept and an acoustic image' or 'recto and verso of a sheet of paper' – which suggest that for every *signifiant* there is a particular positive concept hidden behind it. When they discuss the meanings of words and sentences, however, linguists generally do not speak in this way: they may talk of the various uses of a word, its range of potential meanings, the paraphrasable content of a sentence, its potential force as an utterance, without implying that for each phonological sequence there is a definable concept attached to it, a meaning invisibly inscribed on it. What then is the semiologist to do in analysing other systems of signs? What sort of *signifié* is he looking for?

In his *Introduction à la sémiologie* Georges Mounin suggests that the semiologist should in fact restrict his investigations to cases where signifiers have clearly defined concepts firmly attached to them by a communicative code. Distinguishing between interpreting and decoding, he argues that one interprets indices and decodes signs: 'the decoding is univocal for all recipients in possession of the code of communication' (p. 14). His paradigm case is something like Morse code or traffic signs, where one can look up a signifier in a code book and discover its signified. But such an approach is very ill-suited to the study of natural languages or other complex systems: one does not take a thought and apply an algorithm to encode it; listeners interpret sentences rather than decode them. Mounin's view seems to rest on a very questionable theory of language and stands condemned by the conclusions that it forces up on him: literature is not a system of signs because one cannot speak of encoding and decoding by fixed codes.

This approach to the *signifié*, of which Mounin is only the extreme representative, derives from what Jacques Derrida calls a 'metaphysics of presence' which longs for a truth behind every sign: a moment of original plenitude when form and meaning were simultaneously present to consciousness and not to be distinguished. Though dissociation is a fact of our post-lapsarian state, it is assumed that we should still try to pass through the signifier to the meaning that is the truth and origin of the sign and of which the signifier is but the visible mark, the outer shell. Even if this view seems appropriate to speech, its inadequacy becomes obvious as soon as we reflect upon writing, and especially literature, where an organized surface of signifiers insistently promises meaning but where the notion of a full and determinate original meaning that the text 'expresses' is highly problematic. Poetry offers the best example of a series of signifiers whose signified is an empty but circumscribed space that can be filled in various ways; but the same is true of ordinary language, though this may be obscured by the fact that the sign itself serves as a name for the *signifié*. The sign *dog* has a signified which we may call the concept 'dog', but that is less of a positive determination than we might wish: its content is difficult to specify since it has a range of applications.

There is, as Peirce says, a fundamental incompleteness to the sign, in that there must always be 'some explanation or argument' which enables the sign to be used. The *signifié* cannot be grasped directly but requires an 'interpretant' in the form of another sign (for 'dog' the interpretant may be a sign like *canine*, or a paraphrase, or a specification of relations with other signifieds such as 'cat', 'wolf', etc.). 'The sign and the explanation together make up another sign, and since the explanation will be a sign, it will probably require an additional explanation' (*Collected Papers*, II, pp. 136–7). There is, as Derrida would say, no full meaning but only *différance* (differences, deferment): the signified can be grasped only as the effect of an interpretive or productive process in which interpretants are adduced to delimit it. This process is what Peirce calls 'development'. It is a familiar fact that one can know the meaning of a word without being able to state that meaning, and the evidence for this knowledge is one's ability to develop the sign; to go on, for example, to say what it does *not* mean. 'The grammar of the word "knows" is evidently closely related to that of "can", "is able to". But also closely related to that of "understands". ("Mastery" of a technique).'[8]

In any system that is more complex than a code – in any system which can produce meaning instead of merely refer to meanings that already exist – there are two ways of thinking of the *signifiant* and *signifié*. One may accept the primacy of the *signifiant*, as the form which is given, and take the *signifié* as that which can be developed from it but only expressed by other signs. Or one may start with the *signifié* by taking any signs which circumscribe or designate effects of meaning as the developments of a *signifié* for which one must find the *signifiant* and the relevant set of conventions. Whether one identify the signified as the meaning promised by a signifier or as an effect whose signifier must be sought, the crucial point is not to limit the study of signs to code-like situations where already defined meanings are univocally related to signifiers. Such an approach, 'would lead to a normative view of the signifying function which would be unable to deal with the multiplicity of signifying practices even if it did not make them pathological cases to be repressed' (Kristeva, *Le Langage, cet inconnu*, p. 26).

Discovery procedures

The attempt to treat other cultural systems as languages might depend simply on the assumption that these basic concepts of *langue* and *parole*, of relations and oppositions, of *signifiant* and *signifié*, could be used with profit in discussing other phenomena. But it might also depend on the stronger claim that linguistics provides a procedure, a method of analysis, which can be applied with success elsewhere. When Barthes speaks of structuralism as 'essentially an *activity*, that is to say the ordered sequence of a certain number of mental operations' he takes as its basis various methods for isolating and classifying units that derive from linguistics (*Essais critiques*, p. 214). When

Paul Garvin writes that 'structural analysis can be applied to any object of cognition which may legitimately be viewed as a structure and for which appropriate analytical starting points can be found', he implies, whatever other questions he begs, that linguistics provides an algorithm which will successfully direct analysis if certain conditions are fulfilled (*On Linguistic Method*, p. 148).

Linguists may have given cause for such an attitude by their suggestions that the task of linguistic theory is to develop 'discovery procedures': 'formal procedures by which one can work from scratch to a complete description of the pattern of a language'.[9] A discovery procedure would be a mechanical method – an explicitly defined series of steps – for actually constructing a grammar, given a corpus of sentences. If properly defined it would permit two linguists, working independently on the same data, to achieve identical (and correct) results.

The procedures proposed were, for the most part, operations of segmentation and classification: ways of dividing an utterance into morphemes and morphemes into phonemes and then of classifying these elements by considering their distribution. Some structural linguists such as Bloch and Trager insisted that the procedures be entirely formal – based exclusively on form with no appeal to meaning – on the assumption that this made the analysis more objective. Generally, however, evidence about similarity or difference of meaning was admitted: /b/ and /p/ are separate and contrasting units because when one replaces another in various contexts differences of meaning result.

But attempts to develop fully explicit discovery procedures have not been successful. Citing 'repeated failures', Chomsky argues that 'it is very questionable whether this goal is attainable in any interesting way, and I suspect that any attempt to meet it will lead into a maze of more and more elaborate and complex analytic procedures that will fail to provide answers for many important questions about linguistic structure' (*Syntactic Structures*, pp. 52–3). What is significant for structuralists is not the linguists' failure to attain this goal, since only the most general procedures would be borrowed, but Chomsky's claim that attempts to work out discovery procedures are fundamentally misguided and raise false problems. For if, as he suggests, fixation on this goal can produce an unwarranted complexity of the wrong kind, this may well have implications for structural analysis in other fields.

First of all, the search for discovery procedures leads one to concentrate on ways of automatically identifying facts which one knows already rather than on ways of explaining them. A proper discovery procedure must assume no prior knowledge of the language, and, as Bloch and Trager observe, 'if we knew nothing about English, it would take us some time to see that *John ran* and *John stumbled* are phrases of a different type and construction from *John Brown* and *John Smith*' (*Outline of Linguistic Analysis*, p. 74). Not only does one waste time, but in order to devise objective procedures for discovering facts about language one must introduce requirements that complicate and even distort description. For example, if morphemes are to be identified by an objective and formal procedure, then one must require that every morpheme have a specifiable phonemic shape (otherwise the identification of morphemes would be a matter of intuitive and 'subjective' judgments). But this rule makes the relationship between *take* and *took* problematic. How can one 'discover' the past morpheme in *took*?[10] The proper concern of the linguist should be to devise the most general and powerful morphophonemic rules governing the form of *verb + past*, and it should be that problem rather than the need objectively to discover the past morpheme in *took* that determines his treatment of the word.

More important, however, an interest in discovery procedures can lead to a basic and dangerous fallacy:

> A common view appears to be that to justify a grammatical description it is necessary and sufficient to exhibit some explicit procedure (preferably, purely formal) by which this description could have been mechanically constructed from the data. This view I find very strange . . . There are undoubtedly perfectly general and straightforward procedures for arriving at the most wild descriptions – e.g. we can define a *morpheme* in a perfectly general, straightforward, and formal way, with no mixing of levels, as any sequence of three phonemes. Clearly it is necessary somehow to justify the procedure itself. (Chomsky, 'A Transformational Approach to Syntax', p. 241)

This pertains to structural analyses in any field and should not be forgotten. A discovery procedure may be a useful heuristic device, but, however well defined, it does not guarantee the correctness or relevance of its results. They must be tested, howsoever they were obtained: 'a linguistic description is a hypothesis, and like hypotheses in other sciences it is of no direct relevance to its truth how it has been arrived at' (Householder, *Linguistic Speculations*, p. 137).

How then does one test grammars? If a rudimentary discovery procedure produces a description of a corpus, how does one evaluate that description? One must have something to check it against and this is, precisely, our knowledge of the language. We would require, for example, that a grammar correctly identify *took* as the past tense of *take*, that it specify the meaning-relation between *The enemy destroyed the city* and *The city was destroyed by the enemy*, and that it account for the different functions of *John* in *John is easy to please* and *John is eager to please*. In short, our linguistic competence provides us with a set of facts about language, and a grammar must account for these facts if it is to achieve descriptive adequacy. As Chomsky says, enunciating the fundamental principle of linguistic analysis, 'without reference to this tacit knowledge there is no such subject as descriptive linguistics. There is nothing for its descriptive statements to be right or wrong about' ('Some controversial questions in phonological theory', p. 103). One must begin with a set of facts to be explained, drawn from the linguistic competence of speakers, and construct hypotheses to account for them.

Although structural linguists often spoke as if their task were simply to describe a corpus of data and suffered in this respect from an inadequate theory, their work itself was not invalidated, for they did not divest themselves of their linguistic competence and thus had a sense of what would be a correct description. Bernard Pottier emphasizes the need for 'common sense' in eliminating ridiculous results, such as a morphemic analogy between *prince*: *princeling*: *boy*: *boiling*, which might be produced if one set out simply to look for patterns in a body of data (*Systématique des éléments de relation*, p. 41). This common sense is nothing other than linguistic competence, and one may suspect that it was generally consulted.

Second, though they may in theory have been based on the study of a corpus, grammars were always generative in the sense that they went beyond the corpus to predict the grammaticality or ungrammaticality of sentences not contained in it. Hjelmslev is quite explicit on this point: 'We require of any linguistic theory that it enable us to describe self-consistently and exhaustively not only a given Danish text, but also all other given Danish texts, and not only all given but also all conceivable or possible Danish texts' (*Prolegomena*, p. 16). He did not explain how this goal was to be attained, and in this respect his theory is inadequate; but his assumption must have been that in constructing a grammar one would take account of one's knowledge of the language and not formulate rules that would exclude possible sentences. To take a concrete example, Martin Joos's study of the English verb is explicitly corpus-based and attempts to proceed as rigorously as possible; but he assumes that his account will be valid for the English verb in general – that it will make explicit 'what every eight-year-old native English speaker already knows'.[11]

Finally, structural linguists did admit that their results had to be checked in some way against speakers' knowledge of the language, although this criterion may not have formed an explicit part of their theory. Zellig Harris observes, for example, that 'one of the chief advantages of working with native speakers over working with written texts . . . is the opportunity to check forms, to get utterances repeated, to test the productivity of particular morphemic relations, and so on' (*Methods in Structural Linguistics*, p. 12). Here there is hesitation, as if this were purely a practical advantage instead of a theoretical necessity, but elsewhere he admits that 'the test of segment substitutability is the action of the native speaker; his use of it or his acceptance of our use of it' (p. 31). Although there were American dissenters, such views were widespread in European linguistics: the commutation test in phonology, for example, was not so much a formal discovery procedure as a way of testing hypotheses about phonological oppositions against a speaker's knowledge of the language.

All this is to say that, despite its different theoretical formulations, structural linguistics can in a Chomskian perspective be seen as an investigation of linguistic competence whose results, however obtained, must be tested against that competence. Although they may have spoken as if their task were to analyse a closed corpus of utterances, linguists clearly expected their grammar to have a validity for other utterances as well and hence to be 'generative'. Nor, obviously, did they believe that just any rigorous procedure would yield valid results. Perhaps because of a desire to use what they took to be 'scientific' methods, they were unwilling to take from their own linguistic competence a set of facts about language to be explained but sought, rather, to develop formal procedures which would 'rediscover' these facts and in the process shed light on the linguistic system. This foreknowledge played an important role in preventing them from producing ridiculous descriptions, and so, in effect, the primacy of evidence about linguistic competence was always assumed. In this sense, structural linguistics presupposed at least part of the general framework within which generative grammar has now placed linguistic inquiry.

'Generative' or 'transformational'

I have so far spoken of 'generative' rather than 'transformational' grammar, and for good reason. Grammars must be and have always been generative in that their rules applied to sequences besides those in a particular corpus. They have simply not been explicit: anyone who has consulted a pedagogical grammar knows that often he cannot deduce from it whether a particular sentence is well formed, despite the author's desire to provide the rules for the language in question. It is not unreasonable to expect those who take linguistics as a model for the study of other systems to make their own 'grammars' as explicit as possible. But grammars have not been transformational, and there is no reason to impose this requirement on structuralists. The need for a transformational component in Chomskian grammar is determined by a variety of considerations, but transformations themselves are specific technical devices designed to take a form generated by one set of rules (in deep structure) and change it, mechanically, into the form that is actually observed. Analogous phenomena will no doubt be found in other, non-linguistic systems; but until the rules of those systems are made more explicit, the attempt to formulate transformations is likely to lead only to confusion. Lévi-Strauss, for example, uses the term to refer to what are, properly speaking, paradigmatic relations between two observed sequences: 'deprivation of food supplied by a sister' in one myth is 'transformed' into 'deprivation of a mother who supplied food' in a second and into 'absorption of anti-food (intestinal gas) "supplied" by a grandmother' in a third (*Le Cru et le cuit*, p. 71). Such transformations have nothing to do with transformational grammar.

Generally it does not seem unfair to say that attempts to use transformations in other areas will become interesting only when base rules of some sort have been formulated with sufficient precision to give one a set of well-defined deep structures which must be related in a rigorous way to observed surface forms. There is little reason to think about transformational rules until one knows what specific problems they would have to solve, for these problems are what determine the form of the rules. Meanwhile, fools rush in . . . Ruwet's proposal that all love poems be thought of as transformations of the proposition 'I love you' is simply modish (*Langage, musique, poésie*, pp. 197–9).

One factor that has tempted structuralists in recent years to shift their allegiance to transformational grammar is the notion that it is more 'dynamic'. Whereas structural linguistics was analytic and reduced a given sequence to its constituents, Chomsky's model is thought to be synthetic and to represent the actual production of utterances (new and old) by a speaker: 'generative grammar has, in its theoretical foundations, the advantage over analytic approaches to language, of introducing a synthetic point of view which presents the act of speech as a generative process'.[12] But, as Chomsky has repeatedly emphasized, this is not the case; the grammar generates structural descriptions but does not represent the actual process of generating sentences.

To avoid what has been a continuing misunderstanding, it is perhaps worthwhile to reiterate that a generative grammar is

not a model for a speaker or a hearer . . . When we speak of a
grammar as generating a sentence with a certain structural
description, we mean simply that the grammar assigns this
structural description to the sentence. (*Aspects of the Theory of
Syntax*, p. 9)

Indeed, one could say that the base component of a transformational
grammar, which begins by rewriting *Sentence* as *Noun phrase + verb
phrase* and continues by breaking down each of these constituents, is
analytic in precisely the same way as the phrase-structure grammars
of structural linguistics.

What is important in transformational grammar for the structuralist is not a notional 'dynamism' nor specific transformational
machinery but its clarification of the nature of linguistic investigation:
the task is not to describe a corpus of data but to account for facts
about language by constructing a formal representation of what is
involved in knowing a language. It should now be possible, in the
light of that suggestion, to offer a preliminary statement of the scope
and limitations of linguistics as a model for the study of other
systems.

Consequences and implications

In an article on 'La structure, le mot, et l'événement', Paul Ricoeur
derives from a discussion of the linguistic model a number of
conclusions about the limits of structural analysis. The method is
valid, he claims, only in cases where one can (a) work on a closed
corpus; (b) establish inventories of elements; (c) place these elements
in relations of opposition; and (d) establish a calculus of possible
combinations. Structural analysis, he argues, can produce only
taxonomies, and Chomsky's new and dynamic conception of structure 'heralds the end of structuralism conceived as the science of
taxonomies, closed inventories, and attested combinations' (*Le
Conflit des interprétations*, pp. 80–1).

But the notion that structural linguistics was a taxonomic science
was refuted by Trubetzkoy in the early days of phonology. Contesting
Arvo Sotavalta's claim that phonemes were comparable to zoological
or botanical classes, he argued that unlike the natural sciences,
linguistics is concerned with the social use of material objects and
therefore cannot simply group items together in a class on the grounds
of observed similarities. It must attempt to determine which similarities and differences are functional in the language (*Principes de
phonologie*, pp. 12–13). One can classify animals in various ways:
according to size, habitat, bone structure, phylogeny. These taxono-

mies will be more or less motivated according to the importance given these features in some theory, but there is no *correct* taxonomy.[13] A particular animal may be correctly or incorrectly classified with respect to a given taxonomy, but the taxonomy itself cannot be right or wrong. In phonology, however, one is trying to determine what differential features are actually functional in the language, and one's classes must be checked by their ability to account for facts attested by linguistic competence. Structural analysis may, of course, produce groupings of little interest or explanatory value, but such failures are not the fault of the linguistic model itself.

Moreover, one cannot, as I have suggested, oppose structural linguistics and generative grammar as Ricoeur does. The latter, aside from important differences of a technical kind, has made explicit and coherent the programme that was always implicit in the former. Linguistics has always attempted to discover the rules of *la langue* and this will always involve segmentation, classification and the formulation of oppositions and rules of combination.

Nor is it true to say, as Ricoeur does, that structuralism is resolutely anti-phenomenological in that it is concerned only with the relations among phenomena themselves and not with the relation of the subject to phenomena. For the utterance itself, as a material object, offers no hold for analysis: one must be concerned with the speaker's judgments about its meaning and grammaticality if one is to reconstruct the system of rules which make it grammatically well formed and enable it to have a meaning. Structuralist disciplines, writes Pierre Verstraeten in his 'Esquisse pour une critique de la raison structuraliste', analyse the object 'by taking into consideration the very criteria of intelligibility that the object involves' (p. 73). They are concerned with the norms by which objects become cultural phenomena and hence signs. Linguistics attempts to formalize the set of rules which, for speakers, are constitutive of their language, and in this sense structuralism must take place within phenomenology: its task is to explicate what is phenomenally given in the subject's relation to his cultural objects.[14]

None the less, structural analysis does offer a particular type of explanation. It does not attempt, as phenomenology might, to achieve empathetic understanding: to reconstruct a situation as it might have been consciously grasped by an individual subject and hence to explain why he chose a particular course of action. Structural explanation does not place an action in a causal chain nor derive it from the project by which a subject intends a world; it relates the object or action to a system of conventions which give it its meaning and distinguish it from other phenomena with different meanings. Something is explained by the system of distinctions which give it its identity.

For Lévi-Strauss the most important lesson of the 'phonological revolution' was the passage 'from the study of conscious phenomena to that of their unconscious infrastructure' (*Anthropologie structurale*, p. 40). A speaker is not consciously aware of the phonological system of his language, but this unconscious knowledge must be postulated if we are to account for the fact that he takes two acoustically different sequences as instances of the same word and distinguishes between sequences which are acoustically very similar but represent different words. The need to postulate distinctions and rules operating at an unconscious level in order to explain facts about social and cultural objects has been one of the major axioms that structuralists have derived from linguistics.

And it is precisely this axiom that leads to what some regard as the most significant consequence of structuralism: its rejection of the notion of the 'subject'.[15] A whole tradition of discourse about man has taken the self as a conscious subject. Descartes, in the most categorical statement of this position, argued that 'I am only, strictly speaking, something which thinks' (*res cogitans*). Others have been reluctant to concede the *res* but have made the self an active pheno-menological subject which endows the world with meaning. But once the conscious subject is deprived of its role as source of meaning – once meaning is explained in terms of conventional systems which may escape the grasp of the conscious subject – the self can no longer be identified with consciousness. It is 'dissolved' as its functions are taken up by a variety of interpersonal systems that operate through it. The human sciences, which begin by making man an object of knowledge, find, as their work advances, that 'man' disappears under structural analysis. 'The goal of the human sciences', writes Lévi-Strauss, 'is not to constitute man but to dissolve him' (*La Pensée sauvage*, p. 326). Michel Foucault argues in *Les Mots et les choses* 'that man is only a recent invention, a figure not yet two centuries old, a simple fold in our knowledge, and that he will disappear as soon as that knowledge has found a new form' (p. 15).

One might reply that this is only true for the French, whose Cartesian conception of man is such as to be destroyed by the discovery of the unconscious; but to reply immediately in that way would be to miss the point, for the claim is not that there is no such thing as 'man'. It is, rather, that the distinction between man and the world is a variable one, which depends on the configuration of knowledge at a given period. It has been made in terms of conscious-ness – the world being everything except consciousness. What the human sciences have done is to chip away at what supposedly belongs to the thinking subject until any notion of the self that is grounded thereon becomes problematic.

Language is once again the privileged, exemplary case. Descartes cited man's use of language as the primary evidence for the existence of other minds and took animals' inability to use language creatively as proof that they were purely mechanistic, non-thinking organisms. Saussure too saw the speaker's ability to produce new combinations of signs as an expression of 'individual freedom' which escaped the rules of an interpersonal system (*Cours*, pp. 172–3). Indeed, one thinks of speech as the prime instance of individuality; it seems the one area where the conscious subject might be master.

But that mastery is easily reduced. A speaker's utterances are understood by others only because they are already virtually contained within the language. 'Die Sprache spricht', claims Heidegger,[16] 'nicht der Mensch. Der Mensch spricht nur, indem er geschicklich der Sprache entspricht.' (Language speaks. Man speaks only in so far as he artfully 'complies with' language.) A generative grammar goes some way to formalizing this view. The construction of a system of rules with infinite generative capacity makes even the creation of new sentences a process governed by rules which escape the subject.

There is, of course, no question of denying the existence or activity of individuals. Though thought thinks, speech speaks and writing writes, nevertheless, as Merleau-Ponty says, in each case there lies between the noun and the verb the gap which one leaps when one thinks, speaks or writes (*Signes*, p. 30). Individuals choose when to speak and what to say (though those possibilities are created and determined by other systems), but these acts are made possible by a series of systems which the subject does not control.

> The researches of psychoanalysis, of linguistics, of anthropology
> have 'decentred' the subject in relation to laws of its desire,
> the forms of its language, the rules of its actions, or the play of
> its mythical and imaginative discourse. (Foucault, *L'Archéologie
> du savoir*, p. 22)

And as it is displaced from its function as centre or source, the self comes to appear more and more as a construct, the result of systems of convention. The discourse of a culture sets limits to the self; the idea of personal identity appears in social contexts; the 'I' is not given but comes to exist, in a mirror stage which starts in infancy, as that which is seen and addressed by others.[17]

What are the effects of this philosophical reorientation? How does the disappearance of the subject shape the structuralist project? The most obvious and pertinent consequences are changes in the requirements of understanding. Not only does structural analysis abandon the search for external causes; it refuses to make the thinking subject an explanatory cause. The self has long been one of the major principles of intelligibility and unity. One could suppose that an act or text was a sign whose full meaning lay in the consciousness of the subject. But if the self is a construct and result it can no longer serve as source. In the case of literature, for example, we can construct an 'author', label as 'project' whatever unity we find in the texts produced by a single man. But as Foucault says, the unit of the author, far from being given *a priori*, is always constituted by particular operations (*L'Archéologie*, p. 35). Indeed, even in the case of a single work, how could the author be its *source*? He wrote it, certainly; he composed it; but he can write poetry, or history, or criticism only within the context of a system of enabling conventions which constitute and delimit the varieties of discourse. To intend a meaning is to postulate reactions of an imagined reader who has assimilated the relevant conventions. 'Poems can only be made out of other poems', says Northrop Frye, but this is not simply a matter of literary influence. A text can be a poem only because certain possibilities exist within the tradition; it is written in relation to other poems. A sentence of English can have meaning only by virtue of its relations to other sentences within the conventions of the language. The communicative intention presupposes listeners who know the language. And similarly, a poem presupposes conventions of reading which the author may work against, which he can transform, but which are the conditions of possibility of his discourse.

To understand a text is not to ask 'what was being said in what was said?', but not for the reasons most often adduced by English and American critics. To say that a poem becomes an autonomous object once it leaves the author's pen is, in one sense, precisely the reverse of the structuralist position. The poem cannot be *created* except in relation to other poems and conventions of reading. It is what it is by virtue of those relations, and its status does not change with publication. If its meaning changes later on, that is because it enters new relations with later texts: new works which modify the literary system itself.

But though structuralism may always seek the system behind the event, the constitutive conventions behind any individual act, it cannot for all that dispense with the individual subject. He may no longer be the origin of meaning, but meaning must move through him. Structures and relations are not objective properties of external objects; they emerge only in a structuring process. And though the individual may not originate or even control this process – he assimilates its rules as part of his culture – it takes place through him, and one can gain evidence about it only by considering his judgments and intuitions.

Linguistics is the surest guide to the complex dialectic of subject and object that structuralism inevitably encounters, for in the case of language three things are clear: first, we have all 'mastered' an extremely complex system of rules and norms which makes possible a range of behaviour, yet we do not fully understand what it is that we have learned, what composes our linguistic competence. Second, there is obviously something to analyse; the system is not a chimera of the enthusiastic analyst. And finally, any account of the system must be evaluated by its ability to account for our judgments about meaning and ambiguity, well-formedness and deviance. It is because we can grasp these propositions in the case of language that linguistics provides a methodological model which can guide research on more obscure and specialized semiotic systems.

In sum then, we might say that linguistics does not provide a discovery procedure which, if followed in automatic fashion, will yield correct results. Whatever one's procedure, results must still be checked by their ability to account for facts about the system in question, and thus the analyst's task is not simply to describe a corpus but to account for the structure and meaning that items of the corpus have for those who have assimilated the rules and norms of the system. Studying signs which, whatever their apparent 'naturalness', have a conventional basis, he tries to reconstruct the conventions which enable physical objects or events to have meaning; and this reconstruction will require him to formulate the pertinent distinctions and relations among elements as well as the rules governing their possibility of combination.

The basic task is to render as explicit as possible the conventions responsible for the production of attested effects. Linguistics is not hermeneutic. It does not discover what a sequence means or produce a new interpretation of it but tries to determine the nature of the system underlying the event.

CHAPTER 2

The Development of a Method: Two Examples

the pale pole of resemblances
Experienced yet not well seen; of how
Much choosing is the final choice made up,
And who shall speak it?
WALLACE STEVENS

To observe the practical consequences of applying linguistic models in other fields we might look at two projects that are exemplary in different ways. Roland Barthes's *Système de la mode* has been praised by other structuralists for its 'methodological rigour': 'it would be difficult to imagine a better illustration of the semiological method'.[1] More explicitly based on linguistics than Barthes's work on literature, it illustrates the difficulties that arise when one tries to use linguistics in a particular way and thus offers a warning that should be heeded in other attempts. Moreover, Barthes sees a close analogy between fashion and literature:

> both are what I should call homeostatic systems: that is to say, systems whose function is not to communicate an objective, external meaning which exists prior to the system but only to create a functioning equilibrium, a movement of signification . . . If you like, they signify 'nothing'; their essence is in the process of signification, not in what they signify. (*Essais critiques*, p. 156)

The second example, Lévi-Strauss's *Mythologiques*,[2] is the most extensive structural analysis ever undertaken, and the obvious affinities between myth and literature make his procedures relevant to any discussion of structuralism in literary criticism.

The language of fashion

Fashion is a social system based on convention. If clothing had no social significance people might wear whatever seemed most comfortable and buy new clothes only when the old wore out. By giving meaning to certain details – calling them stylish or appropriate for certain occasions and activities – the fashion system enforces distinctions among garments and speeds up the process of replacement: 'c'est le sens qui fait vendre'. The semiologist is interested in the mechanisms by which this meaning is produced.

In order to study the workings of this system, Barthes chooses to concentrate on the captions beneath photographs in fashion magazines ('la mode écrite'), because the language of captions isolates the features which make a particular garment fashionable, orients perception and divides continuous phenomena into discrete categories. The widths of lapels on suits form a continuum, but if the caption speaks of the wide lapels on a particular suit it introduces a distinctive feature to characterize those which are *à la mode*. The description is, as Barthes says, 'un instrument de structuration': language permits one to pass from the material objects to the units of a system of signification by bringing out, through the process of naming, meaning that was merely latent in the object (*Système de la mode*, p. 26).

Barthes's linguistic model requires him to collect a corpus of data from a single synchronic state of the system, and fashion, of course, is eminently suitable for such treatment since it changes abruptly once a year when designers bring out their new collections. By taking captions from a year's issues of *Elle* and *Jardin des Modes*, Barthes creates a manageable corpus which, he hopes, will contain the different possibilities of the system at that stage.

What is one to do with the corpus? What are the effects to be explained? They turn out to be rather complex. Consider the two captions, *Les imprimés triomphent aux courses* (Prints win at the races) and *Une petite ganse fait l'élégance* (Slim piping is striking). One can identify a variety of *signifiés* that they produce. In the first place, the presence of *imprimés* and *ganse* in the captions tells us that these features are fashionable. At a second level, the combination of *imprimés* and *courses* signifies that they are appropriate for this particular social situation. Finally, there is 'a new sign whose signifier is the complete fashion utterance and whose signified is the image of the world and of fashion that the journal has or wants to convey' (p. 47). The rhetoric of these two captions implies, for example, that piping has not simply been labelled 'elegant' but actually produces elegance, and that prints are the crucial and active agents of social triumphs (it is your clothes, not you, who triumph). These meanings are connotations, certainly; but they are not for that haphazard or personal phenomena. The term 'connotation' is insidious if it suggests that they are unsystematic and peripheral. One could define connotations, rather, as meanings produced by conventions other than those of natural languages. As a sentence of French *Les imprimés triomphent aux courses* means that prints triumph at the races, but as a caption it has other meanings that are produced by the fashion system.

But what is one to do with these meanings? Barthes quite properly distinguishes between two levels of the system: the 'vestimentary code', in which the pertinent features of fashionable garments are expressed, and the 'rhetorical system', which includes the other elements of the sentence. In studying the latter one can investigate the vision of the world presented by the captions (the signifieds of the rhetorical system) or the procedures by which this vision is conveyed (the process of signification itself). The serious methodological problems arise at the more basic level of the vestimentary code. Here all sequences have the same meaning: the presence of an item in a caption signifies that it is fashionable. And there is little to be said about the process of signification: the fact that the picture is presented in a fashion magazine is what connects the signifier and the signified *Mode*.

The problem that offers scope for detailed investigation is which elements of the sequence are pertinent at the level of the vestimentary code and which are rhetorical. In *Une petite ganse fait l'élégance* does 'petite' determine the fashionableness of piping or is it used for its rhetorical connotations (humble, unpretentious, pretty)? In *La vraie tunique chinoise plate et fendue* is 'vraie' a rhetorical intensifier? To answer these questions one must investigate the rules of fashion operative in the given year. Taking sequences describing fashionable garments as 'well-formed', one asks what are the rules which produce these sequences but would not produce sequences describing garments that happen to be unfashionable at that time. To reduce sequences to their constituents and to write rules of combination that would account for well-formed captions is the course of investigation that the linguistic model suggests.

To proceed thus one needs information about unfashionable garments. Without it, like a linguist attempting to construct a grammar solely on the basis of a corpus of well-formed sentences, one does not know what changes in a sequence would make it deviant and therefore cannot determine its pertinent features. If the corpus speak of a *Veste en cuir à col tailleur*, one cannot tell whether it is fashionable because of the leather, the collar or the combination of the two. The obvious solution would be to rely on the judgments of those who are fashion-conscious and have in some sense mastered the system, but Barthes seems to assume that a rigorous structural analysis of a corpus forbids this. At one point he tries to resolve the problem of pertinence with a highly specious argument:

> every description of a garment is subject to a certain end,
> which is to manifest or, better still, to transmit Fashion . . .
> to alter a fashion sequence (at least in its terminology),
> to imagine, for example, a bodice buttoning *in front* rather than
> *behind*, is thereby to pass from the fashionable to the
> unfashionable. (pp. 32–3)

But it does not follow that each descriptive term designates a feature without which the garment would be unfashionable. Because Barthes thinks that his task is to describe the corpus, he neglects the primary problem of determining which elements in the sequences carry functional distinctions. Assuming that linguistics provides a discovery procedure of sorts, he does not try to resolve an obvious empirical problem.

His strategy is indeed one of neglect. He is not concerned, he says, with what was fashionable in this particular year but only with the general mechanisms of the system and therefore does not provide rules which distinguish the fashionable from the unfashionable. The decision is regrettable, first, because it makes his whole project rather obscure. Why choose a single synchronic state if one is not interested in describing that state? If one is concerned only with fashion in general, then surely one requires evidence from other years when different combinations would be recorded, lest one mistake the particularities of one year's fashion for general properties of the system. The choice of a corpus, it seems, is determined only by the linguists' assertion of the priority of synchronic description and the desire to give an impression of fidelity and rigour.

Second, refusal to investigate what is fashionable and what is not makes his results indeterminate. He argues, for example, that 'petite' in *petite ganse* is rhetorical because *grande ganse* does not figure in the corpus and hence 'petite' figures in no opposition. But the opposition might be precisely that between *petites ganses* which were fashionable and *grandes ganses* which were not and so did not appear in fashion magazines. Such questions cannot be decided on purely distributional grounds.

Finally, his results cannot be checked. If the function of the system is to transmit fashion then it should be described as doing just that, and one could evaluate the analysis by calling upon the evidence of other sequences from the same year or the judgments of the fashion-conscious and seeing whether Barthes's rules successfully distinguished the fashionable from the unfashionable. In the absence of such a project there is simply no way to test the adequacy of his descriptions.

What, then, does Barthes do in describing the corpus? The fullest description would be a list of the sequences which occur, but since this would be of no interest he sets out to reduce them to a series of syntactic schemes and to establish a number of paradigm classes corresponding to syntactic positions: 'one must first determine what are the syntagmatic (or sequential) units of the written garment and then what are the systematic (or virtual) oppositions' (p. 69).

Study of the distribution of items leads Barthes to postulate a basic syntagmatic structure consisting of three slots: 'object', 'support' and 'variant'. In *Un chandail à col fermé*, 'chandail' (sweater) is the object, 'fermé' (closed) the variant, and 'col' (collar) the support of the variant. This structure has an intuitive validity in that when speaking of a fashionable garment one may well tend to name it, identify the part in question, and specify the feature that makes it fashionable. The schema is subject to various modifications: in *ceinture à pan* the effective variant, 'existant', is not expressed; in *Cette année les cols seront ouverts* object and support are fused. In fact, there is no conceivable sequence which could not be described by one of the modified schemas that he lists, and his claim that the model 'is justified in so far as it permits us to account for *all* sequences according to certain *regular* modifications' (p. 74), is not a strong hypothesis about the form of fashion captions.

More interesting and pertinent is the attempt to establish paradigm classes of items which can fill these three syntagmatic slots. First of all, a whole series of items, such as skirt, blouse, collar, gloves, may serve either as object or as support. Items which can fill either slot Barthes calls 'species', and he argues that a distributional analysis enables one to group them into sixty different *genera* or 'kinds'. Garments or parts of garments which are syntagmatically incompatible – which cannot be combined as elements of a single outfit – are placed in paradigmatic contrast within a single kind. Each paradigm is a repertoire of contrasting items from which only one may be chosen at a single time: 'a dress and a ski-outfit, although formally very different, belong to the same kind since one must "choose" between them' (p. 103). Barthes's kinds seem adequate as a representation of syntagmatic incompatibilities: no two members of a single kind will appear as object and support in a single sequence. But a proper description should specify co-occurence relations in considerably greater detail. For example, if a member of the kind 'collar' is the support, then the object must belong to one of a limited set of kinds: roughly, garments which have collars. Inversely, if 'collar' is the object, then the support must be taken from 'material', 'edge', 'cut', 'motif', 'colour', etc.

One might expect that if the division into kinds is correct, then these classes will be the units on which such rules of combination operate. But Barthes's categories seem unlikely to serve. Dress, ski-outfit and bikini are placed in a single paradigm class, but as objects they would take very different supports. If one would require a totally different set of classes in order to write rules of combination, then those which Barthes proposes have only the weakest justification.

Variants are classed according to the same principles: 'wherever there is syntagmatic incompatibility there is established a system of signifying oppositions, that is to say, a paradigm' (p. 119). A collar cannot be both open and closed but it can be both wide and open. Compatibilities and incompatibilities of this kind lead him to postulate thirty groups of variants which cannot be realized simultaneously on the same support. He does not, however, use these classes to formulate explicit rules of combination.

Barthes seems to have been misled by linguistics into thinking that distributional analysis could produce a set of classes which need not be justified by any explanatory function. But even without explanatory efficacy, his inventories would be interesting as examples of what distributional analysis can achieve had he proceeded in a rigorous way. But instead of determining which items are never *in the corpus* simultaneously predicated of the same support, he refers to general compatibilities and incompatibilities determined by the nature of the garments themselves. Strictly speaking, if his corpus contains brown collars and open collars but no brown open collars, he ought to place 'brown' and 'open' within a paradigm class; he does not do so, because he knows that in fact collars can be both open and brown.

Barthes's failure to adhere to his theoretical programme illustrates the difficulties inherent in distributional analysis. If he were trying to determine what items were compatible and incompatible according to the fashions of a given year, then he would need to call on information from outside the corpus since the absence of a particular combination from the corpus would not necessarily mean that it was unfashionable. If he is not interested in the combinations permitted by fashion in a particular year, but only in general compatibilities and incompatibilities of garments, he should not in the first place have taken his corpus from a single year; but even with a wider corpus he would have to draw on supplementary information so as to note combinations which physically are quite possible (pyjama tops and ski-trousers) but do not appear in the corpus because they have never been fashionable. In either case, then, the analyst must go beyond the corpus to information provided by those who are knowledgeable either in fashion or in clothing. This knowledge of compatibilities and incompatibilities – like the competence of native speakers – is the true object of analysis and one should focus on it directly rather than draw upon it occasionally and surreptitiously.

What we have, then, is a rather confused, incomplete, and unverifiable account of the vestimentary code which cannot serve even as a specimen of formal analysis. It does not offer a system of rules which would specify what is fashionable; nor does it attempt rigorous distributional analysis of a corpus. Misled by the linguistic model, Barthes went about his task in precisely the wrong way and then was unwilling to follow a formal method through to the end. He neglected to decide what he was trying to explain and stopped without having explained anything.

It is extremely important to note Barthes's failure because of the tendency among both critics and admirers to accept this work as a model of structuralist procedure. The pernicious ignorance of Roger Poole's 'but it must be admitted that the *Système* is a correct piece of analysis' can only lead to a misunderstanding of structuralism.[3] Barthes's own comment is much more apposite: 'I passed through a euphoric dream of scientificity' ('Réponses', p. 97). It is scarcely surprising that a linguistic model perceived in a euphoric dream should yield confused and inadequate results.

Fortunately, Barthes's discussion of the rhetorical level of the system is more pertinent and successful than his account of the vestimentary code. What are the implications of the ways in which fashion sequences are presented? What can be discovered about the system from an investigation of its process of signification? Just as the most important feature of a poem may not be its meaning but the way in which that meaning is produced, so the rhetorical strategy of fashion is more interesting than the fashions themselves. One of the most striking features of the system is the variety of procedures designed to 'motivate' its signs: 'it is obviously because Fashion is tyrannical and its signs arbitrary that it must convert them into natural facts or rational laws' (p. 265). First of all, the system assigns functions to garments, asserting their 'practicality' (*A linen coat for cool summer evenings*) without explaining why they should be more appropriate than unfashionable garments. It can, moreover, use particularizing descriptions (*A raincoat for evening strolls along the docks at Calais*) which, because the functions they propose are so contingent, even pointless, appear the more 'natural'.

> It is the very preciseness of the reference to the world that makes the function unreal; one encounters here the paradox of the art of the novel: any fashion so detailed becomes unreal, but at the same time, the more contingent the function the more 'natural' it seems. Fashion-writing thus comes back to the postulate of realist style, according to which an accumulation of small and precise details confirms the truth of the thing represented. (p. 268)

Finally, the system may use various syntactic forms to naturalize its signs. Present and future tenses convert arbitrary decisions about what shall be fashionable into facts which simply exist in their own right or are the result of an inscrutable natural process (*This summer dresses will be of silk*; *Prints win at the races*). Reflexive verbs make the garments themselves agents of their stylishness (*Les robes se font longues*; *Le vison noir s'affirme*; cf. *Dresses are becoming longer*; *Black mink asserts itself*). The arbitrary decisions about what shall be fashionable are concealed by a rhetoric which does not name the agents responsible, which takes effects and, concealing their causes, treats them as facts that have been observed or as phenomena which develop in accordance with some independent and autonomous process. The essence of fashion as a semiotic system lies in the energy with which it naturalizes its arbitrary signs.

But that energy is matched by the insistence with which fashion constantly produces distinctions that have no utilitarian correlate. There must not, of course, be important functional differences between one year's style and the next, lest people refuse to change. And consequently fashion must give significance to the most trivial modifications: *Cette année les étoffes velues succèdent aux étoffes poilues*. It doesn't matter that a 'hairy' fabric has the same properties as a 'shaggy' one, or that the observable differences be noted only by those who are fashion-conscious. It is the distinction itself rather than any content of the distinction that fashion prizes. But the proliferation of empty distinctions increases potential meanings in a way that denies intrinsic value to the material garment: fashionableness lies in the description rather than in the object itself.

> The system of fashion thus offers the splendid paradox of a semantic system whose only goal is to undermine the meaning which it so luxuriantly elaborates . . . without content, it thus becomes the spectacle to which men treat themselves of the power they have to make the insignificant signify. Fashion thus becomes an exemplary form of the act of signification and in this way unites with the essence of literature, which is to make one read the *signifying* of things rather than their meaning. (p. 287)

It is at this level that the study of fashion is especially rewarding and suggests something of the paradoxical nature of semiotic systems. A society, as this and Barthes's other works show, devotes considerable time and resources to the elaboration of systems designed 'to make the world heavy with meaning', to convert objects into signs. But on the one hand it seems that 'men deploy an equal energy in masking the systematic nature of their creations and reconverting the semantic relation into a natural or rational one' (p. 285). Yet, on the other hand, the very energy employed in the proliferation and naturalization of signs – the desire to make everything signify and yet to make all those meanings inherent and intrinsic – finally undermines the meaning accorded to objects. These two processes which seek in opposite ways to affirm meaning, by creating and naturalizing it, contribute to what becomes, in effect, a self-contained activity. Absorbing and undermining the two contributary forces, the process of signification becomes an autonomous play of meaning. One has only to think of the way in which the rallying cry of 'realism' has served to justify changes in literary artifice, and of the ways in which the desire to make the real signify has led to the creation of autonomous worlds, to see that such paradoxes are not the property of fashion alone.

Mythological logic

The four volumes of Lévi-Strauss's *Mythologiques* are the most extensive and impressive example of structural analysis to date. The very *grandeur* of the project – an attempt to bring together the myths of the North and South American continents, to display their relations so as to offer proof of the unifying powers of the human mind and the unity of its products – make it a work that one could not hope to evaluate or even describe in brief compass. But one may approach it with more limited ambitions: to see in what ways the linguistic model might animate and support an analysis of fictional discourse.

The investigation of myth is part of a long-term project which uses ethnographic material to study the fundamental operations of the human mind. At the conscious and especially the unconscious level, Lévi-Strauss argues, the mind is a structuring mechanism which imposes form on whatever material it finds to hand. Whereas Western civilizations have developed abstract categories and mathematical symbols to facilitate intellectual operations, other cultures use a logic whose procedures are similar but whose categories are more concrete and hence metaphorical. To take a purely hypothetical example, instead of saying that two groups are similar but distinct, yet not in competition, they might call the first 'jaguars' and the second 'sharks'.

In his work on *La Pensée sauvage* and *Totémisme* Lévi-Strauss tried to show that anthropologists have failed to explain numerous facts about primitive peoples because they have not understood the rigorous logic that underlies them. Atomistic and functionalist explanations fail in a wide range of cases and make other peoples appear excessively primitive and credulous. If a clan has a particular animal as a totem it is not necessarily because they grant it special economic or religious significance. The feeling of reverence or particular taboos connected with a totem may be results rather than causes. 'To say that clan A is "descended" from the bear and clan B is "descended" from the eagle is only a concrete and abbreviated way of stating the relationship between A and B as analogous to the relationship between the two species' (*Le Totémisme aujourd'hui*, p. 44). To explain a totem is to analyse its place in a system of signs. Bear and eagle are logical operators, concrete signs, with which statements about social groups are made.

Myth has been chosen as the area for a 'decisive experiment' in the investigation of this concrete logic because in most activities it is difficult to tell which regularities of the system are due to common mental operations and which to external contraints. But in the realm of mythology all constraints are internal; in principle anything can happen in a myth, so if we can discover an underlying system this system, Lévi-Strauss argues, may be attributed to the mind itself:

> if it were possible to show in this instance too that the apparent arbitrariness of myths, the supposed freedom of inspiration, the seemingly uncontrolled process of invention, implied the existence of laws operating at a deeper level, then the conclusion would be inescapable . . . if the human mind is determined even in its creation of myths, *a fortiori* it is determined in other spheres as well. (*Le Cru et le cuit*, p. 18)

The first postulate, therefore, is that myths are the *parole* of a symbolic system whose units and rules of combination can be discovered. 'Experience proves that the linguist can work out the grammar of the language he is studying from a ridiculously small number of sentences', and in a similar way the anthropologist should be able to produce an account of the system from the study of a limited corpus (*ibid.*, p. 15). The example of phonology suggests that the structures studied need not be known to any of the participants that the elements isolated need have no intrinsic meaning but may derive their significance entirely from their relations with one another, and that systematic operations of segmentation and classification should lead one to a system of terms.

In an early essay on 'La structure des mythes' which set out to follow the methods of phonology, Lévi-Strauss asked how one could recognize and determine the constituents of myth and decided that they were not individual relational terms but 'bundles of relations'. If the phoneme is called a 'bundle of distinctive features', that is because an individual phoneme participates in a number of oppositions at once, but Lévi-Strauss's bundle is in practice a set of items which share a single functional trait. There is no automatic procedure for isolating these bundles or 'mythemes' and consequently Lévi-Strauss must begin with a hypothesis about the meaning of a myth if he is to discover in it a set of mythemes that would account for that meaning. He postulates that myths explain or reduce a contradiction by relating its two terms to another pair of items in a four-term homology. Given this rather formal and abstract *signifié*, one knows what to look for in analysing a myth and can, as Lévi-Strauss does, identify the four mythemes by grouping items under four headings in such a way that each group will possess a common trait which can form part of the homological structure. The Oedipus myth, for example, is treated as follows (*Anthropologie structurale*, p. 236):

A	B	C	D
Cadmos seeks his sister Europa	Spartoi kill one another	Cadmos kills the dragon	Labdacos = Lame
Oedipus marries Jocasta	Oedipus kills Laius	Oedipus 'kills' the Sphinx	Laius = Left-sided
Antigone buries her brother Polynices	Eteocles kills his brother Polynices		Oedipus = Swollen-footed

The incidents of the first column share the trait of giving kinship more than its due ('rapports de parenté sur-estimés') and so contrast with the patricide and fratricide of the second column ('rapports de parenté sous-estimés'). The third column concerns the slaying of anomalous monsters, which are half-human and born of the earth. To destroy them, Lévi-Strauss says, is to deny the autochthonous origin of man; whereas the final column shows the persistence of autochthonous origins in the inability, apparently typical of chthonian man, to walk properly. Man supposedly emerged from the earth, but individuals are born from the union of man and woman. The myth relates this contradiction to the opposition between overestimation and underestimation of kinship ties, which are both observed in social life, and thereby supposedly renders it more acceptable: 'experience may give the lie to the theory of autochthonous origin, but social life verifies cosmology in that both display the same contradictory structure' (*ibid.*, p. 239).

This method is unsatisfactory for a number of reasons. First, by taking myths individually it provides no obvious way of relating them to one another. Second, the need to select those incidents which will fit into the proposed structure makes it rather arbitrary: a number of important items are omitted. But finally and most important, it does not really advance our understanding of the logic of myth: the only logic revealed is that of the homologous structure postulated in advance and an elementary logic of class membership. Consequently, when he undertakes a full-scale study of myth Lévi-Strauss abandons – though he does not explicitly reject – this early approach. In particular, the attempt to discover a four-term homology within or behind each myth yields to a comparison of myths designed to reveal the logic of the 'codes' they use.

A code is a set of objects or categories drawn from a single area of experience and related to one another in ways that make them useful logical tools for expressing other relations. 'The goal of this book', Lévi-Strauss writes in the introduction to his first volume, 'is to show how empirical categories – such as the "raw" and the "cooked", the "fresh" and the "decayed", the "moistened" and the "burned" . . . – can serve as conceptual tools for working out abstract notions and combining them in propositions' (*Le Cru et le cuit*, p. 9). One can think of his task, therefore, as that of explaining the presence of various items or incidents in myths by identifying the codes from which they derive and showing what these codes express. Our most familiar examples of this procedure come from literary criticism. We might say, for instance, that in his sonnet 144, 'Two loves I have of comfort and despair', Shakespeare takes the basic opposition good/evil and explores it in a number of codes: the religious (angel/ devil, saint/fiend), the moral (purity/pride) and the physical (fair/ coloured ill). To explain the presence of any one of these items is to show that in the code drawn from a particular area of experience it is part of a binary opposition whose function is to express an underlying thematic contrast.

In the case of literature we know more or less how to proceed. We know that in our own culture dark hair and blond hair are opposed or that angel and devil contrast in the religious code, and we grasp the meanings which the poem conveys so that we can check our explanation of details by their relevance to those meanings. In the case of myths, however, the situation is quite different: considerable effort and perspicacity is required to construct the cultural context that provides clues to the nature of possible codes, and we start without a firm sense of meaning which would enable us to evaluate the description of myths. The analyst must therefore discover both structure and meaning. This requirement produces what Lévi-Strauss calls a spiral movement, in which one myth is used to elucidate another, and this leads on to a third which, in turn, can only be interpreted when read in the light of the first, etc. The final result ought to be a coherent system in which each myth is studied and understood in its relations with the others: 'the context of each myth comes to consist more and more of other myths' (*Du Miel aux cendres*, p. 305). To explain an item or incident in a particular myth the analyst must not only consider its relations to other elements in that myth; he must also try to determine how it is related to elements appearing in similar contexts in other myths.

Lévi-Strauss would argue that his procedure is analogous to the study of a linguistic system: in both cases one compares syntagmatic sequences in order to construct paradigmatic classes and examines those classes so as to determine the pertinent oppositions between members of each paradigm. From the point of view of the analyst, he argues, a single syntagmatic chain is meaningless; one must either 'divide the syntagmatic chain into segments which can be superposed and which one can show to constitute so many variations on a single theme', which was the procedure in his early essay; or one must 'set an entire syntagmatic chain, that is to say a whole myth, against other myths or segments of myths'. Whichever procedure is chosen, the effect is to replace a single syntagmatic chain by a paradigmatic set, whose members then acquire significance from the very fact that they are opposed to one another (*Le Cru et le cuit*, p. 313).

Linguistics teaches that two items can be taken as members of a paradigm class only when they can replace one another in a given context. If one had two versions of a myth which differed only at one point, then one could, by comparing the two variant elements, discover respects in which they differed and, if one knew whether the two versions of the myth had the same or different meanings, one would have discovered either an instance of free variation or of functional opposition which ought to be included in an account of the system. Alternatively, if one had several myths with the same meaning, one could compare them in order to discover the formal similarities responsible for this meaning. Where this is the case Lévi-Strauss's method seems unimpeachable and his arguments convincing. For example, he cites folkloric rituals in England and France in which, when a younger sister married before an elder, the latter was, in one case, lifted up and placed on the oven, made to dance barefoot in another and, in a third, required to eat a salad of onions, roots and clover. Lévi-Strauss argues that one should not attempt to interpret these customs separately and that one will succeed in understanding them only if one sets them in relation to one another and discovers their common features (*ibid.*, p. 341). The paradigm uses the opposition between the raw and the cooked to encode the distinction between nature and culture. The rite either expresses the raw, unsocialized status of the elder daughter (dancing barefoot, eating a raw salad) or else socializes her through a symbolic 'cooking'.

Though it does not involve myths as such, this example illustrates several problems crucial to the analysis of myth. First, the analysis seems validated by the 'plausibility' of the meaning attributed to the rituals. We know enough of the Western culture from which these examples come to prescribe certain conditions that a viable interpretation must meet: that the elder's celibacy be seen as undesirable, and that anything required of her be either symbolic penance or symbolic cure. It is thus, in a sense, our own competence which serves as a very general standard against which explanations must be tested. Second, it is obviously significant that the groups in question should know on what occasion to practise these particular rituals, for by knowing the occasion we already know something of what the rituals mean. We do not, therefore, need to inquire into what the people actually think about the rituals or what explanations they would themselves offer – unless, of course, they offered explanations which applied to the other cases as well. The operative system may function in a perfectly unconscious way: people's feelings that these rituals are appropriate for these occasions are sufficient empirical correlates for us to assume the existence of a system. Finally, the terms used in the explanation – 'raw', 'cooked', 'nature', 'culture' – are justified not simply by the fact that they seem to apply to this particular range of cases but by their pertinence and applicability to other phenomena as well. They are not *ad hoc* terms invented for the occasions but general distinctions whose importance is otherwise attested. In sum, this example of Lévi-Strauss's method works because we approach the facts with a strong presumption of unity and sense of the conditions of plausible explanation, including at least a rudimentary awareness of the meanings of the rituals and of the explanatory terms which might be pertinent to them.

But suppose that the three cases did not so obviously 'go together'; suppose, for example, that we were presented with three short stories involving weddings: in the first the guests exclaim during the festivities, 'You'll be next, Ursula!' and hoist the elder sister onto the stove; in the second, the elder sister takes off her shoes and dances barefoot around the newly-weds; in the third the father says, 'No wedding cake for you until you find yourself a husband', and gives the daughter a salad of lettuce and onions. Each tale would contain a curious feature that invited explanation, but it would not be obvious that they required a common explanation, and the critic who sought to elucidate one incident by comparing it with the others might well be accused of excessive ingenuity. This is the problem continually posed by Lévi-Strauss's analyses: if two myths go together in some sense – if they have the same meaning or perform the same function – then any formal similarities that can be discovered are likely to be pertinent; but if they do not go together the analysis remains extremely questionable. Two items can be compared on a variety of grounds; which grounds will yield pertinent relations?

Consider, for example, the first comparison in *Le Cru et le cuit*. Myth 1 may be summarized as follows:

> A boy rapes his mother and as punishment is set various difficult tasks, which he accomplishes with the aid of animals, birds, etc. In anger the father proposes an expedition to capture parrots and, when the boy is half-way up the cliff, removes the ladder and leaves him stranded. The boy manages to climb a vine to the top of the cliff and, after a series of privations and misfortunes, returns in disguise to his people. That night a storm extinguishes all the fires in the village except that of his grandmother. To gain revenge on his father the boy has him organize a hunt and, changing himself into a stag, charges the father and throws him into a lake where he is devoured by fish, except for the lungs which float to the surface and become aquatic plants. In another version he sends wind and rain to punish his father's tribe. (pp. 43–5)

Lévi-Strauss compares this with a second myth from the same tribe:

> Witnessing the rape of his mother, a boy reports this to his father who kills the two guilty parties. While searching for his dead mother the boy changes into a bird whose droppings, falling on the father's shoulder, cause a large tree to grow there. Humiliated, the father wanders, and wherever he stops to rest lakes form; the tree, reciprocally, shrinks until eventually it disappears. The father remains in these pleasant surroundings, surrendering his tribal post to his own father, and manufacturing ornaments and noise-makers which he gives to members of his former tribe. (*ibid.*, pp. 56–8)

One can observe various relations between the two myths at different levels of abstraction. For example, one could treat them as similar in structure except for certain inversions of their terms. Putting the inverted terms of the second myth in parentheses, one would have: Participation (non-participation) in the rape of his mother creates hostile (non-hostile) relations between a boy and his father, which lead to the son's (father's) isolation from the tribe by human (natural) forces. Lévi-Strauss, however, perceives a different parallelism:

> Each tale involves a Tugare hero who creates either water of celestial origin after having moved in an upwards direction

(by climbing up a hanging vine), or water of terrestrial origin after having been pushed in a downwards direction (weighed down as the tree whose weight he supports grows larger). Moreover, the celestial water is harmful . . . whereas the terrestrial water is beneficent . . . the first hero is involuntarily separated from his village through his father's malevolence; the second voluntarily separates himself from his village, prompted by kindly feelings towards his father. (*ibid.*, p. 58)

Both proposals involve only a few details of each myth (Lévi-Strauss uses others in later comparisons) and treat the details as manifestations of more general categories. Obviously other groups of relations could be produced by such methods, and their status depends on the grounds of particular comparison. To one nurtured on Western literature the opposition between *upwards* and *downwards* movement suggested by Lévi-Strauss seems rather factitious, since the striking feature of the father's predicament in the second story is not downward movement itself but the tree growing out of his shoulder and weighing him down. Lévi-Strauss's reading does receive some justification, though, from ethnographic evidence. The Bororo distinguish three original classes of plants: hanging vines, the Jatoba tree and marsh plants, which correspond, respectively, to the elements of heaven, earth and water. The opposition between the hanging vine in the first myth and the Jatoba tree which grows from the father's shoulder in the second may well be pertinent as an expression of the opposition between up and down, heaven and earth. Such information provides grounds for comparison because it bears on how members of the tribe in question might read their myths. Once such grounds are established it becomes possible to work out relations between myths.

One might distinguish, then, between three different analytical situations. Given two myths with similar meanings or functions, it should be possible to establish relations between them. Alternatively, when two myths are taken from the same culture and information about the distinctions used in the culture is available, one also has grounds for comparison. But when, as is so often the case, Lévi-Strauss compares two myths from different cultures and claims to derive their meaning from the relations between them, his analysis may become very problematic indeed. There is no *a priori* reason to think that the myths have anything to do with one another.

In an early chapter of *L'Origine des manières de table*, for example, Lévi-Strauss collects a set of myths from the most diverse regions of North and South America which contain the motif of 'la femme-crampon' – a woman who literally attaches herself to a man. Since several of these myths relate this woman to the frog in one way or another, Lévi-Strauss feels justified in adding to this group other myths containing the motif of a frog-woman.

> We have available two paradigms, that of the *femme-crampon* and that of the frog-woman, whose area of distribution is North and South America. The paradigms are independently associated with one another in each hemisphere. Indeed, we have shown that here and there the *femme-crampon* is a frog. We can now understand the reason for this union: the one says explicitly what the other says metaphorically. The *femme-crampon* attaches herself physically and in the most abject way to the back of her bearer, who is or whom she wishes to make her husband. The frog-woman, an abusive foster-mother, or often an ageing mistress unable to resign herself to the departure of her gallant, evokes a type of woman who, as we ourselves would say, 'sticks', giving the word in this case its figurative meaning. (p. 57)

It is by comparing these myths, he argues, that one can determine their underlying structure and hence their meaning. Some myths will express portions of the structure which others do not. But of course this exercise of devising a common schema which represents the meaning of this group of myths depends on a prior assumption that they all have the same meaning.

According to Lévi-Strauss they assert that it is culpable and dangerous to confuse the physical differences among women with the specific features which distinguish men from animals or one species of animal from another. Women, whether beautiful or ugly, are all human and all deserve a husband (p. 60). Now if it were known from ethnographic evidence that all these myths had the same meaning, Lévi-Strauss might well claim to have discovered it; or if the myths were all taken from a single culture, then he would be justified in seeking a single explanation for the various *femmes-crampon*. But in this case there is no particular reason to think that the motif should have a similar meaning in each culture or myth.

It is clear, therefore, that even at the most general level Lévi-Strauss's problems and procedures are rather different from those of the linguist. Lévi-Strauss is trying to show that myths from various cultures do go together, as the *parole* of a general mythological language; but the linguist does not have to prove that the sentences of English should be treated as a group. He knows that there is a grammar of English because speakers of the language understand one another and make use of formal differences to communicate different meanings. The linguist can discover what functional differences are correlated with and responsible for differences of meaning by comparing and analysing sequences because he has information about the judgments of speakers and the meaning of sentences. Comparison of /bet/ and /bed/ reveals a functional opposition which is used to communicate two different meanings. Lévi-Strauss claims that meaning is revealed by comparing myths, but the differences between two myths drawn from different cultures are not used to communicate anything.

More than anything else, it is the lack of data about meaning that vitiates the analogy with linguistics, for in the study of language the structural and the semiological cannot be dissociated: the relevant structures are those which enable sequences to function as signs. The lack of a semiological perspective leads Lévi-Strauss to concentrate on the structural, to find patterns and modes of organization in his material, but without evidence about meaning it is difficult to show that these patterns are more relevant than others. Although he has drawn from linguistics a few basic principles – that social phenomena may be governed by a subconscious system, that the analyst must attempt to establish paradigm classes so as to determine the variant features of members of the paradigm, that the relations among terms are more important than the terms themselves – the absence of anything corresponding to linguistic competence, which would provide the data to be explained and a standard against which to check one's results, is so crucial a difference that one cannot concur with Jean Viet's suggestion that what inspires confidence in Lévi-Strauss's method is the example furnished by structural linguistics.[4] Here, as in *Système de la mode*, one can observe the insufficiencies of a particular interpretation of structural linguistics: the notion that in studying a corpus one can discover the grammar or logic of a system through the division and comparison of forms may lead to a neglect of the basic problem of determining precisely what is to be explained.

But Lévi-Strauss's difficulties are not, like Barthes's, due to inadvertence or methodological confusion. He could have set out to study the system of myths in a particular society and tried to isolate those differences which are functional within that society. But he has deliberately chosen another perspective: that of mythology in general. In his earlier study of kinship he had faced a similar problem: societies attach very different meanings to their marriage rules, but the anthropologist cannot simply accept these meanings and turn a blind eye to the underlying relationships that he perceives among the rules of different societies. When he describes and compares kinship systems as procedures for ensuring the circulation of women and creating social solidarity – when he uses that general meaning to ground his analysis of particular systems – the conclusions and the approach itself cannot, as he says, be justified inductively. 'We are concerned here not with facts but with significance. The question which I asked myself was that of the *meaning* of the prohibition of incest (what the eighteenth century would have called its "spirit")' (*Leçon inaugurale*, p. 28). The object of study is not the meaning of a rule for the society which follows it but the meaning of phenomena themselves, in their interrelations. In the case of mythology the crux of the issue lies here also. When Lévi-Strauss says that myths resolve oppositions 'one must ask whether the opposition is resolved *for the myth* or, in fact, *for the natives*'.[5] Lévi-Strauss has resolutely chosen the former: 'I thus do not aim to show how men think in myths but how myths think in men, unbeknownst to them' (comment les mythes se pensent dans les hommes, et à leur insu) (*Le Cru et le cuit*, p. 20).

To justify this choice one must explain why assertions about meaning are not reducible to statements about the reactions of individuals, and here literature provides a useful analogy. There is a sense in which the resolution of oppositions that takes place in a metaphor is the thought of the poem itself rather than the thought of a group of readers, and the critic studying the structure of that poem or a series of poems does not begin by taking surveys to discover the reactions of readers. The reason is that texts have meaning for those who know how to read them – those who, in their encounters with literature, have assimilated the conventions that are constitutive of literature as an institution and a means of communication. It is in terms of literature or poetry that poems have meaning, and one could say, paraphrasing Lévi-Strauss, that the critic's task is to show 'comment la littérature se pense dans le hommes'.

This analogy may, in fact, provide the key both to a sympathetic understanding of Lévi-Strauss's project and to an identification of its difficulties. For he is concerned not with the meanings myths have for individuals who know only the myths of their own society but with the meanings myths might have within the global system of myths: within mythology as an institution. In this respect his project is as justifiable as that of a modern critic who does not attempt to reconstruct the meaning a poem might have had for a sixteenth-century audience but explores the meanings it can have now, within a greatly enriched institution of literature. But whereas the institution of literature is fostered and maintained by literary education, and whereas literature has many experienced readers who are aware of the range of its products, the institution of mythology leads an uncertain existence and few could be said to have assimilated its system. To put it quite plainly, we know how to read literature but do not know how to read myths. And this is crucial, because though the meanings of myths or of poems may not be reducible to the judgments of individuals, those judgments are the only evidence we have concerning the nature of the conventions which function within the institutions to produce meaning. To discover how poetry works we must think about how we read poems; for that we have evidence, but we know little about how to read myths.

In fact, the question which Lévi-Strauss seems to have asked himself is 'How can myth have a meaning?' 'What are the conventions and procedures of reading that would enable the institution of mythology to become as real and as present as the institution of literature?' He is trying to teach himself and his readers the language of myth, which as yet has no native speakers. He is creating, as it were, a theory of reading: postulating various codes and logical operations which will permit us to read one myth against another and produce a coherent system from which meaning will emerge. This is clearly what has happened in the case of the *femme-crampon*. Too good a structuralist to make the elementary error of assuming that a given element must necessarily have the same meaning in different contexts, his use of the motif as a connecting device represents a claim that these myths become interesting and intelligible when read against one another, *as if* they had the same meaning. If the procedures he develops succeed in making myths intelligible it will no doubt be due to some fit between method and object. And this fit will illustrate what was, after all, the general goal of his project: the specificity of the mind's operations and the unity of its products, be they myths or theories of myth.

> It makes little difference whether, in this book, the thought of South American Indians takes shape through the operations of my thought or my thought through the operations of theirs. What matters is that the human mind, regardless of the identity of those who are, for the moment, its representatives, should here display an increasingly intelligible structure from the progression of this doubly-reflexive movement of two thoughts interacting with one another. (*ibid.*, p. 21)

The techniques of reading that he develops will of course manifest and shed light upon the operations of the mind.

Taken as a theory of reading, Lévi-Strauss's account of myth offers the student of literature the rare spectacle of an attempt to invent and test conventions for the reading of fictional discourse. Since myth and literature share, at the very least, a 'logic of the concrete', one should consider his proposals concerning the reading of myth as hypotheses about semiotic operations that may be performed intuitively in the reading of literature.

From his discussion of codes, for example – culinary, gustatory, olfactory, astronomical, acoustic, zoological, sociological, cosmological –, the hypothesis emerges that elements of a text acquire meaning as a result of oppositions into which various areas of experience have been organized and which, once recognized by a reader who has assimilated the relevant codes, can be correlated with other, more abstract oppositions. If the heroine of a story appears dressed in white, this detail can be given a meaning because the opposition between white and black is a codified logical operator. Extended to literature, Lévi-Strauss's work on codes might lead to the claim that what we speak of as 'connotations' are not meanings associated atomistically with individual terms but the result of contrasts within codes, on which the process of symbolic interpretation is finally dependent.

The discussion of 'sun' and 'moon' is a case in point. Lévi-Strauss sees this opposition as a powerful mythological operator with great semantic potential: 'so long as it remains an opposition, the contrast between the sun and the moon can signify almost anything'. The meaning of *sun* is not determined by any actual or intrinsic properties of the object but by the fact that it contrasts with *moon* and that this contrast may be correlated with others. Thus, the distinction may be sexual: the sun will be male and the moon female, or vice versa; they can be husband and wife, sister and brother. Or, they can be of the same sex, two women or two men opposed in character or power.[6] Although myths may well exploit binary contrasts with more freedom than does literature, the ease with which poets use *day* and *night* to express a variety of oppositions suggests that Lévi-Strauss's theory should not be restricted to the realm of mythology.[7]

The basic principle on which the analysis of codes rests is the fundamentally Saussurian notion that matter is only the instrument of signification, not the signifier itself. 'In order that it may fulfil this role, one must first reduce it, retaining only a few of its elements which are suitable for expressing contrasts and forming oppositional pairs' (*Le Cru et le cuit*, pp. 346–7). This is fundamentally an hypothesis about the structuring process of reading which, in order to make the text signify, organizes its elements into oppositional series which can then be correlated with other oppositions. This process has one extremely important consequence: the extraction of pertinent features leaves a residue which can itself be organized into various oppositions, producing the kind of plurivalency or ambiguity that many have taken to be constitutive of literary language. Because of the very principle on which codes are constructed, it is possible in reading to multiply the codes that might be relevant to any particular stretch of discourse.

A second aspect of Lévi-Strauss's theory is the claim that there are some basic semantic contrasts which it is the task of various codes to express. In discussing myths he generally takes statements about kinship or social relations as the more important meanings, but he does not attempt to justify this preference and observes, in fact, that 'it is pointless to try to isolate privileged semantic levels in myths' (*ibid.*, p. 347). But it does not seem entirely pointless. Not only is it implicit in his theory of codes but it is confirmed by the analogy with literature. There can be little doubt that in reading poems or novels one does establish a hierarchy of semantic features. We may interpret statements about the weather as metaphors for states of mind, but none ever read statements about moods as metaphors for the weather. The opposition between good and bad weather is not, shall we say, recognized as fundamental in itself and therefore is taken as expressing some other, more important contrast. One of the tasks of criticism might be to determine what semantic features enjoy this privileged status and seem worthy to serve as the ultimate *signifiés* of symbols.

Precisely because it deals with unfamiliar materials – texts from outside our own culture – Lévi-Strauss's work exposes some of the basic problems of reading which in other cases may not become the object of explicit reflection since they are largely solved by a rich cultural experience. The very oddity of the myths he cites, the difficulty of achieving what we would ordinarily think of as satisfactory understanding, makes clear just how much we rely, in the reading of texts from Western culture, on a series of codes and conventions of which we are not fully aware. The initial strangeness of the myth is somewhat reduced when Lévi-Strauss sets it against other myths and supplies the codes which enable its elements to signify and fall into patterns; and that process of naturalizing the myth serves as an image of the operations which we are accustomed to perform on our own fictional texts. To make these operations explicit, to describe the structuring process, the codes employed, and the goals which direct the activity, should be easier for literature than for myth, since there is to hand, in the judgments of experienced readers, considerable evidence about how it functions. For this 'language', that is to say, there are more 'native speakers', and we need not, like Lévi-Strauss, invent a method of reading while investigating it.

These two examples confirm some of the preliminary conclusions about the application of linguistic models to the study of other cultural systems. They both illustrate that linguistics does not provide a discovery procedure which could be followed mechanically and that attempts to use it as if it did may lead one to neglect the basic problem of determining what one wishes to explain. *Système de la mode* shows the indeterminacy that results if one sets out simply to describe a corpus rather than formulate the rules of a generative system which would represent 'competence' of some kind. *Mythologiques* does not encounter precisely this difficulty but suffers from the fact that there is as yet very little evidence about the meanings of items in the general system that it would reconstruct. In neither case does a corpus of sequences itself provide the analyst with sufficient evidence. He needs to call upon judgments about similarity and difference of meaning, about well-formedness and deviance, if he is to do more than identify patterns. Both Barthes and Lévi-Strauss seem to formulate relations and patterns without sufficient consideration of their explanatory value, and for that reason neither offers a model of what structural analysis ought to be.

In the study of literature it should, in theory, be possible to avoid most of these problems, but, as we shall see, many of the same difficulties arise due to misconceptions about the nature and efficacy of linguistic methods.

CHAPTER 3

Jakobson's Poetic Analyses

I wished beauty to be considered as
regularity or likeness tempered by
irregularity or difference

GERARD MANLEY HOPKINS

For anyone interested in applying linguistic methods to the study of literature an obvious procedure would be to use the categories of linguistics to describe the language of literary texts. If literature is, as Valéry said, 'a kind of extension and application of certain properties of language',[1] then the linguist might contribute to literary studies by showing what properties of language were being exploited in particular texts and how they were extended or reorganized. The claim that this activity might be central to the study of literature is part of a general position shared by the Russian formalists, the Prague aestheticians, and contemporary structuralists; and the link between these groups – the man who has done more than anyone else to sustain this claim – is Roman Jakobson, whose theoretical statements and practical analyses are the basic texts of that variety of structuralism which seeks to apply the techniques of structural linguistics directly to the language of poems.

Since literature is first of all language and since structuralism is a method based on linguistics, the most likely meeting place, as Genette observes, is that of the linguistic material itself (*Figures*, p. 149). The linguist might analyse the phonological, syntactic, and semantic structures of sentences in poems, but it would be left to the critic to analyse the special functions this linguistic material acquires when it is organized as a poem. Jakobson insists, however, that such restrictions on the role of linguistics 'are based on an outmoded prejudice which either takes away from linguistics its fundamental aim, that is to say the study of the verbal form in relation to its functions, or else cedes to linguistic analysis only one of the diverse functions of language: the referential function' (*Questions de poétique*, p. 485). All instances of language fulfil at least one of the six functions: the referential, the emotive, the phatic, the conative, the metalingual and the poetic. And the linguist cannot neglect one of these six if he would achieve a comprehensive theory of language. Indeed, for Jakobson poetics is an integral part of linguistics and can be defined as 'the linguistic study of the poetic function in the context of verbal messages in general and in poetry in particular' (*ibid.*, p. 486).

In every speech act

> the *addresser* sends a *message* to the *addressee*. To be operative the message requires a *context* referred to, seizable by the addressee, and either verbal or capable of being verbalized; a *code* fully, or at least partially, common to the addresser and the addressee; and, finally, a *contact*, a physical channel and psychological connection between the addresser and the addressee, enabling both of them to enter and stay in communication. ('Linguistics and Poetics', p. 353)

Focus on any one of these six factors produces a particular linguistic function, and the poetic function is defined as 'focus on the message for its own sake'. By 'message' Jakobson does not, of course, mean 'propositional content' (that is stressed by the referential function of language) but simply the utterance itself as a linguistic form. In Mukarovsky's words, 'the function of poetic language consists in the maximum foregrounding of the utterance.'[2] Foregrounding may be accomplished in various ways, including the use of deviant or ungrammatical constructions, but for Jakobson the principal technique is the use of highly patterned language. Whence his famous definition of the linguistic criterion by which the poetic function is to be identified: 'The poetic function projects the principle of equivalence from the axis of selection into the axis of combination' ('Linguistics and Poetics', p. 358). Or, in a somewhat later version: 'One might state that in poetry similarity is superimposed on contiguity, and hence "equivalence is promoted to the constitutive device of the sequence"' ('Poetry of grammar and grammar of poetry', p. 602). In other words, the poetic use of language involves placing together in sequence items which are phonologically or grammatically related. Patterns formed by the repetition of similar items will be both more common and more noticeable in poetry than in other kinds of language.

These patterns, Jakobson argues, can be revealed by the linguistic analysis of a text:

> Any unbiased, attentive, exhaustive, total description of the selection, distribution and interrelation of diverse morphological classes and syntactic constructions in a given poem surprises the

examiner himself by unexpected, striking symmetries and
anti-symmetries, balanced structures, efficient accumulation of
equivalent forms and salient contrasts, finally by rigid
restrictions in the repertory of morphological and syntactic
constituents used in the poem, eliminations which, on the other
hand, permit us to follow the masterly interplay of the
actualized constructions. (*ibid.*, p. 603)

This striking and optimistic passage suggests that if one follows
patiently the procedures of linguistic analysis – and follows them
mechanically so as to avoid bias – one can produce a complete
inventory of the patterns in a text. The claim seems to be, first, that
linguistics provides an algorithm for exhaustive and unbiased
description of a text and, second, that this algorithm of linguistic
description constitutes a discovery procedure for poetic patterns in
that if followed correctly it will yield an account of the patterns which
are objectively present in the text. These patterns will surprise the
analyst himself, but since the procedures which revealed them are
objective and exhaustive he can enjoy the surprise of discovery and
need not worry about the status and pertinence of these unexpected
results.

There are, however, good reasons for concern. Leaving aside for
the moment the relevance of the patterns discovered in this way, one
must seriously question the claim that linguistics provides a determinate procedure for exhaustive and unbiased description. A complete
grammar of a language will, of course, assign structural descriptions
to every sentence, and if the grammar is explicit two analysts using it
will assign the same description to a given sentence; but once one
goes beyond this stage and undertakes a distributional analysis of a
text, one enters a realm of extraordinary freedom, where a grammar,
however explicit, no longer provides a determinate method. One can
produce distributional categories almost *ad libitum*. One might, for
example, begin by studying the distribution of substantives and
distinguish between those which were objects of verbs and those which
were subjects. Going one step further, one might distinguish between
those which were objects of singular verbs and those which were
objects of plural verbs, and then one might subdivide each of these
classes according to the tense of the verbs. This process of progressive
differentiation can produce an almost unlimited number of distributional classes, and thus if one wishes to discover a pattern of symmetry
in a text, one can always produce some class whose members will be
appropriately arranged. If one wants to show, for example, that the
first and last stanzas of a poem are related by a similar distribution of
some linguistic item, one can always define a category such that its

members will be symmetrically distributed between the two stanzas. Such patterns, needless to say, are 'objectively' present in the poem, but they are not for that reason alone of any importance.

None has done more than Jakobson to show the importance of syntactic parallelism and grammatical tropes in poetry, and that aspect of his work is not in question here. The claim contested is both more specific and more universal: that linguistic analysis enables one to identify, as a distinctive feature of the poetic use of language, the ways in which stanzas or couplets are linked by the symmetrical distribution of grammatical units. A consideration of Jakobson's analysis of one of Baudelaire's 'Spleen' poems will show how, with a little inventiveness, symmetries of all kinds can be discovered and will illustrate the speciousness of some of the patterns identified in this way.

I   Quand le ciel bas et lourd pèse comme un couvercle
     Sur l'esprit gémissant en proie aux longs ennuis,
     Et que de l'horizon embrassant tout le cercle
     Il nous verse un jour noir plus triste que les nuits;

II Quand la terre est changée en un cachot humide,
     Où l'Espérance, comme une chauve-souris,
     S'en va battant les murs de son aile timide
     Et se cognant la tête à des plafonds pourris;

III Quand la pluie étalant ses immenses traînées
     D'une vaste prison imite les barreaux,
     Et qu'un peuple muet d'infâmes araignées
     Vient tendre ses filets au fond de nos cerveaux,

IV Des cloches tout à coup sautent avec furie
     Et lancent vers le ciel un affreux hurlement,
     Ainsi que des esprits errants et sans patrie
     Qui se mettent à geindre opiniâtrement.

V   – Et de longs corbillards, sans tambours ni musique,
     Défilent lentement dans mon âme; l'Espoir,
     Vaincu, pleure, et l'Angoisse atroce, despotique,
     Sur mon crâne incliné plante son drapeau noir.

(When the low and heavy sky weighs like a lid
On the spirit groaning from the tedious anxieties that prey on it,
And when, embracing the whole rim of the horizon,
It pours on us a black day, more dismal than night;

When the earth is changed into a damp dungeon,
Where hope, like a bat,
Goes battering its timid wings against the walls
And dashing its head against mouldy ceilings;

When the rain stretching down its long streaks
Imitates the bars of a vast prison,
And a silent horde of loathsome spiders
Come to spin their webs inside our brains,

Suddenly the bells leap out in a fury
And fling a hideous howling at the sky,
Like wandering and homeless spirits
Who begin to wail relentlessly.

– And long trains of hearses, without drums or music,
File slowly through my soul; Hope,
Vanquished, weeps, and vile, despotic Anguish
Plants her black flag in my bowed skull.)

Jakobson's basic technique in analysing poems is to divide them
into stanzas and show how symmetrical distribution of grammatical
items organizes the stanzas into various groupings, especially the odd
stanzas and the even, the anterior and the posterior, the outer and
the inner.[3] In his discussion of 'Spleen' he looks first at the distribution of pronominal forms. A complete list by stanzas would be as
follows: I: *Il, nous*; II: *s', son, se*; III: *ses, ses, nos*; IV: *se, qui*;
V: *mon, mon, son*. The symmetry is not obvious, although of course
one might say that the first and fourth stanzas are linked and set off
from the remainder by the fact that the former each contain two
pronominal forms and the latter three. But Jakobson prefers more
symmetrical types of organization and argues instead that the
odd-numbered stanzas are set off against the even by virtue of the fact
that only the former contain first-person pronouns (*nous* in the first,
nos in the third, and two *mon* in the fifth) (*Questions de poétique*,
p. 421). One can easily find other patterns in the material: III, which
contains plural pronominal adjectives (*ses, ses, nos*), is, as the central
stanza, set off from the others, which contain none; III and V, which
contain no pronouns proper but only pronominal (possessive)
adjectives, contrast with I, II, and IV, which do contain ordinary
personal pronouns. But Jakobson cites neither of these contrasts
since he is interested above all in the symmetry of odd versus even.

Another pattern which links together the odd stanzas is, according
to Jakobson, the distribution of qualifiers. The distribution of
adjectives is as follows: I: *bas, lourd, longs, tout, noir, triste* (6);
II: *humide, son, timide, pourris* (4); III: *ses, immenses, vaste, muet,
infâmes, ses, nos* (7); IV: *affreux, errants* (2); V: *longs, mon, atroce,
despotique, mon, incliné, son, noir* (8). There is no initial symmetry
here, but with a little ingenuity one can discover patterns. First of all,
Jakobson argues that four substantives in each of the odd stanzas are

directly modified by an adjective or participle, but in order to produce
these figures he drops possessive adjectives from the class of adjectives, drops *tout* from the list of adjectives, though it is clearly an
adjectival form here,[4] and adds *gémissant* to the list of adjectival
participles, which is at best a questionable decision since it seems
probable that *gémissant* does not directly modify *esprit* but is the verb
of a participial phrase which taken as a whole modifies *esprit*.
Moreover, Jakobson suggests that adjectival participles ('participes
épithètes') are symmetrically distributed in the odd stanzas: I:
gémissant; III: *étalant*; V: *incliné*. Now if *étalant* really were a
direct qualifier, Jakobson would be forced to add *pluie*, which it
modifies, to the list of substantives with direct qualifiers, which would
give him four in the first stanza, five in the third, and four in the
fifth – not so satisfying a symmetry as his original figure of four in
each. In reply to this criticism,[5] Jakobson admits that *étalant* is not a
direct qualifier but argues that it can be classed with them because it is
only 'a less advanced stage of the transformation of verb into adjective'. This is, of course, perfectly true, but if he admits *étalant* on
those grounds he must also include *vaincu*, which is at least as close to
adjectival status, and he would be hard put to justify exclusion of the
participle *embrassant*, which is also a 'less advanced stage of the
transformation of verb into adjective'.

When he comes to the distribution of qualifiers themselves, he
achieves a nice symmetry by extending the class to include adverbs of
manner and continuing to exclude possessive adjectives and the
adjective *tout*. The even stanzas now each contain three qualifiers,
since *son* has been omitted from the second and *opiniâtrement* added
to the fourth. The external stanzas contain six, since *gémissant* has
replaced *tout* in the first and *lentement* has been added to the fifth
after exclusion of *mon, mon* and *son*. And the middle stanza, with the
omission of *ses, ses* and *nos*, now contains either four or five, depending on whether *étalant* is retained (*Questions de poétique*, p. 422).

However unpromising the distribution of the more obvious
grammatical categories, one can, it seems, find ways of producing
symmetry. But the point is not that in his zeal to display balanced
figures Jakobson treats grammar carelessly – such quibbling would be
of little interest and would not, in any case, impugn the method itself.
It is rather that Jakobson's way of proceeding indicates the tenuous-
ness and even irrelevance of this kind of numerical symmetry. To
grant importance to such numerical balance implies, for example,
that the poem is better organized if one read *gémissant* as a qualifier
or if one condition oneself to think of manner adverbs but not
possessive adjectives as qualifiers. If one agree that recognizing the
true character of these elements does not weaken the poem or alter its

effect, one has, in essence, rejected Jakobson's claim that this pattern which he perceives makes a significant contribution to the unity and poeticality of the text. He offers no arguments to convince us of the importance of numerical symmetry, and the patterns themselves do not contribute to any such conviction.

In addition to discovering patterns which link the stanzas of poems in a variety of combinations, Jakobson generally undertakes to show that the central line or lines of the text are in some way distinguished and set off from the rest, as if a well-made poem required an identifiable centre around which it turns. In 'Spleen' there is little evidence to support the isolation of the two middle lines,

> D'une vaste prison imite les barreaux,
> Et qu'un peuple muet d'infâmes araignées,

and although he points out some similarities between these two lines, his claim that they are set off from the rest of the poem depends upon an argument about the distribution of transitory grammatical forms (verb forms unmarked for person and adverbialized adjectives): 'one notes in the first half of "Spleen" five active participles and in the second half a pair of infinitives followed by two adverbs and finally by two participles now in the past, while the two middle lines are devoid of any transitory form' (p. 429).

This is an extremely curious argument, for the simple reason that the first two lines of the second stanza and the first three lines of the fourth stanza are also devoid of transitory forms, so that this criterion scarcely suffices to distinguish the two middle lines from the rest of the poem. But the point is of interest precisely because Jakobson's willingness to use so specious an argument seems to imply that it is extremely important to find some distributional pattern which sets off the centre of the poem, and one may not be wrong in attributing to him the implicit claim that 'Spleen' would be a better poem, or at least better organized, if the middle lines were in fact the only ones without transitory forms. The suggestion seems to be that if we were to introduce transitory forms into the first three lines of the fourth stanza, which now lack them as surely as do the middle lines of the third, the prominence of the latter would be enhanced and the organization of the poem strengthened. Replacing *tout à coup* by the adverbialized adjective *subitement* and changing the non-transitory adjective *errants* to a participle with an appropriate complement (e.g. *errant sans compagnie* for *errants et sans patrie*) introduces two new transitory forms and makes the poem adhere more closely to the pattern of organization that Jakobson would see in it. But it is doubtful whether changes of this sort in the fourth stanza succeed in altering the effect of the middle lines of the third stanza. And if one thinks that introducing these transitory forms does not make the two middle lines of the poem stand out more clearly and contrast with the rest of the text, then one is implicitly rejecting Jakobson's claim about the importance of this particular distributional pattern.

Jakobson's assertions of the relevance of various patterns are undermined first of all by the fact that the presence or absence of a given pattern seems often to depend upon factors (such as whether one should read *gémissant* as a direct qualifier) which bear little relation to the effects of the poem and, second, by the fact that linguistic categories are so numerous and flexible that one can use them to find evidence for practically any form of organization. If one takes the stanza as the basic unit, a five-stanza poem like 'Spleen' can be organized in a limited number of ways: the odd stanzas may be opposed to the even (1, 3, 5/2, 4), the external to the internal (1, 5/2, 3, 4), and the central to the peripheral (3/1, 2, 4, 5). In addition, there are four linear divisions (1/2, 3, 4, 5), (1, 2/3, 4, 5), (1, 2, 3/4, 5) and (1, 2, 3, 4/5). Jakobson finds five of these seven possible configurations in the poem, and thus his claim might seem to be that there are two possible forms of organization that have not been exploited: (1/2, 3, 4, 5) and (1, 2/3, 4, 5). However, it is not difficult to show that by the criteria of a Jakobsonian analysis the poem contains these structures as well.

First of all, the structure (1/2, 3, 4, 5): the opening stanza is clearly set off from the other four by the fact that it is the only stanza to contain non-reflexive personal pronouns, which are placed together for added emphasis (*il nous* verse un jour noir).

Second, the structure (1, 2/3, 4, 5): if one looks at the distribution of verbal forms one finds a symmetry which links the first two stanzas and sets them off from the rest of the poem. Both of these stanzas contain two finite verbs (I: *pèse, verse*; II: *est changée, va*) and two present participles (I: *gémissant, embrassant*; II: *battant, cognant*) but no other verbal forms. This ordered symmetry is opposed to the disorder of the last three stanzas which contain, in addition to finite verbs asymmetrically distributed, an assortment of present participles, past participles and infinitives.

These categories and symmetries are no less natural and evident than Jakobson's, and one is forced to conclude either that the poem is organized in all seven possible ways or that Jakobson's method permits one to find in a poem any type of organization which one looks for. If one adopts the second conclusion, it follows that the structures which one discovers in a poem by these methods have not the relevance of distinguishing characteristics since one could have found other structures by using different methods.

It might well be, however, that Jakobson would not object to such

a conclusion. Indeed, despite his numerous theoretical discussions
and analyses of particular poems it is not clear exactly what claims
he would make for his analytical method. If he is maintaining that
linguistic analysis enables one to discover precisely which forms of
organization, out of all possible structures, are actualized in a given
poem, then one may contest his claim by showing that there is no
type of organization which could not be found in a particular poem.
On the other hand – and this is perhaps more likely, given the fact
that he tends to find the same organizational symmetries in the
different poems he analyses – his position may be rather that since
the poetic function makes equivalence the constitutive device of the
sequence, one will be able to find innumerable symmetries in any poem,
and that it is precisely this fact which distinguishes poetry from prose.

To counter that argument one would need only to show that using
Jakobson's analytical methods one can find the same symmetries of
odd and even, external and internal, anterior and posterior in a given
piece of prose. If one takes, for example, the opening page of
Jakobson's 'Postscriptum' to *Questions de poétique* and, leaving aside
the first sentence which is unusually short, takes the following four
sentences as units, one can discover striking symmetries and anti-
symmetries which knit together and oppose the units in all the likely
ways (p. 485).

    I D'un côté, la science du langage, évidemment appelée à
      étudier les signes verbaux dans tous leurs arrangements
      et fonctions, n'est pas en droit de négliger la *fonction*
      poétique qui se trouve coprésente dans la parole de
      tout être humain dès sa première enfance et qui joue
      un rôle capital dans la structuration du discours.
    II Cette fonction comporte une attitude introvertie à
      l'égard des signes verbaux dans leur union du signifiant
      et du signifié et elle acquiert une position dominante
      dans le langage poétique.
    III Celui-ci exige de la part du linguiste un examen
      particulièrement méticuleux, d'autant plus que le vers
      paraît appartenir aux phénomènes universaux de la
      culture humaine.
    IV Saint Augustin jugeait même que sans expérience en poétique
      on serait à peine capable de remplir les devoirs d'un
      grammairien de valeur.

  (I) On the one hand, the science of language, which clearly is
destined to study verbal signs in all their arrangements and
functions, has no right to neglect the poetic function, which is

present in the speech of every human being from childhood and which plays a central role in structuring discourse.
(II) This function involves an introverted attitude towards verbal signs with respect to the fusion of the signifier and the signified, and it takes on a dominant role in poetic language.
(III) This use of language demands particularly careful analysis from the linguist, especially since verse seems to be one of the universals of human culture. (IV) Saint Augustine even believed that without a knowledge of poetics one could scarcely carry out the duties of a competent grammarian.)

The odd units are related and opposed to the even by virtue of the fact that the only two adverbialized adjectives in the passage are symmetrically distributed in the odd sentences (I: *évidemment*; III: *particulièrement*). There are no adverbs of this sort in the even-numbered sentences.

The outer sentences are related to one another and opposed to the inner by the distribution of finite verbs: first of all, the outer sentences each contain one main verb (I: *est*; IV: *jugeait*) while the inner contain two, linked by a co-ordinating conjunction or a comparative conjunction with co-ordinating rather than subordinating force (II: *comporte . . . et . . . acquiert*; III: *exige . . . d'autant plus que . . . paraît*); second, the only finite verbs in subordinate clauses appear in the outer sentences (I: *se trouve, joue*; IV: *serait*); finally, the only forms of the verb *être* occur in symmetrical distribution in the outer sentences, occupying inverse positions as the main verb in I (*est*) and the subordinate verb in IV (*serait*).

The first two sentences are linked and set off from the last two by a series of patterns. The former contain the only possessive adjectives in the passage (I: *leurs, sa*; II: *leur*). The subjects of all finite verbs in the former are grammatically feminine (I: *la science, la fonction poétique*; II: *Cette fonction, elle*), whereas those in the latter sentences are masculine (III: *Celui-ci, le vers*; IV: *Saint Augustin, on*). The third and fourth sentences are linked by the distribution of substantives: not only do they contain the same number (six, as opposed to fourteen and nine in the first and second), but their distribution by number and gender is rigorously symmetrical (one masculine plural and no feminine plurals in each of the two sentences; three masculine and two feminine singulars in the third but two masculine and three feminine singulars in the fourth). The four co-ordinating conjunctions are restricted to the first two sentences, again in symmetrical distribution, two in each (I: *et, et*; II: *et, et*).

No doubt other symmetries and anti-symmetries could be discovered if one wished to continue looking. These should suffice to illustrate the possibility of isolating, in prose that is not especially poetic, 'unexpected, striking symmetries and anti-symmetries, balanced structures, efficient accumulation of equivalent forms, and salient contrasts'. This sort of numerical symmetry cannot in itself serve as a defining characteristic of the poetic function of language.

The same kind of problem is encountered at the level of sound patterns. We have only the crudest ideas of what makes a line euphonious or successful and of how phonological modulations from one line to another contribute to the effects of a poem; and clearly linguistics should be of some help here. But to suggest that the methods of phonological analysis give us a procedure for the discovery of poetic patterns begs more questions than it resolves. Linguistics offers a first step, certainly: rewrite the poem or stanza as a series of distinctive-feature matrices. But linguistics does not tell us how to go on from there. What will count as a relationship of equivalence? How many distinctive features must two phonemes share if they are to count as related? How far apart can two phonemes be if their relationship is to take effect, and is this distance proportional to the number of distinctive features they share or does it depend on syntactic and semantic considerations? Linguistic method does not itself provide an answer to these questions, and arguments drawn from linguistics may well run counter to what we know to be true. For example, in analysing Racine's line, 'Le jour n'est pas plus pur que le fond de mon cœur', Nicolas Ruwet claims that linguistics authorizes us to consider only the lexical items in determining sound patterns and thus limits his description to the relationships between the sounds of *jour*, *pur*, *fond* and *cœur* (*Langage, musique, poésie*, p. 213). But every schoolboy knows that the alliteration of '*pas plus pur*' and the assonance of '*le fond de mon*' are crucial to the sound pattern of the line, as can be seen if one alters the non-lexical items to produce a verse with different resonances, such as: 'Le jour n'est guère si pur que le fond d'un tel cœur'.

In his analysis of 'Spleen' Jakobson quite rightly insists on the intensity of the phonetic play and displays numerous examples of repetitions, often between widely dispersed lines. But he takes one no further towards a general theory of the pertinent and irrelevant relationships among sounds. Even where linguistics provides definite and well-established procedures for classing and describing elements of a text it does not solve the problem of what constitutes a pattern and hence does not provide a method for the discovery of patterns. *A fortiori*, it does not provide a procedure for the discovery of poetic patterns.

If one rejects Jakobson's claims that linguistics provides a determinate analytical procedure for discovering the organization of poetic texts and that the patterns thus discovered are necessarily relevant by virtue of their 'objective' presence in the text, one can still salvage much from his theory, for it is primarily the importance granted to numerical symmetry that leads to the indiscriminate postulation of structures. To place other aspects of his work in a perspective that will give them their proper value, one might put a different construction on his definition of the poetic function. For, as will be obvious in the light of Jakobson's analytical procedures, repetition of similar constituents may be observed in any text and thus cannot in itself serve as the distinguishing feature of the poetic function.

Indeed, when Jakobson is analysing individual lines or particular phrases rather than complete poems, he does not simply note distributional patterns but explains the poetic function with respect to the effect of these patterns. The slogan 'I like Ike' deploys a high degree of phonetic repetition, and this repetition also has a function: it presents 'a paronomastic image of feeling which totally envelops its object . . . a paronomastic image of the loving subject enveloped by the beloved object' ('Linguistics and Poetics', p. 357). The indissoluble relation between *I*, *like* and *Ike* suggests that it is perfectly natural, even inevitable, that I like Ike. One might say, using Jakobson's own example as a guide, that one has an instance of the poetic function only when one can point to effects which might be explained as the result of particular projections of the principle of equivalence from the axis of selection into the axis of combination.

One can find evidence for this stronger interpretation in Jakobson's theoretical statements. Although rhyme is a prime instance of phonological repetition, 'it would be an unsound oversimplification to treat rhyme merely from the point of view of sound. Rhyme necessarily involves the semantic relationship between rhyming units' (*ibid.*, p. 367). And again, 'In poetry, any conspicuous similarity in sound is evaluated in respect to similarity and/or dissimilarity in meaning' (*ibid.*, p. 372). It is precisely the 'set towards the message' in poetry, as opposed to the orientations with which one approaches varieties of discursive prose, that gives phonological repetition this function of posing the question of semantic relationship. Thus, the reader of the preceding sentence does not draw semantic consequences from the phonological repetition in 'ap*pro*aches . . . *pro*se', but the rhyme in the first stanza of 'Spleen' between 'ennuis' and 'nuits' enforces a possible semantic connection. Similarly, in the first stanza of Baudelaire's 'La Géante' –

Du temps que la Nature en sa verve puissante
Concevait chaque jour des enfants monstrueux,

J'eusse aimé vivre auprès d'une jeune géante,
Comme aux pieds d'une reine un chat voluptueux.

(In the days when a powerful and zestful Nature
Brought forth each day monstrous children,
I should have liked to live by a young giantess,
Like a voluptuous cat at a queen's feet.)

– although the nouns which *monstrueux* and *voluptueux* modify are
in a different relationship, the rhyme between the two adjectives
implies an intimate association of the gigantic and the voluptuous
which is not at all out of place in the poem.

At one point Jakobson argues quite explicitly that

> equivalence in sound, projected into the sequence as its
> constitutive principle, inevitably involves semantic equivalence,
> and on any linguistic level any constituent of such a sequence
> prompts one of two correlative experiences which Hopkins
> neatly defines as 'comparison for likeness' sake' and 'comparison
> for unlikeness' sake'. (*ibid.*, pp. 368–9)

Emphasis on the 'experience' prompted by equivalence strikes a
salutary note which is too often lacking in his practical analyses.
One is seldom certain exactly what sort of experiences are supposed
to be prompted by the symmetrical distribution of transitory grammatical forms or of nouns modified by direct qualifiers. It would
seem not unreasonable to suggest that patterns discovered are
relevant only when they can be correlated with some experience that
they explain, but here one treads an ill-marked path. Michael
Riffaterre argues, for example, that many of Jakobson's patterns
involve components which cannot be perceived by the reader and thus
remain foreign to the poetic structure ('Describing poetic structure',
p. 207). But his 'law of perceptibility', as he calls it, can scarcely
advance the argument or provide a way of distinguishing between
poetic and non-poetic structures, for the simple reason that it is an
extremely awkward strategy to point to a particular pattern and then
to claim that it cannot be perceived. Nor can one take as one's
standard what readers *have* perceived, first because readers do not
themselves necessarily know which constituents or patterns may have
contributed to the effects experienced, second, because one does not
wish to eliminate on grounds of principle the possibility of a critic
pointing out to us something we had not observed in the text but
whose importance we are willing to grant, and third, because one
would have to set up rather arbitrary rules in order to exclude
Jakobson and others like him from the company of readers whose
perceptions serve as the standard of perceptibility.

Moreover, Jakobson himself does not claim that the structures in question are consciously perceived: they can function perfectly well at a subliminal level, he says, without deliberate decisions or conscious knowledge on the part of either author or reader (*Questions de poétique*, p. 292). Of course, it is even more difficult to argue about what might have subliminal effect than about what might be perceptible, but Jakobson is not, I think, trying by this formulation to escape all possibility of falsification. In replying to the complaint that the reader does not perceive these complex relations between grammatical items, he argues that

> speakers employ a complex system of grammatical relations
> inherent in their language without being able to isolate and
> define them, and this task is left to linguistic analysis. Like
> those who listen to music, the reader of the sonnet takes delight
> in its stanzas, and even if he experiences and feels the
> agreement of the two quatrains or of the two tercets, no reader
> without special training will be capable of determining the
> latent agents of this agreement. (*ibid.*, p. 500)

The claim of the first sentence makes the point very nicely. Speakers of a language experience the meaning of sentences and know whether they are grammatical or ungrammatical, though they are not able to explain the complex system of grammatical relations that produce these effects. But it is only because speakers do have these experiences that linguists have something to explain. The most elegant grammatical analysis would be rejected as irrelevant if it made no contribution to the project of accounting for the grammaticality of sentences and the meaning-relations of their components. When Jakobson employs this analogy and speaks of readers' 'capacity to grasp the effects immediately and spontaneously without rationally isolating the processes by which they are produced', he makes it clear that his theory does not fall outside the realm of verification. His view that grammatical patterning is important commits him to the claim that it has effects and thus places the problem at a level where it is at least possible to argue. The poetic function is still a communicative function, and to test whether patterns isolated are in fact responsible for particular effects one may attempt to alter the patterns to see whether they change the effects in question. It is not, of course, always easy to test claims in this way, since effects may be difficult to grasp or isolate; but the more difficult it is to perceive changes in effect, the more implausible the claim that certain patterns play a crucial role in the poetic text.

In his theoretical statements Jakobson is often quite explicit about the effects of grammatical devices. He stresses that syntactic parallelism, as Hopkins says, begets or passes into parallelism of thought, and he shows much the same to be true for marked phonological parallelism ('Linguistics and Poetics', pp. 368–72). The juxtaposition of contrasting grammatical categories can be compared, he says, with 'dynamic cutting' in film montage:

> a type of cutting which, e.g. in Spottiswoode's definition, uses the juxtaposition of contrasting shots or sequences to generate ideas in the mind of the spectator, which these constituent shots or sequences by themselves do not carry. ('Poetry of grammar', p. 604)

This suggests that the function of grammatical analysis might be to explain how it is that in particular cases ideas are generated in the minds of readers which would not have been generated if other combinations of grammatical or phonological types had been used. In other words, rather than attempt to use linguistic analysis as a technique for discovering patterns in a text, one might start from data about the effects of poetic language and attempt to formulate hypotheses which would account for these effects. Jakobson himself is quite adept at using linguistics in this way as a critical tool: when asked not to analyse a whole poem but to explain a particular effect he outstrips most literary critics. Thus, when at the Indiana conference on style in language John Lotz asked why the title of I. A. Richards's poem 'Harvard Yard in April/April in Harvard Yard' was so much superior to its converse, 'April in Harvard Yard/Harvard Yard in April', Richards floundered but Jakobson came to the rescue with a precise and doubtless correct explanation: that whereas in the former the six stressed syllables are all separated from one another by unstressed styllables, 'an inverted order of the two sentences would abolish their rhythmic continuity by a clash of two stressed syllables ". . . Yard/Harvard . . ." ' and would destroy the symmetry which puts a stress on the first and last syllables of the line (Sebeok, *Style in Language*, p. 24). One might add that the inverted order would produce the monotony of six identical (or slightly varying, depending on pronunciation) vowels in immediate sequence. Claims of this sort can be tested by changing vowel and stress patterns, as in 'May in Memorial Court/Memorial Court in May' which seems at least as poetically effective as 'Memorial Court in May/May in Memorial Court'.

But if one uses linguistics as a critical tool in this way, how does that affect the definition of the poetic function? No longer the key to a method of analysis, it becomes a hypothesis about the conventions of poetry as an institution and in particular about the kind of attention to language which poets and readers are allowed to assume.

Jakobson's definition would imply, for example, that one of the things readers of poetry do, and are allowed to do, when confronted with striking phonetic or grammatical parallelism is to attempt to set the two items in a semantic relationship and take them as either equivalent or opposed. Samuel Levin, whose theory of 'couplings' is drawn directly from Jakobson's work, has explored the semantic consequences of non-semantic parallelisms which couple two items. When one reads Pope's line, 'A soul as full of worth as void of pride', one assumes that pride is a vice. That effect is produced by the kind of attention one pays to parallelism in poetry: since 'full of worth' and 'void of pride' are set in strict grammatical relation and display structural correspondence, one assumes that they are either equivalent or opposed in meaning (as much of one good quality as another or as much of one good quality as of a bad). One opts for equivalence, since the context seems to be one of praise. And since 'full' and 'void' positionally equivalent and antonyms, 'worth' and 'pride', which are also positionally equivalent, must become antonyms if one's expectations about the parallelism of the larger constituents are to be fulfilled (*Linguistic Structures in Poetry*, p. 30). What really confirms this analysis, however, is the fact that the alternative interpretation is to take pride as a definite virtue, thus retaining the effects of parallelism, rather than to say that pride is neither virtue nor vice.

To see the force of such expectations one might consider a case where they are not fulfilled and where this failure produces a sense of incoherence. Gérard de Nerval's sonnet 'El Desdichado' (the disinherited) begins with a statement of loss and a negatively defined identity: 'Je suis le ténébreux, – le veuf, – l'inconsolé' (I am the dark one, the widower, the unconsoled). The sestet offers a series of possible identities and some of the relevant evidence:

> Suis-je Amour ou Phébus? . . . Lusignan ou Biron?
> Mon front est rouge encor du baiser de la reine;
> J'ai rêvé dans la grotte où nage la sirène . . .
>
> Et j'ai deux fois vainqueur traversé l'Achéron:
> Modulant tour à tour sur la lyre d'Orphée
> Les soupirs de la sainte et les cris de la fée.

(Am I Love or Phoebus? . . . Lusignan or Biron? My forehead is still red from the queen's kiss; I have dreamed in the grotto where the siren swims . . . And I have twice victoriously crossed Acheron: tempering in turn on Orpheus's lyre the saint's sobs and the fairy's cries.)

In the first line of the sestet the strict grammatical parallelism sets up expectations which must be tested at the semantic level. Since the two questions are positionally equivalent one might assume that the choice between Love and Phoebus is parallel to that between Lusignan and Biron and hence that Love and Lusignan share some feature which differentiates them from Phoebus and Biron (although, as Léon Cellier points out, a chiasmus which set Love and Biron against Phoebus and Lusignan would be theoretically possible).[6] But it is extremely difficult to discover appropriate distinguishing features. If, like Jacques Geninasca, who subjects the sonnet to an exhaustive Jakobsonian analysis, one takes the grammatical parallelism for granted and assumes that there must be a semantic parallel, one can exercise great ingenuity in choosing among the Birons known to history and among the escapades of Phoebus (*Analyse structurale des 'Chimères' de Nerval*, pp. 49-100). But this attempt runs counter to the evidence provided by the rest of the sonnet, where there is a marked opposition between the classical world on the one hand (Love, Phoebus) and the world of medieval French legends on the other (Lusignan, Biron). Since the citation of these two pairs is directly followed by two lines which continue this opposition (the queen's kiss and the siren's grotto), we may conclude that the first line of the tercets turns on this opposition as well, but that by grouping its items thus, in a way which establishes expectations that are not fulfilled, it both reinforces the impression that the quest for a viable identity cannot be compassed by the clear form of the *either/or* and promotes a fusion rather than isolation of categories: the alternatives proposed by the syntax are not significantly distinctive and the choices which the rest of the poem sets forth are not so mutually exclusive as to be joined and separated by a disjunctive *or*. If Jakobson's theory is taken as bearing on the process of reading it helps to account for poetic effects of this kind.

Indeed, it is in this perspective, as a theory of the operations which grammatical figures can induce readers to perform, that Jakobson's account of poetic language is most usefully considered. To say that there is a great deal of parallelism and repetition in literary texts is of little interest in itself and of less explanatory value. The crucial question is what effects patterning can have, and one cannot approach an answer unless one incorporate within one's theory an account of how readers take up and structure elements of a text.

A final example of the usefulness of Jakobson's theory and of the difficulties he encounters through applying it incorrectly, can be taken from his analysis of Shakespeare's 129th sonnet.

> Th'expense of Spirit in a waste of shame
> Is lust in action, and till action, lust
> Is perjured, murderous, bloody, full of blame,

Savage, extreme, rude, cruel, not to trust,
Enjoyed no sooner but despised straight,
Past reason hunted, and no sooner had,
Past reason hated, as a swallowed bait,
On purpose laid to make the taker mad.
Mad in pursuit, and in possession so,
Had, having, and in quest to have, extreme,
A bliss in proof, and proved, a very woe,
Before a joy proposed, behind a dream.
  All this the world well knows, yet none knows well
  To shun the heaven that leads men to this hell.

Approaching the sonnet from a linguistic point of view, Jakobson discovers an instance of grammatical parallelism and draws from it semantic conclusions:

Only the even strophes display hypotaxis and end in
multileveled 'progressive' structures, i.e. constructions with
several degrees of subordinates, each of them postponed to the
subordinating constituent:

II A) hated B) as a swallowed bait C) on purpose laid
    D) to make E) the taker F) mad.
IV A) none knows well B) to shun C) the heaven
    D) that leads E) men F) to this hell.
The penultimate constituents of both progressive structures are
the only animate nouns of the sonnet (II the taker, IV men),
and both constructions finish with the only substantival tropes:
bait and *taker*, *heaven* and *hell* instead of heaven's sovereign
and hellish torment. (*Shakespeare's Verbal Art in 'Th'Expence of
Spirit'*, p. 21)

Given this parallelism, Jakobson argues that the first centrifugal line of the sonnet 'introduces the hero, *the taker*', who is manifestly a victim, and that 'the final centrifugal line brings the exposure of the malevolent culprit, *the heaven that leads men to this hell*, and thus discloses by what perjurer the joy was proposed and the lure laid' (*ibid.*, p. 18).

From a structural parallelism Jakobson deduces the equivalence of individual constituents. He therefore relates 'on purpose laid' to 'the heaven' and suggests that heaven's sovereign is the culprit who has deliberately laid the bait. This mistaken interpretation arises from a confusion about the nature and function of parallelism. The reader does not consider the grammatical structure of the sonnet in isolation, allowing it to override all other considerations. He takes in syntactic features together with other features and thus will find an obvious thematic and grammatical parallel between 'to make the taker mad' and 'leads men to this hell': the second is a generalized version of the first. This relation of equivalence suggests that whatever makes the taker mad should be related to what leads men to this hell, and hence that 'bait' is the equivalent in the second quatrain of 'heaven' in the couplet. The natural interpretation is thus to take 'heaven' as the vision of 'bliss' and 'joy proposed' which baits the taker and not as a trope for 'heaven's sovereign'.

Jakobson, thinking in distributional terms, takes position to be the crucial factor: since 'on purpose laid' directly precedes 'to make' he relates it to 'heaven' which directly precedes 'that leads'. But the reader would make this connection only if he approached the poem without paying any attention to logical and thematic relations. Position does play a role, but not in the way that Jakobson implies; it is subordinated to thematic considerations. The reader can notice that the phrase 'on purpose laid', which appears between 'bait' and 'to make', has no constituent corresponding to it in the final line of the sonnet. The logical parallelism has been violated, and this has considerable significance: the vituperative and accusatory tone of 'on purpose laid' has vanished by the time we reach the couplet. No longer is lust 'past reason hated', with a passion that leads to random and undirected accusations. The fault lies, it is suggested, not with some unknown culprit who has deliberately laid this bait, but with men themselves who cannot move from one sort of knowledge to another – from *connaître* to *savoir*. The grammatical structure reinforces this effect by making one aware of the fact that a particular constituent has, by the time we reach the couplet, been repressed or overcome.

Jakobson's misinterpretation is quite instructive because it shows clearly how a mistaken assumption vitiates the application of his theory. The readiness with which he accepts his interpretation suggests that he thinks it is correct *because* it has been reached by linguistic analysis. If one assumes that linguistics provides a method for the discovery of poetic patterns, then one is likely to blind oneself to the ways in which grammatical patterns actually operate in poetic texts, for the simple reason that poems contain, by virtue of the fact that they are read as poems, structures other than the grammatical, and the resulting interplay may give the grammatical structures a function which is not at all what the linguist expected. It is only by starting with the effects of a poem and attempting to see how grammatical structures contribute to and help to account for those effects that one can avoid the mistakes which result if one thinks of grammatical analysis as an interpretive method.

For even in its own province the task of linguistics is not to tell us what sentences mean; it is rather to explain how they have the meanings which speakers of a language give them. If linguistic analysis were to propose meanings which speakers of the language could not accept, it would be the linguists who were wrong, not the speakers. Much the same is true in the study of the poetic function of language: poetic effects constitute the data to be explained. Jakobson has made an important contribution to literary studies in drawing attention to the varieties of grammatical figures and their potential functions, but his own analyses are vitiated by the belief that linguistics provides an automatic discovery procedure for poetic patterns and by his failure to perceive that the central task is to explain how poetic structures emerge from the multiplicity of potential linguistic structures.

CHAPTER 4

Greimas and Structural Semantics

Mais si le langage exprime autant par
ce qui est entre les mots que par les
mots? Par ce qu'il ne 'dit' pas que
par ce qu'il 'dit'? *
MERLEAU-PONTY

One might expect semantics to be the branch of linguistics which
literary critics would find most useful. If there is any realm where the
methods of linguistic description could with profit be applied to the
language of literature, it is that of meaning. What critic does not in
his moments dream of a scientifically rigorous way of characterizing
the meaning of a text, of demonstrating with tools of proven appropriateness that certain meanings are possible and others impossible?
And even if semantic theory did not suffice to account for all meanings
observed in literature, would it not, at least, form a primary stage in
literary theory and critical method by indicating what meanings must
be characterized by supplementary rules? If semantics could provide
a description of the semantic structure of a text it would certainly be
of great use to critics, even if it were not a panacea.

Such hopes, however well-founded, have been vain. Semantics has
not yet reached the stage where it can characterize the meaning of a
text, and even the more modest goals it has set for itself have scarcely
been achieved. Katz and Fodor, who like most transformational
grammarians are not known for the modesty of their theoretical
claims, see the task of semantics as that of describing selected aspects
of a speaker's competence: his ability to determine the literal meaning
of sentences, to recognize synonymous sentences and to reject
anomalous readings. They are concerned with the meaning of
sentences only, not of utterances nor of connected discourse, and they
do not attempt to characterize in detail the meaning of deviant (e.g.
metaphorical) strings.[1] The literary critic who hopes that semantics
might make a substantial contribution to the understanding of

* But what if language speaks as much by what is between words as by the
words themselves? As much by what is does not 'say' as by what it 'says'?

meaning in literature will doubtless concur with Uriel Weinreich's view that they are 'concerned with an extremely limited part of semantic competence', and that 'whether there is any point to semantic theories which are accountable only for special cases of speech – namely humourless, prosaic, banal prose – is highly doubtful' ('Explorations in Semantic Theory', pp. 397–9).

The critic would prefer a more ambitious theory, even if it be less systematic; and therefore it is surprising that A. J. Greimas's *Sémantique structurale* has received so little attention,[2] for it attempts to account for verbal meaning of all kinds, including that of metaphors, of sentences in connected discourse and even the 'totalité de signification' of a text or set of texts. Starting with the meanings of words or lexical items, Greimas attempts to formulate rules and concepts to account for the meanings produced when they combine in sentences or in complete texts; and his book concludes with a study of 'the imaginative world' of the novelist Georges Bernanos, 'a nearly complete specimen of description, carried out on a given corpus, specifying the procedures used, and proposing, in the end, definitive models of organization for a semantic micro-universe' (*Sémantique structurale*, p. 222). If, as this passage implies, Greimas's theory did provide an algorithm for the semantic and thematic description of a literary corpus, it would be extremely valuable indeed; and one may as well say at once, rather than raise false hopes, that such claims are unjustified. But by examining the difficulties his theory encounters, the ways in which it fails, one may hope to shed some light on the possibilities and limitations of semantic theories of this kind. Greimas's work is only the most ambitious example of a particular way of applying linguistic models to the description of literary language, and one must attempt to determine how far it is possible to account for meaning in literature on the hypothesis that minimal semantic features combine in rule-governed ways to produce large-scale semantic effects.

A semantic theory must aim at both operational and descriptive adequacy; that is to say, it must use concepts which can be defined in terms of empirical techniques or operations and it must account for intuitively attested facts about meaning. A theory of description is operationally adequate only if it is sufficiently explicit for different linguists using its apparatus to reach the same results or, more precisely, for a computer to be programmed to use its techniques in producing descriptions. If the theory were formulated as a set of instructions which produced readings, its descriptive adequacy would depend on the 'correctness' of those readings. In the present state of semantics any theory will fail in at least one of these respects: either it will use a coherent and explicit metalanguage but fail to account for certain semantic effects, or it will develop concepts which specify the effects to be explained but which are not themselves explicitly defined in operational terms. The initial problem in evaluating Greimas's theory – and which perhaps explains why, despite his reputation as a leading structuralist, so little has been written about it – is that one is not sure in which way it fails. When introducing a new concept he defines it both in terms of other concepts of the theory and in terms of the semantic effects it is designed to explain, but often these two definitions do not coincide and one must choose which is to be the crucial specification. Is his theory a set of interlocking concepts which fail to explain a range of semantic effects, or is it rather a specification of aspects of semantic competence whose terms must be given a more adequate operational definition? In either case, his example illustrates with considerable clarity the difficulty of bridging the gap between the semantic features of words and the meanings of sentences or texts.

At the base of Greimas's theory, as of any serious semantics, is an opposition between 'immanence' and 'manifestation': between a conceptual 'map' of possible features of the world, independent of any language, and the actual groupings of these features in the words and sentences of a language. The plane of immanence consists of minimal semantic features or 'semes' which are the result of oppositions (masculine/feminine, old/young, human/animal, etc.). The lexical items or 'lexemes' of a particular language manifest certain combinations of these features: *woman*, for example, combines a phonological shape and the semes 'female' and 'human', which are the result of immanent oppositions. Any semantic theory will require a hierarchically organized set of semantic features, but none has even approached this goal, since it would require one to devise an ordered list of all possible attributes. However, the minimum condition of adequacy for an analysis into semes is quite simply stated: for any two lexical items that differ in meaning there must be one or more semes which account for that difference.

Since the meaning of a lexical item can vary from one context to another, Greimas postulates that the semantic representation of a lexeme consists of an invariant core (*le noyau sémique*), made up of one or more semes, and a series of contextual semes, each of which will be manifested only in specific contexts. To determine the semantic composition of a particular lexical item, one considers all the readings or 'sememes' that the lexeme has in a corpus and extracts, as components of the *noyau sémique*, those features shared by all sememes. The variations in meaning are reduced to a series of alternative contextual semes. This first stage of description, the analysis of lexemes in terms of semantic features, may be thought of as the formalization of a dictionary of the language. All semantic theories rest on a base of this sort, and at this level Greimas's work is not particularly distinctive. The crucial question is how, given some representation of the meaning of words, one is to account for the meanings of sentences and sequences of sentences.

The most elementary case is the combination of a subject and verb or of an adjective and noun. How will semantics account for the fact that *bark* has a different meaning in *The dog barked at me* and *The man barked at me* or that the sense of *colourful* is not the same in *a colourful dress* and *a colourful character*? A speaker who knows the meanings of the individual words has no difficulty in extracting the correct meaning from their combinations. What representation of this ability can linguistics offer? Greimas argues that the choice among the contextual semes attached to one lexical item is determined by the presence of one of these semes in the other item. Thus, the lexeme *bark* would have as its core something like 'a sharp vocal noise' and as its contextual variants the features 'human' and 'animal'. One selects whichever of these features, 'human' or 'animal', is present in the subject of the verb (p. 50). If this were so, then the process of determining the correct reading for pairs of words could be represented as an explicit procedure: look up each lexeme in the dictionary and write its semantic specification; then take each of the contextual semes of the first lexeme in turn and see if they are present in the second lexeme; if so, retain them; if not, abandon them.

Some process of this sort is no doubt at work in semantic competence, but Greimas's formulation encounters several difficulties. First of all, it does not work even for the lexical item he cites as example: *aboyer* (to bark, bay, clamour after) contains the nucleus 'a kind of cry' and the contextual semes 'animal' and 'human', so that *Le chien aboie après le facteur* means 'The dog barks at the postman' and *L'enfant aboie après sa mère* means 'The child clamours for his mother'. But selection does not always work in this simple fashion: though the police are human, *La police aboie après le criminel* does not mean that they clamour for him, uttering human cries, but that they pursue him with the tenacity of hounds that have taken the scent and are in full cry. If it is to account for effects of this kind, the theory must become considerably more complex, for in its present state it can explain only those metaphorical readings which it has built into words at the lexical level. In *That man is a lion*, an example which Greimas cites, the correct metaphorical meaning is produced only if one has included in the dictionary entry for the lexeme *lion* the contrasting contextual semes 'human' and 'animal', so that the presence of a human subject may select the features 'human', 'courageous', etc. This means, for example, that every animal or vegetable term which can be used to insult or praise a human being must have this metaphorical meaning listed in the lexicon as one of its contextual variants. The case of poetic language, however, would seem to indicate both the futility of trying to incorporate in a lexicon all possible metaphorical meanings (since new metaphors are always being produced) and the unnecessary character of such a procedure (since new metaphors can be understood). We shall consider below other ways of accounting for metaphorical meanings; for the moment the point is simply that Greimas's attempt to work from minimal units to larger units encounters difficulties because he must try to build in at lower levels all meanings that might be encountered at higher levels.

Another problem stemming from the same cause is the general constraint imposed on sememes by Greimas's theory: in order to assign the correct meanings to *colourful dress* and *colourful character* we must invent some feature which is present in both *colourful* and *dress* and another present in both *colourful* and *character*, and since the distinction between *dress* and *character* which induces the different meanings of *colourful* seems to be 'physical object' as against 'human', the lexical entry for colourful must specify as part of its meaning the alternatives 'physical object' and 'human'. This is counter-intuitive, to say the least, and one would prefer some kind of generalizable rule which would indicate how a set of adjectives behave in the presence of items with these features; for 'human' does not seem to be part of a meaning of *colourful* in the sense that 'human' and 'physical object' are part of two alternative meanings of *cutter* (one who cuts/that which cuts).

It is, however, crucial to Greimas's theory that correct readings be selected by an actual repetition of semes, for the semes which are thus repeated in a text are called 'classemes' and are largely responsible for the coherence of texts. Just as the repetition of semes leads to the formation of classemes, so the repetition of classemes in a text enables the reader to identify a level of coherence or an 'isotopy' which unifies it.

> Such a conception of classemes, as items whose characteristic is to be repeated, can have definite explanatory value if only in making more comprehensible the still vague yet very necessary concept of *meaningful whole* (*totalité de signification*) . . .
> We shall attempt to show, by the use of the concept of *isotopy*, how it is that whole texts are situated at homogeneous semantic levels, how the global meaning of a set of signifiers, instead of

being postulated *a priori*, can be interpreted as a real structural property of linguistic manifestation. (p. 53).

If he could succeed in showing how the total meaning of a text might be derived by some definable operations from a set of signifiers, his work would indeed be of great moment to the literary critic; but unfortunately the notion that repetition of classemes leads to a particular form of unity is simply not borne out by the examples he cites.

Jokes, he argues, provide excellent evidence of the functioning of isotopies since the joke is a form which deliberately displays and plays with the linguistic operations that comprehension involves. At a splendid and elegant evening party one guest remarks to another, 'Ah! belle soirée, hein? Repas magnifique, et puis jolies toilettes, hein?' (Splendid evening, isn't it? Magnificent food, and the dresses (toilets) are lovely, eh?). To which comes the not unpredictable reply: 'Ça, je n'en sais rien . . . je n'y suis pas allé' (Couldn't say, really . . . I haven't been) (p. 70). Greimas claims, quite correctly, that the first part of the joke, introducing the situation, establishes one context and level of coherence and that the reply of the second speaker 'destroys its unity in suddenly opposing a second isotopy to the first'. Certainly this is what happens, but it is difficult to see how this could be explained as the result of the repetition of classemes. The reading 'dresses' for *toilettes* is determined by rather more subtle features of the context than the sort of classeme previously discussed. To see that no feature of *brillante soirée mondaine* suffices in itself to determine this reading of *toilettes* one need only turn the joke around and have the first speaker ask for directions – 'Où sont les toilettes' or 'Avez-vous vu les toilettes' – with the reply, 'They're all around you.' In this case the reader selects the correct meanings with no difficulty even though the seme 'sanitary facility' or whatever relates to nothing in the introduction to the joke. He knows that one is not likely to ask where the dresses are at a fashionable evening party.

It is extremely important for a theory of discourse to be able to account for readers' abilities to choose among alternative readings and establish levels of coherence, but the process involves some rather complex notions of *vraisemblance* and appropriateness which cannot be rendered, it would seem, by a list of the classemes which appear more than once in a particular stretch of text. Greimas seems to recognize this when he writes in a later chapter that

> the need for a *cultural grid* to resolve difficulties concerning the discovery of isotopies . . . calls into question the very possibility of objective semantic analysis. For the fact that in the present state of knowledge it is difficult to imagine such a

grid which would meet the requirements of a mechanical
analysis indicates that description itself still depends, to a large
extent, on the subjective decisions of the analyst. (p. 90)

In other words, Greimas sees that the proposed scheme is not in
itself a procedure for semantic analysis. Isotopies, if they are indeed
to capture the levels of coherence of a text, cannot be automatically
identified by noting the repetitions of classemes. They do, however,
represent an important aspect of the reader's competence – one which
certainly requires explanation – and the use of the concept will be
discussed in greater detail below.

Once one has identified the various isotopies of a text one can in
theory divide a text into its isotopic strata. As Greimas sadly notes,
this procedure is still very much determined by the subjective perceptions of the analyst, but he claims that by exercising great care and
going back repeatedly over the text one can hope to avoid omissions
(pp. 145–6). This assumes, of course, that one knows what one is
looking for, which is far from clear. For example, Greimas has
identified what he calls the basic isotopies: the 'practical', which is a
manifestation of the 'cosmological' or the outer world, and the
'mythic', which concerns the 'noological' or inner world (p. 120).
The example which illustrates this distinction – a *heavy sack* versus a
heavy conscience – is clear enough, and no doubt the distinction could
be made in a large number of cases, especially where two senses of a
word are correlated with inner and outer references. But there are
vast numbers of cases where the distinction seems irrelevant – how
does one decide whether the sentences on this page are practical,
mythic or both? – or where little is gained by attempting to fragment
a unitary meaning (*La police aboie après le criminel* is both internal
and external without being ambiguous). Greimas appears to assume
that phrases will already be marked with the relevant classemes,
intéroceptive and *extéroceptive*, by the time one reaches this stage,
but this simply transfers the problem to a lower level. The procedure
has an obvious intuitive validity: in interpreting a poem, for example,
one will extract and relate to one another all the sequences relating
to a classeme such as *human* in order to determine what meanings
cluster around this semantic core. But Greimas has not even approached a formal definition of the operation: how long, for example,
is a sequence?

The next step in semantic description is the 'normalization' of
series which have been constructed by isolating the sequences
belonging to a single isotopy. This is essentially a process of reducing
the sentences to a series of subjects and predicates which will be cast
in a constant form so that they can be related to one another and, as it

were, added up. Everything referring to the act of enunciation is first eliminated: first and second person pronouns (which are replaced by 'the speaker' and 'the listener'), all references to the time of the message, deictics, in so far as they are dependent on the situation of the speaker and not simply on other parts of the message (pp. 153–4). Each sequence is then reduced to a set of nominal phrases (*actants*) and a predicate which is either a verb or predicate adjective (Greimas calls them 'dynamic' and 'static' predicates or *functions* and *qualifications*). Predicates may also include modal operators and an adverbial element of some kind (*aspect*). *Actants* or nominal groups will fit into one of six different roles: subject, object, *destinateur* (sender), *destinataire* (receiver), *opposant* (opponent) and *adjuvant* (helper). A single sentence, then, will contain up to six *actants*, a function or qualification, and possibly a modal operator and adverbial element.

One function of this scheme is to make the structure of the sentence roughly homologous to the 'plot' of a text. The story of a quest, for example, will have a subject and an object, opponents and helpers, and perhaps other actants whose function is to give or receive. Ideally, such a plot might be conceived as an ordered and discriminating sum of the actantial relations manifested in those sentences which are located on the appropriate isotopy. However, it is clear that one could not simply transcribe sentences in this notation and conflate the results, for the hero will not be the subject of every sentence, nor will other characters necessarily occupy the thematically appropriate actantial roles in sentences.

The application of the actantial model to the analysis of narrative will be discussed in chapter 9, but that is not its only function. It also offers a representation, though again perhaps more in theory than in practice, of the process of reading which, by the hypothesis that this notation implies, involves going through the text and grouping together the various actantial roles in which a particular nominal group appears, the series of qualifications appended to particular nominal groups, and the series of functions or actions which are combined to form the action of a text. Whether an analysis carried out in these terms would offer a pertinent representation of the process of semantic synthesis is not known, since there has apparently been no systematic attempt to transcribe a text according to these formulae and then show how a formalized process of synthesis would operate.[3] But there seem at least two important obstacles. First of all, at the level of the sentence itself, the debates concerning case grammar, which is formally analogous to Greimas's approach in that it makes the sentence a predicate with a constellation of nominals in various logical slots, show that the number of the actantial roles that are required if one is to represent the relations among sentence constituents cannot be determined without considerable empirical experimentation.[4] Greimas gives very few examples to show the adequacy of his model of the sentence. And second, he gives no indication as to how his model would deal with all the problems of relationships between sentences which make discourse analysis such a daunting and as yet unformalized activity. Even supposing that isotopic stretches of discourse were isolated, all the problems of formalizing relations of anaphora and presupposition between sentences remain to be solved.[5]

Greimas does claim that this 'normalization' of the text helps one to 'discover more easily its redundancies and structural articulations' (p. 158), and in his last chapter he attempts to determine the structure of the 'imaginary universe' of the novelist Georges Bernanos as a way of illustrating his method of semantic description. Unfortunately, he does not take the texts themselves and show how one might start from semantic features and go on to determine classemes, isotopies, and finally, global structures of meaning. He bases his study on an Istanbul thesis by Tahsin Yücel on *L'Imaginaire de Bernanos* whose results, he rather disarmingly claims, 'permit us *not to avoid* the difficulties that any description involves' (p. 222). This is true only in the sense that he does not overcome them, and the reader who would like to see how one could 'normalize' a text and then, by some well-defined procedure, determine its structural articulations and redundancies is very much aware that the difficulties of such a proposal have indeed not been avoided. No stretch of text, however short, is presented and analysed.

Greimas claims that his procedure is as follows: he chooses as his basic isotopy the opposition between *life* and *death* and extracts from the corpus all the qualifications situated on this isotopy. Taking the items which qualify *life*, one reduces them to a limited set of sememes and then, by a second process of extraction, collects all the contexts in which each of these appears. He is thus undertaking a distributional analysis of the most traditional kind. If, for example, one has a sequence such as *Life is beautiful* one asks in the second extraction what other nominal groups in the text are qualified by *beautiful* and thus obtains a class of items which are equivalent with respect to this particular distributional feature. Less skilful analysts would no doubt encounter sequences such as *Marie is beautiful* or *That dress is beautiful* and thus be forced to relate *life* to *Marie* and *dress*, but for some reason Greimas obtains no irritating collocations of this kind and discovers, rather, the distributional equivalence of *vie* (life), *feu* (fire) and *joie* (joy), which are as a class opposed to *mort* (death), *eau* (water) and *ennui*. He can then proceed to determine the qualifications which appear with the four new terms, 'and so on until the corpus has been exhausted, that is to say until the last extraction (n) using the last inventory (n-l) makes no new qualifications appear' (p. 224). This spurious rigour would not be so objectionable if Greimas deigned to indicate by a single example how he proposes to deal with sentences such as those which contain the first instances of *vie* in Bernanos's *Sous le soleil de Satan*: 'It was the hour of the poet who distilled life in his head so as to extract its secret, perfumed, poisoned essence.' 'He still broods in melancholy fashion on the paradise lost of middle-class life.' 'The Marquis of Cardigan led in the same place the life of a king without a kingdom.' It is not at all clear which items would be extracted as qualifications of *life* by Greimas's procedure.

The semantic features which Greimas extracts from his series of inventories are arranged in a system of oppositions representing the associations of life and death. Or rather, the results of projecting this fundamental opposition into other semantic spheres are captured in the form of corresponding disjunctions: transparent versus opaque, hot versus cold, lightness versus heaviness, rhythm versus monotony, etc. The tableaux have considerable intuitive validity since the oppositions themselves are inherent in the semantic structure of the language and the values assigned to the poles of the oppositions seem not unrelated to the eccentricities of Bernanos's imaginary world. But the crucial question is what claims might be made for an analysis of this sort. What is the difference, for example, between the status of the results Greimas has obtained and that of more traditional analyses of imagery as undertaken, for example, by Jean-Pierre Richard?[6] What is gained, that is to say, by attempting to derive the structure of an imaginative world from an analysis of discourse carried out in a supposedly formal and rigorous way rather than from the more intuitive consideration of sets of images? Greimas gives no direct reply, but one might suppose that he would simply claim a greater objectivity, as the necessary virtue of an exhaustive study of qualifications. But as anyone who has attempted such work on even a short piece of prose can testify, systematic inventories produce collocations which seem irrelevant to the purposes in hand and which are generally eliminated in the final statements of patterns. The collocation of *life* and *middle-class* (*bourgeoise*), does not, for example, appear in any of Greimas's schema, though it is found in the sentence of *Sous le soleil de Satan* that was cited above; and the reason is presumably that Greimas has eliminated it for the same kind of reasons that would lead the more impressionistic student of imagery not to take note of it in the first place. To be convinced of the superiority of Greimas's method one would not only need to see the procedures of extraction at work on actual texts so as to gain some sense of their effective rigour; one would also require some explanation of the ways in which the selection of pertinent collocations was carried out.

A set of ten categories suffices, Greimas argues, to describe Bernanos's mythical universe (p. 246). One tests such a claim by determining whether anything which one takes to be a true statement about this imaginative world can be represented as a relationship among these categories and whether the relationships among categories, as defined by Greimas, are such as to exclude statements about the imaginative world which one takes to be false. But even if Greimas's results were to pass this test with flying colours, that would give them only the status of a successful critical statement. The larger claim which Greimas would wish to make, the suggestion that his theory provides a determinate procedure for the description of meaning, cannot be substantiated without precise examples of descriptive procedures and formalization of the rules of analysis. No one would expect Greimas, in the present state of knowledge, to have reached that stage, and he clearly has not done so; but the ways in which he fails cast doubt on the viability of the project itself: it may be impossible, in principle as well as in practice, to construct a model which would derive the meaning of a text or of a set of texts from the meaning of lexical items.

If one wishes to profit from Greimas's example, the best strategy is to invert his perspective and, starting from the supposition that the meaning of texts is not automatically derivable from the meanings of lexical items, focus on the gaps in Greimas's theory, which help one to define, by virtue of the environment in which they occur, the supplementary considerations that an adequate theory of reading would require. By looking at the broken links in Greimas's algorithmic chain one can see what needs to be supplied from outside the realm of linguistic semantics if the chain is to be completed.

Three problematic regions have so far been identified: procedures to account for the selection of readings at the classematic level where two or more lexical items are united in a phrase, methods for identifying isotopies or levels of coherence, and ways of accounting for the organization of meaning above the isotopic level or, in other words, within the text itself as semantic universe. Although the concepts of Greimas's theory label and thus identify the operations which readers must be presumed to perform they do not go very far towards explicating them.

The difficulty of accounting for one's ability to select readings at the phrasal level is most forcibly illustrated by metaphor. Greimas's machinery requires, as was noted above, that lexical items which can serve as the vehicle of a metaphor have the metaphorical potential incorporated in their lexical entries, so that, for example, the production of the correct reading for *This man is a lion* depends on the presence of the contextual seme *human* in the lexical entry for *lion*. Not only is this requirement in itself exceedingly cumbersome and counter-intuitive; it has the unfortunate consequence of entailing the suppression of semantic features on which the point of the metaphor may depend. For to call someone a lion is not merely to say that they are courageous; it is also to imply that their boldness has an animal quality to it. Yet this effect is lost if we incorporate in the lexical entry for *lion* an opposition between the contextual semes *human* and *animal* such that selection of one excludes the other. In Donne's line, 'For I am every dead thing', which brings together the animate and the inanimate, we have an effect that cannot be captured by semantic machinery which forces us to select for both subject and predicate either the classeme *animate* or the classeme *inanimate* but not both. The identification with the inanimate has point to it only if the *I* retains some of its animate character.

The ability of readers to find metaphorical readings for the most surprising collocations indicates the futility of trying to account for metaphors at the level of lexicon and suggests, rather, that one should attempt to define the semantic operations which metaphorical interpretation involves. These are, of course, extremely complex: in the sentence *Golf plays John*, a canonical example for the violation of selection-restrictions, we know that *plays* requires an animate subject and therefore assign the feature *animate* to *golf*. But that is by no means all that we do: rejecting the meaning of *play* which takes a human direct object (to compete with), we deprive John of some of his human status and make him an object of the activity (only when one is so degraded as to become oneself an object can the inanimate *golf* become a subject that exercises and sports with its unfortunate victim). The requirements of metaphorical coherence bring about readjustments in the semantic value of all three terms, so one cannot represent the process simply as bringing the semantic content of one term into line with that of another. Were that so, we should hold firm the content of *play* and *John* and simply rework that of *golf*, yielding 'Golf competes with John'. Instead, our awareness of the ordinary relations between *play* and *golf* establishes an expected structure into which we mould the rearranged terms, inverting the roles which would be assigned to *John* and *golf* in *John plays golf*. The semantic features which are added to each item in the process of metaphorical interpretation do not suppress the old, which they contradict, but coexist with them, producing a tension between the animate and inanimate within each lexical item which is the source of whatever piquancy the metaphor has.

Greimas seems to recognize the importance of retaining contradictory semes when he proposes the notion of positive and negative isotopies (pp. 99–100). When the narrator of a poem compares himself to a drunken boat the classeme *human*, which establishes the 'positive' isotopy, remains dominant, while the present but repressed classeme *non-human* establishes a negative isotopy. In the case of a madman who thinks he is a chandelier, however, the classeme *non-human*, which establishes the negative isotopy, would be dominant.

Retention of non-dominant semes is a considerable improvement but is still not an adequate analysis of the process by which readings are selected. We would require, for example, some representation of the way in which the dominant classeme is chosen. In metaphors of the form A is B, which are far from being the most complex and interesting, semantic features of the first term generally dominate, but *A mighty fortress is our God* does not mean that we worship the castle as if it were a god. In genitive metaphors, the A of B, the features of the first term which do not fit in with those of the second are generally suppressed, but again this is not always the case: 'From his eyes of flame/Ruby tears there came.' In cases like these it is features of the context that are decisive, and there is no reason to think that the selection of readings can be accounted for as an automatic readjustment of classemes prior to the establishment or identification of isotopies or levels of coherence.

'The principal difficulty of reading', Greimas writes, 'consists in discovering the isotopy of the text and in remaining at that level' (p. 99). Literary theory and semantics face the same problem: 'the struggle against the logomachic character of texts, the search for conditions for objectively establishing the isotopies which permit reading, is one of the principal worries of semantic description in its initial phases' (*Du Sens*, pp. 93–4). In reading a text one gains a sense of what it is about; one isolates a semantic field in which a number of items fall as the topic of the text and hence as the central point of reference to which other items one encounters should, if possible, be related. But, as Greimas notes, one can choose at random a series of elements in a text, treat them as a set, and construct some general category encompassing them all: 'it is always possible to reduce an inventory, taken on its own, to a constructed sememe' (*Sémantique structurale*, p. 167). What, then, prevents the reader's activity from being totally arbitrary, though logical? Ideally, the explicit description of the isotopies of a text 'should account for all possible coherent readings. Without going so far as explicitly listing each reading, it would define the conditions of each.'[7] If such a goal is to be even remotely possible, one must formulate some general rules to account for the fact that not every conceivable isotopy is valid for a given text. What are, then, 'the conditions for objectively establishing the isotopies'?

In some simple cases one might accept Greimas's claim that repetition of a particular classeme suffices to account for the isotopy. Baudelaire's second 'Spleen' poem, 'J'ai plus de souvenirs que si j'avais mille ans', begins with a paratactic sequence of sentences, each containing a pronominal form in the first person singular, and in each case the relationship between the pronoun and the predicate is that of container to contained. Thus, when the reader comes to the line, 'Je suis un vieux boudoir plein de roses fanées' (I am an old boudoir full of faded roses), he will, as Greimas says, 'attempt, more or less consciously, to extract from the "physical" description of the boudoir all the semes which can develop and maintain the second isotopy, which has been postulated from the beginning, of the poet's inner space' (*ibid.*, p. 97).

But in other instances it is considerably more difficult to explain what happens or how a dominant isotopy comes to assert itself. François Rastier has applied Greimas's theory to Mallarmé's 'Salut' in an analysis which shows the intuitive validity of the concept of isotopy but also the formidable problems involved in specifying how it is isolated.

Salut
Rien, cette écume, vierge vers
A ne désigner que la coupe;
Telle loin se noie une troupe
De sirènes, mainte à l'envers.

Nous naviguons, ô mes divers
Amis, moi déjà sur la poupe
Vous l'avant fastueux qui coupe
Le flot de foudres et d'hivers;

Une ivresse belle m'engage
Sans craindre même son tangage
De porter debout ce salut

Solitude, récif, étoile
A n'importe ce qui valut
Le blanc souci de notre toile.

(*Toast/Safety/Salvation*
Nothing, this froth, virgin verse
To indicate only the cup;
So in the distance many a troupe
Of sirens drown themselves, topsy-turvy.

We sail, O my varied friends,
I already on the poop
You the gaudy prow that cuts
The seas of winters and lightning;

A lovely intoxication engages me
Without fear even of the pitching
To offer this toast

Solitude, reef, star
To whatever was worth
The white care of our canvas.)

'The work of the reader', Rastier writes, 'consists of listing and naming in metalinguistic fashion the semes that characterize the chosen isotopy ('Systématique des isotopies', p. 88). The first of these can be designated as *banquet*. Any item which can be read as bearing a relation to the general semantic field surrounding the concept is extracted from the text and given an interpretation that integrates this isotopy. For example: '*rien* = these lines (connotes the modesty required of speakers); *écume* = champagne bubbles; *vierge vers* = a toast offered for the first time . . .' (p. 86). A second isotopy is that of navigation (e.g. *salut* = saved from the sea; *écume* = the froth of waves). And finally, a third level is postulated, 'which can be designated by the word *writing*' (p. 92).

But these isotopies are not simply the result of classemes that have been repeated. For one thing, in constructing the first the reader requires knowledge of the semiotic system defining the rituals of banquets. In order to be able to extract 'modesty' from *rien*, 'champagne' from *écume* and 'tablecloth' from *toile* he must know what takes place at banquets and have a strong desire to read the poem in these terms. Moreover, to read the sonnet as about writing one requires considerable evidence from Mallarmé's other poems, which couple, for example, writing and negativity (*rien*). This last isotopy cannot be the result of the repetition of features since the only element in the text which directly relates to it is *vierge vers*. That is to say, if we imagine a reader who knows French but has no experience of poetry and its conventions and *a fortiori* no knowledge of Mallarmé's poems, it is impossible to believe that he would find, in reading this poem, a series of items which repeatedly propose that the poem be interpreted as about writing. The experienced reader of poetry, on the other hand, knows that poems, especially poems by Mallarmé, are likely to be about poetry, that neither banquets nor sea voyages serve as satisfactory final isotopies, in that banquets always celebrate something and voyages are traditionally metaphors for other types of quest. It is only because he possesses knowledge of this kind – only because he approaches the poem with implicit models of this sort – that he is able to read the poem as about writing.

The importance of readers' expectations about poetry is even clearer in another case discussed by Rastier. 'In Gerard Manley Hopkins' "The Windhover", no semantic interpretant enables one to read anything other than the obvious isotopy which may be crudely stated as "a falcon rises and then swoops" ' (p. 100). How is it, then, that readers are not satisfied with this interpretation? What enables them to 'go on'? Committed as he is to the view that levels of coherence are manifested by a repetition of features, Rastier is forced to argue that

> the presence . . . of a large number of lexemes of foreign origin, French for the most part, indicates a foreignness whose connotations, for an Englishman, are aristocratic and, for a Jesuit, sacred (through the Latin origin); whence the discovery of a second isotopy crudely summed up as 'Christ rises in the heavens and comes to earth.' (p. 100)

By this criterion, of course, it would follow that one could read any text containing many words of Latin origin as a text on a sacred subject. However 'objective' such a procedure, it fails on the simple count of empirical adequacy. Moreover, the hypothesis is totally unnecessary. The reader of poetry knows that when such metaphorical energy is expended on a bird the creature itself is exalted and becomes metaphor, so that he would in any case seek analogues through which to generalize and grasp the splendour of 'buckling'; and if the religious isotopy did not propose itself in the interpretive search, it might be justified by general expectations concerning the author, whose poems demand at least an attempt at a religious reading. As Rastier's attempt at analysis shows, there is no reason to believe that the process of constructing levels of coherence can be explained without reference to some general literary models which guide the reader's approach to the text.

In discussing an example of a different kind, a joke drawn from Freud, Greimas demonstrates that even in prose texts consisting of perfectly comprehensible well-formed sentences the process of reading may consist of seizing upon a single feature of the text and building upon it an elaborate conceptual hypothesis for which there is really extraordinarily little evidence in the language itself – though everyone would agree that the interpretation was correct.

A horse-dealer offers a client a horse:
– If you take this horse and leave at four in the morning

you'll be at Presbourg at half-past six.
– And what will I do at Presbourg at six-thirty in the
morning?

The reader recognizes that there is a conflict of isotopies between the dealer's remark and the client's and that this is what creates the joke. But the text itself contains very little evidence indeed for this interpretation. The reader does not know where the exchange takes place, whether the journey to Presbourg is long or short, or how swiftly a fast horse could cover the distance. There is thus little objective reason for the natural and correct reaction of taking the dealer's remark as an illustration of the speed of the horse. The crucial factor, although Greimas does not mention it, is probably the closure of the text. If the dealer's and the client's remarks were on the same isotopic level the text would not end where it does, but since it comes so abruptly to a halt there must be meaning enough in the few sentences presented and that meaning will probably be generated by an oppositional structure. If the passage is to be of any interest at all there must be a contrast between the dealer's statement and the client's reply, and this expectation is strong enough to make us reject plausible literal readings in order to discover a conflict. We can take the brief introductory statement as establishing an isotopy which suggests that what follows will be a statement by the dealer about the horse and that, given our cultural models, it will concern some posi-tive quality of the horse. Thus, when we encounter in the next sentence the opposition between departure and arrival, this deter-mines, as Greimas says, 'the choice of one of the variables within the class of positive qualities of riding horses' (*Sémantique structurale*, p. 92). We can then read the client's remark as a misinterpretation – either foolish or deliberate – and do so with such confidence as to laugh at one of the two figures.

This case provides excellent evidence both that isotopies are not produced by the simple repetition of semantic features and that it may be misleading to think of texts as 'organic wholes'. Their unity is produced not so much by intrinsic features of their parts as by the intent at totality of the interpretive process: the strength of the expectations which lead readers to look for certain forms of organiza-tion in a text and to find them. A semantic theory which would account for the coherence of texts cannot afford to ignore the models which permit the production and organization of content.

From time to time Greimas recognizes that he cannot, in fact, move automatically from lower to higher levels, that a problem he encounters 'calls into question once again the diachronic status of description considered as a procedure'. Although theoretically it should be possible first to reduce the text to a series of sememes and then to show how these sememes combine to form classemes, isotopies, and finally the structured content which is the 'global meaning' of a text, in fact, it is clear that 'reduction presupposes the hypothetical representation of structures to be described, but that structuration, in its turn, if it is to be successfully carried out, presupposes a completed reduction' (*ibid.*, p. 167). From Greimas's point of view this kind of reciprocal implication is an obstacle to the formulation of a descriptive algorithm, but for the critic this is a useful specification of the importance of hypothetical representations of structures to the process of understanding. As Merleau-Ponty says, the meaning of the whole is not produced by an inductive summing up of the meanings of parts; it is only in the light of hypotheses about the meaning of the whole that the meaning of parts can be defined. Understanding 'n'est pas une série d'inductions – C'est *Gestaltung* et *Rückgestaltung* . . . Cela veut dire: il y a *germination* de ce qui *va avoir été* compris' (is not a series of inductions – it is the postulation and repostulation of wholes . . . That is to say, there is germination of what is *going to have been* understood) (*Le Visible et l'invisible*, p. 243). One attempts a reduction in terms of one hypothesis and if that does not work one tries another. Semantic description must provide a representation of the structuring activity of the reader.

Structural hypotheses for the recognition of meaning are extremely important at all levels, but especially once one has recognized isotopies and must organize the semes into content. Although Greimas does not propose a formal procedure, he does offer a number of suggestions about the 'conditions de la saisie du sens' – the conditions for the perception of meaning.

In constructing cultural objects, he argues, the mind is subject to various constraints which define the 'conditions of existence for semiotic objects'. The most important of these is the 'elementary structure of signification' which has the form of a four-term homology (A:B: :—A:—B) and 'furnishes a semiotic model designed to account for the initial articulations of meaning within a semantic micro-universe' (*Du Sens*, p. 161). Since meaning is diacritical any meaning depends on oppositions, and this four-term structure relates an item to both its converse and its contrary (black:white: :non-black: : non-white). This basic configuration holds also, Greimas argues, for the simplest representation of the meaning of a text as a whole. It is grasped as a correlation between two pairs of opposed terms. This structure can be either static or dynamic, depending on whether the text is read syntagmatically or paradigmatically: that is, as narrative or as lyric.

'To have a meaning a narrative must form a signifying whole and thus is organized as an elementary semantic structure' in which a temporal opposition is correlated with the homologous thematic opposition: *avant*: *après*: : *contenu inversé*: *contenu posé* (*ibid.*, p.187). In other words, the relation between an initial state and a final state is correlated with the opposition between an initial thematic situation or problem and a thematic conclusion or resolution. The claim is, roughly speaking, that the reader can grasp the *récit* as a whole only by fitting it into this structure and relating a thematic development to the development of the plot. And this structural expectation, of course, helps to make possible the interpretation of individual incidents or sentences of the text.

Lyrics, however, may often be grasped as a whole without any reference to temporal development; there need be no movement from A to B. Modern poetry in particular, Greimas writes, is the 'discursive manifestation of a taxonomy'. The reader is faced with phrases or images, linked in rudimentary discursive fashion, from which he must extract features that he can use to organize the text into oppositional classes. The sememes of poetic discourse 'bear, on the one hand, the semes that are constitutive of the poetic isotopy and, on the other hand, serve as semic relays, that is to say, as places where the substitution of semes takes place'. Items become equivalent with respect to the poetic structure and interchange semantic features, and the particular combination of semes which any individual word bears becomes much less important than the features that serve as links between words and therefore as the bases of the poem's semantic classes. It is more important, for example, that the semes *fluidity* and *luminosity* are used to link words and to establish meaningful oppositions than that they are both manifested in the sememe *sky* or *lake*. 'This can be explained only if one considers the production of homologous semic classes as the primary fact and the sememic structure of the linguistic manifestation as secondary' (*Sémantique structurale*, pp. 135–6).

The fundamental structure of a poem will thus, by Greimas's hypothesis, be a pair of semantic classes which in their opposition to one another are correlated with another pair of classes so as to produce a thematic interdependence. The major constraint on the formation of thematic classes is that they be binary: 'an inventory of items cannot be reduced to a class and denoted by a single sememe except in so far as another inventory is, at the same time, constituted and named' (*ibid.*, p. 167). And the reason is quite simple: to class a series of elements together is to claim that some feature which they share is pertinent to the meaning of the poem; if that feature is indeed pertinent it is because of the opposition between it and another feature which is, in turn, the common denominator of another class. Van Dijk, applying Greimas's methods to the analysis of a poem, reaches a similar conclusion: 'One may postulate that the occurrence of a thematic seme requires the existence of an opposing thematic seme which serves as its partner.'[8] Binary constraints govern the process of thematic construction.

Moreover, just any opposition will not suffice. One is not necessarily satisfied with a reading of a poem just because one has succeeded in correlating two oppositions. Cultural models enable us to read towards intuitively felt goals which tell us under what conditions we may be considered to have done enough. Figurative interpretation, Greimas argues,

> consists of retaining in the process of extraction only those
> semes which are pertinent to the construction of models. Thus,
> the description of poetic language will abandon, for example,
> the figures of *attic* and *cellar*, retaining only the semes *high* and
> *low*, useful for the construction of axiological sememes . . .
> such as *euphoria of heights* and *dysphoria of depths*. (*ibid.*, p. 138)

Since the 'axiological' is defined as a 'mythic' isotopy (concerning the inner world) manifested in qualifications (and hence, roughly, evaluative description), the suggestion is that figurative interpretation is a process of discovering oppositions which can be correlated with opposed values. One does not simply seek oppositions within a poem but seeks those oppositions upon which the poem seems to set some value, so that the latter may serve as the second opposition of one's four-term homology. Thus, Van Dijk, analysing a poem by du Bouchet, discovers two thematic classes, *paysage* and *maison*, which are correlated with opposing values, and this is more satisfying than an interpretation which set *paysage* and *maison* in relation to, shall we say, *grass* and *carpet*. If we are to account for the production of meaning we may well be forced to postulate, as Greimas says, 'a hierarchy of semantic isotopies, some more "profound" than others',[9] but the problem of relative profundity and dominance will be, at least in part, a specifically literary question.

Although some of these concepts will prove useful in the later discussions of poetics, one is tempted to say that Greimas's real contribution lies in the problems he tackles and the difficulties he encounters. The strong hypothesis about semantic description which he attempts to test is that if words and sentences are transcribed in terms of semantic features it should be possible to define a series of operations which would lead, in algorithmic fashion, from these minimal features to a series of readings for the text as a whole. But if, as has been argued, the reader's ability to recognize isotopies cannot be represented as a process of noting which classemes are repeated, then the notion of an algorithm for semantic description is called into question. Linguistic analysis does not provide a method by which the meaning of a text can be deduced from the meaning of its components. And the reason is not simply that sentences have different meanings in different contexts: that is only the problem with which one began. The difficulty is, rather, that the context which determines the meaning of a sentence is more than the other sentences of the text; it is a complex of knowledge and expectations of varying degrees of specificity, a kind of interpretive competence which could in principle be described but which in practice proves exceedingly refractory. For it consists on the one hand of various assumptions concerning coherence and general models of semantic organization and on the other of expectations concerning particular types of texts and the kind of interpretation they require. If a newspaper editorial be set down on a page as a poem, the semantic features of its elements remain in one sense the same but are subjected to different interpretive treatment and organized at different isotopic levels; and a theory which attempts to derive the meaning of a text from the meaning of its constituents, however perspicuous and explicit it may be, will fail to account for differences of this kind.

Both Jakobson and Greimas start from the assumption that linguistic analysis provides a method for discovering the patterns or meanings of literary texts, and though the problems they encounter are different the lessons which their examples offer are substantially the same: that the direct application of techniques for linguistic description may be a useful approach if it begins with literary effects and attempts to account for them, but that it does not in itself serve as a method of literary analysis. The reason is simply that both author and reader bring to the text more than a knowledge of language and this additional experience – expectations about the forms of literary organization, implicit models of literary structures, practice in forming and testing hypotheses about literary works – is what guides one in the perception and construction of relevant patterns. To discover the nature and forms of this supplementary knowledge is the task of poetics; but before considering what has been and might be done in this area we should look at one other way in which linguistics has been used in structuralist literary criticism.

CHAPTER 5

Linguistic Metaphors in Criticism

I fear we are not getting rid
of God because we still believe
in grammar.
NIETZSCHE

If one does not apply the techniques of linguistic description directly
to the language of literature, how can one make use of linguistics in
criticism? Barthes has observed that 'structuralism has emerged from
linguistics and in literature it finds an object which has itself emerged
from language', but how does this 'emergence' affect the relationship
between the study of language and the study of literature? Barthes's
reply is decidedly ambiguous: on the one hand, he suggests that 'at
every level, be it that of the argument, the discourse or the words, the
literary work offers structuralism the picture of a structure perfectly
homological with that of language itself'; yet on the other hand he
sees structuralism as an attempt 'to found a science of literature, or,
to be more exact, a linguistics of discourse whose object is the "language" of literary forms, grasped at many levels' ('Science versus
literature', pp. 897–8).

In other words, there is definite hesitation about which is the
pertinent and fruitful analogy: is the individual literary work like a
language or is literature as a whole like a language? In the first case,
the analogy rests on the fact that a number of linguistic concepts can
be applied by extension or in a metaphorical way to literary works:
one can speak of the work as a system, whose elements are defined by
their relations to one another, of syntagmatic and paradigmatic
relations, of sequences whose functions in the work correspond to
those of nouns, vrbes and adjectives in the sentence. In the second
case, the analogy is stronger and more interesting: since literature
itself is a system of signs and in this respect like a language, one
postulates a poetics which would study literature as linguistics studies
language, taking its cue from linguistics wherever that seemed
possible.

Part of the hesitation may be due to the ambiguity of the linguistic model itself, as it was presented in the days before Chomsky. In so far as structural linguistics was defined as a way of analysing a corpus of data, it offered no guidelines as to what could legitimately be considered a corpus by those attempting to apply linguistic methods in other fields. Why not works of one author, works on a particular theme or even a single work conceived as a corpus of stanzas, chapters or sentences? The model might easily have been interpreted as justifying the study of any corpus.

Whatever its causes, this hesitation produces two different views of the structuralist project. If one postulates a global homology between linguistics and poetics it follows that one's task is not to elucidate the meaning of individual works, any more than it is the linguist's task to study individual sentences and tell us what they mean, but to study works as manifestations of a literary system and show how the conventions of that system enable the works to have meaning. If, on the other hand, one postulates an analogy between a language and an individual work or group of works, then analysis of the work is no longer means to an end but the end itself. One's task is to deconstruct and understand it, just as the linguist's task is to understand the language he is studying; and one may, to this end, draw upon whatever linguistic concepts seem useful.

In *Critique et vérité* Barthes labelled these two activities 'science of literature' and 'criticism', recognizing that the former was the more appropriate application of the linguistic model but that the latter, in its attempt to produce or define the meaning of a work, was closer to the traditional task of criticism (pp. 56–75). Structuralists have not eschewed criticism, though they have perhaps aimed less at interpretation than at what Barthes calls 'ordered transformations' of the work, by which there comes to 'float above the primary language of the work a second language, a cohesion of signs' (p. 64). Before passing on to poetics proper one should briefly examine this kind of criticism and especially the ways in which the linguistic and semiotic orientation of structuralism informs the study of individual texts.

From this point of view one can distinguish two general categories into which critical works may be grouped. The first type, based on the metaphor which makes a work or a group of works a language, treats its object as a system whose rules and forms must be elucidated. Criticism of this kind has marked affinities with more traditional studies which treat individual works as 'organic wholes' or the works of a given author as the variants of a single project, but it may perhaps be distinguished by the 'esprit de système' which animates it and its willingness to establish relations that are based not on identity of substance but homology of differences. The second approach takes the work not as a language but as locus in which theoretical or practical analyses of languages are carried out. The work is studied as the vehicle of an implicit theory of language or of other semiotic systems and is interpreted in those terms.

The work as system

Barthes's *Sur Racine*, which treated Racinian tragedy 'as a system of units and functions' (p. 9), falls squarely within the first category. Although it became, by virtue of Picard's violent attack on it in *Nouvelle critique ou nouvelle imposture*, the focal point for the controversy concerning *la Nouvelle critique* in the mid-1960s, it can scarcely be cited as an exemplary structural analysis. Barthes himself admits that it represents a moment of transition between thematic criticism and the adumbration of a system. None the less, precisely because it does in certain respects take its distance from thematic criticism of a more phenomenological stripe it helps to indicate the character of structuralist criticism.

In his early study of Michelet, isolating themes of dryness, heat, fecundity, emptiness, fullness, vagueness, etc., Barthes seemed inclined to identify the structure of an imaginative world with the obsessions of the writer as subject: 'one must first display this man's coherence . . . discover the structure of an existence (I do not say "of a life"), a thematics, as it were, or better still, an organized network of obsessions' (*Michelet par lui-même*, p. 5). The perspective is that of phenomenological critics like Jean-Pierre Richard, Jean Starobinski and J. Hillis Miller, whose thematic studies are explicitly directed towards the writer's 'way of experiencing the world and of experiencing himself in relation to it' and insist that one must 'investigate objectivized structures as the expression of a structuring consciousness'.[1] In *Sur Racine*, however, Barthes is no longer willing to make the individual subject the source of the structures he discovers in the works. Reading individual tragedies as moments of a system, he is interested in the common structures that may be derived from them and that serve as the functional oppositions and the rules of combination of the system. Since, however, he adopts a 'somewhat psychoanalytic language' the distinctiveness of his orientation is obscured and his study of 'Racinian man' could without much difficulty be presented as an account of Racine's own thematic universe. What I have tried to set forth, he writes,

is a kind of Racinian anthropology, which is both structural and analytic: structural in essence, because tragedy is here treated as a system of units (the 'figures') and functions;

analytic in its presentation, because it seemed to me that only a
language such as that of psychoanalysis, which is able to pick
up the fear of the world, would be appropriate for an encounter
with imprisoned man. (pp. 9–10)

Although linguistic concepts play little role in the analysis itself,
the linguistic model does offer a structural metaphor for the organization of the work. The first part, Barthes says, is paradigmatic in
nature – it analyses the various roles and functions of Racinian
tragedy considered as a system – and the second part is syntagmatic –
it takes up the paradigmatic elements and shows how they are
combined in sequence at the level of individual works (p. 9). More
important, however, the linguistic model suggests that what Barthes
should look for are relations and oppositions rather than substantive
features or themes that are repeated throughout the plays. Thus, when
he maintains that there are three formal 'spaces' in Racine, the
Chamber or seat of power, the Anti-Chamber where characters wait
and confront one another and the Outside, which is the locus of
death, flight and events, the claim is not that each of the plays contains, specifically, a chamber and an anti-chamber and no other
spaces but the outside world. The claim is rather that the two oppositions, between the actual seat of power and the space where people
talk, and between the place where characters are isolated and the
external world which exists only potentially as a space where other
things happen, have a central function in producing the tragic
situation. The space in which characters find themselves is, functionally, an Anti-Chamber: 'trapped between the world, the place of
action, and the Chamber, the place of silence, the Anti-Chamber is the
place of language' whose enclosure enforces the tragic destiny (pp.
15–19).

Similarly, when Barthes writes that the story of the primal horde –
in which rival sons band together and kill the father who has domi-
nated them and prevented them from taking wives – 'is the whole of
Racine's theatre', he is not claiming that each tragedy contains,
independently, an expression of this theme but rather that his theatre
finds its unity and 'becomes coherent only at the level of this ancient
fable', which may be suppressed and transformed in many individual
plays (p. 21). If Racinian tragedy is a system, then in order to analyse
it one must be able to determine what are the functional oppositions,
and for this one must grasp the 'centre' of the system, which functions
as a principle of inclusion and exclusion. Barthes has presumably
postulated that the centre is tragedy itself and then has asked what are
the oppositions or relations which produce the tragedy. Finding that
they are three – the relation of authority, the relation of rivalry and

the relation of love, he is then in a position to determine what roles the various combinations of these relations produce.

Although neither his argument nor his analysis is as clear as one might wish, the importance accorded to the myth of the primal horde depends on the fact that it seems to him to manifest the relation of authority which makes love problematic (an instance of disobedience or incest) and the relation of rivalry between those subjected to authority. It thus contains the basic oppositions which produce the roles of Racinian theatre. The characters themselves 'receive their differences not from their status in the world but from their place in the general configuration of forces which imprisons them', and that configuration, he argues, is composed of various combinations of the three fundamental relations (p. 21).

Although *Sur Racine* is marred by a misleading psychoanalytic language, a needless methodological obscurity and the laconic style of one delighting in the opportunity to say shocking things about the greatest French classic, most of the attacks on the book have been based on a failure to appreciate the formal nature of Barthes's proposal. Picard, for example, assumes that the relation of authority should be identical in substance in each of the plays and has no difficulty in showing that 'under the same descriptive and explanatory rubric M. Barthes groups extremely diverse realities' (*Nouvelle Critique ou nouvelle imposture*, p. 40). That, of course, is the point of this relational concept: the various plays express in different ways what, from the point of view of the tragic situation, is a single function. In each case the contrast which produces the dramatic situation and defines the roles of the protagonists is the opposition between he who wields authority and he who is subject to it. These functions, and here lies both the interest of Barthes's analysis and the trace of the linguistic model, are not defined by identity of substance but by the presence of an opposition which is taken to be functional in the system as a whole.

Linguistics serves more as a source of metaphors in Barthes's essays on Sade. Once again the object of analysis is the corpus of an author's works, but in this case the 'centre' of the system is not a product of the thematic development of each work, as it was in the case of Racine. Sade's narratives have what Barthes calls a 'rhapsodic structure': development in time is the result of the linear nature of the text rather than any inner necessity, and to tell the tale is 'to juxtapose repetitive and mobile segments' (*Sade, Fourier, Loyola*, pp. 143–4). Consequently, the system is an immense paradigm of sequences which are well formed as members of the system in that they organize and codify the erotic. To analyse the system is to determine the minimal functional elements and see how they combine: 'il y a une grammaire

érotique de Sade (une pornogrammaire) – avec ses érotèmes et ses
règles de combinaison' (there is a Sadian grammar of the erotic (a
pornogrammar) – with its erotemes and its rules of combination)
(p. 169). The minimal unit is the *posture*, 'the smallest possible combination since it unites only an action and its point of application'.
In addition to sexual poses there are various 'operators' such as
kinship links, social status and physiological variables. Postures can
be combined to form 'operations' or composite erotic tableaux, and
when operations are given a temporal development they become
'episodes' (pp. 33–4).

All these units, Barthes writes,

> are subject to rules of combination or composition. These rules
> would easily permit a formalization of the erotic language,
> analogous to the 'tree structures' used by linguists . . . In the
> Sadian grammar there are two principal rules: these are, as it were,
> regular procedures by which the narrator mobilizes the units
> of his 'lexicon' (postures, figures, episodes). The first is a rule of
> exhaustivity: in an 'operation' the greatest possible number of
> postures should be accomplished simultaneously . . . The second
> is a rule of reciprocity . . . all functions can be exchanged,
> everyone can and should be in turn actor and victim,
> flagellator and flagellated, coprophagist and coprophagized, etc.
> This rule is central, first because it makes Sadian eroticism truly
> a formal language, in which there are only classes of actions
> and not groups of individuals, which very much simplifies the
> grammar . . . and secondly because it prevents us from
> dividing Sadian society according to sexual roles. (pp. 34–5)

In fact, the difference between masters and victims lies in the former's
appropriation of a second code, which is that of speech – especially in
the long 'dissertations' which occupy whatever space is not taken by
operations and episodes. But according to Barthes 'the code of the
phrase and that of the figure (erotic) continually link up and form a
single line, along which the libertine moves with the same energy'
(p. 37). A mode of order, speech transforms actions into crimes by
naming them, images into scene by detailing them, and scenes into
discourse by writing them. Sade's writing, using the erotic code as its
generative device, takes up and contaminates language itself – 'the
criminal contamination touches all styles of discourse' by lodging
within them moments of erotic paradigms; it thus ensures the force
of its transgression, for 'society can never recognize a mode of writing
that is structurally linked to crime and sex' (p. 39).

Linguistics here serves as model, of course, but it is perhaps less
important in determining an analytic procedure than in offering a set

of terms which, because they are already linked by a theory, can create coherence when used as the target language in analytic translation. The coherence is, as it were, ready made, giving the allure of a system to what is essentially an interpretation that stresses the order and the combinatory exhaustiveness of the Sadian vision.

Another and perhaps superior example of the criticism which derives a system from a corpus is Genette's study of baroque imagery in his essay 'L'or tombe sous le fer'. This is distinguished from usual accounts of imagery by its insistence that in baroque poetry 'qualities are organized into differences, differences into contrasts, and the sensible world is polarized according to the strict laws of a kind of geometry of material' (*Figures*, p. 30). Whereas the poems of Ronsard and earlier poets move towards a fusion of categories, 'baroque poetry, on the contrary, seems by vocation to resist any assimilation of this kind': in a line like 'L'or tombe sous le fer' (Gold falls beneath iron), the metals are used 'for their most superficial and abstract function – a kind of valency defined by a system of discontinuous oppositions' (pp. 31–3). In this system gold is opposed to iron, giving the line a kind of natural rigour, but aside from this the qualities of the two metals or the possible connotations of the two terms are not used by the poem: each term is simply a synecdoche which permits the poem to state in the code of images the meaning, 'Wheat falls beneath the sickle'.

Genette's analysis enables him to produce a diagram of the system of oppositions according to which some fifteen terms are organized, thus putting to work the linguistic concept of a system of terms whose value is purely formal and differential. Again, it is the notions of system, binary opposition, distinctive feature and relational term which are important.

In an essay entitled 'Comment lire?' Todorov speaks of an operation called 'figuration', which consists of taking a text or group of texts as a system determined by a particular figure or structure functioning at various levels. He cites as example Boris Eichenbaum's study of the Russian poet, Anna Akhmatova: 'at all levels this poetic opus obeys the figure of oxymoron . . . it is reflected not only in stylistic details but also in the subject.' The narrator that the poems project is simultaneously passionate sinner and saintly nun; 'the lyric tale of which she is the centre moves by antithesis, paradox; it evades psychological formulation, becomes strange by the incoherence of mental states. The image becomes enigmatic, upsetting' (*Poétique de la prose*, p. 249). The discovery of such homologies is, of course, a familiar technique of criticism, but structuralists are perhaps more willing to make the feature which they trace through the levels of a text or set of texts a formal structure.

A good example of this approach is Genette's essay on Saint Amant and the baroque which takes the figure of inversion as the fundamental device of the system. The poetic diction which makes birds 'fish of the air' is not an isolated phenomenon; it derives from the general concept of a reversible universe in which one thing is the mirror image of another. Ocean, for example, is symmetrical with sky; not only does it reflect the natural world but it contains beneath its surface another and inverted world. In Saint Amant's *Moïse sauvé* the passage through the Red Sea offers the occasion for the description of

> a word which is new and virginal rather than foreign, answer and replica to our world, but richer, more highly coloured . . . more disturbing by its familiarity than by its strangeness, which offers itself to the Jewish people both as a reminder of Eden and as an anticipation of the promised land. (*Figures*, pp. 15–16)

For Saint-Amant, 'every difference is resemblance by surprise, the Other is a paradoxical version of the Same', and the baroque universe is so rigidly structured that the strange, the new, the marvellous, can only be imagined and presented as an inversion or reversal of ordinary combinations of terms. This striking claim is the result of a desire to reach systematic formulation.

Another example of this procedure, which illustrates how little supposedly structuralist criticism may differ from more familiar modes, is Todorov's work on Henry James's short stories. There is, he argues, a particular structural property which the stories share, a 'figure which organizes both themes and syntax, the composition of the tale as much as the point of view'. Traceable at various levels, the secret of the Jamesian tale 'is precisely the existence of an essential secret, of something unnamed, of an absent and all-powerful force which sets in motion the present machinery of narration' (*Poétique de la prose*, p. 153). Called upon to lecture on structuralism and the study of literature at Oxford, Todorov used this study as his example,[2] but one can say that the search for an invariant pattern in the works of an author is not a distinctively structuralist approach, nor is it the same as treating a corpus of works as a semiotic system. When linguistics ceases to be used as a heuristic device, structuralist criticism loses much of its distinctiveness.

The work as semiotic project

The second approach, which involves a more extensive application of linguistic concepts, does not postulate an analogy between a set of works and a language but takes the work itself as the investigation of a semiological system and attempts to formulate more explicitly the insights it provides. Barthes has argued, for example, that one of the most important features of Brecht's theatre is his demonstration that 'revolutionary art must admit the arbitrariness of signs, must allow a certain "formalism" in the sense that it must treat form according to the proper method, which is a semiological method' (*Essais critiques*, p. 87). It is Brecht himself who is the semiologist, who displays a particular theory of the sign in his practice of aesthetic distancing and his use of costumes and decor: 'what Brechtian drama as a whole postulates is that today at least drama has not to express the real so much as to signify it. It is therefore necessary that there be a certain distance between the signifier and the signified.'

A more fully developed example is Barthes's account of Loyola, whom he sees as a 'Logothete or founder of a language'. Following in part the model of natural languages, Loyola isolates a semiological space, divides his material into discrete articulations and provides an order or syntax for the combination of signs. 'The invention of a language, such is the object of the *Spiritual Exercises*'; Loyola wants to construct a 'language of interrogation' whereby the practitioner can find something to say to God, 'encode' his request in the proper way so that divine guidance will be forthcoming. 'The enormous and uncertain labour of a logo-technician or constructor of languages' involves producing general rules that will generate well-formed spiritual utterances and make prayer an ordered but interminable activity. To this end there is a proliferation of oppositions and syntagmatic categories, *topoi* and narrative structures, which 'derive from the need to occupy the whole territory of the mind and thereby to refine the channels through which the practitioner's request is articulated and taken up by the energy of speech' (*Sade, Fourier, Loyola*, pp. 7–9 and 50–9).

If Loyola's work can be seen as the invention and study of a devotional semiotic system, Proust's *A la recherche du temps perdu* may be read as an account of the narrator's semiotic initiation. Proust's work, writes Gilles Deleuze in his brilliant *Proust et les signes*, 'is founded not on the exposition of memory but on the learning of signs' (p. 9). The narrator encounters signs of the social world, signs of love, signs of the tangible world and signs of art which take up and transform the others. Not only does Deleuze study the way in which the narrator learns to recognize and interpret these signs and thus to situate himself in the various realms of experience which they structure; he derives from the novel a general theory of the features which distinguish these four types of sign and which account for the various responses and experiences of the narrator. The functional criteria are the type of material support, the devices which permit interpretation, the characteristic emotional response, the type of meaning they yield, the faculties involved in interpretation, the temporal structure of the sign, and finally, the relation of sign and essence (pp. 102–7). The full exploration of these distinctions yields a metalanguage which succeeds better than any other in relating the theoretical speculations of the novel to the different types of action and experience that are deployed in progressive narration; and thus Deleuze's interpretation is not simply an account of Proust's implicit semiological thought but a superb integration of the Proustian narrator's investigation of signs and his production of signs in the discourse of the novel.

Many of Deleuze's insights are confirmed by Genette's study of 'le langage indirect' in Proust. The *Recherche* is an account of the narrator's progressive mastery of the indirect languages by which people express and conceal the self. Madame Verdurin's 'Je vous gronde' means 'I thank you' rather than 'I scold you'; 'the figures of worldly rhetoric, like all figures, are declared forms of the lie, presented as such and expected to be deciphered according to a code recognized by both parties' (*Figures II*, pp. 251–2). Gestures also constitute a language which must be learned and which exhibits a definite semiotic complexity: as soon as the meaning of a gesture is codified it is no longer a 'true' or natural meaning and the gesture may indicate, above all else, a desire to produce the expected impression. Marcel, waiting to be introduced to the 'jeunes filles en fleurs', prepares to display 'the kind of questioning glance which reveals not surprise but the desire to look surprised – such bad actors are we, or such accomplished physiognomists'.[3] So it is with many signifying acts. The index-made conventional sign

> comes almost invariably to indicate the opposite of what it is
> supposed to mean; in extreme cases the causal relation is even
> inverted, to the great detriment of the signifying intention . . .
> Marcel looks surprised, therefore he is not. (p. 267)

We find 'a language which "reveals" what it does not say – precisely because it does not say it.'

Genette discovers, therefore, a double semiotic critique in Proust: on the one hand, we are shown the hopelessness of attempting to identify sign and referent (places are never as words led the narrator to imagine); on the other hand, the passage from signifier to signified is subject to the most devious and misleading mediations. But the work of art, as a semiotic act, compensates for these two modes of dislocation by taking them as its subject and making these two gaps the space of literary exploration.

Alternatively, structuralist criticism may treat the work not as an analysis of other semiotic systems but as an investigation of language itself. Elaborating in the practice of its writing a critique and subversion of ordinary communicative codes, the work offers the critic the occasion to theorize its practice and to propose, as an interpretation of the work, a description of the adventures of meaning in the text. Such studies are quite common, for they merge easily with the general investigation of the properties of literary discourse, but among the works which function primarily as studies of particular texts, one might cite Stephen Heath's 'Ambiviolences' and Michel Foucault's *Raymond Roussel*.

The former subjects *Finnegans Wake* to what seems the only kind of reading that can encompass both detailed explication of sentences and general thematic synthesis: it takes the problem which the text poses (it is 'unreadable') as its own solution. The unreadability, the violent ambivalence of the work, is not an obstacle to be overcome by judicious translation into an interpretive language but rather the mark of a thematic project which determines the practice of writing. The work undertakes a 'theatralization of language', a foregrounding of the word in the network of its potential differential relations. The signifier is no longer a transparent form through which one accedes to meaning; it is displayed as an object in its own right which bears the traces of possible meanings: its relations to other words, its relations to various types of discourse which press around it. The multiplicity of these relations makes meaning not something already accomplished and waiting to be expressed but a horizon, a perspective of semiotic production. In place of a communicative use of language Joyce presents 'a working of language in which the limits of communication come undone, are set out and fractured in the play of the signifier, whose productions allow a glimpse of "the throb of meaning" ' (p. 65). This, writes Joyce, 'is nat language in any sinse of the world'; it is the *other* of language, its repressed complement, now liberated on pages where it can spawn freely: 'birth of an otion', 'for inkstands', 'Stay us wherefore in our search for tighteousness'. The play of the letter produces a play of meaning and subjects any clear and distinct ideas which might seem to lie outside language, as the furniture of the world, to the indeterminacy of dislocation and contradiction. *Finnegans Wake*, writes Heath, is 'la construction d'une écriture qui sillonne le langage (les langues), faisant sans cesse basculer le signifié dans le signifiant, pour, à tout moment, trouver le drame du langage, sa production' (the construction of a mode of writing which ploughs through language (languages) leaving a wake, perpetually making the signified teeter in the signifier, so as to attain at every moment the drama of language, its productive activity) (p. 71). This drama enacted at the level of the sentence becomes, under the action of the critic's language, both the semiotic theory of the work and its thematic result: those categories which might contribute to the illusion of a world in which meaning is already there as something to be recovered instead of an activity to be pursued are deconstructed and set in motion.

The closest equivalent to Joyce in French literature is perhaps Raymond Roussel, and Foucault's reading yields comparable themes. To purify his texts, to give them an order which was not that of a communicative intention, Roussel resorted to formal procedures which could serve as generative devices. Punning on one phrase to produce another (an English example would be 'The sons raise meat' and 'The sun's rays meet'), he then writes a story to bring the two together. *Locus Solus* is the ultimate game of this sort: the story of machines invented to create a world which is itself created by linguistic machinery. Thus, the machine which, responding to the minutest variations in the weather, picks up teeth and deposits them in a complicated mosaic representing a knight, is itself produced by punning on 'demoiselle à prétendants' (a girl with suitors) to yield 'demoiselle à reître en dents' (paving beetle for a knight in teeth). Such procedures make the text a closed system which is a veritable parody of language as a system of differences. On the one hand, the text manifests, in its senseless puns, 'difference gathered up into itself, in single, dual, ambiguous, Minotaurine form'; and on the other hand it displays the infinite play of differences by which a word sends us off to other words instead of linking directly with a world: 'this marvellous quality which makes language rich in its poverty' (*Raymond Roussel*, p. 23). Roussel's work shows that the response of imagination to language, when language is freely displayed as a system of differences, permits the production of so many meanings as to undermine the notion of positive and determinate signs. 'Inventor of a language which speaks only itself', 'he opened to literary language a strange space, which one could call linguistic if it were not the inverted image, the dreamlike, enchanted, and mythic use of linguistic space' (pp. 209–10). Once again notions of the linguistic system are deployed in interpretation when the critic finds that the most radical texts can only be unified as a special kind of subversive linguistic project.

Less subversive linguistic projects can, of course, be found in more traditional works. In these cases the linguistic orientation of structuralism leads the critic to focus, as an interpretive strategy, on the role accorded to language in a particular work and to make the theory of language which he discovers a major part of its theme. In 'L'orgie langagière' Josette Rey-Debove explores the ways in which the sign becomes an erotic object in Molière's *Les Femmes savantes*. Per Aage Brandt examines the role and implications of speech in

'*Dom Juan* ou la force de la parole'. Michel Arrivé studies Jarry as a writer fascinated by problems of the sign in *Les Langages de Jarry*. Todorov devotes a portion of *Littérature et signification* to the letter as a signifying medium in *Les Liaisons dangereuses* and includes in *Poétique de la prose* a series of articles, which illustrate both the virtues and dangers of this approach, on language in *The Odyssey*, *The Thousand and One Nights* and Constant's *Adolphe*.

In his discussion of *The Odyssey* he tries to adduce linguistic evidence to make Ulysses' lies a central feature of the text. The distinction between *énonciation* (the action of speaking) and *énoncé* (the utterance itself) is manifested, he suggests, in an opposition between 'la parole action' (speech as action) and 'la parole récit' (speech as narration); then, in a rather questionable step, he identifies these modes of language with performative and constative utterances: 'speech as narration derives from the world of constative discourse, whereas speech as action is always performative' (*Poétique de la prose*, pp. 71-2). This is not, as it turns out, a harmless metaphorical reformulation but an attempt to bring into play the qualities of performative and constative utterances so as to make lies or 'la parole feinte' anomalous:

> one the one hand, it cannot but belong to the constative mode: only the constative can be true or false; the performative escapes these categories. On the other hand, to speak in order to lie is not to speak in order to state (*constater*) but in order to act: any lie is necessarily performative. Feigning speech is both narration and action. (p. 72)

But so are most other speech acts. To produce a constative utterance is to perform an act, and lying is not a special case. If in selling someone a car I tell him that it has a new transmission I am performing an act of persuading (speaking in order to act) whether or not the statement is true, and the fact that I am using it to persuade does not in any way prevent it from being true or false. Performative utterances, as Austin defined them, are statements which themselves accomplish the acts to which they refer: thus in 'I promise to pay you ten pounds' the act of promising is the uttering of the sentence.[4] Lies are not performative in this sense; they are statements which happen to be false. And though they may well play a privileged role in the text, the linguistic argument is pure obfuscation.

Todorov's other conclusions bear primarily on the value assigned to speech in the works he is considering. In *The Odyssey* 'dutifulness corresponds to silence, speech is linked with revolt'; 'to speak is to take on a responsibility and therefore also to run a danger' (pp. 69-70). In *The Thousand and One Nights*, on the other hand, 'narration equals life, the absence of narration, death', and therefore, by extension, 'man is only a narrative; when narration is no longer necessary he may die' (pp. 86–7). This identification of a character with his speech is also found in *Adolphe*, which, as Todorov shows in one of his better articles, contains a subtle theory of language. As in *The Thousand and One Nights*, 'death is nothing other than the inability to speak', but here speech is a tragic force as well: 'Constant opposes the notion that words designate things in an adequate way', for to speak is either to alter the feelings of which one speaks, or else to produce the feelings which one feigns in speech; thus, false speech becomes true and supposedly true speech becomes false. The paradoxical structure of this phenomenon, he argues, is homologous to that of desire, as presented in *Adolphe*: 'words imply the absence of things, just as desire implies the absence of its object . . . Both lead to an impasse: that of communication, that of happiness. Words are to things as desire is to the object of desire' (p. 116).

An interest in language, coupled with a penchant for abstraction, can lead to the formulation of schemas of this kind which serve as thematic interpretations of the work in question. The value of such conclusions and interpretations is, however, totally independent of the linguistic model which may have served as source of metaphors or as heuristic device. Linguistics does not, as the preceding examples should amply show, provide a method for the interpretation of literary works. It may provide a general focus, either suggesting to the critic that he look for differences and oppositions which can be correlated with one another and organized as a system which generates the episodes or forms of the text, or offering a set of concepts in which interpretations may be stated. Both cases have their dangers. In the latter, the prestige of linguistics may lead the critic to believe that simply applying linguistic labels to aspects of the text is necessarily a worth-while activity, but of course when used metaphorically or in isolation such terms enjoy no privileged status and are not necessarily more revealing than other concepts which the critic might import or create. In the former case, while it could be argued that any factor which helps the critic to increase the range of relationships which he is able to perceive is of *prima facie* value, the discovery of formal structures is an infinite process and must, if it is to be fruitful, be grounded on a theory of how the literary text functions. A work has a structure only in terms of a theory which specifies the ways in which it functions, and to formulate that theory is the task of poetics.

PART TWO

Poetics

CHAPTER 6

Literary Competence

To understand a sentence means
to understand a language. To
understand a language means to
be master of a technique.
WITTGENSTEIN

When a speaker of a language hears a phonetic sequence, he is able
to give it meaning because he brings to the act of communication an
amazing repertoire of conscious and unconscious knowledge. Mastery
of the phonological, syntactic and semantic systems of his language
enables him to convert the sounds into discrete units, to recognize
words, and to assign a structural description and interpretation to the
resulting sentence, even though it be quite new to him. Without this
implicit knowledge, this internalized grammar, the sequence of sounds
does not speak to him. We are nevertheless inclined to say that the
phonological and grammatical structure and the meaning are
properties of the utterance, and there is no harm in that way of
speaking so long as we remember that they are properties of the
utterance only with respect to a particular grammar. Another
grammar would assign different properties to the sequence (according
to the grammar of a different language, for example, it would be
nonsense). To speak of the structure of a sentence is necessarily to
imply an internalized grammar that gives it that structure.

We also tend to think of meaning and structure as properties of
literary works, and from one point of view this is perfectly correct:
when the sequence of words is treated *as a literary work* it has these
properties. But that qualification suggests the relevance and importance of the linguistic analogy. The work has structure and meaning
because it is read in a particular way, because these potential properties, latent in the object itself, are actualized by the theory of discourse
applied in the act of reading. 'How can one discover structure without
the help of a methodological model?' asks Barthes (*Critique et
vérité*, p. 19). To read a text as literature is not to make one's mind a
tabula rasa and approach it without preconceptions; one must bring

to it an implicit understanding of the operations of literary discourse which tells one what to look for.

Anyone lacking this knowledge, anyone wholly unacquainted with literature and unfamiliar with the conventions by which fictions are read, would, for example, be quite baffled if presented with a poem. His knowledge of the language would enable him to understand phrases and sentences, but he would not know, quite literally, what to *make* of this strange concatenation of phrases. He would be unable to read it *as* literature – as we say with emphasis to those who would use literary works for other purposes – because he lacks the complex 'literary competence' which enables others to proceed. He has not internalized the 'grammar' of literature which would permit him to convert linguistic sequences into literary structures and meanings.

If the analogy seems less than exact it is because in the case of language it is much more obvious that understanding depends on mastery of a system. But the time and energy devoted to literary training in schools and universities indicate that the understanding of literature also depends on experience and mastery. Since literature is a second-order semiotic system which has language as its basis, a knowledge of language will take one a certain distance in one's encounter with literary texts, and it may be difficult to specify precisely where understanding comes to depend on one's supplementary knowledge of literature. But the difficulty of drawing a line does not obscure the palpable difference between understanding the language of a poem, in the sense that one could provide a rough translation into another language, and understanding the poem. If one knows French, one can translate Mallarmé's 'Salut' (see chapter 4), but that translation is not a thematic synthesis – it is not what we would ordinarily call 'understanding the poem' – and in order to identify various levels of coherence and set them in relation to one another under the synoptic heading or theme of the 'literary quest' one must have considerable experience of the conventions for reading poetry.

The easiest way to grasp the importance of these conventions is to take a piece of journalistic prose or a sentence from a novel and set it down on the page as a poem (see chapter 8). The properties assigned to the sentence by a grammar of English remain unchanged, and the different meanings which the text acquires cannot therefore be attributed to one's knowledge of the language but must be ascribed to the special conventions for reading poetry which lead one to look at the language in new ways, to make relevant properties of the language which were previously unexploited, to subject the text to a different series of interpretive operations. But one can also show the importance of these conventions by measuring the distance between the lang-

uage of a poem and its critical interpretation – a distance bridged
by the conventions of reading which comprise the institution of
poetry.

Anyone who knows English understands the language of Blake's
'Ah! Sun-flower':

> Ah, Sun-flower, weary of time,
> Who countest the steps of the Sun,
> Seeking after that sweet golden clime
> Where the traveller's journey is done:
>
> Where the Youth pined away with desire,
> And the pale Virgin shrouded in snow
> Arise from their graves, and aspire
> Where my Sun-flower wishes to go.

But there is some distance between an understanding of the language
and the thematic statement with which a critic concludes his discussion of the poem: 'Blake's dialectical thrust at asceticism is more than
adroit. You do not surmount Nature by denying its prime claim of
sexuality. Instead you fall utterly into the dull round of its cyclic
aspirations.'[1] How does one reach this reading? What are the operations which lead from the text to this representation of understanding?
The primary convention is what might be called the rule of significance: read the poem as expressing a significant attitude to some
problem concerning man and/or his relation to the universe. The
sunflower is therefore given the value of an emblem and the metaphors
of 'counting' and 'seeking' are taken not just as figurative indications
of the flower's tendency to turn towards the sun but as metaphorical
operators which make the sunflower an instance of the human
aspirations compassed by these two lines. The conventions of
metaphorical coherence – that one should attempt through semantic
transformations to produce coherence on the levels of both tenor and
vehicle – lead one to oppose time to eternity and to make 'that sweet
golden clime' both the sunset which marks the closure of the daily
temporal cycle and the eternity of death when 'the traveller's journey
is done'. The identification of sunset and death is further justified by
the convention which allows one to inscribe the poem in a poetic
tradition. More important, however, is the convention of thematic
unity, which forces one to give the youth and virgin of the second
stanza a role which justifies choosing them as examples of aspiration;
and since the semantic feature they share is a repression of sexuality,
one must find a way of integrating that with the rest of the poem.
The curious syntactic structure, with three clauses each depending on
a 'where', provides a way of doing this:

The Youth and the Virgin have denied their sexuality to win the allegorical abode of the conventionally visualized heaven. Arriving there, they arise from their graves to be trapped in the same cruel cycle of longings; they are merely at the sunset and aspire to go where the Sun-flower seeks his rest, which is precisely where they already are.[2]

Such interpretations are not the result of subjective associations. They are public and can be discussed and justified with respect to the conventions of reading poetry – or, as English allows us to say, of *making* sense. Such conventions are the constituents of the institution of literature, and in this perspective one can see that it may well be misleading to speak of poems as harmonious totalities, autonomous natural organisms, complete in themselves and bearing a rich immanent meaning. The semiological approach suggests, rather, that the poem be thought of as an utterance that has meaning only with respect to a system of conventions which the reader has assimilated. If other conventions were operative its range of potential meanings would be different.

Literature, as Genette says, 'like any other activity of the mind, is based on conventions of which, with some exceptions, it is not aware' (*Figures*, p. 258). One can think of these conventions not simply as the implicit knowledge of the reader but also as the implicit knowledge of authors. To write a poem or a novel is immediately to engage with a literary tradition or at the very least with a certain idea of the poem or the novel. The activity is made possible by the existence of the genre, which the author can write against, certainly, whose conventions he may attempt to subvert, but which is none the less the context within which his activity takes place, as surely as the failure to keep a promise is made possible by the institution of promising. Choices between words, between sentences, between different modes of presentation, will be made on the basis of their effects; and the notion of effect presupposes modes of reading which are not random or haphazard. Even if the author does not think of readers, he is himself a reader of his own work and will not be satisfied with it unless he can read it as producing effects. One would find very strange the notion of a poet saying, 'when I reflect on the sunflower I have a particular feeling, which I shall call "p" and which I think can be connected with another feeling which I shall call "q" ', and then writing 'if p then q' as a poem on the sunflower. This would not be a poem because even the poet himself cannot read the meanings in that series of signs. He can take them as referring to the feelings in question, but that is very much another matter. His text does not explore, evoke or even make use of the feelings, and he will be unable to read it as if it did. To experience any of the satisfactions of having written a poem he must create an order of words which he can read according to the conventions of poetry: he cannot simply assign meaning but must make possible, for himself and for others, the production of meaning.

'Every work', wrote Valéry, 'is the work of many things besides an author'; and he proposed that literary history be replaced by a poetics which would study 'the conditions of the existence and development of literature'. Among all the arts, it is 'the one in which convention plays the greatest role', and even those authors who may have thought their works due only to personal inspiration and the application of genius

> had developed, without suspecting it, a whole system of habits
> and notions which were the fruit of their experience and
> indispensable to the process of production. However little they
> might have suspected all the definitions, all the conventions,
> the logic and the system of combinations that composition
> presupposes, however much they believed that they owed
> nothing but to the instant itself, their work necessarily called
> into play all these procedures and these inevitable operations of
> the mind.[3]

The conventions of poetry, the logic of symbols, the operations for the production of poetic effects, are not simply the property of readers but the basis of literary forms. However, for a variety of reasons it is easier to study them as the operations performed by readers than as the institutional context taken for granted by authors. The statements authors make about the process of composition are notoriously problematic, and there are few ways of determining what they are taking for granted. Whereas the meanings readers give to literary works and the effects they experience are much more open to observation. Hypotheses about the conventions and operations which produce these effects can therefore be tested not only by their ability to account for the effects in question but by their ability, when applied to other poems, to account for the effects experienced in those cases. Moreover, when one is investigating the process of reading one can make alterations in the language of a text so as to see how this changes literary effects, whereas that kind of experimentation is not possible if one is investigating the conventions assumed by authors, who are not available to give their reactions to the effects of proposed altera- tions in their texts. As the example of transformational grammar suggests, the best way of producing a formal representation of the implicit knowledge of both speakers and hearers is to present sen- tences to oneself or to colleagues and then to formulate rules which account for the hearers' judgments about meaning, well-formedness, deviance, constituent structure, and ambiguity.

To speak, therefore, as I shall do, of literary competence as a set of conventions for reading literary texts is in no way to imply that authors are congenital idiots who simply produce strings of sentences, while all the truly creative work is done by readers who have artful ways of processing these sentences. Structuralist discussions may seem to promote such a view by their failure to isolate and praise an author's 'conscious art', but the reason is simply that here, as in most other human activities of any complexity, the line between the conscious and the unconscious is highly variable, impossible to identify, and supremely uninteresting. '*When* do you know how to play chess? All the time? or just while you are making a move? And the *whole* of chess during each move?'[4] When driving a car is it consciously or unconsciously that you keep to the correct side of the road, change gears, apply the brakes, dip the headlights? To ask of what an author is conscious and of what unconscious is as fruitless as to ask which rules of English are consciously employed by speakers and which are followed unconsciously. Mastery may be largely unconscious or it may have reached a stage of highly self-conscious theoretical elaboration, but it is mastery in both cases. Nor does one in any way impugn the author's talent in speaking of his mastery as an ability to construct artefacts which prove extremely rich when subjected to the operations of reading.

The task of a structuralist poetics, as Barthes defines it, would be to make explicit the underlying system which makes literary effects possible. It would not be a 'science of contents' which, in hermeneutic fashion, proposed interpretations for works,

> but a science of the conditions of content, that is to say of
> forms. What interests it will be the variations of meaning
> generated and, as it were, capable of being generated by works;
> it will not interpret symbols but describe their polyvalency.
> In short, its object will not be the full meanings of the work
> but on the contrary the empty meaning which supports them all.
> (*Critique et vérité*, p. 57)

In this sense structuralism effects an important reversal of perspective, granting precedence to the task of formulating a comprehensive theory of literary discourse and assigning a secondary place to the interpretation of individual texts. Whatever the benefits of interpretation to those who engage in it, within the context of poetics it becomes an ancillary activity – a way of using literary works – as opposed to the study of literature itself as an institution. To say that is in no way to condemn interpretation, as the linguistic analogy should make perfectly evident. Most people are more interested in using language to communicate than in studying the complex linguistic system which underlies communication, and they need not feel that their interests are threatened by those who make the study of linguistic competence a coherent and autonomous discipline. Similarly, a structuralist poetics would claim that the study of literature involves only indirectly the critical act of placing a work in situation, reading it as a gesture of a particular kind, and thus giving it a meaning. The task is rather to construct a theory of literary discourse which would account for the possibilities of interpretation, the 'empty meanings' which support a variety of full meanings but which do not permit the work to be given just any meaning.

This would not need to be said if interpretive criticism had not tried to persuade us that the study of literature means the elucidation of individual works. But in this cultural context it is important to reflect on what has been lost or obscured in the practice of an interpretive criticism which treats each work as an autonomous artefact, an organic whole whose parts all contribute to a complex thematic statement. The notion that the task of criticism is to reveal thematic unity is a post-Romantic concept, whose roots in the theory of organic form are, at the very least, ambiguous. The organic unity of a plant is not easily translated into thematic unity, and we are willing to admit that the botanical gaze be allowed to compare one plant with another, isolating similarities and differences, or to dwell on formal organization without immediately invoking some teleological purpose or thematic unity. Nor has discourse on literature always been so imperiously committed to interpretation. It used to be possible, in the days before the poem became pre-eminently the act of an individual and emotion recollected in tranquillity, to study its interaction with norms of rhetoric and genre, the relation of its formal features to those of the tradition, without feeling immediately compelled to produce an interpretation which would demonstrate their thematic relevance. One did not need to move from poem to world but could explore it within the institution of literature, relating it to a tradition and identifying formal continuities and discontinuities. That this should have been possible may tell us something important about literature or at least lead us to reflect on the possibility of loosening interpretation's hold on critical discourse.

Such loosening is important because if the analyst aims at understanding how literature works he must, as Northrop Frye says, set about 'formulating the broad laws of literary experience, and in short writing as though he believed that there is a totally intelligible structure of knowledge attainable about poetry, which is not poetry itself, or the experience of it, but poetics' (*Anatomy of Criticism*, p. 14).

Few have put the case for poetics more forcefully than Frye, but in his perspective, as this quotation shows, the relationship between poetry, the experience of poetry and poetics remains somewhat obscure, and that obscurity affects his later formulations. His discussions of modes, symbols, myths and genres lead to the production of taxonomies which capture something of the richness of literature, but the status of his taxonomic categories is curiously indeterminate. What is their relation to literary discourse and to the activity of reading? Are the four mythic categories of Spring, Summer, Autumn and Winter devices for classifying literary works or categories on which the experience of literature is based? As soon as one asks why these categories are to be preferred to those of other possible taxonomies it becomes evident that there must be something implicit in Frye's theoretical framework which needs to be made explicit.

The linguistic model provides a slight reorientation which makes apparent what is needed. Study of the linguistic system becomes theoretically coherent when we cease thinking that our goal is to specify the properties of objects in a corpus and concentrate instead on the task of formulating the internalized competence which enables objects to have the properties they do for those who have mastered the system. To discover and characterize structures one must analyse the system which assigns structural descriptions to the objects in question, and thus a literary taxonomy should be grounded on a theory of reading. The relevant categories are those which are required to account for the range of acceptable meanings which works can have for readers of literature.

The notion of literary competence or of a literary system is, of course, anathema to some critics, who see in it an attack on the spontaneous, creative and affective qualities of literature. Moreover, they might argue, the very concept of literary competence, which carries the presumption that we can distinguish between competent and incompetent readers, is objectionable for precisely those reasons which lead one to propose it: the postulation of a norm for 'correct' reading. In other human activities where there are clear criteria for success and failure, such as playing chess or climbing mountains, we can speak of competence and incompetence, but the richness and power of literature depend, precisely, on the fact that it is not an activity of this kind and that appreciation is varied, personal, and not subject to the normative legislation of self-styled experts.

Such arguments, however, would seem to miss the point. None would deny that literary works, like most other objects of human attention, can be enjoyed for reasons that have little do with understanding and mastery – that texts can be quite blatantly misunderstood and still be appreciated for a variety of personal reasons. But to reject the notion of misunderstanding as a legislative imposition is to leave unexplained the common experience of being shown where one went wrong, of grasping a mistake and seeing why it was a mistake. Though acquiescence may occasionally be disgruntled yielding to a higher authority, none would maintain that it was always thus; more often one feels that one has indeed been shown the way to a fuller understanding of literature and a better grasp of the procedures of reading. If the distinction between understanding and misunderstanding were irrelevant, if neither party to a discussion believed in the distinction, there would be little point to discussing and arguing about literary works and still less to writing about them.

Moreover, the claims of schools and universities to offer literary training cannot be lightly dismissed. To believe that the whole institution of literary education is but a gigantic confidence trick, would strain even a determined credulity, for it is, alas, only too clear that knowledge of a language and a certain experience of the world do not suffice to make someone a perceptive and competent reader. That achievement requires acquaintance with a range of literature and in many cases some form of guidance. The time and effort devoted to literary education by generations of students and teachers creates a strong presumption that there is something to be learned, and teachers do not hesitate to judge their pupil's progress towards a general literary competence. Most would claim, no doubt with good reason, that their examinations are designed not simply to determine whether their students have read various set works but to test their acquisition of an ability.

'Everyone who has seriously studied literature', Northrop Frye maintains, 'knows that the mental process involved is as coherent and progressive as the study of science. A precisely similar training of the mind takes place, and a similar sense of the unity of the subject is built up' (*ibid.*, pp. 10–11). If that seems overstated it is no doubt because what is explicit in the teaching of science usually remains implicit in the teaching of literature. But it is clear that study of one poem or novel facilitates the study of the next: one gains not only points of comparison but a sense of how to read. One develops a set of questions which experience shows to be appropriate and productive and criteria for determining whether they are, in a given case, productive; one acquires a sense of the possibilities of literature and how these possibilities may be distinguished. We may speak, if we like, of extrapolating from one work to another, so long as we do not thereby obscure the fact that the process of extrapolation is precisely what requires explanation. To account for extrapolation, to explain what are the formal questions and distinctions whose relevance the student learns, would be to formulate a theory of literary competence. If we are to make any sense at all of the process of literary education and of criticism itself we must, as Frye argues, assume the possibility of 'a coherent and comprehensive theory of literature, logically and scientifically organized, some of which the student unconsciously learns as he goes on, but the main principles of which are as yet unknown to us' (p. 11).

It is easy to see why, from this perspective, linguistics offers an attractive methodological analogy: a grammar, as Chomsky says, 'can be regarded as a theory of a language', and the theory of literature of which Frye speaks can be regarded as the 'grammar' or literary competence which readers have assimilated but of which they may not be consciously aware. To make the implicit explicit is the task of both linguistics and poetics, and generative grammar has placed renewed emphasis on two fundamental requirements for theories of this kind: that they state their rules as formal operations (since what they are investigating is a kind of intelligence they cannot take for granted intelligence used in applying rules but must make them as explicit as possible) and that they be testable (they must reproduce, as it were, attested facts about semiotic competence).

Can this step be taken in literary criticism? The major obstacle would seem to be that of determining what will count as evidence about literary competence. In linguistics it is not difficult to identify facts that an adequate grammar must account for: though one may need to speak of 'degrees of grammaticalness' one can produce lists of sentences which are incontestably well formed and sentences which are unquestionably deviant. Moreover, we have a sufficiently strong intuitive sense of paraphrase relations to be able to say roughly what a sentence means for speakers of a language. In the study of literature, however, the situation is considerably more complex. Notions of 'well-formed' or 'intelligible' literary works are notoriously problematic, and it may be difficult to secure agreement about what should count as a proper 'understanding' of a text. That critics should differ so widely in their interpretations might seem to undermine any notion of a general literary competence.

But in order to overcome this apparent obstacle we have only to ask what we want a theory of literature to account for. We cannot ask it to account for the 'correct' meaning of a work since we manifestly do not believe that for each work there is a single correct reading. We cannot ask it to draw a clear line between the well-formed and the deviant work if we believe that no such line exists. Indeed, the striking facts that do require explanation are how it is that a work can have a variety of meanings but not just any meaning whatsoever or how it is that some works give an impression of strangeness, incoherence, incomprehensibility. The model does not imply that there must be unanimity on any particular count. It suggests only that we must designate a set of facts, of whatever kind, which seem to require explanation and then try to construct a model of literary competence which would account for them.

The facts can be of many kinds: that a given prose sentence has different meanings if set down as a poem, that readers are able to recognize the plot of a novel, that some symbolic interpretations of a poem are more plausible than others, that two characters in a novel contrast with one another, that *The Waste Land* or *Ulysses* once seemed strange and now seems intelligible. Poetics bears, as Barthes says, not so much on the work itself as on its intelligibility (*Critique et vérité*, p. 62) and therefore problematic cases – the work which some find intelligible and others incoherent, or the work which is read differently in two different periods – furnish the most decisive evidence about the system of operative conventions. Any work can be made intelligible if one invent appropriate conventions: the most obscure poem could be interpreted if there were a convention which permitted us to replace every lexical item by a word beginning with the same letter of the alphabet and chosen according to the ordinary demands of coherence. There are numerous other bizarre conventions which might be operative if the institution of literature were different, and hence the difficulty of interpreting some works provides evidence of the restricted nature of the conventions actually in force in a culture. Moreover, if a difficult work later becomes intelligible it is because new ways of reading have been developed in order to meet what is the fundamental demand of the system: the demand for sense. A comparison of old and new readings will shed light on the change in the institution of literature.

As in linguistics, there is no automatic procedure for obtaining information about competence, but there is no dearth of facts to be explained.[5] To take surveys of the behaviour of readers would serve little purpose, since one is interested not in performance itself but in the tacit knowledge or competence which underlies it. Performance may not be a direct reflection of competence, for behaviour can be influenced by a host of irrelevant factors: I may not have been paying attention at a given moment, may have been led astray by purely personal associations, may have forgotten something important from an earlier part of the text, may have made what I would recognize as a mistake if it were pointed out to me. One's concern is with the tacit knowledge that recognition of a mistake would show rather than with the mistake itself, and so even if one were to take surveys one would still have to judge whether particular reactions were in fact a direct reflection of competence. The question is not what actual readers happen to do but what an ideal reader must know implicitly in order to read and interpret works in ways which we consider acceptable, in accordance with the institution of literature.

The ideal reader is, of course, a theoretical construct, perhaps best thought of as a representation of the central notion of acceptability. Poetics, Barthes writes, 'will describe the logic according to which meanings are engendered in ways that can be *accepted* by man's logic of symbols, just as the sentences of French are *accepted* by the linguistic intuitions of Frenchmen' (*Critique et vérité*, p. 63). Though there is no automatic procedure for determining what is acceptable, that does not matter, for one's proposals will be sufficiently tested by one's readers' acceptance or rejection of them. If readers do not accept the facts one sets out to explain as bearing any relation to their knowledge and experience of literature, then one's theory will be of little interest; and therefore the analyst must convince his readers that meanings or effects which he is attempting to account for are indeed appropriate ones. The meaning of a poem within the institution of literature is not, one might say, the immediate and spontaneous reaction of individual readers but the meanings which they are willing to accept as both plausible and justifiable when they are explained. 'Ask yourself: How does one *lead* anyone to comprehension of a poem or of a theme? The answer to this tells us how meaning is to be explained here.'[6] The paths by which the reader is led to comprehension are precisely those of the logic of literature: the effects must be related to the poem in such a way that the reader sees the connection to be just in terms of his own knowledge of literature.

One cannot therefore emphasize too strongly that every critic, whatever his persuasion, encounters the problems of literary competence as soon as he begins to speak or write about literary works, and that he takes for granted notions of acceptability and common ways of reading. The critic would not write unless he thought he had something new to say about a text, yet he assumes that his reading is not a random and idiosyncratic phenomenon. Unless he thinks that he is merely recounting to others the adventures of his own subjectivity, he claims that his interpretation is related to the text in ways which he presumes his readers will accept once those relations are pointed out: either they will accept his interpretation as an explicit version of what they intuitively felt or they will recognize from their own knowledge of literature the justice of the operations that lead the critic from text to interpretation. Indeed, the possibility of critical argument depends on shared notions of the acceptable and the unacceptable, a common ground which is nothing other than the procedures of reading. The critic must invariably make decisions about what can in fact be taken for granted, what must be explicitly defended, and what constitutes an acceptable defence. He must show his readers that the effects he notices fall within the compass of an implicit logic which they are presumed to accept; and thus he deals in his own practice with the problems which a poetics would hope to make explicit.

William Empson's *Seven Types of Ambiguity* is a work from a non-structuralist tradition which shows considerable awareness of the problems of literary competence and illustrates just how close one comes to a structuralist formulation if one begins to reflect on them. Even if Empson were content to present his work as a display of ingenuity in discovering ambiguities, his enterprise would still be governed by conceptions of plausibility. But of course he wants to make broader claims for his analysis and finds that to do so entails a position very like that recommended above:

> I have continually employed a method of analysis which jumps the gap between two ways of thinking; which produces a possible set of alternative meanings with some ingenuity, and then says it is grasped in the preconsciousness of the reader by a native effort of the mind. This must seem very dubious; but then the facts about the apprehension of poetry are in any case very extraordinary. Such an assumption is best judged by the way it works in detail. (p. 239)

Poetry has complex effects which are extremely difficult to explain, and the analyst finds that his best strategy is to assume that the effects he sets out to account for have been conveyed to the reader and then to postulate certain general operations which might explain these effects and analogous effects in other poems. To those who protest against such assumptions one might reply, with Empson, that the test is whether one succeeds in accounting for effects which the reader accepts when they are pointed out to him. The assumption is in no way dangerous, for the analyst 'must convince the reader that he knows what he is talking about' – make him see the appropriateness of the effects in question – and 'must coax the reader into seeing that the cause he names does, in fact, produce the effect which is experienced; otherwise they will not seem to have anything to do with each other' (p. 249). If the reader is brought to accept both the effects in question and the explanation he will have helped to validate what is, in essence, a theory of reading. 'I have claimed to show how a properly-qualified mind works when it reads the verses, how those properly-qualified minds have worked which have not at all understood their own working' (p. 248). Such claims about literary competence are not to be verified by surveys of readers' reactions to poems but by readers' assent to the effects which the analyst attempts to explain and the efficacy of his explanatory hypotheses in other cases.

It is Empson's self-awareness and outspokenness as much as his brilliance which make his work invaluable to students of poetics; he has little respect for the critical piety that meanings are always implicitly and objectively present in the language of the poem, and thus he can attend to the operations which produce meanings. Discussing the translation of a Chinese fragment,

> Swiftly the years, beyond recall.
> Solemn the stillness of this spring morning.

he notes that

> these lines are what we should normally call poetry only by virtue of their compactness; two statements are made as if they were connected, and the reader is forced to consider their relations for himself. The reason why these facts should have been selected for a poem is left for him to invent; he will invent a variety of reasons and order them in his own mind. This, I think, is the essential fact about the poetical use of language. (p. 25)

This is indeed an essential fact, and one should hasten to point out what it implies: reading poetry is a rule-governed process of producing meanings; the poem offers a structure which must be filled up and one therefore attempts to invent something, guided by a series of formal rules derived from one's experience of reading poetry, which both make possible invention and impose limits on it. In this case the most obvious feature of literary competence is the intent at totality of the interpretive process: poems are supposed to cohere, and one must therefore discover a semantic level at which the two lines can be related to one another. An obvious point of contact is the contrast between 'swiftly' and 'stillness', and there is thus a primary condition on 'invention': any interpretation should succeed in making thematic capital out of this opposition. Moreover, 'years' in the first sentence and 'this morning' in the second, both located in the dimension of time, provide another opposition and point of contact. The reader might hope to find an interpretation which relates these two pairs of contrasts. If this is indeed what happens it is no doubt because the experience of reading poetry leads to implicit recognition of the importance of binary oppositions as thematic devices: in interpreting a poem one looks for terms which can be placed on a semantic or thematic axis and opposed to one another.

The resulting structure or 'empty meaning' suggests that the reader try to relate the opposition between 'swiftly' and 'stillness' to two ways of thinking about time and draw some kind of thematic conclusion from the tension between the two sentences. It seems eminently possible to produce in this way a reading which is 'acceptable' in terms of poetic logic. On the one hand, taking a large panoramic view, we can think of the human life-span as a unit of time and of the years as passing swiftly; on the other, taking the moment of consciousness as the unit, we can think of the difficulty of experiencing time except discontinuously, of the stillness of a clock's hand when one looks at it. 'Swiftly the years' implies a vantage point from which one can consider the passage of time, and the swiftness of passage is compensated for by what Empson calls 'the answering stability of self-knowledge' implicit in this view of life (p. 24). 'This morning' implies other mornings – a discontinuity of experience reflected in the ability to separate and name – and hence an instability which makes 'stillness' the more valued. This process of binary structuring, then, can lead one to find tension within each of the lines as well as between the two lines. And since thematic contrasts should be related to opposed values we are led to think about the advantages and disadvantages of these two ways of conceiving of time. A variety of conclusions are of course possible. The claim is not that competent readers would agree on an interpretation but only that certain expectations about poetry and ways of reading guide the interpretive process and impose severe limitations on the set of acceptable or plausible readings.

Empson's example indicates that as soon as one reflects seriously on the status of critical argument and the relation of interpretation to text one approaches the problems which confront poetics, in that one must justify one's reading by locating it within the conventions of plausibility defined by a generalized knowledge of literature. From the point of view of poetics, what requires explanation is not the text itself so much as the possibility of reading and interpreting the text, the possibility of literary effects and literary communication. To account for the notions of acceptability and plausibility on which criticism relies is, as J.-C. Gardin emphasizes, the primary task of the systematic study of literature.

> This is in any case the only sort of objective that a 'science'
> may set for itself, even if it be a science of literature: the
> regularities unveiled by natural phenomena correspond, in the
> literary field, to certain convergences of perception for
> members of a given culture. ('Semantic analysis procedures in
> the sciences of man', p. 33)

But one should stress that even if the analyst showed little explicit interest in notions of acceptability and merely set out to explain in a systematic way his own reading of literature, the results would be of considerable moment for poetics. If he began by noting his own interpretations and reactions to literary works and succeeded in formulating a set of explicit rules which accounted for the fact that he produced these interpretations and not others, one would then possess the basis of an account of literary competence. Adjustments could be made to include other readings which seemed acceptable and to exclude any readings which seemed wholly personal and idiosyncratic, but there is every reason to expect that other readers would be able to recognize substantial portions of their own tacit knowledge in his account. To be an experienced reader of literature is, after all, to have gained a sense of what can be done with literary works and thus to have assimilated a system which is largely inter-personal. There is little reason to worry initially about the validity of the facts which one sets out to explain; the only risk one runs is that of wasting one's time. The important thing is to start by isolating a set of facts and then to construct a model to account for them, and though structuralists have often failed to do this in their own practice, it is at least implicit in the linguistic model: 'Linguistics can give literature the generative model which is the principle of all science, since it is a matter of making use of certain rules to explain particular results' (Barthes, *Critique et vérité*, p. 58).

Since poetics is essentially a theory of reading, critics of every persua-sion who have tried to be explicit about what they are doing have made some contribution to it and indeed in many cases have more to offer than structuralists themselves. What structuralism does provide is a reversal of critical perspective and a theoretical framework within which the work of other critics can be organized and exploited. Granting precedence to the task of formulating a theory of literary competence and relegating critical interpretation to a secondary role, it leads one to reformulate as conventions of literature and operations of reading what others might think of as facts about various literary texts. Rather than say, for example, that literary texts are fictional, we might cite this as a convention of literary interpretation and say that to read a text as literature is to read it as fiction. Such a reversal may, at first sight, seem trivial, but to restate propositions about poetic or novelistic discourse as procedures of reading is a crucial reorienta-tion for a number of reasons, wherein lie the revitalizing powers of a structuralist poetics.

First of all, to stress literature's dependence on particular modes of reading is a firmer and more honest starting point than is customary in criticism. One need not struggle, as other theorists must, to find some objective property of language which distinguishes the literary from the non-literary but may simply start from the fact that we can read texts as literature and then inquire what operations that involves. The operations will, of course, be different for different genres, and here by the same model we can say that genres are not special varieties of language but sets of expectations which allow sentences of a language to become signs of different kinds in a second-order literary system. The same sentence can have a different meaning depending on the genre in which it appears. Nor is one upset, as a theorist working on the distinctive properties of literary language must be, by the fact that the boundaries between the literary and the non-literary or between one genre and another change from age to age. On the contrary, change in modes of reading offers some of the best evidence about the conventions operative in different periods.

Second, in attempting to make explicit what one does when reading or interpreting a poem one gains considerably in self-awareness and awareness of the nature of literature as an institution. As long as one assumes that what one does is natural it is difficult to gain any understanding of it and thus to define the differences between oneself and one's predecessors or successors. Reading is not an innocent activity. It is charged with artifice, and to refuse to study one's modes of reading is to neglect a principal source of information about literary activity. By seeing literature as something animated by special sets of conventions one can attain more easily a sense of its specificity, its peculiarity, its difference, shall we say, from other modes of discourse about the world. Those differences lie in the work of the literary sign: in the ways in which meaning is produced.

Third, a willingness to think of literature as an institution composed of a variety of interpretive operations makes one more open to the most challenging and innovatory texts, which are precisely those that are difficult to process according to received modes of understanding. An awareness of the assumptions on which one proceeds, an ability to make explicit what one is attempting to do, makes it easier to see where and how the text resists one's attempts to make sense of it and how, by its refusal to comply with one's expectations, it leads to that questioning of the self and of ordinary social modes of understanding which has always been the result of the greatest literature. My readers, says the narrator at the end of *A la recherche du temps perdu*, will become 'les propres lecteurs d'eux-mêmes': in my book they will read themselves and their own limits. How better to facilitate a reading of oneself than by trying to make explicit one's sense of the comprehensible and the incomprehensible, the significant and the insignificant, the ordered and the inchoate. By offering sequences and combinations which escape our accustomed grasp, by subjecting language to a dislocation which fragments the ordinary signs of our world, literature challenges the limits we set to the self as a device or order and allows us, painfully or joyfully, to accede to an expansion of self. But that requires, if it is to be fully accomplished, a measure of awareness of the interpretive models which inform one's culture. Structuralism, because of its interest in the adventures of the sign, has been exceedingly open to the revolutionary work, finding in its resistance to the operations of reading confirmation of the fact that literary effects depend on these conventions and that literary evolution proceeds by displacement of old conventions of reading and the development of new.

And so, finally, structuralism's reversal of perspective can lead to a mode of interpretation based on poetics itself, where the work is read against the conventions of discourse and where one's interpretation is an account of the ways in which the work complies with or undermines our procedures for making sense of things. Though it does not, of course, replace ordinary thematic interpretations, it does avoid premature foreclosure – the unseemly rush from word to world – and stays within the literary system for as long as possible. Insisting that literature is something other than a statement about the world, it establishes, finally, an analogy between the production or reading of signs in literature and in other areas of experience and studies the ways in which the former explores and dramatizes the limitations of the latter. In this kind of interpretation the meaning of the work is what it shows the reader, by the acrobatics in which it involves him, about the problems of his condition as *homo significans*, maker and reader of signs. The notion of literary competence thus comes to serve as the basis of a reflexive interpretation.

The pages that follow have the dual function of indicating and evaluating the work which structuralists themselves have done on various aspects of the literary system and of proposing areas where investigation might well be fruitful. The theoretical programme has attracted more attention and effort than what one might call the axioms of the middle range, and so what is offered is best considered as a framework into which the investigations of many critics – not structuralists alone – might fit, rather than as a presumptuous account of 'literary competence' itself.

CHAPTER 7

Convention and Naturalization

(Stoop) if you are abcedminded, to
this claybook, what curios of signs
(please stoop), in this allaphbed!
Can you rede (since We and Thou had
it out already) its world?
JOYCE

Ecriture, lecture

'Today the essential question is no longer that of the *writer* and the *work*', writes Philippe Sollers, 'but that of *writing* and *reading*' (*Logiques*, pp. 237–8). The concepts of *écriture* and *lecture* have been brought to the fore so as to divert attention from the author as source and the work as object and focus it instead on two correlated networks of convention: writing as an institution and reading as an activity. Emphasis on the author's relation to his work may lead one to think of literature as a version of the communicative speech act, endowed with more permanence than is usual, and to neglect the particularities of writing. But as Thibaudet pointed out long ago, the starting point for a study of literature should be a recognition that it is not just language but, especially in our day, a set of written texts printed in books.[1]

> Criticism and literary history often make the mistake of placing in the same series or mixing as of the same order what is spoken, what is sung, what is read. Literature takes place as a function of the Book, and yet there are few things to which a man of books gives less thought than the Book.

The physical presentation of a text gives it a stability which separates it from the ordinary circuit of communication in which speech takes place, and this separation has important implications for the study of literature. If these implications are not often accorded full weight, it is, as Jacques Derrida has argued, because the assimilation of writing to speech is deeply rooted in the metaphysics of Western culture. To think of the written word as simply a record of the spoken word is but one version of a 'metaphysics of presence' which locates truth in what is immediately present to consciousness with as little mediation as possible. Thus, the Cartesian *cogito*, in which the self is immediately present to itself, is taken as the basic proof of existence, and things directly perceived are apodictically privileged. Notions of truth and reality are based on a longing for an unfallen world in which there would be no need for the mediating systems of language and perception but everything would be itself, with no gap between form and meaning.[2] Interpretation, on this model, is a matter of making present what is absent, of restoring an original presence which is the source and truth of the form in question. The tendency is thus to treat a text as if it were spoken and to try to move through the words to recover the meaning which was present in the speaker's mind at the moment of utterance, to determine what the speaker, in that revealing phrase, 'had in mind'.

However appropriate this model may seem to speech, the written word cannot be thought of in this way. Plato condemned writing because the written word was cut loose and liberated from the communicative presence which alone could be the source of meaning and truth.[3] But this distance, this independence of the written word, is one of the constitutive features of literature.

> To write is to produce a mark which constitutes in its turn a
> kind of productive mechanism, which my absence will not, as a
> matter of principle, prevent from functioning and provoking
> reading, from yielding itself up to reading and rewriting . . .
> For writing to be writing it must continue to 'act' and be
> readable even if what we call the author of the writing be
> provisionally absent or no longer uphold what he has written,
> what he appears to have signed . . . The situation of the writer
> or underwriter is, with respect to the writing, fundamentally the
> same as that of the reader. This essential drift, which is proper
> to writing as a structure of repetition, a structure cut off from
> any absolute responsibility or from consciousness as ultimate
> authority, orphaned and separated since birth from the support
> of the father, is indeed what Plato condemned in the *Phaedrus*.
> (Derrida, *Marges de la philosophie*, p. 376)

The meaning of a sentence, one might say, is not a form or an essence, present at the moment of its production and lying behind it as a truth to be recovered, but the series of developments to which it gives rise, as determined by past and future relations between words and the conventions of semiotic systems. Some texts are more 'orphaned' than others because the conventions of reading are not so firm as to provide a stepfather. To read a political speech, for example, is to submit to a teleology, to take the text as governed by a communicative end which one reconstructs with the help of the conventions of discourse and of the relevant institutions. But literature, foregrounding the text itself, gives freer play to the 'essential drift' and autonomous productivity of the language. Writing involves a *différance*, which Derrida spells with an 'a' to highlight the difference perceptible only within the written language and to emphasize the relation between difference and deferment. The written word is an object in its own right: different from meanings which it defers in a play of differences (*ibid.*, pp. 3–29). If in language there are only differences with no positive terms, it is in literature that we have least cause to arrest the play of differences by calling upon a determinate communicative intention to serve as the truth or origin of the sign. We say instead that a poem can mean many things.

Derrida wants to take his argument a step further and, having maintained that writing cannot be treated on the model of speech, show that the features which he has first isolated in writing are also present in speech, which must, therefore, be conceived according to the new model of writing (*ibid.*, pp. 377–81). But this further move is a purely logical point, which someone concerned with the social facts can afford to neglect: even if Derrida shows that we ought to think of speech as a kind of writing, we may arrest the play of his concepts by saying, simply, that within Western culture there are crucial differences between the conventions of oral communication and those of literature which deserve study whatever their ideological basis. To replace a metaphysic of presence by a metaphysic of absence, to invert the relation between speech and writing so that writing engulfs speech, is to lose the distinction which translates a fact of our culture. Communication does take place. Many instances of language are firmly situated in the circuit of communication. This page, for example, asks to be read not as an infinite play of differences which defers meaning but as a communicative act which explains to the reader my view of Derrida's own communication. It calls upon conventions of reading which are different from those of lyric poetry.

To study writing, and especially literary modes of writing, one must concentrate on the conventions which guide the play of differences and the process of constructing meanings. Barthes emphasizes that all modes of writing have a monumentality which is foreign to spoken language: 'writing is a hardened language which leads an independent existence' and whose task is less to carry or give access to a thought than 'to thrust upon us, by the solid unity and shadows of its signs, the image of a linguistic form constructed before it was invented. What opposes writing to speech is that the former always *appears* symbolic' (*Le Degré zéro de l'écriture*, p. 18). Writing has something of the character of an inscription, a mark offered to the world and promising, by its solidity and apparent autonomy, meaning which is momentarily deferred. Precisely for that reason it calls for interpretation, and our modes of interpretation are essentially ways of constructing communicative circuits into which we can fit it.

Thus, the distinction between speech and writing becomes the source of the fundamental paradox of literature: we are attracted to literature because it is obviously something other than ordinary communication; its formal and fictional qualities bespeak a strangeness, a power, an organization, a permanence which is foreign to ordinary speech. Yet the urge to assimilate that power and permanence or to let that formal organization work upon us requires us to make literature into a communication, to reduce its strangeness, and to draw upon supplementary conventions which enable it, as we say, to speak to us. The difference which seemed the source of value becomes a distance to be bridged by the activity of reading and interpretation. The strange, the formal, the fictional, must be recuperated or naturalized, brought within our ken, if we do not want to remain gaping before monumental inscriptions.

And the first step in the process of naturalizing or restoring literature to a communicative function is to make *écriture* itself a period and generic concept. This is how Barthes uses the term in his early *Le Degré zéro de l'écriture*, where he recognized the correlation between the apparent monumentality and autonomy of writing and the institutional conventions which situate it. As opposed to his language, which an author inherits, and his style, which Barthes defines as a personal and subconscious network of verbal obsessions, an *écriture* or mode of writing is something an author adopts: a function he gives his language, a set of institutional conventions within which the activity of writing can take place. Thus, for example, Barthes argues that from the seventeenth to the early nineteenth century French literature employed a single *écriture classique*, characterized primarily by its confidence in a representational aesthetic (p. 42). To read is essentially to take up or construct a reference, and when Madame de Lafayette writes of the Comte de Tende that upon learning that his wife was pregnant by another man, 'il pensait d'abord tout ce qu'il était naturel de penser en cette occasion' (he thought everything that it was natural to think in such circumstances), she displays the immense confidence in her readers that this mode of writing implies.[4] Language need only gesture towards the world. A century and a half later Balzac offers more information about that towards which he is gesturing, but he shows the same kind of confidence in the representational function of his writing: Eugène de Rastignac was 'un de ces jeunes gens façonnés au travail par le malheur' (one of those young men moulded for work by misfortune); Le Baron Hulot was 'un de ces hommes dont les yeux s'animent à la vue d'une jolie femme' (one of those men whose eyes light up at the sight of a pretty woman). To understand the language of a text is to recognize the world to which it refers.

Moreover, given that function, formal qualities become ornaments which, if they do not obscure the reference, do not affect the meaning. Classical rhetoric defines a series of operations which enable one to move from the textual surface, with its metaphors and synecdoches, to the meanings which are essentially references. La Fontaine's line, 'Sur les ailes du temps la tristesse s'envole' (Sadness flies off on the wings of time), means, a rhetorician tells us, that sadness does not last.[5] We know that this is what it means because we know that in the world time does not have wings nor does sadness fly; and by performing the translation which rhetorical theory requires we isolate the ornament which serves as decoration. Indeed, one might say that debates about rhetoric and the appropriateness of particular expressions in specific genres are possible only because there are various ways of saying the same thing: the figure is an ornament which does not trouble the representational function of language.[6]

This mode of writing depends heavily on readers' ability to naturalize it and to recognize the common world which serves as point of reference; and consequently changes in the social situation, which make it clear that the world is not one, undermine this *écriture*. One can no longer say 'he thought what was natural on such an occasion' without writing an obscure and problematic sentence; and it becomes obvious that, in the absence of this unambiguous referential foundation, a change in expression is a change in thought. A variety of interpretive strategies become necessary, and consequently Barthes identifies a range of *ècritures modernes*. In each case 'what it is first necessary to grasp is not the idiolect of the author but of the institution (literature)' ('Style and its Image', p. 8).

One can, of course, multiply the number of *écritures* until one produces as many distinctions as seem necessary to account for the different ways in which texts must be read, the different contracts which the institution of literature makes available. Such distinctions must take account both of the historical changes from one period to another and of the differences between genres in any given period. Fontanier, for example, argues that tropes are generally more suitable in poetry than in prose because they, like poetry, are 'the children of fiction' and because poetry aims more to please than to instruct about the real world (*Les Figures du discours*, p. 180). In other words, the institution of literature permits a different relation between text and world in the case of poetry and thus makes appropriate certain types of naturalization or operations of reading which are not admitted in prose. Tropes may be literally absurd but they thereby connote an intensity of passion or vivacity of imagination which is the prerogative of the poetic narrator. Poetic 'folly' is made natural and readable by the conventions of genre, and hence tropes are most appropriate in the ode, the epic and tragedy (*ibid.*, p. 181).

A genre, one might say, is a conventional function of language, a particular relation to the world which serves as norm or expectation to guide the reader in his encounter with the text.

> It is indeed this word (novel, poem) placed on the cover of the book which (by convention) genetically produces, programmes, or 'originates' our reading. We have here (with the genre 'novel', 'poem') a *master word* which from the outset reduces complexity, reduces the textual encounter, by making it a function of the type of reading already implicit in the law of this word.
> (Pleynet, 'La poésie doit avoir pour but . . .', pp. 95–6)

To read a text as a tragedy is to give it a framework which allows order and complexity to appear. Indeed, an account of genres should be an attempt to define the classes which have been functional in the processes of reading and writing, the sets of expectations which have enabled readers to naturalize texts and give them a relation to the world or, if one prefer to look at it in another way, the possible functions of language which were available to writers at any given period. As Claudio Guillén observes, 'the theoretical orders of poetics should be viewed, at any moment in their history, as essentially mental codes, with which the practising writer comes to terms through his writing' (*Literature as System*, p. 390).

A genre, in other words, is not simply a taxonomic class. If one groups works together on the basis of observed similarities one does indeed have purely empirical taxonomies of the sort which have helped to bring the notion of genre into disrepute. A taxonomy, if it is to have any theoretical value, must be motivated; but there seems to be considerable confusion about the type of motivation required. For example, in criticizing Northrop Frye's account of genres Todorov argues that without a coherent theory 'we remain prisoners of prejudices transmitted from century to century and according to which (this is an imaginary example) there is a genre such as comedy, when in fact that might be pure illusion' (*Introduction à la littérature fantastique*, p. 26). But a theory which demonstrates that there is no such thing as comedy is not at all what is required. It is not, of course, clear what such a statement would mean or how it could be substantiated, but in any case one may assert that any theory which led to this conclusion would thereby prove its own inadequacy, just as any theory which 'proved' that *King Lear* was not a tragedy would be wrong. If a theory of genres is to be more than a taxonomy it must attempt to explain what features are constitutive of functional categories which have governed the reading and writing of literature. Comedy exists by virtue of the fact that to read something as a comedy involves different expectations from reading something as a tragedy or as an epic.

Indeed, to be fair to Todorov, one should mention that in his discussion of *la littérature fantastique* he does found his genre on the operations of reading. One may isolate a set of works in which the reader is forced to hesitate between a naturalistic and a supernatural explanation of curious events. 'The fantastic occupies this space of uncertainty; as soon as one chooses either reply one leaves the fantastic and enters a neighbouring genre, the strange or the supernatural' (p. 29). The existence of this genre would be confirmed, for example, by the general recognition that there are stories, such as 'The Turn of the Screw', which require us to remain in this state of uncertainty rather than assimilate them as examples of the strange but explicable or of the explicitly supernatural. When we recognize this production of uncertainty as a possible function of language and no longer assume that the 'real meaning' must be either a natural or supernatural explanation we have helped to constitute a new genre. And we have done so by accepting the possibility of a type of meaning or relation of text to the world which previously we might have been inclined to dismiss in favour of other choices.

As this example should make clear, what we speak of as conventions of a genre or an *écriture* are essentially possibilities of meaning, ways of naturalizing the text and giving it a place in the world which our culture defines. To assimilate or interpret something is to bring it within the modes of order which culture makes available, and this is usually done by talking about it in a mode of discourse which a culture takes as natural. This process goes by various names in structuralist writing: recuperation, naturalization, motivation, *vraisemblablisation*. 'Recuperation' stresses the notion of recovery, of putting to use. It may be defined as the desire to leave no chaff, to make everything wheat, to let nothing escape the process of assimilation; it is thus a central component of studies which assert the organic unity of the text and the contribution of all its parts to its meanings or effects. 'Naturalization' emphasizes the fact that the strange or deviant is brought within a discursive order and thus made to seem natural. 'Motivation', which was the Russian formalists' term, is the process of justifying items within the work itself by showing that they are not arbitrary or incoherent but quite comprehensible in terms of functions which we can name. *Vraisemblablisation* stresses the importance of cultural models of the *vraisemblable* as sources of meaning and coherence.

Whatever one calls the process, it is one of the basic activities of the mind. We can, it seems, make anything signify. If a computer were programmed to produce random sequences of English sentences we could make sense of the texts it produced by imagining a variety of functions and contexts. If all else failed, we could read a sequence of words with no apparent order as signifying absurdity or chaos and then, by giving it an allegorical relation to the world, take it as a statement about the incoherence and absurdity of our own languages. As the example of Beckett shows, we can always make the meaningless meaningful by production of an appropriate context. And usually our contexts need not be so extreme. Much of Robbe-Grillet can be recuperated if we read it as the musings or speech of a pathological narrator, and that framework gives critics a hold so that they can go on to discuss the implications of the particular pathology in question. Certain dislocations in poetic texts can be read as signs of a prophetic or ecstatic state or as indications of a Rimbaldian 'dérèglement de tous les sens'. To place the text in such frameworks is to make it legible and intelligible. When Eliot says that modern poetry must be difficult because of the discontinuities of modern culture, when William Carlos Williams argues that his variable foot is necessary in a post-Einsteinian world where all order is questioned, when Humpty-Dumpty tells Alice that 'slithy' means 'lithe' and 'slimy', all are engaged in recuperation or naturalization.

The next two chapters will investigate particular conventions which underlie the lyric and the novel, but before turning to those special modes one should look at the various levels at which naturalization is carried out and the cultural and literary models which make texts readable. The common denominator of these various levels and models is the notion of correspondence: to naturalize a text is to bring it into relation with a type of discourse or model which is already, in some sense, natural and legible. Some of these models have nothing specifically literary about them but are simply the repository of the *vraisemblable*, whereas others are special conventions used in the naturalization of literary works. One can, however, emphasize their similarity of function by grouping them all, as structuralists have done on occasion, under the heading of the *vraisemblable*.

In the introduction to the special number of *Communications* devoted to the topic, Todorov offered three definitions: first, 'the *vraisemblable* is the relation of a particular text to another general and diffuse text which might be called "public opinion" '. Second, the *vraisemblable* is whatever tradition makes suitable or expected in a particular genre: 'there are as many versions of *vraisemblance* as there are genres'. And finally,

> one can speak of the *vraisemblance* of a work in so far as it attempts to make us believe that it conforms to reality and not to its own laws. In other words, the *vraisemblable* is the mask which conceals the text's own laws and which we are supposed to take for a relation with reality. (pp. 2–3)

Retaining these three meanings is not an attempt to achieve profundity at the cost of ambiguity; there are good reasons for grouping them under a single heading, for in each case *vraisemblance* is 'a principle of integration between one discourse and another or several others'.[7] It is important to assert that a work's relation to other texts of a genre or to certain expectations about fictional worlds is a phenomenon of the same type – or a problem of the same order – as its relation to the interpersonal world of ordinary discourse. From the point of view of literary theory, the latter is also a text. 'The world is all that is the case'; it is a set of propositions.[8] And though Wittgenstein did not mean a set of propositions generally held to be true, his position helps to indicate why one might wish to speak of a socially given reality as a text.

The *vraisemblable* is thus the basis of the important structuralist concept of *intertextualité*: the relation of a particular text to other texts. Julia Kristeva writes that 'every text takes shape as a mosaic of citations, every text is the absorption and transformation of other texts. The notion of intertextuality comes to take the place of the notion of intersubjectivity' (*Semiotikè*, p. 146). A work can only be read in connection with or against other texts, which provide a grid through which it is read and structured by establishing expectations which enable one to pick out salient features and give them a structure. And hence intersubjectivity – the shared knowledge which is applied in reading – is a function of these other texts.

> Ce 'moi' qui s'approche du texte est déjà lui-même une pluralité d'autres textes, de codes infinis, ou plus exactement: perdus (dont l'origine se perd) . . . La subjectivité est une image pleine, dont on suppose que j'encombre le texte, mais dont la plénitude, truquée, n'est que le sillage de tous les codes qui me font, en sorte que ma subjectivité a finalement la généralité même des stéréotypes.
>
> (The 'I' which approaches the text is itself already a plurality of

other texts, of infinite, or more precisely, lost codes (whose origins are lost) . . . Subjectivity is generally thought of as a plenitude with which I encumber the text, but in fact this faked plenitude is only the wash of all the codes which make up the 'I', so that finally, my subjectivity has the generality of stereotypes.) (Barthes, *S/Z*, pp. 16–17)

Though it is difficult to discover the sources of all the notions or expectations which make up the 'I' or the reader, subjectivity is not so much a personal core as an intersubjectivity, the track or the furrow left by the experience of texts of all kinds. To characterize the various levels of the *vraisemblable* is to define the ways in which a work can be traversed by or brought into contact with other texts and thus to isolate different manifestations of this textual intersubjectivity which assimilates and naturalizes the work.

One might distinguish five levels of *vraisemblance*, five ways in which a text may be brought into contact with and defined in relation to another text which helps to make it intelligible. First there is the socially given text, that which is taken as the 'real world'. Second, but in some cases difficult to distinguish from the first, is a general cultural text: shared knowledge which would be recognized by participants as part of culture and hence subject to correction or modification but which none the less serves as a kind of 'nature'. Third, there are the texts or conventions of a genre, a specifically literary and artificial *vraisemblance*. Fourth, comes what might be called the natural attitude to the artificial, where the text explicitly cites and exposes *vraisemblance* of the third kind so as to reinforce its own authority. And finally, there is the complex *vraisemblance* of specific intertextualities, where one work takes another as its basis or point of departure and must be assimilated in relation to it. At each level there are ways in which the artifice of forms is motivated or justified by being given a meaning.

The 'real'

The first type of *vraisemblance* is the use of 'the text of the natural attitude of a society (the text of *l'habitude*), entirely familiar and in this very familiarity diffuse, unknown as text'.[9] This is best defined as a discourse which requires no justification because it seems to derive directly from the structure of the world. We speak of people as having minds and bodies, as thinking, imagining, remembering, feeling pain, loving and hating, etc., and do not have to justify such discourse by adducing philosophical arguments. It is simply the text of the natural attitude, at least in Western culture, and hence *vraisemblable*. When a text uses such discourse it is to that extent inherently intelligible, and when it deviates from such discourse the reader's tendency is to translate its 'metaphors' back into this natural language. The most elementary paradigms of action are located at this level: if someone begins to laugh they will eventually stop laughing, if they set out on a journey they will either arrive or abandon the trip. If a text does not explicitly mention these terminations we grant it the benefit of doubt and take them for granted as part of its intelligibility. Should it explicitly violate them, we are forced to place the action in another and fantastic world (which is itself, of course, a way of providing a context which makes the text intelligible by making it *vraisemblable*).

Recognition of this first level of *vraisemblance* need not depend on the claim that reality is a convention produced by language. Indeed, the danger of that position is that it may be interpreted in too sweeping a fashion. Thus, Julia Kristeva argues that anything expressed in a grammatical sentence becomes *vraisemblable* since language is constitutive of the world (*Semiotikè*, pp. 215 and 208–45). It would be more appropriate to say, with Barthes, that whatever meanings a sentence liberates, it always seems as though it ought to be telling us something simple, coherent and true, and that this initial presumption forms the basis of reading as a process of naturalization (*S/Z*, p. 16). 'John cut out his thought and fastened it to his tibia' gains a certain *vraisemblance* from its expression as a grammatical sentence, and we are lead to try to invent a context or to relate it to a text which would make it intelligible, but it is not *vraisemblable* in the way 'John is sad' would be, since it does not form part of the text of the natural attitude, whose items are justified by the simple observation, 'but Xs are like that'.

Cultural *vraisemblance*

Second, there is a range of cultural stereotypes or accepted knowledge which a work may use but which do not enjoy the same privileged status as elements of the first type, in that the culture itself recognizes them as generalizations. When Balzac writes that the Count of Lanty was 'petit, laid et grêlé, sombre comme un Espagnol, ennuyeux comme un banquier' (small, ugly and pock-marked, as gloomy as a Spaniard and as boring as a banker), he is using two different types of *vraisemblance*. The adjectives are intelligible as qualities which it is quite natural and possible for someone to possess (whereas 'he was small, green and demographic' would violate this first-order *vraisemblance* and require us to construct a very curious world indeed). The two comparisons, however, involve cultural references and stereotypes which are accepted as *vraisemblable* within the culture ('as gloomy as an Italian' and 'as boring as a painter' would be *invraisemblable* in these terms) but which are still open to question: a banker need not be boring, and we accept that possibility along with the stereotype. Most elements of the second level function in this way: one is aware of them as generalizations or cultural categories which may oversimplify but which at least make the world initially intelligible and consequently serve as a target language in the process of naturalization.

Proust speaks of a café owner who 'always compared everything he heard or read with a certain already-familiar text and whose admiration was aroused if he found no differences'.[10] Much of a work's *vraisemblance* comes from its citation of this 'collective, anonymous voice, whose origin is a general human knowledge' (Barthes, *S/Z*, p. 25). And it is at this level that the traditional concept of *vraisemblance* is located. Barthes notes, for example, that Aristotle's *Rhetoric* is essentially a codification of a general social language, with all the maxims and *topoi* which contribute to an approximate logic of human actions and enable the orator, for example, to argue from action to motive or from appearance to reality. 'It may seem very flat indeed (and no doubt false) to say that young men anger more swiftly than old', but to do so is to make one's argument *vraisemblable*: 'passions are ready-made pieces of language which the orator must simply be familiar with . . . passion is nothing but what people say about it: pure intertextuality' '(L'ancienne rhétorique', p. 212). Discussing this level of *vraisemblance* in Balzac, Barthes notes that it is as though the author had at his disposal seven or eight school manuals which contained the knowledge that constitutes popular bourgeois culture: a handbook of practical medicine (with notions of various illnesses and conditions), a rudimentary psychological treatise (generally accepted propositions about love, hatred, fear, etc.), a compendium of Christian and Stoic ethics, a logic, an anthology of proverbs and maxims on life, death, suffering, women, etc., and histories of literature and of art which provide both a set of cultural references and a repertoire of types (characters) which may serve as exempla. 'Although they may be entirely of bookish origin, these codes, by a reversal proper to bourgeois ideology, which turns culture into nature, serve as the foundation of the real, of "Life" ' (*S/Z*, p. 211).

Citing this general social discourse is a way of grounding a work in reality, of establishing a relationship between words and world which serves as guarantee of intelligibility; but more important are the interpretive operations which it permits. When a character in a novel performs an action, the reader can give it a meaning by drawing upon this fund of human knowledge which establishes connections between action and motive, behaviour and personality. Naturalization proceeds on the assumption that action is intelligible, and cultural codes specify the forms of intelligibility. When Balzac tells us that Sarrasine 'rose with the sun, went to his studio and didn't emerge until night', we naturalize that action by reading it as a direct manifestation of character and interpret it as 'excess' (in terms of the normal working day) and as artistic commitment (in terms of cultural and psychological stereotypes). When, on coming out of the theatre, he is 'overcome by an inexplicable sadness', we can explain it as the cultural mark of his extreme involvement. These operations bring the text's notation into a context of coherence and, by that fundamental tautology of fiction which allows us to infer character from action and then to be pleased at the way in which action accords with character, make it *vraisemblable*.

Conceptions of the world operative at this level also control what has been called the 'threshold of functional relevance, that which divides the narratable from the non-narratable, sequences below which are taken-for-granted' (Heath, 'Structuration of the Novel-Text', p. 75). There is a level of generality at which we ordinarily speak of our engagement with the world: we 'walk to the store' rather than 'raise our left foot two inches off the ground while swinging it forward and, displacing our centre of gravity so that the foot hits the ground, heel first, stride off on the ball of the right foot, etc.' The latter description, which goes below the level of functional relevance, is an instance of what the Russian formalists called 'defamiliarization': a way of making strange. The process of reading naturalizes and reduces that strangeness by recognizing and naming: this passage describes 'walking'. Of course, the fact that such operations are required in the reading of a particular text produces a surplus of potential meaning which must be justified and interpreted at another level, but the threshold of functional relevance serves as a 'natural' foundation or firm point of departure from which one can work out towards other meanings. A long description of a baroque assemblage of planes and joints is made intelligible by deciding that it is a description of a chair and then inquiring why the chair should have been described in this unusually detailed way. A natural foundation permits the identification of strangeness.

Vraisemblance at this level involves what a recent writer on realism calls the 'middle distance': an optic which neither brings us too close to the object nor lifts us too far above it but views it in precisely the way that we ordinarily do in the daily business of living. What determines this middle distance, he writes, is one of the most familiar functions of all literature: 'the fictional creation of *people*, of individual characters and lives informed by what in any one age is agreed to constitute a certain integrity and coherence'.[11] Whether or not, as he thinks, this can be viewed as the goal of literature, it is certainly the substratum of literature: most literary effects, particularly in narrative prose, depend on the fact that readers will try to relate what the text tells them to a level of ordinary human concerns, to the actions and reactions of characters constructed in accordance with models of integrity and coherence.

In what is perhaps the best article on *vraisemblance* of this kind, Gérard Genette notes that in seventeenth-century discussions *vraisemblance* is what we should today call an ideology: 'a body of maxims and prejudices which constitute both a vision of the world and a system of values'. An action is justified by its relation to a general maxim, and 'this relationship of implication functions also as a principle of *explication*: the general determines and thus explains the particular; to understand a character's conduct, for example, is to refer it to an accepted maxim, and this reference is taken as a move from effect to cause'. In *Le Cid* Rodrigue challenges the Count because 'nothing can prevent a noble son from avenging the honour of his father', and his action becomes intelligible when it is related to this maxim. In *La Princesse de Clèves*, however, the heroine's confession to her husband is, for the seventeenth century, *invraisemblable* and unintelligible because it is 'an action without a maxim' (*Figures II*, pp. 73–5).

The body of maxims may be either assumed implicitly by a text (as what is 'natural' within the culture) or explicitly cited and proffered. In the latter case we have what Genette calls 'un vraisemblable artificiel': the text itself performs the operations of naturalization but simultaneously insists that the laws or explanations which it offers are the laws of the world. A sentence which is initially *invraisemblable*, such as 'The Marquise called for her carriage and then went to bed' (*invraisemblable* because it deviates from an accepted logic of human actions), can be naturalized by additions which would bring it within the pale of accepted cultural models: 'for she was extremely capricious' (where labelling makes deviation intelligible) or 'for, like all women who have never encountered opposition to their desires, she was extremely capricious' (which produces the relevant maxim) (*ibid.*, pp. 98–9). The Balzacian novel, with its proliferation of pedagogic clauses and generalized categories, is the best example of this type of text, which describes characters and actions while creating the fund of social knowledge which justifies its descriptions and makes them intelligible. But, of course, if this artificial *vraisemblance* seems markedly different from that which the social and cultural models make natural, we will relegate it to the third level and speak of it as the purely literary *vraisemblance* of a particular imaginative world.

Models of a genre

The third level or set of models does indeed involve a specifically literary intelligibility: a set of literary norms to which texts may be related and by virtue of which they become meaningful and coherent. One type of norm is that invoked when speaking of an author's imaginative world: we allow works to contribute to a semi-autonomous world, whose laws are not precisely those of our own but which nevertheless has laws and regularities which make actions and events within it intelligible and *vraisemblable*. Our intuitive sense of this *vraisemblance* is extremely powerful: we know, for example, that it would be totally inappropriate for one of Corneille's heroes to say, 'I'm fed up with all these problems and shall go and be a silversmith in a provincial town'. Actions are plausible or implausible with respect to the norms of a group of works, and reactions which would be thoroughly intelligible in a Proustian novel would be extremely bizarre and inexplicable in Balzac. Out of context, Père Goriot is a hopelessly exaggerated character who makes no sense; but in terms of the laws of the Balzacian universe he is immediately intelligible. One might say, in fact, that at this level of *vraisemblance* one should identify series of constitutive conventions which enable various sorts of novels or poems to be written. Henry James's novels, for example, are based on the convention that human beings are sensitive to incredibly subtle ramifications of interpersonal situations and that, whatever their difficulties, they tend to cherish this subtlety and refrain from violating it by the grossness of direct speech. Balzac's novels could not have been written as they were but for two conventions: first, the convention of determination, that the world is fundamentally intelligible and that everything which happens can be explained by recourse to certain types of models, and second, that in a given synchronic state of society the determining force is energy, of which each individual possesses a particular amount (that he can hoard or spend) in addition to that which he can draw from others.[12] Flaubert's novels, one might say, are made possible by the convention that nothing can resist irony except complete innocence, which is the residue left by irony. And thus, if in reading *Madame Bovary* we feel that Emma is indeed doomed, it is not because a convincing analysis has been presented but because we have become accustomed to Flaubert's prose. We know that intensity of aspiration will be given its due but that the particular forms of aspiration will be forced through the crucible of irony, which they cannot survive except as pure form.[13]

We could, of course, speak of such conventions as theories or views of the world, as if it were the task of novels to express them, but such an approach would do scant justice to the novels themselves or to the experience of reading them, for it is the nature of such conventions to remain unexpressed since they are generally indefensible or at least implausible as explicit theories. And we do not read the novels in order to discover such theories; they function, rather, as means to other ends, which are the novels themselves. It may be more useful to speak of myths which are necessary if the novel is to come into being or of formal devices which generate the novel than of theories which it is the novel's function to express. The former naturalizes at the level of the literary system whereas the latter naturalizes in terms of a biographical or communicative project.

The latter is, of course, an extremely familiar mode of naturalization, and we might give it a literary slant which would justify including it at this level of *vraisemblance* by saying that our model of literature as an expressive but not didactic form permits us to explain literary texts in terms of implicit theories or networks of obsessions to which we would not be willing to grant the same importance in non-literary discursive texts. If we explain the death of Charles in *Madame Bovary* by saying that Flaubert's juvenilia show an obsession with the notion that one might bring about one's own death by a purely mental negation of life, we are implying that literature is more closely connected to the unconscious self than other modes of writing. If we explain Balzac's castrating females, who must make men tame children before they can love them, by looking at Balzac's own relations with his mistresses, we are again claiming that there is here a more direct channel between the text and personal affective structures than obtains in the case of other forms. We are postulating, that is to say, as a constitutive convention of the institution of literature, that the text stands in a certain relation to its author and that it may therefore be naturalized or made intelligible by relating its elements to a particular pyschological *vraisemblance*.

Closely allied to this kind of naturalization, though less dependent on the notion of an empirical author, is that which relies on the creation of narrative *personae*. As a linguistic object the text is strange and ambiguous. We reduce its strangeness by reading it as the utterance of a particular narrator so that models of plausible human attitudes and of coherent personalities can be made operative. Moreover, extrapolating from the postulated figure, we may tell ourselves empirical stories which make elements in the text intelligible and justified: the narrator is in a particular situation and reacting to it, so that what he says may be read within a general economy of human actions and judged by the logic of those actions. He is arguing, or praising, or expostulating, or describing, or analysing or ruminating, and the poem will find its coherence at the level of that action.

More generally, one might say that our notion of the range of possible speech acts which a literary text might perform is the very basis of literary naturalization, because it provides us with a set of purposes which might determine the coherence of a particular text. Once a purpose is postulated (praise of a mistress, meditation on death, etc.) one has a focal point which governs the interpretation of metaphor, the organization of oppositions and the identification of relevant formal features. And it is clear that we are dealing with literary conventions here, for our notions of literature do not permit just any speech act to serve as the determinant of a poem. It is perfectly possible to write a poem in order to invite a friend to dinner, but if we admit the poem to the institution of literature we thereby contract to read it as a statement which coheres on another level. Thus, Ben Jonson's 'Inviting a Friend to Supper' becomes the evocation of a particular style of life and is read as enacting through the tone and posture of the verse the values that support and recommend this mode of life. The invitation becomes a formal device rather than thematic centre, and what might have been explained as elements of an invitation are given another function.

But the ways of producing coherence in individual texts may seem at some remove from ordinary notions of the *vraisemblable*, and since they will be the principal burden of the next two chapters one may for the moment simply note that they are devices by which texts are naturalized and move on to the last set of conventions operative at this level of *vraisemblance*: those of genre.

Aristotle himself recognized that each genre designates certain kinds of action as acceptable and excludes others: tragedy can present men as better than they are and comedy as worse than they are without violating *vraisemblance*, because each genre constitutes a special *vraisemblance* of its own. The function of genre conventions is essentially to establish a contract between writer and reader so as to make certain relevant expectations operative and thus to permit both compliance with and deviation from accepted modes of intelligibility: 'it is essentially a matter of making the text as *perceptible* as possible; one can see what role this conception gives to the notions of genre and model: that of archetypes, of partly abstract models which serve as guide to the reader' (Genot, 'L'écriture libératrice', p. 49). A statement will be taken differently if found in an ode and in a comedy. The reader attends to characters in a different way if he is reading a tragedy or if he is reading a comedy which he expects to end in multiple marriages.

The detective story is a particularly good example of the force of genre conventions: the assumption that characters are psychologically intelligible, that the crime has a solution which will eventually be revealed, that the relevant evidence will be given but that the solution will be of some complexity, are all essential to the enjoyment of such books. In fact, these conventions are especially interesting because of the large place they grant to the irrelevant. It is only at the level of solution that coherence is required: everything deviant and suspicious must be explained by the resolution which produces the key to the 'real' pattern, but all other details can at this point be set aside as of no consequence. The conventions make possible the adventure of discovering and producing a form, of finding the pattern amid a mass of details, and they do so by stipulating what kind of patttern one is reading towards.

The expectations enshrined in the conventions of genre are, of course, often violated. Their function, like that of all constitutive rules, is to make meaning possible by providing terms in which to classify the things one encounters. What is made intelligible by the conventions of genre is often less interesting than that which resists or escapes generic understanding, and so it should be no surprise that there arises, over and against the *vraisemblance* of genre, another level of *vraisemblance* whose fundamental device is to expose the artifice of generic conventions and expectations.

The conventionally natural

The fourth level involves an implicit or explicit claim that one is not following literary convention or producing texts which find their intelligibility at the level of generic *vraisemblance*. But of course, as it is customary to say in this connection, the forms that such claims take are also literary conventions. The introductions to eighteenth century novels which explain how the diary or manuscript came into the narrator's possession, the use of external narrators who vouch for the truth of the tale told by another, are, of course, conventions in their own right which play upon the opposition between truth and fiction. Alternatively, the narrator may simply exhibit his awareness of the conventions of literary *vraisemblance* and insist that the improbability of what he is recounting guarantees its truth. Balzac expends considerable discursive energy in such a cause:

> It is frequently the case that certain actions in human life
> appear quite literally *invraisemblable*, though they are true.
> But is this not because we almost always fail to cast upon our
> spontaneous actions a kind of psychological illumination and

fail to explain those reasons of mysterious origin which necessitated them. (*Eugénie Grandet*, chapter 3)

The improbable is labelled and objections thereby disarmed, as the narrator appeals to common notions of explanation and mystery: if the reader is a reasonable man like the narrator, it is suggested, he will not be upset by the improbable and will allow the narrator's frankness and proffered explanation to convince him of its truth.

Jacques le fataliste offers another version of this bold metalinguistic step which makes deviation from the literary norm a criterion of *vraisemblance*. Jacques and his master meet a group of men armed with pitchforks and clubs:

> You will suppose that it was the people from the inn, their servants, and the brigands of whom we spoke . . . You will suppose that this little army will set upon Jacques and his master, that there will be a bloody skirmish . . . and it lies entirely within my power to make all that happen; but farewell the truth of the story! . . . It is obvious that I am not writing a novel since I neglect what a novelist would never fail to use. He who takes what I write for the truth will perhaps be less in error than he who takes it for a fable. (Garnier edition, pp. 504–5)

The narrator announces his freedom from the expectations of the genre and offers the incoherence of his *récit* (the appearance of this group of men serves no function in the plot) as proof of its veracity.

But as this example already suggests, such a procedure hovers on the brink of a move away from mimesis. The reference to the power of the writer to set down what he likes ('il ne tiendrait qu'à moi que tout cela n'arrivât') could easily be expanded to the claim that the true order is not that of the conventions of a genre but that of the narrative act itself, whose freedom is governed only by the limits of language. Repeatedly, the narrator proposes contradictory lines of development, emphasizing his power to choose one or the other: 'What prevents me from having the master marry and be cuckolded, from sending Jacques off to the colonies?' 'What prevents me from producing a violent quarrel between these three characters?' 'It depends only on me to make you wait a year, two years, three years, for the story of Jacques' loves, by separating him from his master and making each meet with whatever accidents take my fancy.'[14] Breaking away from novelistic necessity to the freedom of the act of writing may entail reliance on the first and second levels of *vraisemblance* which specify the possibilities of action. But these levels are taken up in a higher *vraisemblance* or level of intelligibility, which is that of writing itself. The text finds its coherence by being interpreted as a narrator's exercise of language and production of meaning. To naturalize it at this level is to read it as a statement about the writing of novels, a critique of mimetic fiction, an illustration of the production of a world by language.

Of course, the denial of conventions of genre does not necessarily take one this far. It is a common device in detective stories for characters to discuss the conventions of the detective story and to contrast the order of that form with the disorder which they perceive in the case that involves them. But generally such conversations do not lead the reader to think that the conventions of the genre have been by-passed; they function, rather, as dramatic irony. A hysterical maid wakes Mrs Bantry to tell her that there is a body in the library and she wakes her incredulous husband: 'Nonsense... There couldn't be... It's that detective story you were reading... Bodies are always being found in libraries in books. I've never known a case in real life.'[15] The Colonel's attitude is not empirically absurd, but we do not take it as a comment on the novel's artificiality. Rather, we laugh at his self-confidence, his mistaken appeal to *vraisemblance*, and we look forward to the moment of revelation, for, as readers of detective stories we know that there will indeed be a body in the library.

Such limited play with generic conventions is a version of what Empson, in a brilliant discussion, calls 'pseudo-parody to disarm criticism': the text shows its awareness of its own artificiality and conventionality, not so as to shift into a new mode devoid of artifice, but so as to convince the reader that it is aware of other ways of looking at the matter in hand and therefore can be trusted not to distort things while taking its own course.[16] Thus the numerous poems which contain disparaging references to the artificiality of poetry – from the Elizabethans to Marianne Moore – do not attempt to go beyond the conventions of poetry or to give their language a different function but only to forestall a possible objection on the reader's part (the reader need not himself think what the narrator has explicitly admitted and thus can focus his attention elsewhere) and to garner additional authority (the narrator is fully aware of possible attitudes towards verse and thus may be presumed to have good reasons for writing in verse). In Ben Jonson's 'On Lucy Countesse of Bedford' the hyperboles of poetic praise are explicitly cited ('timely rapt with hold fire', I set out, 'as Poets use', to imagine the most divine creature possible), and this praise is not cancelled by the apparent rejection of poetic elaboration:

Such when I meant to faine, and wished to see,
My Muse bad, *Bedford* write, and that was she.

But these final lines do affect the process of naturalization: we move from one level of *vraisemblance* (the lyric of praise) to another (the act of praise, in relation to its conventional modes) and read the poem as more discriminating praise precisely because it can assume the conventions with an awareness of their fragility. Similarly, Marianne Moore's 'Poetry', with its famous 'there are things that are important beyond all this fiddle', does not involve a rejection or exposure of genre conventions, especially since the 'fiddle' is admirably manifested in her elaborate syllabic form; but it does shift the process of naturalization onto another level by forcing us to consider, if we are to make the poem intelligible, the relation between the meaning of statements such as 'I, too, dislike it' in ordinary discourse and their transmutation by the poetic context.

The best way to explain this level of *vraisemblance* and naturalization may be to say that citing or opposing conventions of genre brings about a change in the mode of reading. We are forced to cast our net wider so as to include more than the third level of *vraisemblance* and intelligibility and must allow the dialectical opposition which the text presents to result in a synthesis at a higher level where the grounds of intelligibility are different. We read the poem or novel as a statement about poems or novels (since it has, by its opposition, adumbrated that theme). To interpret it is to see how it uses various types of content or devices to make a statement about the imaginative ordering of the world that takes place in literature. We expect the text to cohere in those terms, and of course once again we have models of the *vraisemblable* at this level which assist the interpretive process: a repertoire of traditional functions of literature and attitudes towards it (the text becomes intelligible at this level when we find these attitudes in it) and a sense of how to read particular elements or images as instances of the literary process. In reading many modern texts this level of *vraisemblance* and naturalization becomes the most important, and in one sense it has the advantage of being less reductive than others, for it need not resolve a difficulty but can recognize that what requires interpretation is the existence of a difficulty more than the difficulty itself.

Every work is clear, provided we locate the angle from which the blur becomes so natural as to pass unnoticed – provided, in other words, we determine and repeat that conceptual operation, often of a very specialized and limited type, in which the style itself originates. Thus the sentence of Gertrude Stein: 'A dog that you have never had has sighed' is transparent on the level of pure sentence formation. (Jameson, 'Metacommentary', p. 9)

Instead of interpreting it, we might describe it as an example of the power of words to create thought or of the peculiar dislocatory force of that linguistic agent which has no existence in nature: the negative.

Fredric Jameson's remarks quoted above describe the process very well. It is a process of naturalization in that what seemed difficult or strange is made natural (a blur so natural as to pass unnoticed) by locating a proper level of *vraisemblance*. And this level is a repertoire of projects. Even the most radical readings of literary works propose a project from whose vantage point the blur becomes clear or natural: the project of illustrating or enacting the practice of writing.[17] In the great Hegelian game of interpretation, where each reader strives to attain the outermost circle that comprehends all else but is not itself comprehended, this level of *vraisemblance* enjoys, at least at our moment in history, a privileged status because of its ability to assume and transform other levels. But it is none the less a mode of conventional naturalization, and attempts to organize it so that it would lie beyond ideology and convention take us, as chapter 10 will argue, beyond the bounds of sense altogether.

Parody and irony

The fifth level of naturalization may be seen as a local and specialized variant of the fourth. When a text cites or parodies the conventions of a genre one interprets it by moving to another level of interpretation where both terms of the opposition can be held together by the theme of literature itself. But the text which parodies a particular work requires a somewhat different mode of reading. Though two different orders must be held together in the mind – the order of the original and the point of view which undermines the original – this does not generally lead to synthesis and to naturalization at another level but rather to an exploration of the difference and resemblance. In fact, the function performed by the fourth level of *vraisemblance* is here performed by the concept of parody itself, which serves as a powerful device of naturalization. In calling something a parody we are specifying how it should be read, freeing ourselves from the demands of poetic seriousness, and making the curious features of the parody intelligible. The amazing alliteration, the thrusting anapestic rhythm, and the absence of content in Swinburne's self-parody, 'Nephelidia', are immediately recuperated and given significance when we read it as parody: we read them as imitations and exaggerations of features of the original.

If it is to avoid burlesque, parody must capture something of the spirit of the original as well as imitate its formal devices and produce through slight variation – usually of lexical items – a distance between the *vraisemblance* of the original and its own. 'I see how this poem works; look at how easy it is to show up the sententiousness of this poem; its effects are imitable and hence artificial; its achievement is fragile and depends on conventions of reading being taken seriously.' That is essentially the spirit of parody. Generally it invites one to a more literal reading, establishing a contrast between the naturalization required for appreciation of the original and the more literal interpretive process appropriate to the parody. Part of this effect is no doubt due to the fact that parody is an imitation and that by making its model explicit it implicitly denies that it is to be read as a serious statement of feelings about real problems or situations, thus freeing us from one type of *vraisemblance* used to enforce metaphorical readings of poems. Henry Reed's 'Chard Whitlow', one of the best parodies of Eliot, uses lines which, in Eliot, would receive proper metaphorical naturalization but places them in a context which leads us to read them differently:[18]

> As we get older we do not get any younger.
> Seasons return, and today I am fifty-five,
> And this time last year I was fifty-four,
> And this time next year I shall be sixty-two.
> And I cannot say I should like (to speak for myself)
> To see my time over again – if you can call it time:
> Fidgeting uneasily under the draughty stair,
> Or counting sleepless nights in the crowded tube.

The series of ages enforces a literal reading of the first line, preventing tautology from finding its function at another level, as seems to happen in *Four Quartets* (As we grow older/The world becomes stranger). And thus 'time' in 'if you can call it time' is only allowed to hover on the edge of metaphysical exploration before teetering back into comic bathos. In other contexts the last two lines might function as powerful non-empirical images, but here we are stopped by the absurdity of the empirical images – of these ways of actually passing one's time. And the brilliant line, 'The wind within a wind unable to speak for wind', which parodies the beginning of section five of 'Ash Wednesday' (Still is the unspoken word, the Word unheard,/The Word without a word, the Word within/The world and for the world), reinforces, by the substitution of 'wind', the suggestion of pomposity which serves as the integrating function of the parody. Whereas the surface pomposities of *Four Quartets* (And what you own is what you do not own/And where you are is where you are not) are located and tempered by immediate shifts into another mode which can be read as indirect comment (The wounded surgeon plies the steel/That questions the distempered part), the *vraisemblance* of the parody insists on a literal reading which displays the distance between the 'natural' interpretation and what is required by Eliot's verse when it is taken seriously.

Parody involves the opposition between two modes of *vraisemblance*, but unlike the fourth case its oppositions do not lead to synthesis at a higher level. Rather, the dominance of the parodist's own *vraisemblance* is temporarily asserted. In this respect, parody resembles irony (though in other respects they are very different: irony relying on semantic rather than formal effects). Kierkegaard maintains that the true ironist does not wish to be understood, and though true ironists may be rare we can at least say that irony always offers the possibility of misunderstanding. No sentence is ironic *per se*. Sarcasm may contain internal inconsistencies which make its purport quite obvious and prevent it from being read except in one way, but for a sentence to be properly ironic it must be possible to imagine some group of readers taking it quite literally. Otherwise there is no contrast between apparent and assumed meaning and no space of ironic play. Situational or dramatic irony quite obviously presupposes two orders in contrast with one another: the order postulated by the proud protagonist is revealed as mere semblance when he falls into the contrary order of poetic justice. The proleptic assertion of one order is undermined by consequences which we feel are 'appropriate' in that they derive from another, though not necessarily preferable, order.

Situational irony is thus a mode of existential recuperation which we use to make the world intelligible when the intelligibility which someone had previously postulated is shown to be false. 'That's exactly what would happen', we say when it begins to rain just as we start a picnic lunch, realizing that it would be woefully comic to expect the universe to conform to our plans but preferring to suggest, even though it be in jest, that it is not wholly indifferent to us but acts in accordance with a contrary order which might be grasped: it will systematically frustrate our plans. And thus dramatic irony in literature involves the contrast between a protagonist's vision of the world and the contrary order which the reader, armed with foreknowledge, can grasp.

Verbal irony shares this oppositional structure but is rather more complex and interesting, for it is not usually explicitly signalled by the events which thrust situational irony before us (or by the 'little did he know that . . .' and 'if only I had realized that . . .' which announce dramatic irony). The perception of verbal irony depends upon a set of expectations which enable the reader to sense the incongruity of an apparent level of *vraisemblance* at which the literal meaning of a sentence could be interpreted and to construct an alternative ironic reading which accords with the *vraisemblance* which he is in the process of constructing for the text. Sometimes it is not difficult to identify the play between two levels of expectation. Balzac writes that Sarrasine, arriving at his first rendez-vous with Zambinella, 'avait espéré une chambre mal éclairée, sa maîtresse auprès d'un brasier, un jaloux à deux pas, la mort et l'amour, des confidences échangées à voix basse, cœur à cœur, des baisers périlleux' (had hoped for a dimly-lit room, his mistress crouching by the fire, a jealous rival near at hand, death and love, secrets exchanged in heart-to-heart whispers, perilous kisses). The superfluity of detail, the heterogeneity of the catalogue – the mixture of the specific and the general – announce that this is noted with some narrative distance, cited as fragments of another 'text' which is being treated ironically. The 'code of passion', a set of cultural stereotypes – 'grounds what Sarrasine is said to feel' (Barthes, *S/Z*, p. 145). For Sarrasine this is the operative level of *vraisemblance*, the kind of coherence and intelligibility which he expects; but the text suggests an ironic reading of this level in proposing, implicitly, another *vraisemblance* presumed to contain more elements of truth: Sarrasine's expectations are foolish and novelistic; well-lit rooms and a lack of jealous rivals are not improbable.

When we cannot locate precise sources for the *vraisemblance* treated ironically the process of irony is more complex. In ordinary conversation the operative expectations are drawn from a shared knowledge of external contexts: knowing both George and Harry one can decide that what George has just said about Harry does not accord with the text of justifiable attitudes about Harry, that George, from one's knowledge of him, can be presumed to be familiar with this text, and therefore that what he has said must be taken ironically. The statement is naturalized by being read ironically, and this can happen even if one does not think of George as 'quoting' someone else's foolish statement with ironic inflection. In the case of literature the contributory expectations depend on an even more complex sum of social and cultural experience.

When Flaubert writes that during her illness Emma Bovary had a vision of heavenly bliss and purity to which she resolved to aspire, his language does not itself offer decisive indications of irony:

> Elle voulut devenir une sainte. Elle acheta des chapelets, elle
> porta des amulettes; elle souhaitait avoir dans sa chambre,
> au chevet de sa couche, un reliquaire enchâssé d'émeraudes,
> pour le baiser tous les soirs.

> (She wanted to become a saint. She bought rosaries; she wore

amulets; she wanted to have in her room, at the head of her bed, a reliquary set in emeralds, in order to kiss it every evening.) (II, xiv)

How do we recognize irony here? What provokes and supports the assumption that these words are to be read with some detachment and with an exploration of possible attitudes towards them?

First of all, we have recourse to general models of human behaviour which we assume that we share with the narrator: one does not simply decide to become a saint, as one decides to become a nurse or a nun; and even if saintliness were the proper object of a decision, the way to become a saint would not be to purchase the equipment. Moreover, our model of sainthood presumably clashes with the concrete forms that Emma's desires take: emeralds on a reliquary do not ensure the progress of the soul, nor should it be purchased in order that one might kiss it. But if there is to be any point to our appeal to these models, we must be willing to grant that there is a plausible attitude sketched in the text: that for some people, among them Emma, the text when read literally is perfectly acceptable.

Thus irony would seem to depend, at least in the first instance, on the referentiality of the text: our first step in recuperation is to assume that it refers to a world with which we are familiar and that therefore we are in a position to judge it; for if it were fantasy or fairy-tale, or if it concerned a primitive tribe in Borneo, we would have no standards by which to recognize the inappropriate and self-indulgent. It is no doubt for this reason that the novel has been thought the form most propitious to irony. Referring us constantly to a world whose reality it asserts, it makes relevant our models of human behaviour and enables us to detect the foolishness of apparent meanings.

But even at this initial stage there is a dialectic between text and world, for our sense of irony is strengthened, perhaps even provoked, by the fact that on the evidence given we expect Emma to be a foolish and self-indulgent woman: a level of coherence established by the text serves as a *point de repère* to which we try to relate any notation of her thoughts and actions.

Given our knowledge of the world and our knowledge of the world of the novel, we are in a position to detect irony whenever the text appears to offer judgments with which we would not concur or whenever, with apparent disinterestedness, it does not pass judgment where we think a judgment would be appropriate. But, of course, we must have formed an impression of narrative *vraisemblance* – a level of coherence at which Flaubert's prose habitually operates – so that we can determine whether the text is actually being ironic or whether, on the contrary, it is describing without irony projects on which we, in our superior wisdom, can pass ironic judgment.

The type of *vraisemblance* or intelligibility which, in an ironic reading, we oppose to that of Emma's attitudes is thus composed of a variety of factors which we tend rather too glibly to group together under the ambiguous heading of 'context': our models of *vraisemblance* at the level of human behaviour, which provide standards of judgment; our expectations about the world of the novel, which suggest how details concerning actions or characters are to be interpreted and thus help to give us something to judge; the apparent assertions which sentences make and whose incongruousness we recuperate by reading them ironically; and finally our sense of the habitual procedures of the text – an ironic *vraisemblance* – which justifies our activity and reassures us that we are only participating in the play to which the text invites us.

Even this complex process involves, essentially, the replacement of an apparent meaning by a 'true' meaning, which we justify on the grounds that the text becomes more coherent thereby. Indeed, this need for a second level of *vraisemblance*, a 'true' reading, seems to Barthes the most unfortunate feature of irony, for it arrests the play of meaning. It is, he writes, extremely difficult to undermine or criticize the stereotype without having recourse to another stereotype, which is that of irony itself. 'Comment épingler la bêtise sans se déclarer intelligent? Comment un code peut-il avoir barre sur un autre sans fermer abusivement le pluriel des codes?' (How can one deflate stupidity without declaring oneself intelligent? How can one code have an advantage over another without improperly setting limits to the plural nature of codes?) (*S/Z*, p. 212). How can the ironist criticize one point of view or attitude for being excessively limited without asserting the completeness and truth of his own view?

This is indeed a crucial question, for from the description offered so far it might seem as though ironic naturalization makes more grandiose claims than the things which it deflates. At the moment when we propose that a text means something other than what it appears to say we introduce, as hermeneutic devices which are supposed to lead us to the truth of the text, models which are based on our expectations about the text and the world. Irony, the cynic might say, is the ultimate form of recuperation and naturalization, whereby we ensure that the text says only what we want to hear. We reduce the strange or incongruous, or even attitudes with which we disagree, by calling them ironic and making them confirm rather than abuse our expectations.

But one might also turn that definition around and, focusing on its less cynical face, say that in calling a text ironic we indicate our desire to avoid premature foreclosure, to allow the text to work on us as fully as it can, to give it the benefit of doubt by allowing it to contain whatever doubts come to mind in reading it. Once expectations of irony are established, that is to say, we can undertake ironic readings which lead to no certainty or 'true attitude' that can be opposed to the apparent statement of the text but only to a formal *vraisemblance* or level of coherence which is that of ironic uncertainty itself. What is set against appearance is not reality but the pure negativity of unarrested irony.

In Stephen Crane, for example, we find many instances of surface incongruities: violations of register, which one tends to assume are ironic; but it is extremely difficult to locate any covert assertion that they make. When we are told in 'The Open Boat' that 'Many a man ought to have a bathtub larger than the boat which here rode upon the sea', we can identify the irony of the inversion: the boat is the size of a bathtub and like a bathtub, full of water, but bathtubs are designed to keep water in and boats to keep water out. But the 'many a man ought' strikes a strange note which is difficult to place: a phrase which seems to connote only narratorial detachment, an unwillingness to be responsible for the prose. 'These waves were most wrongfully and barbarously abrupt and tall, and each froth-top was a problem in small-boat navigation.' Here again there is a fundamental problem of tone, a suggestion of irony; but the waves *are* barbarously tall, and does one really want to maintain that the narrator is turning an ironic eye on the men in the boat, making them think of the waves as wrongfully abrupt and deflating the self-centredness of that view? Does the slightly pompous understatement of 'a problem in small-boat navigation' really make light of their difficulty in steering the boat and keeping it from swamping? One could multiply examples almost indefinitely, and the only satisfactory solution is to naturalize these strange notations at the level of an uncertain irony.

Barthes says that Flaubert,

en maniant une ironie frappée d'incertitude, opère un malaise salutaire de l'écriture: il n'arrête pas le jeu des codes (ou l'arrête mal), en sorte que (c'est là sans doute la *preuve* de l'écriture) *on ne sait jamais s'il est responsable de ce qu'il écrit* (s'il y a un sujet *derrière* son langage); car l'être de l'écriture (le sens du travail qui la constitue) est d'empêcher de jamais répondre à cette question: *Qui parle*?

(in welding an irony fraught with uncertainty, brings about a salutary uneasiness in the writing: he refuses to halt the play of codes (or does so badly), with the result that (and this is no doubt the true test of writing as writing) one never knows whether he is responsible for what he writes (whether there is an individual subject behind his language): for the essence of writing (the meaning of the work which constitutes writing) is to prevent any reply to the question: who is speaking?) (*S/Z*, p. 146)

This is precisely what one seems to be dealing with in Crane: unable to arrest the play of meaning and compose the text, or even its fragments, as spoken from an identifiable position by someone with identifiable attitudes, one is forced to recognize that the act of writing, of moving out of the communicative circuit of speech, has been successful, and that the level of *vraisemblance* at which the story becomes coherent is that of irony itself as project. Narrative dislocation, we might say, displays language as a kind of indifferent fate, which can put everything to the test with a distance and detachment that is unjustifiably cruel. The reader's passage through the waves of this irony is a voyage of discovery, certainly, in that he is made to test all the ways of deflating the experience of the men in the boat and to pass through the various pomposities by which language blurs experience or makes it fragile and vulnerable to the sneer. To offer a reading at this level is to naturalize elements in the text by giving them a function in this pattern, but that pattern is not so much a positive precipitate of irony as the action of irony itself as a means of hesitation.

To naturalize at these various levels is to make the text intelligible by relating it to various models of coherence. Although in structuralist parlance naturalization tends to be thought of as a bad thing, it is an inevitable function of reading; and it may at least be worth noting that when the Russian formalists – whose work on this topic structuralists have not rejected – spoke of naturalization under the heading of 'motivation', they took it to be a very good thing indeed. An element was motivated if it had a function in the literary text, and in principle everything in a successful work of art should be motivated. The humblest function was 'realistic motivation': if in the description of a room there occur items which tell us nothing about a character and play no role in the plot this very absence of meaning enables them to anchor the story in the real by signifying, this is reality. This function rests, as Barthes observes, on the assumption, deeply engrained in Western culture, that the world is simply there and can thus best be denoted by objects whose sole function is to be there ('L'effet de réel', p. 87). The Russian formalists also identified 'compositional motivation', where an element is justified by its contribution to plot structure or to the portrayal of character, and 'artistic motivation', where an element or device contributes to special artistic effects, of which the most frequently discussed was 'defamiliarization' or renewal of perception.[19] But as should by now be clear, these varieties of motivation represent different ways of naturalizing the text, of relating it to models of intelligibility: realistic motivation involves my first and second levels of *vraisemblance*, compositional motivation the second and third, and artistic motivation the second, third, fourth and fifth. Criticism values motivation in so far as it sees its task as constructing a coherent and intelligible simulacrum of the text.

Structuralist dissatisfaction with naturalization does not entail an ability to go beyond it: one cannot avoid naturalization if one seeks to speak of literary works but can only postpone it and ensure that it takes place at a higher and more formal level. There is here, however, a desire to avoid premature foreclosure, to allow the text to differentiate itself from ordinary language, to grant maximum scope to the play of formal features and of semantic uncertainties. Instead of attempting to resolve difficulties so as to produce themes or statements by a persona about a particular problem one may seek to preserve those difficulties by organizing the text as an illustration of certain problems. At the highest level they are problems of language itself.

Discussion of the process of reading as naturalization does, of course, produce a disposition towards this kind of criticism, because if one has made oneself aware of the various naturalizing operations that reading and criticism involve, one will become newly attentive to the ways in which the text resists the operations which one seeks to perform on it and exceeds the meaning which one can discover at any given level of *vraisemblance*. Consequently, the most interesting features of a text – the features on which a structuralist *criticism* may choose to dwell – become those by which it asserts its otherness, its difference from what is already dealt with by the cultural models of literature as an institution. But that is a subject which must be left for the last chapter. There is still much to be said about poetics itself before moving on to a criticism which derives from poetics. If structuralists have been rather too hasty to move beyond systems of convention, one is not obliged to follow their example, especially since the violations of norms which interest them are only made possible by norms which they have been too impatient to investigate in detail. One must now try to set forth the work that has been done on the systems of the lyric and the novel and indicate where more work needs to be done.

CHAPTER 8

Poetics of the Lyric

Heavenly hurt it gives us—
We can find no scar,
But internal difference,
Where the Meanings are.
EMILY DICKINSON

If one takes a piece of banal journalistic prose and sets it down on a page as a lyric poem, surrounded by intimidating margins of silence, the words remain the same but their effects for readers are substantially altered.[1]

> Hier sur la Nationale sept
> Une automobile
> Roulant à cent à l'heure s'est jetée
> Sur un platane
> Ses quatre occupants ont été
> Tués.

> (Yesterday on the A7 an automobile travelling at sixty miles per hour crashed into a plane tree. Its four occupants were killed.)

To write this as a poem brings into play a new set of expectations, a set of conventions determining how the sequence is to be read and what kind of interpretations may be derived from it. The *fait divers* becomes a minor but exemplary tragedy. 'Hier', for example, takes on a completely different force: referring now to the set of possible yesterdays, it suggests a common, almost random event. One is likely to give new weight to the wilfulness of 's'est jetée' (literally, 'threw itself') and to the passivity of 'its occupants', defined in relation to their automobile. The lack of detail or explanation connotes a certain absurdity, and the neutral reportorial style will no doubt be read as restraint and resignation. We might even note an element of suspense after 's'est jetée' and discover bathos in the possible pun on 'platane' ('plat' = flat) and in the finality of the isolated 'tués'.

This is clearly different from the way in which journalistic prose is interpreted, and these differences can only be explained by the expectations with which one approaches lyric poetry, the conventions which govern its possible modes of signification: the poem is a-temporal (hence the new force of 'hier'); it is complete in itself (hence the significance of the absence of explanation); it should cohere at a symbolic level (hence the reinterpretation of 's'est jetée' and 'ses occupants'); it expresses an attitude (hence the interest in tone as deliberate posture); its typographic arrangements can be given spatial or temporal interpretations ('suspense' or 'isolation'). When one reads the text as a poem new effects become possible because the conventions of the genre produce a new range of signs.

These interpretive operations are not in any sense structuralist; they are very much those which readers and critics apply with greater subtlety to poems of greater complexity. But the crudity of the example has the virtue of emphasizing the extent to which the reading and interpreting of poems is based on an implicit theory of the lyric. 'Do not forget', writes Wittgenstein, 'that a poem, even though it is composed in the language of information, is not used in the language-game of giving information.'[2] But remembering this is scarcely sufficient; one must inquire what is the nature of the language-game in question.

Poetry lies at the centre of the literary experience because it is the form that most clearly asserts the specificity of literature, its difference from ordinary discourse by an empirical individual about the world. The specific features of poetry have the function of differentiating it from speech and altering the circuit of communication within which it is inscribed. As the traditional theories tell us, poetry is making; to write a poem is a very different act from speaking to a friend, and the formal order of poetry – the conventions of line-endings, rhythms and phonetic patterns – help to make the poem an impersonal object, whose 'I' and 'you' are poetic constructs. But the fact that a text is a poem is not the necessary result of its linguistic properties, and attempts to base a theory of poetry on an account of the special properties of the language of poems seem doomed to failure.

Cleanth Brooks, for example, propounded one theory of poetic discourse in his famous phrase, 'the language of poetry is the language of paradox' (*The Well-Wrought Urn*, p. 3). By its very nature poetic discourse is ambiguous and ironical, displays tension, especially in its modes of qualification; and close reading, together with knowledge of connotations, will enable us to discover the tension and paradox of all successful poems. Thus, in Gray's line, 'The short and simple

annals of the poor', we may note a tension between the usual connotations of 'annals' and the semantic features of the context 'short',
'simple', and 'the poor' (p. 102). Although Brooks and others have
found tension and paradox in poetry of all sorts, the theory fails
as an account of the nature of poetry because one can find similar
tension in language of any kind. Quine's *From a Logical Point of
View* is seldom mistaken for a lyric poem, but its opening sentence
reads, 'A curious thing about the ontological problem is its simplicity'.
There is tension between the associations of 'ontological' and the
assertion of simplicity, especially since the essay shows it to be far
from simple. Moreover, there is a nice irony in the use of the word
'thing', generally associated with physical objects but here used for
what is ontologically problematic: a fact or relational property.
Indeed, the tension in this example seems greater than that in Gray's
line; and the critic who wants to make Gray a poet and exclude
Quine from this company is obliged, I think, to say that the tension
is relevant in the first case in a way that it is not in the second, that
one must attend to the former but need not attend to the latter.

Of course, if Quine's sentence were used in a different language-
game, absorbed by different conventions, the irony would indeed
become thematically dominant:

From a Logical Point of View
A curious

        thing
about the

        ontological
problem

        is
its

        simplicity

The typographical arrangement produces a different kind of attention
and releases some of the potential verbal energy of 'thing', 'is' and
'simplicity'. We are dealing less with a property of language (intrinsic
irony or paradox) than with a strategy of reading, whose major
operations are applied to verbal objects set as poems even when their
metrical and phonetic patterns are not obvious.

This is not to deny, of course, the importance of formal patterns.
As Jakobson has stressed, in poetic discourse equivalence becomes
the constitutive device of the sequence, and phonetic or rhythmic
coherence is one of the major devices which distances poetry from the
communicative functions of ordinary speech. The poem is a structure
of signifiers which absorbs and reconstitutes the signified. The
primacy of formal patterning enables poetry to assimilate the mean-

ings which words have in other instances of discourse and subject them to new organization. But the significance of formal patterns is itself a conventional expectation, the result as well as the cause of a kind of attention specific to poetry. As Robert Graves argues,[3]

> One doesn't 'listen' when reading standard prose; it is only in poetry that one looks out for metre and rhythmic variations on it. The writers of *vers libre* rely on their printers to call your attention to what is called 'cadence' or 'rhythmic relation' (not easy to follow) which might have escaped you if written as prose; *this* sentence, you'll find, has its thumb to its nose.

In reading poetry we are disposed not only to recognize formal patterns but to make them something more than ornament attached to communicative utterances; and thus, as Genette says, the essence of poetry lies not in verbal artifice itself, though that serves as catalyst, but more simply and profoundly in the type of reading (*attitude de lecture*) which the poem imposes on its readers:

> a motivating attitude which, beyond or prior to prosodic or semantic features, accords to the whole or part of the discourse that intransitive presence and absolute existence which Eluard calls 'poetic prominence' (*l'évidence poetique*). Here poetic language would seem to reveal its true 'structure', which is not that of a particular *form* defined by its specific attributes but rather that of a *state*, a degree of presence and intensity to which, as it were, any sequence can be brought, if only there is created around it that *margin of silence* which isolates it in the middle of ordinary speech (but not as a deviation). (*Figures II*, p. 150)

This is to say that neither the formal patterns nor linguistic deviation of verse suffices in itself to produce the true structure or state of poetry. The third and crucial factor, which can operate effectively even in the absence of the others, is that of conventional expectation, of the type of attention which poetry receives by virtue of its status within the institution of literature. To analyse poetry from the point of view of poetics is to specify what is involved in these conventional expectations which make poetic language subject to a different teleology or finality from that of ordinary speech and how these expectations or conventions contribute to the effects of formal devices and of the external contexts that poetry assimilates.

Distance and deixis

First, there is the fact of distance and impersonality. To read a poem by a poet who is not an acquaintance is very different from reading one of his letters. The latter is directly inscribed in a communicative circuit and depends on external contexts whose relevance we cannot deny even if we are ignorant of them. The 'I' of the letter is an empirical individual, as is the 'You' whom it addresses; it was written at a particular time and in a situation to which it refers; and to interpret the letter is to adduce those contexts so as to read it as a specific temporal and individual act. The poem is not related to time in the same way, nor has it the same interpersonal status. Although in the act of interpreting it we may appeal to external contexts, telling ourselves empirical stories (one morning the poet was in bed with his mistress and, when wakened by the sun which told him that it was time to be up and about his affairs, he said, 'Busie old foole, unruly Sunne . . .'), but we are aware that such stories are fictional constructs which we employ as interpretive devices. The situation to which we appeal is not that of the actual linguistic act but that of a linguistic act which we take the poem to be imitating – directly or deviously. We appeal to models of human personality and human behaviour in order to construct referents for the pronouns, but we are aware that our interest in the poem depends on the fact that it is something other than the record of an empirical speech act. And if we say that the lyric is not heard but overheard we have no illusions that we are engaged in listening at the keyhole; we are simply using this fiction as interpretive device. Indeed, the fact that we develop such strategies to overcome the impersonality of poetic discourse is the strongest confirmation of that impersonality.

This aspect of the poetic function is best observed in the ways in which our expectations about the lyric alter the effects of deictics or shifters. Deictics are 'orientational' features of language which relate to the situation of utterance, and for our purposes the most interesting are first and second person pronouns (whose meaning in ordinary discourse is 'the speaker' and 'the person addressed'), anaphoric articles and demonstratives which refer to an external context rather than to other elements in the discourse, adverbials of place and time whose reference depends on the situation of utterance (here, there, now, yesterday) and verb tenses, especially the non-timeless present.[4] The importance of such deictics as technical devices in poetry can scarcely be overestimated, and in our willingness to speak of a poetic persona we recognize from the outset that such deictics are not determined by an actual situation of utterance but operate at a certain distance from it. When Blake's first four *Poetical Sketches* ('To Spring', 'To Summer', 'To Autumn' and 'To Winter') address each season in turn and ask it either to hasten or to stay its visit, we do not simply accept this as the context of the discourse (Blake is addressing the seasons) but recognize that such a procedure is a device whose implications must be incorporated within our interpretation of the poem. How can we construct a poetic 'I' which addresses the seasons and what can we make of the 'thou' that is addressed? As Geoffrey Hartman writes,

> If calling the seasons is a gratuitous or ritual act, this but helps to move into the foreground the lyric pathos, the *ore rotundo*, of their style. Here voice calls upon itself, calls up images of its previous power. Blake indulges in a continuous reminiscence of that power by offering us a splendid pastiche of echoes and themes from the Bible, the classics, and even the high odic tradition of the eighteenth century. It is all poetic diction, but poetic diction in search of its truth – which is the identity, now lost, of the poetical and the prophetic spirit. (*Beyond Formalism*, p. 194)

The deictics do not refer us to an external context but force us to construct a fictional situation of utterance, to bring into being a voice and a force addressed, and this requires us to consider the relationship from which the qualities of the voice and the force could be drawn and to give it a central place within the poem. The conventions which enable us to abandon an actual situation of discourse for an invocational-prophetic mode put this latter framework back into the poem as an instance of the energy of anticipation that characterizes the poetical spirit: a spirit which can envision what it calls for. Our ability to perceive that spirit is partly due to the conventions which remove the poem from an ordinary circuit of communication.

Phenomena of this kind are encountered in a range of cases where the specific thematic effects may be very different. Were it not for conventional expectations we should be upset to find that the 'I' in Shelley's 'The Cloud' is in fact a cloud; were the conventions less powerful we should be content simply to have identified the situation of utterance. But since the 'I' is a poetic construct our preliminary identification must be brought back into the poem, and we must try to decide what it means to make a cloud speak, what kind of 'I' the poem secretes, and give the answer a central place in our interpretation. Wallace Stevens's 'Anecdote of a Jar' gives us but a single deictic to work with: the 'I' of the opening line.

> I placed a jar in Tennessee,
> And round it was, upon a hill.

Any speaker whom the reader fills in or imagines will be a poetic construct. His identity depends on the significance given to the action of placing the jar in Tennessee, in that he must be someone who could be the agent of that action. And the fact that the deictic appears in the poem indicates that agency is of some importance and must be integrated with any interpretation.

A whole poetic tradition uses spatial, temporal and personal deictics in order to force the reader to construct a meditative persona. The poem is presented as the discourse of a speaker who, at the moment of speaking, stands before a particular scene, but even if this apparent claim was biographically true it is absorbed and transformed by poetic convention so as to permit a certain kind of thematic development. The drama will be one of mind itself when faced with external stimuli, and the reader must take account of the gap between object and feeling, if only in order that the fusion which the poem may enact be taken as an achievement. Coleridge's 'The Eolian Harp' asserts its context with first and second person pronouns, verbs in the present tense, and indications of time and place:

> My pensive Sara! thy soft cheek reclined
> Thus on mine arm, most soothing sweet it is
> to sit beside our Cot (. . .)
> And watch the clouds (. . .)
>   How exquisite the scents
> Snatched from yon bean-field! (. . .)

The setting is a point of departure for the work of the imagination, but the reader must convert the situation into an instance of security, serenity, fulfilment; for after the diffident pantheism gives way before religious scruples the poem returns to its deictics ('this cot, and thee, heart-honoured Maid!'), anchoring itself in its situation of discourse. Though there is no such explicit return in Wordsworth's 'Tintern Abbey', the function of the deictics is much the same, and the reader must take the situation which the opening lines force him to construct not as an external framework but as the proleptic assertion of the major thematic structure: the imagination's assimilation of and response to particulars of the world. Similarly, in Yeats's 'Among School Children' the opening line, 'I walk through the long school-room questioning' and the later 'I look upon one child or t'other there' do not simply give us the situation of discourse but force us to construct a poetic narrator who can fulfil the thematic demands of the rest of the poem.

In short, even in poems which are ostensibly presented as personal statements made on particular occasions, the conventions of reading enable us to avoid considering that framework as a purely biographical matter and to construct a referential context in accordance with demands of coherence that the rest of the poem makes. The fictional situation of discourse must be constructed so as to have a thematic function. These changes in the reading of deictics which

poetic conventions produce are no less evident in poems where the
'I' of the speaker is not explicit. Yeats's 'Leda and the Swan'
contains an unusual number of anaphoric definite articles in its
opening lines:

> A sudden blow: the great wings beating still
> Above the staggering girl, the thighs caressed
> By the dark webs, her nape caught in his bill,
> He holds her helpless breast upon his breast.
>
> How can those terrified vague fingers push
> The feathered glory from her loosening thighs?

The ordinary function of such articles is not destroyed: we must
construct a reference for them (the wings of the swan, the girl in the
scene, her thighs, the dark webs of the swan's feet, etc.).[5] But we
cannot simply say that the poet is looking at the scene or a representation of it and therefore is taking it for granted, because that use of
deictics is the result of a choice (he knows the readers will not be
looking at the scene); and so we must consider the implications of
assuming such a stance, of choosing to make the event into a relatively
static scene used as point of departure for the questions about knowledge and power, about the relation of incarnation and historical
determinism. Or again, when a poem like Ben Jonson's 'On my first
Daughter' begins with an adverb of place,

> Here lies to each her parents ruth,
> Mary, the daughter of their youth

that deictic does not primarily give us a spatial location but tells us,
as soon as we have identified its reference to the grave, what kind of
fictional act we are dealing with and hence how the poem is to be
taken. It functions as the traditional *siste viator* of the epitaph, and
because the conventions of poetry have made us accustomed to
separate the fictional situation of enunciation from an empirical act of
enunciation, we can read the poem as epitaph and understand the
shift from the 'my' of the title to the 'their' of the second line.
Although 'inscriptions' of this kind make up a sub-genre of verse,
closely related to the epigram, the enunciative distancing that the
conventions of poetic deixis make possible permit one to think of
lyric poetry in general as an approach to the inscription – though an
inscription which tells a figured story of its own genesis.

In contemporary poetry, of course, impersonality is exploited to
more disruptive ends. Play with personal pronouns and obscure
deictic references which prevent the reader from constructing a
coherent enunciative act is one of the principal ways of questioning

the ordered world which the ordinary communicative circuit assumes. A single example from John Ashbery will illustrate very well the difficulties that arise when referential uncertainties pose obstacles to the construction of a fictional enunciative context.[6]

> They dream only of America
> To be lost among the thirteen million pillars of grass:
> 'This honey is delicious
> *Though it burns the throat.*'
>
> And hiding from darkness in barns
> They can be grownups now
> And the murderer's ash tray is more easily –
> The lake a lilac cube.

We have difficulty composing a scene or situation because too much is assumed: 'They', 'the thirteen million pillars', 'This honey', the same or another 'They', 'The murderer's ash tray' and 'The lake'. We are challenged to make them all givens of a single situation and seem doomed to failure. But we can observe the effects of our expectations here, because we can produce readings by making certain assumptions. If the 'They' of line one are the same as the 'They' of line six, and if the latter governs 'hiding' in line five, then we can say that dreaming of America is a grown-up form of hiding from darkness, a desire to lose oneself in Whitman's leaves of grass that have now become institutionalized – numerous but countable pillars. And if we assume the murderer not to fit into this particular situation but to come from another context we can relate this form of hiding to that reassuring ritual of concealment and discovery evoked by the parodistic fragment of a detective story (the murderer's ash as a clue). If we take 'This' in line three to refer not to an external context but to the dream of the first line, we can say that dreaming of America is a bitter-sweet experience; or if we take lines three and four as a juxtaposed quotation from another context we can make it an instance of the grown-ups' experience – who have learned to value the sweet despite its aftertaste. Set against all this human fuss is the lake (what lake?), phonetically at one with its description (the *lake a lilac c*ube), crystalline and resisting attempts to relate it to other elements of a situation.

Connections are multiple and tenuous, especially since the plethora of deictics prevents us from constructing a discursive situation and determining which are its prime constituents. These objects provoke a more rewarding exploration of one's modes of ordering than is usual, and of course such exploration would not begin were it not for the initial conventions that enable us to construct fictive personae to satisfy the demands of internal coherence and relevance. 'In reading we must become aware of what we write unconsciously in our reading', says Philippe Sollers (*Logiques*, p. 220). Our 'unconscious writing' is our attempt to order and naturalize the text, which in poems like Ashbery's is challenged and questioned.

Our major device of order is, of course, the notion of the person or speaking subject, and the process of reading is especially troubled when we cannot construct a subject who would serve as source of the poetic utterance. There is thus an initial plausibility to Julia Kristeva's claim that poetic language involves a constant passage from subject to non-subject, and that 'in this *other* space where the logic of speech is unsettled, the subject is dissolved and in place of the sign is instituted the collision of signifiers cancelling one another' (*Semiotikè*, p. 273). But as the above examples have shown, it is only the empirical individual speaker who is dissolved, or better, displaced, shifted into a different and impersonal mode. The poetic persona is a construct, a function of the language of the poem, but it none the less fulfils the unifying role of the individual subject, and even poems which make it difficult to construct a poetic persona rely for their effects on the fact that the reader will try to construct an enunciative posture. As Henri Meschonnic argues in an apt critique of Kristeva, it is more fruitful to stress the impersonality of writing and the meaning that is produced by the attempt to construct a fictional persona than to speak of the disappearance of the subject (*Pour la poétique*, II, p. 54). Even in poems like Ashbery's the naturalizing process is not definitively blocked: one may shift deictic references into another mode and say that the lines are fragments of language which could be used referentially but which here are simply inscribed (the hand that writes, having writ, moves on), and that the enunciative situation is that of language working itself out in fragments which are gathered and ordered by formal patterns. If we take this course we can still postulate, as the unifying function, a poetic persona whose speech announces, as Ashbery writes elsewhere,[7]

> that the carnivorous
> Way of these lines is to devour their own nature, leaving
> Nothing but a bitter impression of absence, which as we
>   know involves presence but still.
> Nevertheless these are fundamental absences, struggling to
>   get up and be off themselves.

Organic wholes

The second fundamental convention of the lyric is what we might call the expectation of totality or coherence. This is, of course, connected with the convention of impersonality. Ordinary speech-acts need not be autonomous wholes because they are but parts of complex situations to which they contribute and from which they derive meaning. But if the enunciative situation of a poem is itself a construct which must be brought back within the poem as one of its components, one can see why critics have generally followed Coleridge in insisting that the true poem is 'one the parts of which mutually support and explain each other' (*Biographia Literaria*, chapter xiv). The notion has, of course, been challenged, especially as the criterion of excellence: 'a poem is much more like a Christmas tree than an organism', says John Crowe Ransom.[8] But even if we adopt his metaphor we might find it difficult to abandon the notion of a harmonious totality: some Christmas trees are more successful than others, and we are inclined to think that symmetry and harmonious arrangement of ornaments makes some contribution towards success.

The crucial point, however, is that even if we deny the need for a poem to be a harmonious totality we make use of the notion in reading. Understanding is necessarily a teleological process and a sense of totality is the end which governs its progress. Ideally, one should be able to account for everything in a poem and among comprehensive explanations we should prefer those which best succeed in relating items to one another rather than offer separate and unrelated explanations. And poems which succeed as fragments or as instances of incomplete totality depend for their success on the fact that our drive towards totality enables us to recognize their gaps and discontinuities and to give them a thematic value. For example, Pound's 'Papyrus',

Spring . . .
Too long . . .
Gongula . . .

is not itself a harmonious whole: the solidarity of vowels and consonants does not succeed in enforcing semantic continuity. We must read it as a fragment, as indeed the dots invite us to do. But we approach it with the presumption of continuity (the assumption, for example, that the four words are part of a single statement) and can extrapolate to read it as a love poem (Gongula as a person addressed), treating the gaps as figures of anticipation or incompletion. To interpret the poem, that is to say, is to assume a totality and then to make sense of gaps, either by exploring ways in which they might be filled in or by giving them meaning as gaps.

Notions of totality take various forms in structuralist writings. Jakobson's insistence that poems display a rigorous symmetry at the level of phonetic and grammatical patterning has already been discussed. Greimas's theory of lyric poetry as the discursive manifestation of a taxonomy involves the claim that the reader moves towards an understanding of the poem by constructing thematic classes and that what he is seeking is a four-term homology in which two opposing classes are correlated with opposed values. This is, of course, a hypothesis about the conventions of reading, about what kind of goal one is reading towards. Todorov speaks of reading as 'figuration' in which one attempts to discover a central structure or generative device which governs all levels of the text. And Barthes says that in modern poetry 'words produce a formal continuity from which there gradually emanates an intellectual or emotional density impossible without them'. The individual words themselves, however, contain all the potential senses and relations among which communicative discourse would be required to choose, and they thus 'institute a discourse full of gaps and flashes, full of absences and voracious signs, without a foreseen and fixed intention' (*Le Degré zéro de l'écriture*, pp. 34 and 38). The concept of totality is central because it is only in these terms that one can define the action of modern poetry: the failure to realize, except momentarily and tenuously, the continuity promised by formal patterns. Like anyone concerned with the act of reading, Barthes must take the drive towards fusion and totality for granted, as an expectation which will often be disappointed by the action of literature itself, but which, for that very reason, is the source of the effects which he prefers to describe.

The intent at totality of the interpretive process is easiest to observe in the case of poems where there is apparent discontinuity. Thomas Nashe's lyric, 'Adieu, farewell earth's bliss', concludes with the following stanza:

> Haste, therefore, each degree
> To welcome destiny.
> Heaven is our heritage,
> Earth but a player's stage;
> Mount we unto the sky.
> I am sick, I must die.
>   Lord, have mercy on us.

Each of the last three lines is itself unambiguous, but they become ambiguous, Empson says, by virtue of the fact that the reader assumes that they are related. One must attempt to reconcile them by fitting them into a structure which functions as a totality. There are, of course, various ways of doing this – various interpretations of the last three lines – but they can be distinguished by the different formal models that they use. First, if the model is the elementary dialectic of thesis, antithesis and synthesis, we can say that the arrogant exaltation of the mystic is set against the mere terror of natural man and that the third line resolves this opposition in a Christian humility. Or, if the model is the series united by a common denominator, we can maintain 'that the experience they convey is too strong to be conceived as a series of contrasts; that one is able to reconcile the different elements; that one is not conscious of their difference but only of the grandeur of the imagination which brought them together' (*Seven Types of Ambiguity*, pp. 115–16). Finally, taking as model the opposition which is not resolved but deflected by a shift into another mode, we might say that the last line acts as an evasion of the contradiction of the two preceding lines by moving out of the realm of feeling and judgment into one of faith. If other interpretations seem less satisfying than these it is no doubt because they fail to attain structures which correspond with one of our elementary models of totalities.

In the example from Nashe models of unity help us to relate three distinct and parallel items in a paratactic sequence, but they can also be used to discover structure in a poem which is already unified, albeit in a somewhat refractory way, by its complex syntax.

Soupir
Mon âme vers ton front où rêve, ô calme soeur,
Un automne jonché de taches de rousseur,
Et vers le ciel errant de ton oeil angélique
Monte, comme dans un jardin mélancolique,
Fidèle, un blanc jet d'eau soupire vers l'Azur!
– Vers l'Azur attendri d'Octobre pâle et pur
Qui mire aux grands bassins sa langueur infinie
Et laisse, sur l'eau morte où la fauve agonie
Des feuilles erre au vent et creuse un froid sillon,
Se traîner le soleil jaune d'un long rayon.

(My soul towards your brow where, O calm sister, dreams an autumn strewn with russet patches, and towards the wandering sky of your angelic eyes, mounts, as in a melancholy garden a faithful fountain of white water sighs toward the blue! – towards the tender blue of pale and pure October which mirrors its infinite languor in large pools and lets, on the dead water where the tawny agony of leaves wanders in the wind and traces a cold furrow, the yellow sun linger in a long ray.)

Mallarmé produces, as Hugh Kenner says, a single effect, and 'the trick of the blending was to make the elements digress from a kernel sentence which holds them firmly in relation to one another and allows the reader's mind to overlay them' ('Some Post-Symbolist Structures', pp. 391–2). But in order to understand the effect and grasp the poem as a whole we must sort out its elements into structures which run counter to the synthesizing organization of the syntax. The first might be the opposition between the vertical and the horizontal: the aspiration of the soul and of the faithful white fountain on the one hand, against the 'dead' water of the pool, the death rattle (*agonie*) of the fallen leaves, the cold furrow of their horizontal wandering. That opposition provides an elementary thematic coherence, but it leaves some features of the poem unaccounted for, and if we would integrate them we must appeal to another model. An autumn strewn with russet leaves 'dreams' in the woman's brow, and the blue sky towards which the fountain aspires is mirrored in the reflecting pond of the fountain, so that in both cases the goal of aspiration is a transformation of the starting point. The above and the below are opposed only to be connected by the vertical movement of aspiration, which is also, of course, the synthesizing act of the poem (the poem creates connections in an act of homage and aspiration). But again we might wish to go beyond this dialectical structure and note that the soul is only mounting, not arriving, and that a fountain does not reach the sky but falls back into the pool. Moreover, in so far as the 'wandering sky of your angelic eye' is identified with the azure, the long, lingering ray of a sun which will set cannot remain divorced from the woman's glance. We may, then, wish to restructure materials previously organized, place them in what is roughly a four-term homology, and say that the woman is to autumn as the soul's aspiration is to its inevitable but unmentioned failure. Winter will come and suns will set.

The intent at totality of the interpretive process may be seen as the literary version of the Gestaltist law of Prägnanz: that the richest organization compatible with the data is to be preferred.[9] Research in the field of artistic perception has confirmed the importance of structural models or expectations which enable one to sort out and organize what one perceives,[10] and there seem good reasons to suppose that if in reading and interpreting poems one is seeking unity one must have at least rudimentary notions of what would count as unity. The most basic models would seem to be the binary opposition, the dialectical resolution of a binary opposition, the displacement of an unresolved opposition by a third term, the four-term homology, the series united by a common denominator, and the series with a transcendent or summarizing final term. It is at least a plausible hypothesis that the reader will not feel satisfied with an interpretation unless it organizes a text according to one of these formal models of unity.

Theme and epiphany

The third convention or expectation governing the lyric, closely related to the notion of unity, is that of significance. To write a poem is to claim significance of some sort for the verbal construct one produces, and the reader approaches a poem with the assumption that however brief it may appear it must contain, at least implicitly, potential riches which make it worthy of his attention. Reading a poem thus becomes a process of finding ways to grant it significance and importance, and in that process we call upon a variety of operations which have come to form part of the institution of poetry. Some lyrics, of course, explicitly announce their concern with themes which occupy a central place in human experience, but many do not; and it is in these cases that we must employ special formal conventions.

The first might be stated as 'attempt to read any brief descriptive lyric as a moment of epiphany'. If an object or situation is the focus of a poem, that implies, by convention, that it is especially important: the 'objective correlative' of an intense emotion or the locus of a moment of revelation. This applies particularly to imagist poems, haiku and other brief poems which allow the lyric form to assert their importance. Pound's 'In a Station of the Metro',

> The apparition of these faces in the crowd;
> Petals on a wet, black bough.

asks to be taken as a perception of 'inscape', a moment of revelation in which form is grasped and surface becomes profundity. Similar procedures are at work in many of William Carlos Williams's lyrics. A note left on a kitchen table which read 'This is just to say I have eaten the plums which were in the icebox and which you were probably saving for breakfast. Forgive me, they were delicious: so sweet and so cold' would be a nice gesture; but when it is set down on the page as a poem the convention of significance comes into play.[11] We deprive the poem of the pragmatic and circumstantial functions of the note (retaining simply this reference to a context as an implicit assertion that this sort of experience is important), and we must therefore supply a new function to justify the poem. Given the opposition between the eating of plums and the social rules which this violates, we may say that the poem as note becomes a mediating force, recognizing the priority of rules by asking forgiveness but also affirming, by the thrust of the last few words, that immediate sensuous experience also has its claims and that the order of personal relations (the relationship between the 'I' and the 'you') must make a place for such experience. We can even go on from there and say that the world of notes and breakfast is also the world of language, which cannot assimilate or stand up to these moments when, as Valéry says, 'le fruit se fonde en jouissance'. The value affirmed by the eating of plums is something that transcends language and cannot be captured by the poem except negatively (as apparent insignificance), which is why the poem must be so sparse and superficially banal.

Such operations are not, of course, restricted to the reading of modern poetry. The lyric has always been based on the implicit assumption that what was sung as a particular experience would be granted greater importance. Consider one of Ronsard's *Amours*:

> Mignonne, levez-vous, vous êtes paresseuse,
> Jà la gaie alouette au ciel a fredonné,
> Et jà le rossignol frisquement jargonné,
> Dessus l'épine assis, sa complainte amoureuse.
> Debout donc, allons voir l'herbelette perleuse,
> Et votre beau rosier de boutons couronné,
> Et vos œillets aimés auxquels aviez donné
> Hier au soir de l'eau, d'une main si soigneuse.
> Hier en vous couchant, vous me fîtes promesse
> D'être plus tôt que moi ce matin éveillée,
> Mais le sommeil vous tient encore toute sillée.
> Ian, je vous punirai du peché de paresse,
> Je vais baiser cent fois votre œil, votre tétin,
> Afin de vous apprendre à vous lever matin.

(Get up, my sweet, you are lazy! Already the gay lark has
trilled in the sky, and the nightingale, perched on the
hawthorn, has already elegantly warbled its amorous lay.
Up then! Let us go and see the pearly lawn and your pretty
rose-bush crowned with buds, and your cherished pinks which
you watered yesterday evening with such attentive hands.
Last night when going to bed you promised me to be awake
earlier than I this morning, but sleep still keeps you hooded.
There! I shall punish you for the sin of laziness; I will a
hundred times kiss your eye, your breast, so as to teach you to
get up early.)

Shifting this out of an implied empirical context, we can read it as a version of pastoral which asserts the value of a matutinal vision of love, a playful tenderness made innocent yet delicately sensuous by the identification of the woman and nature. In order to achieve a reading which justifies the poem, one must transform its content (watering of flowers, teaching you to get up, etc.) into constituents of a generalized ethos.

Another convention of a different kind, especially useful in the case of obscure or minimal poems where the fact that they are presented as poems is the one thing we can be certain of, is the rule that poems are significant if they can be read as reflections on or explorations of the problems of poetry itself. Apollinaire's famous one-line poem is an excellent case in point:

Chantre
Et l'unique cordeau des trompettes marines
(Singer/And the single string of marine trumpets.)

In the absence of any other significant subject, one must exploit the fact that 'singer' is a traditional metaphor for 'poet'. Since, as Jean Cohen says, co-ordination in poetry relates two items in terms of an implicit subject,[12] one must try to construct the implicit subject which brings together singer and instrument, and the obvious candidate is something like 'poetry' or 'artistic activity'. The binary structure of the alexandrine suggests that we relate the two noun phrases to one another, and by stressing the pun (*cordeau/cor d'eau* (trumpet of water)) and the ambiguity of *trompettes marines* (wooden stringed instrument/marine trumpet), we can make them equivalent. Reading this punning activity and creation of equivalences as synecdoche for poetic activity generally, and calling upon the basic convention which allows us to relate what the poem says to its status as a poem, we can produce a unified interpretation: that the poem has a single line because the marine trumpet has only a single string, but that the fundamental ambiguity of language allows the poet to make music with a single line of verse. Such an interpretation depends upon three general conventions – that a poem should be unified, that it should be thematically significant, and that this significance can take the form of reflection on poetry – and four general interpretive operations: that one should try to establish binary relations of opposition or equivalence, that one should look for and integrate puns and ambiguities, that items may be read as synecdoches (or metaphors, etc.) in order to attain the level of generality required, and that what a poem says can be related to the fact that it is a poem.

The convention that poems may be read as statements about poetry is extremely powerful. If a poem seems utterly banal it is possible to take banality of statement as a statement about banality and hence to derive a suggestion that poetry can go no further than language, which is inevitably distinct from immediate experience, or, alternatively, that poetry should celebrate the objects of the world by simply naming them. The ability of this convention to assimilate anything and endow it with significance may give it a dubious status, but its importance can be attested, for example, by most critical writings on Mallarmé and Valéry. There is a sense in which all representational poetry – all poetry which is not presented as taking place wholly within the mind itself – is allegorical: an allegory of the poetic act and the assimilation and transformation it performs.[13]

There are, of course, other conventions about the kind of significance to be discovered in poems, but these generally become the property of particular schools. A biographical convention tells the reader to make the poem significant by discovering in it the record of a passion, thought or reaction and hence by reading it as a gesture whose significance lies in the context of a life. There are analogous psychoanalytical and sociological conventions. Proponents of the New Criticism, who sought to read each poem on its own terms, substituted a common liberal humanism for more explicit conventions of significance (though the notion of balanced or resolved tensions was extremely important[14]) and thus deployed what R. S. Crane calls a 'set of reduction terms' towards which the analysis of ambivalence, tension, irony and paradox was to move: 'life and death, good and evil, love and hate, harmony and strife, order and disorder, eternity and time, reality and appearance, truth and falsity . . . emotion and reason, complexity and simplicity, nature and art' (*The Languages of Criticism and the Structure of Poetry*, pp. 123–4). These oppositions function as rudimentary models of the kind of thematic significance that the reader attempts to find in poems. A structuralist criticism, on the other hand, as opposed to a structuralist poetics which does not aim at interpretation, tends to use as models of significance notions of language, of literature itself, and of the sign. The successful critical act will show what the poem implies about the status of the sign and the poetic act itself. There is, of course, no way to escape from such models altogether, for the simple reason that one must have a sense, however undefined, of what one is reading towards.

Resistance and recuperation

It is at this level, where the notion of the 'ultimate significance' of a work becomes important, that one encounters critical pluralism. But prior to this stage there are common operations of reading which make possible the discovery of various types of significance and which can be defined as modes of naturalization. The conventions of impersonality, unity and significance set the stage, as it were, for the reading of poetry and determine the general orientation of reading, but more specific and local conventions are at work in the processing of the text itself.

'The poem must resist the intelligence/Almost successfully', says Wallace Stevens; and its distinctiveness lies in that resistance: not necessarily the resistance of obscurity, but at least the resistance of patterns and forms whose semantic relevance is not immediately obvious. Criticism in this century may be seen as an attempt to increase the range of formal features that can be made relevant and to find ways of analysing their effects in terms of meaning. But of course the reading of poetry has always involved operations to make the poetic intelligible, and poetics has always attempted, if only implicitly, to specify the nature of such operations.

Rhetoric, for example, structuralism's 'august forebear', was essentially an attempt 'to analyse and classify the forms of speech and to make the world of language intelligible' (Barthes, 'Science versus literature', p. 897). Rhetorical theory sought to justify various features of literary works by naming them and specifying which figures were appropriate to particular genres. It was animated, Genette argues, by a desire 'to discover at the second level of the system (literature) the transparency and rigour which already characterize the first (language)' (*Figures*, p. 220). Indeed, it seems likely that the disrepute into which rhetoric has fallen – or had fallen until the attempts of structuralists to revive it – is due to a misunderstanding about its function. Since one cannot go through a text and label rhetorical figures without having already understood the text, it may well seem that rhetorical analysis, as a classificatory discipline, is a sterile and ancillary activity which makes no significant contribution to criticism. But a semiological or structuralist theory of reading enables us simply to reverse the perspective and to think of training in rhetoric as a way of providing the student with a set of formal models which he can use in interpreting literary works. When he encounters Malherbe's line,

Le fer mieux employé cultivera la terre
(Iron better employed will cultivate the earth),

he will find that the rhetorical figures with which he is familiar define a series of operations which he can perform on *fer* until he discovers that the best reading (the most *vraisemblable*) is one involving two synecdoches (iron→weapon; iron→plough). Though structuralists have not made this point as firmly as they might, their discussions imply that rhetorical figures are instructions about how to naturalize the text by passing from one meaning to another – from the 'deviant' to the integrated – and by labelling this transformation as appropriate to a particular poetic mode. When a lover is 'slain' by the glance of his beloved, the reader must perform a semantic transformation to make the text intelligible – otherwise, like Helena in *Faust* part II, he will mistake hyperbolic compliment for tragedy; but he must also recognize the text's semantic detour as a generic form of praise.

The rhetorical figure, says Genette, 'is nothing other than an aware ness of the figure, and its existence depends wholly on the reader being conscious, or not being conscious, of the ambiguity of the discourse before him' (*ibid*., p. 216). One has a rhetorical figure when the reader perceives a problem in the text and takes certain rule-governed steps to devise a solution.

The productivity of rhetorical operations is best illustrated by taking a phrase and seeing how various figures permit one to develop it. If a poem were to begin, 'Tired of the oak, I wandered . . .', one might subject 'oak' to a variety of semantic operations which lead to a wide range of potential meanings. The *Groupe de Liège* have done much to formalize rhetorical operations, and if one follows the analysis in their *Rhétorique générale* one can see why rhetorical figures lie at the basis of interpretation. There are, according to this analysis, two types of 'decomposition' used in constructing semantic figures: the whole may be divided into its parts (tree: trunk, roots, branches, leaves, etc.), or a class may be divided into its members (tree: oak, willow, elm, chestnut, etc.). The most basic rhetorical figure, synecdoche, uses both these relations and allows one to move from part to whole, from whole to part, from member to class and from class to member. These four operations, when applied to 'oak', produce a variety of readings:

> part   →   whole: woods, garden, door, table, etc. (things containing or made of oak).
>
> whole →   part: leaf, trunk, acorn, roots, etc.
>
> member→   class: tree, strong things, tall things, non-animate organisms, etc.
>
> class   →   member: common oak, holm oak, holly oak, dyer's oak, etc.

Only a few of these meanings, of course, would be possible in context, and it is obvious that the generalizing operations are the more important; to move from vehicle to tenor is often to take the vehicle as a member of a general class. The move from class to member or from whole to part, however, is perhaps better described as a recognition of reference than as figurative interpretation: in 'the old tree' we read 'oak' for 'tree' only when the context indicates that the tree in question is in fact an oak. But there are none the less cases where one makes a trope intelligible by noting that an action or condition predicated of a whole in fact apertains only to a part: 'the state was angry' means that the government or the leaders of the state were angry.

Metaphor is a combination of two synecdoches: it moves from a whole to one of its parts to another whole which contains that part, or from a member to a general class and then back again to another member of that class. Starting again from 'oak' we have:

```
member →      class  → member
  oak   →   tall things  → any tall person or object
            strong things  any strong person or object
whole   →     part  → whole
  oak   →   branches  → anything with branches (banks?)
            roots        anything with roots
```

The move from member to class to member is the most common procedure for interpreting metaphors.

Of the other two ways of combining a pair of synecdoches, the move from class to member to class again is generally illicit; it has not been honoured with a name and interpretations which followed this model would usually be thought highly questionable: the class of dogs has members who are also members of the class of brown animals, but 'I like dogs' cannot, except in exceedingly unusual circumstances, be taken to mean 'I like brown animals'. The fourth possibility, however – the move from part to whole to part again – is metonymy: in 'George has been chasing that skirt' the skirt and the girl are related as parts of a notional or visual whole; in other instances cause can stand for effect or vice versa because both are parts of a single process.

The repertoire of rhetorical figures serves as a set of instructions which readers can apply when they encounter a problem in the text, though in some cases it is not so much the operations themselves that are important as the reassurance which rhetorical categories offer the reader: reassurance that what seems odd is in fact perfectly acceptable since it is figurative expression of some kind and therefore capable of being understood. If one knows that hyperbole, litotes, zeugma, syllepsis, oxymoron, paradox and irony are possible, one will not be surprised to find words or phrases that must be dealt with in the ways that these figures suggest. One can subtract emphasis from hyperbole or add it to litotes, supply two meanings for a single word in zeugma, differentiate the meanings of two instances of a word in syllepsis, assume the truth of the expression and try to find ways out of the contradiction in oxymoron and paradox, and reverse a literal meaning in the case of irony.[15] Of course readers no longer learn to perform these operations by learning to name rhetorical figures, but the processes of comprehension in which they become adept are very similar to those that Fontanier recommends for the identification of tropes:

examine whether the sentence as a whole, or any of the

propositions that compose it, or finally any of the words which
serve the utterance, should not be taken in a sense different
from the literal and normal meaning; or if to this latter
meaning there has not been joined another which is precisely
that which was principally intended. In both cases it is a trope . . .
what is its species? . . . that depends on its particular way of
signifying or expressing or on the relationship which is its basis.
Is it based on a resemblance between two objects? Then it is a
metaphor. (*Les Figures du discours*, p. 234)

One identifies phrases which require semantic transformation and
considers what kind of move seems justified in each case; the set of
possible moves is partly composed of the set of rhetorical figures.

It is essential to stress, of course, that understanding poetry is not
simply a process of replacing what does not make sense with what
does. Our conventions lead us to expect and to value metaphorical
coherence and thus to preserve the vehicles of rhetorical figures and
to structure them while we are investigating possible meanings.
Empson's work on ambiguity has provided admirable support for the
claim that poetic effects depend to a considerable extent on the
interaction of various half-formed meanings derived from a consideration of figurative language, and that value is to be located in the
exploratory process rather than in any semantic conclusion. Quoting
lines from *Hamlet*, III iii,

> but tis not so above;
> There is no shuffling, there the Action lies
> In his true Nature, and we ourselves compelled
> Even to the teeth and forehead of our faults
> To give in evidence,

he remarks that in 'the teeth and forehead of our faults' 'all we are
given is two parts of the body and the Day of Judgment; these have
got to be associated by the imagination of the reader. There is no
immediate meaning, and in spite of this there is an impression of
urgency and practicality . . .' This is due, no doubt, to 'a sense that
the words themselves, in such a context, include, as part of the way in
which they are apprehended, the possibility of flashes of fancy' in
various directions (*Seven Types*, p. 92). Of course metaphors using
genitive constructions are among the most powerful, since 'the X of
Y' may express many different relationships.[16] And here, although
we may want to say that, given the form 'compelled even to the X of
our faults to give in evidence', the main meaning must be something
like 'the most determined, vicious, essential aspects of our faults',
if we are to allow the metaphors their full power we must let them

work on us by forcing an implicit exploration of the relation of our teeth and our forehead to our faults: 'A *forehead*, besides being a target for blows, is used both for blushing and frowning . . . *Teeth*, besides being a weapon of offence, are used in making confessions, and it is a mark of contempt . . . that you are struck there . . . the *forehead* covers the brain where the *fault* is planned, while the *teeth* are used in carrying it out' (*ibid.*, p. 91). Empson's work, one might say, is based on a double conviction: that literary effects can be explained in terms of meaning, so that paraphrase is the basic analytical device, and yet that one must preserve as much of the literal meaning of metaphors as one can by offering simultaneous translations in various different directions.

Apparent contradictions, obscurities or deviations from require-ments of ordinary logic are powerful means, as Empson says, of forcing the reader 'to adopt a poetical attitude to words'. For Empson this attitude to the word is an exploratory attention, an ordered process of invention in which the activity may be more important than the results but in which the results can be ordered. For struct-uralists, discursive ordering is less important; they tend to think of poetry as a way of liberating the word from the constraints which discursive order imposes on it and not as a way of imposing new constraints: the word 'sparkles with infinite freedom and is ready to radiate towards a thousand uncertain and possible rela-tions'.[17] It thus becomes difficult for structuralists to write about particular poems except to argue that they illustrate the ways in which poetry undermines the functions of ordinary language. Fortu-nately, however, the 'work of the signifier' on which structuralists place so much stress does not simply produce disorder but absorbs and reorders semantic contexts, and one of the main functions of criticism has been to naturalize this process by attempting to explain the semantic value or semantic effects of various types of formal organization.

The most obvious feature of poetry's formal organization is the division into lines and stanzas. The break at the end of a line or the space between stanzas must be accorded some kind of value, and one strategy is to take poetic form as a mimesis: breaks represent spatial or temporal gaps which can be thematized and integrated with the poem's meaning. So, in Book I of *Paradise Lost* the passage recount-ing the classical myth of Satan's fall can be read as imitative form:

>   and how he fell
> From Heaven, they fabled, thrown by angry Jove
> Sheer o'er the crystal battlements: from morn
> To noon he fell, from noon to dewy eve,

> A summer's day; and with the setting sun
> Dropped from the zenith like a falling star,
> On Lemnos the Aegean isle. (lines 740–6)

The breaks between 'fell/From Heaven', 'from morn/To noon', and 'setting sun/Dropped' are the ones generally regarded as particularly expressive, figuring spatial gaps by typographic space. Or, to take a more modern example, in Robert Lowell's 'Mr Edwards and the Spider' a stanza break separates a preposition from its object:

> Faith is trying to do without

> faith.

One critic illustrates the naturalization of formal features by commenting that 'typography neatly imitates the decline of Faith into faith, yet suggests a paradox: that "Faith" comes to "faith" (the minor provisional assumptions that underpin any living), with difficulty and across (just barely across) the great distance that the gap between the stanza enacts.'[18] To read thus is to naturalize in terms of external contexts: to assume that typographic space reproduces a space in the world or at least a gap in the mental processes. Poetry of this sort assumes that readers will undertake this kind of naturalization – assumes that such procedures form part of the institution of poetry.[19]

Another way of naturalizing line endings which does not move so quickly from word to world is based on what one might call the phenomenology of reading. The break at the end of the line represents a pause in reading and hence brings about syntactic ambiguity: one attempts to compose into a whole the sequence preceding the pause and then, after passing over the pause, discovers that the construction was not in fact complete and that the elements preceding the pause must be given a different function in the new whole. Book IV of *Paradise Lost* offers an especially clear example:

> Satan, now first inflamed with rage, came down,
> The Tempter ere th'Accuser of mankind,
> To wreck on innocent frail man his loss

At this pause 'his loss' is read as man's fall, but with the next line we must readjust the thematic and syntactic conclusions:

> Of that first Battle, and his flight to Hell. (lines 9–12)

As John Hollander says, in the most thorough and perceptive treatment of the subject, 'the enjambment revealed itself reveals the true antecedent, but the ambiguity of the pronoun reflects the fact that, in the poem, Satan's loss is not only the type of Adam's, but a cause of it' ('Sense Variously Drawn Out', p. 207). Or again, in Book III, the lines 'Then feed on thoughts, that voluntary move/Harmonious numbers' (lines 37–8), produce a 'flicker of hesitation about whether the thoughts move only themselves, or something else', and thus make us see that the numbers 'are the very thoughts themselves, seen under a new aspect; the placing of "move", which produces the momentary uncertainty about its grammar, ties together "thoughts" and "numbers" in a relation far closer than cause and effect'.[20]

This kind of naturalization takes place at a different, and many would say more appropriate, level than the former, for it allows the poem's organization to absorb and restructure meanings instead of taking that organization as the representation of a state of affairs. It is certainly at this level that most attempts to deal with rhythm and sound patterns must be located, for despite the interesting work of Ivan Fónagy on the association between phonic and visual or tactile sensations,[21] the analysis of poetry cannot go very far if it restricts itself to mimetic effects (onomatopoeia) and sound symbolism. Although these matters are very obscure, it would seem that rather than try to move directly from form to meaning in that way we should try to explicate the conventions which enable formal features to organize semantic structures and thus to have meaning of a more indirect kind. There are three operations that we can perform. The first is to justify a phonetic or rhythmical figure as a way of stressing or throwing into relief a particular form and thus emphasizing its meaning. In Baudelaire's line, 'Je sentis ma gorge serrée par la main terrible de l'hystérie' (I felt my throat seized by the terrible hand of hysteria), the final word brings together sounds which are scattered throughout the line and thus serves as summation. Blake's 'To the Evening Star' asks this 'bright torch of love' to

> scatter thy silver dew
> On every flower that shuts its sweet eyes
> In timely sleep. Let thy west wind sleep on
> The lake; speak silence with thy glimmering eyes,

and the metrical pattern of 'In timely sleep. Let thy west wind sleep on', where 'on' receives terminal stress and thus comes to mean 'continue to sleep', intensifies the image of the wind sleeping on the lake and sleeping on.

The second operation is to use metrical or phonetic patterns to produce what Samuel Levin calls 'couplings', in which parallelism in sound or rhythm begets or passes over into parallelism of meaning. In Valéry's 'La Dormeuse' the poem focuses on the first line of the sestet, 'Dormeuse, amas doré d'ombres et d'abandons', and we might at first be tempted to say that euphony is a metaphor for the beauty experienced by the beholder as he gazes upon the 'Sleeping girl, golden mass of shadows and yieldings'. But the phonetic pattern connects *Dor*, *doré*, *d'ombres*, *dons*, and the rhyme word of the following line, *dons* (gifts), thus bringing into relation a set of semantic elements – sleep, gold, shadows, gifts – and posing the possibility of fusion. Moreover, *amas* takes up *âme* (soul) which appears twice in the sonnet in positions of stress, and *amie*, which refers to the sleeping girl. As Geoffrey Hartman says, the syllable *am* migrates through the poem, bringing about a coupling of these elements, and it is this presence of *âme* in *amas* which 'leads us to the poem's fundamental theme: that the beauty of things is independent of our sense for what is human', that the soul is both present and absent in the 'mass' (*amas*) and is at its most powerful when it is hidden and exercises an aesthetic rather than sentimental attraction.[22]

Or, to take an instance of rhythmical coupling, in Pound's 'The Return' a strong rhythmic figure holds together the lines which tell us how the gods once were:

> Góds of the wíngèd shóe!
> Wíth them the sílver hóunds
>   sníffing the tráce of aír!

We need not worry about the identity of these hounds; the important thing is the coherence or continuity provided by the rhythm which knits these three lines together and opposes their firmness to the hesitant and disconsolate movement of the gods' return:[23]

>   ah, see the tentative
> Movements, and the slow feet,
> The trouble in the pace and the uncertain
> Wavering!
> See, they return, one, and by one

Finally, in cases where neither of these operations can be performed with confidence – where the specific thematic effects of prosodic or phonetic patterns are difficult to discern – we can fall back on the convention of unity and symmetry and justify formal features in these terms. The attractions of nonsense poetry are no doubt due in large measure to the satisfaction of seeing order emerge from the semantically inchoate, and we can naturalize such poems by speaking of them in just this way: as artifice which subjects language to another order, whose purposes we cannot quite grasp, but which is at least an alternative order and by virtue of that fact alone sheds an oblique light on the order of other languages. Max Jacob's famous line,

'Dahlia, dahlia, que Dalila lia' does not assimilate the external context and transform it, as do our previous examples: the notion of Delilah binding dahlias is scarcely germane. We have, rather, a phonetic solidarity which uses fragments of meaning (the 'binding' or 'tying up' is important) to suggest the irrelevance of other meaning. In this respect surrealism is not far from poetry of the sublime. Consider the final stanza of Shelley's 'The Cloud':

> I am the daughter of Earth and Water,
>   And the nursling of the Sky;
> I pass through the pores of the ocean and shores;
>   I change, but I cannot die.
> For after the rain when with never a stain
>   The pavilion of Heaven is bare,
> And the winds and sunbeams with their convex gleams
>   Build up the blue dome of air,
> I silently laugh at my own cenotaph,
>   And out of the caverns of rain,
> Like a child from the womb, like a ghost from the tomb,
>   I arise and unbuild it again.

Donald Davie speaks of this as a poem 'ruined by licentious phrasing', by which he means a lack of semantic coherence: 'oceans and shores', for example, is, he claims, 'unthinkable in speech or prose'.[24] We might go some way towards defending Shelley but we should, I think, be obliged to concede defeat in the end, for it is obvious that 'shores' is determined by the rhyme with 'pores', 'cenotaph' by the rhyme with 'laugh' and that there is no coherent cosmology at work here. 'Shelley pitches his poem in a high key, to advise us not to expect nicety of discrimination and prosaic sense', says Davie, and in those expectations we can see one convention of the lyric at work: the use of a prosodic and phonetic order to lift us away from empirical contexts and to impose another order which we can call, precisely, the sublime.

We naturalize such poems in a very formal and abstract way by showing how various features contribute to patterns which help to assert the monumentality and impersonality of poetry, but we can also provide a general context in which they become meaningful by saying that their job is to break out of the 'middle distance' of realism and to assert, as Wallace Stevens says, that 'gaiety of language is our seigneur' and that the making of fictions is a worthy activity.

> Si les mots n'étaient que signes
> timbres-poste sur les choses
> qu'est-ce qu'il en resterait

poussières
gestes
temps perdu
il n'y aurait ni joie ni peine
par ce monde farfelu

(If words were only signs/postage stamps on things/what would
there remain/dust/gestures/lost time/there would be neither joy
nor pain/in this crazy world).[25]

Structuralists have done relatively little work on poetry, as the
paucity of quotations from their writings will no doubt have indicated,
and with the exception of Paul Zumthor's monumental *Essai de
poétique médiévale*, which sets out to reconstruct the conventions of
poetry in the medieval period, there has been no attempt to produce a
systematic account of the operations of reading or the assumed
conventions of the lyric. One is therefore bound to take from
structuralism a theoretical framework and to fill it in by drawing on
the writings of critics from other traditions who have worked to
greater purpose on the lyric. But of course, as I have already suggested, to reorganize critical discussions in this way may in itself be a
step forward in that it indicates what problems require further work
if we are to reach an understanding of the conventions of poetry.
In the case of the novel, to which we now turn, structuralists themselves have rather more to say, and the next chapter can take a more
properly expository form.

CHAPTER 9

Poetics of the Novel

L'homme poursuit noir sur blanc.*
MALLARMÉ

'Le roman', writes Philippe Sollers, 'est la manière dont cette société se parle.' More than any other literary form, more perhaps than any other type of writing, the novel serves as the model by which society conceives of itself, the discourse in and through which it articulates the world. And it is no doubt for this reason that structuralists have concentrated their attention on the novel. It is here that they can most easily study the semiotic process in its fullest scope: the creation and organization of signs not simply in order to produce meaning but in order to produce a human world charged with meaning. For the basic convention which governs the novel – and which, *a fortiori*, governs those novels which set out to violate it – is our expectation that the novel will produce a world. Words must be composed in such a way that through the activity of reading there will emerge a model of the social world, models of the individual personality, of the relations between the individual and society, and, perhaps most important, of the kind of significance which these aspects of the world can bear. 'Our identity', Sollers continues, 'depends on the novel, what others think of us, what we think of ourselves, the way in which our life is imperceptibly moulded into a whole. How do others see us if not as a character from a novel?' (*Logiques*, p. 228). The novel is the primary semiotic agent of intelligibility.

Lisibilité, illisibilité

The way in which novels participate in the production of meaning would itself be a sufficiently worthy object of investigation, but the very fact that the novel is conventionally tied to the world in a way

* Man pursues black on white.

that poetry is not gives it a range of critical functions which have interested structuralists even more. Precisely because the reader expects to be able to recognize a world, the novel he reads becomes a place in which models of intelligibility can be 'deconstructed', exposed and challenged. In poetry deviations from the *vraisemblable* are easily recuperated as metaphors which should be translated or as moments of a visionary or prophetic stance; but in the novel conventional expectations make such deviations more troubling and therefore potentially more powerful; and it is here, on the edges of intelligibility, that structuralist interest has come to focus. In *S/Z* Barthes begins his discussion of Balzac with a distinction between readable and unreadable texts – between those which are intelligible in terms of traditional models and those which can be written (*le scriptible*) but which we do not yet know how to read (p. 10). And although Barthes's own analysis suggests that this distinction is not itself a useful way of classifying texts – every 'traditional' novel of any value will criticize or at least investigate models of intelligibility and every radical text will be readable and intelligible from some point of view – it does at least indicate the appropriateness and fecundity of taking the play of intelligibility as the focal point of one's analysis. Even when the novel is not explicitly engaged in undermining our notions of coherence and significance, by its creative use of these notions it participates in what Husserl would call the 'reactivation' of models of intelligibility: that which is taken as natural is brought to consciousness and revealed as process, as construct.[1] Given the range of novels available to us, it would be extremely surprising if we were able to avoid recognizing, even when reading pre-twentieth-century texts, that they imply and force us to deploy different models of personality, causality, and significance. Even when novels themselves do not question the models on which they rely, the variety of models with which a reader will be confronted performs a critical function by provoking comparison and reflection.

The distinction between the readable and the unreadable text, between the 'traditional' or 'Balzacian' novel and the modern novel (usually represented by the *nouveau roman*), between – and this is its latest avatar – what Barthes calls the *texte de plaisir* and the *texte de jouissance*, has been so central to structuralist work on the novel that, despite its usefulness in leading to concentration on modes of order and intelligibility, it threatens to establish a distorted opposition which would seriously hamper our work on the novel. Fortunately, Barthes himself implicitly admits that these are functional concepts rather than classes of texts. Some people, he observes, would appear to desire a text which was fully modern and properly unreadable, 'a text with no shadow, severed from the dominant ideology', but this would be 'a text with no fertility, with no productivity, a sterile text' which could give rise to nothing. 'The text needs its shadow' – 'some ideology, some mimesis, some subject'. It needs at least pockets, streaks, suggestions of this kind: subversion requires a *chiaroscuro* (*Le Plaisir du texte*, p. 53). And inversely, the 'readable' or traditional text cannot, without becoming sterile, be wholly predictable and obviously intelligible; it must challenge the reader in some way and lead to a re-reading of the self and the world. When discussing the *nouveau roman* as a radical break with the 'Balzacian' novel, Stephen Heath cites Michel Butor's claim that the *nouveau roman*, through its practice of writing, reveals the world as a series of systems of articulation: 'the system of signification within the book will be an image of the system of meanings within which the reader is caught in his daily life' (*The Nouveau Roman*, p. 39). But of course all defences of the novel have assumed that there was a relation of this kind: that the meanings experienced when reading a novel would have a bearing on the reader's own life and would enable him to look upon it in new ways. For all its opposition to models of intelligibility and coherence, the radical novel relies on the link between text and ordinary experience just as traditional novels did.

There are, as Barthes recognizes, two ways in which we might think of this opposition which structuralists have made their basic critical device. We might say that between the traditional and the modern text, between the pleasure of the *texte de plaisir* and the rapture of the *texte de jouissance*, there is only a difference of degree: the latter is only a later and freer stage of the former; Robbe-Grillet develops out of Flaubert. But on the other hand we might say that pleasure and rapture are parallel forces which do not meet and that the modernist text is not a logical historical development but the trace of a rupture or scandal, so that the reader who enjoys both is not synthesizing in himself a historical continuity but living a contradiction, experiencing a divided self (*Le Plaisir du texte*, pp. 35–6). But perhaps one should go a step further than Barthes and say that the facts which lead him to propose these two views indicate that we are dealing not so much with a historical process in which one kind of novel replaces another as with an opposition which has always existed within the novel: a tension between the intelligible and the problematic. As Julia Kristeva observes, from its very beginnings the novel has contained the seeds of the anti-novel and has been constructed in opposition to various norms (*Le Texte du roman*, pp. 175–6). It is certainly striking that when structuralists write about classical texts they end by discovering gaps, uncertainties, instances of subversion and other features which it is rather too easy to consider as specifically modern. To recognize that there is in this respect a continuity within the novel – between Flaubert and Robbe-Grillet, between Sterne and Sollers – does not force us to abandon the notion of *jouissance* as a rapture of dislocation produced by ruptures or violations of intelligibility.

If we organize our approach to the novel in this way we make structuralist writings properly germane to the novel as a whole and not just to a particular class of modernist texts, and we centre the study of the novel on models of coherence and intelligibility which it employs and challenges. There are three domains or sub-systems where cultural models are particularly important: plot, theme and character. Before turning to these models, however, we should consider the general structuralist theory of the novel as a hierarchy of systems, the basic conventions of narrative fiction which this approach identifies, and the distinctions and categories that have been applied in the study of narration itself.

If we apply to the novel Benveniste's principle that 'the meaning of a linguistic unit can be defined as its capacity to integrate a unit of a higher level', we can say that units of novelistic discourse must be identified by their function in a hierarchical structure. To understand a text, Barthes says,

> is not only to follow the unwinding of the story, it is also to identify various levels, to project the horizontal links of the narrative sequence onto an implicitly vertical axis; to read a narrative is not only to pass from one word to another, it is also to pass from one level to another. ('Introduction à l'analyse structurale des récits', p. 5)

Though too little attention has been paid to the way in which readers pass from one level to another, the importance of levels in linguistic systems has led to the assumption that in order to carry out a structural analysis in other areas 'one must first distinguish several descriptive levels and place them in the perspective of a hierarchy or of integration' (*ibid.*). The conventions of the genre may be thought of as expectations about levels and their integration; the process of reading is that of implicitly recognizing elements as of a particular level and interpreting them accordingly. By way of illustration we might look at two levels which are widely separated – a level of trivial detail and a level of the narrative speech act.

Narrative contracts

If the basic convention governing the novel is the expectation that readers will, through their contact with the text, be able to recognize a world which it produces or to which it refers, it ought to be possible to identify at least some elements of the text whose function it is to confirm this expectation and to assert the representational or mimetic orientation of fiction. At the most elementary level this function is fulfilled by what one might call a descriptive residue: items whose only apparent role in the text is that of denoting a concrete reality (trivial gestures, insignificant objects, superfluous dialogue). In a description of a room items which are not picked up and integrated by symbolic or thematic codes (items which tell us nothing about the inhabitant of the room, for example) and which do not have a function in the plot produce what Barthes calls a 'reality effect' (*l'effet de réel*): deprived of any other function, they become integrated units by signifying 'we are the real' ('L'effet de réel', pp. 87–8). The pure representation of reality thus becomes, as Barthes says, a resistance to meaning, an instance of the 'referential illusion', according to which the meaning of a sign is nothing other than its referent.

Elements of this kind confirm the mimetic contract and assure the reader that he can interpret the text as about a real world. It is possible, of course, to trouble this contract by blocking the process of recognition, preventing one from moving through the text to a world, and making one read the text as an autonomous verbal object. But such effects are possible only because of the convention that novels do refer. Robbe-Grillet's famous description of a tomato slice, which tells us first that it is perfect and then that it is flawed, plays on the fact that this description at first appears to have a purely referential function, which is troubled when the writing introduces uncertainties and thus lifts our attention away from a supposed object to the process of writing itself (*Les Gommes*, III, iii). Or again, in the opening paragraph of Robbe-Grillet's *Dans le labyrinthe*, description of the weather seems at first to establish a context ('Outside it is raining') but when the next sentence introduces a contradiction ('Outside the sun is shining') we are forced to realize that the only reality in question is that of writing itself which, as Jean Ricardou says, uses the concept of a world in order to display its own laws.[2]

If the process of recognition is not blocked at this level then the reader will assume that the text is gesturing towards a world which he can identify and will, after assimilating this world, attempt to move back from world to text so as to compose and give meaning to what has been identified. This second move in the cycle of reading can be troubled if the text undertakes an excessive proliferation of elements whose function seems purely referential. Enumerations or descriptions of objects which seem determined by no thematic purpose enable the reader to recognize a world but prevent him from composing it and leave him with flawed or incomplete meanings which are still applied to the world or to his own experience by virtue of prior recognition. The fundamental character of a truly 'realistic' or referential discourse is, as Philippe Hamon says, to deny the story or to make it impossible by producing a thematic emptiness (*une thématique vide*) ('Qu'est-ce qu'une description?', p. 485). Consider, for example, Flaubert's description of the scene which confronts Bouvard and Pécuchet when, on their first morning in their newly acquired country house, they arise and gaze out the window:

> Directly ahead were the fields, on the right a barn, and the steeple of a church, and on the left a screen of poplars.
> Two main paths, in the form of a cross, divided the garden into four parts. The vegetables were arranged in beds, from which rose, here and there, dwarf cypresses and trained fruit-trees. On one side an arbour-way led to a bower; on the other a wall held up espaliers; and a lattice fence, at the back, opened onto the countryside. There was beyond the wall an orchard; behind the bower a thicket; beyond the lattice fence a small track. (chapter 2)

It is difficult to discover a thematic purpose to this description. The sentences lead us through a garden and reveal, at the end of their adventure, an orchard, a thicket, a small track. A mania of precision produces *une thématique vide*. By blocking access to concepts Flaubert shows his mastery of what Barthes calls the indirect language of literature: 'the best way for a language to be indirect is to refer as constantly as possible to things themselves rather than to their concepts, for the meaning of an object always flickers, but not that of the concept' (*Essais critiques*, p. 232). Relying on this referential function, Flaubert produces descriptions which seem determined only by a desire for objectivity and thus leads the reader to construct a world which he takes as real but whose meaning he finds difficult to grasp.

The referential function may be affirmed by descriptive details but it also depends to a considerable extent on the narrative stance implied by the text. The difficulty of reading a novel like Pierre Guyotat's *Éden, Éden, Éden* derives in part from the fact that we are unable to identify any narrator and so do not know how to situate its language. If we could read it as some speaker's account of a situation, real or imagined, we would be some way towards organizing it; but instead we have a sentence which lasts for two hundred and fifty-five pages, 'as if it were a question of representing, not imagined scenes, but the scene of language, so that the model of this new mimesis is no longer the adventures of a hero but the adventures of the signifier:

what happens to it.'³ There are, however, few novels of this kind. In most cases we can order the text as the discourse of an explicit or implicit narrator who tells us about events in a world. Sartre maintains that the nineteenth-century novel is told from the viewpoint of wisdom and experience and listened to from the viewpoint of order. Whether in the role of social analyst or of an individual who looks back, all passion spent, the narrator has mastered the world and tells a civilized company of listeners about a series of events which now can be composed and named (*Qu'est-ce que la littérature ?*, pp. 172–3).

This is perhaps the simplest case, where the narrator identifies himself and the audience which joins him in looking at events of the past; but even where the framework of the fireside tale is missing we can, thanks to what Barthes calls 'the code through which the narrator and reader are signified throughout the story itself',⁴ make the text into a communication about a world situated with respect to narrator and reader. For example, on the first page of George Eliot's *Silas Marner* we are told that 'in the days when the spinning wheels hummed busily in the farmhouses . . . there might be seen, in districts far away among the lanes, or deep in the bosom of the hills, certain pallid undersized men.' The definite articles and the 'there might be seen' affirm an objective situation, which is set at a distance from the narrator and from the readers who must be told that in those days superstition clung easily round every unwonted person. As the image of the narrator begins to emerge, that of an imaginary reader is also sketched. The narrative indicates what he needs to be told, how he might have reacted, what deductions or connections he is presumed to accept. Thus, in Hardy's *The Mayor of Casterbridge* sentences which assert the objectivity of the scene indicate what the reader might have observed had he been present: 'What was really peculiar, however, in this couple's progress, and would have attracted the attention of any casual observer otherwise disposed to overlook them, was the perfect silence they preserved.' There are attempts to establish the reality of the scene by deducing information from it, as if the narrator enjoyed no special knowledge but were an observer like the reader:

> that the man and woman were husband and wife, and the
> parents of the girl in arms, there could be little doubt. No other
> than such relationship would have accounted for the atmosphere
> of stale familiarity which the trio carried along with them like a
> nimbus as they moved down the road. (chapter 1)

Similarly, the stylistic tics of Balzac's prose are almost all ways of evoking and solidifying the contract with the reader, insisting that the narrator is only a more knowledgeable version of the reader and that they share the same world to which the language of the novels refers. The demonstratives followed by relative clauses (she was one of those women who . . .; on one of those days when . . .; the façade is painted that yellow colour which gives Parisian houses . . .) create categories while implying that the reader knows them already and can recognize the kind of person or object about which the narrator speaks. The hypostatized observers act as personae for the reader and suggest how he would have reacted to the spectacle that is being presented: 'From the way in which the Captain accepted the coachman's help to get down from the carriage one could have told that he was fifty years old' (*on eût reconnu le quinquagénaire*). Such constructions assert that the meanings extracted from the scene are the common property of narrator and reader: wholly *vraisemblable*. Madame Vauquer's skirt 'résume le salon, la salle à manger, le jardinet, annonce la cuisine et fait pressentir les pensionnaires' (sums up the salon, the dining room, the garden, adumbrates the kitchen and foreshadows the residents). 'Fait pressentir' to whom? To whom does it announce or encapsulate these things? Not to the narrator alone, who will not take responsibility for this synthesis, but to the reader who, as someone conversant with the great social text, is presumed to be capable of making such connections. 'Who speaks here?' asks Barthes when we are told that 'Zambinella, *as if* terror-stricken . . .' It is not an omniscient narrator. 'What is heard here is the *displaced* voice which the reader grants, by proxy, to the narrative . . . it is specifically the voice of reading' (*S/Z*, p. 157).

Novels become problematic when the voice of reading is inaudible. In Robbe-Grillet's *La Jalousie*, for example, descriptions are not conducted according to what a reader would notice or might conclude if he were present, and consequently it becomes impossible to organize the text as communication between an implied 'I' and an implied 'you'. 'Nearly all statements', says Empson, 'assume in this way that you know something but not everything about the matter in hand and would tell you something different if you knew more' (*Seven Types*, p. 4). When a text behaves as though the reader were not familar with tables set for dinner – when it presents descriptions without regard for the 'order of the notable' – the reader must assume that it is trying to tell him more and has difficulty in discovering what in fact is 'the matter in hand'. There is a surplus of potential meaning and a lack of communicative focus.

Novels which comply with mimetic expectations assume that readers will move through language to a world, and since there are various ways of referring to the same thing they can allow a variety of rhetorics. At the beginning of *Le Père Goriot*, for example, Balzac's narrator moves into what is explicitly a reflection on his tale, and no sooner has the image of 'the chariot of civilization' led to an appropriate metaphorical development, running over hearts, breaking them and continuing its 'glorious march', than we are assured that the story itself contains no exaggeration: 'Sachez-le: ce drame n'est ni une fiction, ni un roman. *All is true.*' And a few pages later, after a Dickensian description of 'the lodging-house smell', which is desperate linguistic exuberance rather than an attempt at precision, he assures us of the reality and indescribability of his referent: 'perhaps it could be described if a procedure were invented for weighing up the nauseous elementary particles contributed by the distinctive catarrhal clouds of each lodger, young and old.' Do not be deceived by my language, he seems to be saying. Whatever its elaborations it is only a gesture to refer you to a world.

Such texts make an internal distinction between story and presentation, between referential object and the rhetoric of a narrator. In employing this opposition in their discussion of novels structuralists have taken their lead from linguistics, relying on Benveniste's distinction between 'two distinct and complementary systems . . . that of story (*l'histoire*) and that of discourse (*discours*)' (*Problèmes de linguistique générale*, p. 238). To say that a literary work is both story and narration seems intuitively just: in reading Raymond Queneau's *Exercices de style*, for example, we recognize that the same story has been told in ninety-nine different ways. But the passage from the linguistic distinction to the literary has been fraught with surprising difficulties which call attention to some interesting aspects of narration.

Benveniste bases his distinction on the system of verb tenses: the difference between the perfect and the aorist (*passé simple* or *passé défini*) is that the former establishes a link between the past event and the present in which one speaks of the event (e.g. John has bought a car). 'Like the present tense, the perfect belongs to the linguistic system of discourse, since its temporal reference is to the moment of speech, whereas the reference of the aorist is to the moment of the event' (*ibid.*, p. 244). The crucial distinction is between forms which contain some reference to the situation of enunciation and forms which do not. First and second person pronouns are therefore excluded from the system of *l'histoire*, as are deictics which depend for their meaning on the situation of enunciation (now, here, two years ago, etc.).

This is not yet a distinction between a story and its mode of presentation because a story could be narrated in the mode of *l'histoire*. As example, Benveniste cites a passage from Balzac's *Gambara*:

After a turn in the arcades, the young man looked at the sky
and then at his watch, made an impatient gesture, entered a
tobacco shop, lit a cigar, placed himself before a mirror, and
glanced at his clothes, somewhat more elaborate than the laws
of taste in France permit. He adjusted his collar and his black
velvet waistcoat, which was criss-crossed by one of those
large golden chains made in Genoa; then, throwing his velvet-
lined coat onto his left shoulder with a single movement and
letting it hang there in elegant folds, he continued his walk,
without allowing himself to be distracted by the leers of
passers-by. When the lights in shops began to go on and the
night seemed to him sufficiently dark, he made his way
towards the square of the Palais Royal like a man who was
afraid of being recognized, for he kept to the side of the square
until the fountain so as to enter the rue Froidmanteau screened
from the hackney cabs.

Apart from one verb in the present tense ('than the laws of taste in
France permit'), this passage contains none of the linguistic signs of
discourse: 'in truth, there is no longer even a narrator', says Benveniste. 'No one speaks here; events seem to tell themselves' (*ibid.*,
p. 241).

This may be true from a linguistic point of view, but the reader of
literature will have recognized a narrative voice: 'one of those large
golden chains made in Genoa' implies a relation of complicity and
shared knowledge between narrator and reader; 'like a man who was
afraid of being recognized, *for* . . .' gives us a narrator who infers a
state of mind from an action and presumes that the reader will
accept the connection as he describes it. If we were to separate the
story from all marks of a personal narrator we would have to exclude,
as Genette says, even the slightest general observation or evaluative
adjective, the most discreet comparison, the most modest 'perhaps',
the most inoffensive logical connection, all of which partake of
discours rather than *histoire* (*Figures II*, p. 67).

Todorov says that Benveniste has identified 'not only the characteristics of two types of speech but also two complementary aspects of
any speech' (*Poétique de la prose*, p. 39), and although this may seem
an evasive attempt to have it both ways, a refusal to consider what the
distinction really involves, there is a sense in which it is an apt comment. We can distinguish between two modes of language – sentences
which contain references to the situation of enunciation and the
subjectivity of the speaker and those that do not – but we also know
that every sequence is both a statement and an enunciative act.
However much a text strives to be pure story in Benveniste's terms,

it will still contain features that characterize a particular narrative stance. The *passé simple* itself serves as the formal sign of the literary (in that it is generally excluded from speech) and 'implies a world that is constructed, elaborated, detached, reduced to its significant lines' and not a dense, confused, open reality which is thrown down before the reader. If the text announces that 'la marquise sortit à cinq heures' the narrator is taking his distance, giving us a pure event stripped of its existential density. Because the novel uses this form, says Barthes, it makes life into destiny and duration into oriented and meaningful time (*Le Degré zéro de l'écriture*, p. 26). Moreover, immense variation in narrative personae results from differences in the degree of knowledge or precision manifested in description. Compare 'he lit a cigarette' and 'taking a thin white cylinder from the box and placing one end between his lips, he lifted a tiny flaming piece of wood to a point one inch below the other end of the cylinder'. Though both of these sentences are *histoire* in Benveniste's terms, they imply different narrative postures by virtue of their relations to the 'threshold of functional relevance' of our second level of *vraisemblance*.

But the most confusing adaptation of Benveniste's discussion is Barthes's attempt in his 'Introduction à l'analyse structurale des récits' to distinguish between 'personal' and 'a-personal' narration. The former, he says, cannot be recognized solely by the presence of first-person pronouns; there are tales or sequences written in the third person which are 'really manifestations of the first person.' How does one decide? One need only rewrite the sequence, replacing *he* by *I*, and if this entails no other alterations one is dealing with a sequence of personal narration (p. 20). Thus, 'he entered a tobacco shop' can be rewritten as 'I entered a tobacco shop', whereas 'he seemed pleased at the distinguished air his uniform gave him' becomes an incongruous 'I seemed pleased at the distinguished air my uniform gave me', which implies a schizophrenic narrator. Examples which resist rewriting are a-personal. This, Barthes says, is the traditional mode of the *récit*, which uses a temporal system based on the aorist and designed to exclude the present of the speaker. 'In the *récit*, says Benveniste, no one speaks.'

This is most confusing. By Benveniste's criteria 'he entered a tobacco shop' is impersonal. Barthes makes it personal. The feature which makes the second example a-personal for Barthes is the 'seemed', which indicates a judgment on the part of the narrator and would make the sentence, by Genette's criteria if not explicitly by Benveniste's, an example of *discours* rather than *histoire*. Barthes has very nearly reversed the categories while claiming to follow Benveniste's example. What prevents a sentence from being rewritten in the first person is the presence of elements which implicitly identify the narrator as someone other than the character mentioned in the sentence, and thus the marking of the narrator becomes, by a curious paradox, the criterion for an 'a-personal' mode of discourse. Barthes's discussion indicates the complexity of subjectivity in narration and the usefulness of distinguishing between cases where no point of view other than that of the protagonist is marked (which he calls personal) and those where another narrator is indicated (a-personal), but the distinction can scarcely be justified by referring to Benveniste's linguistic analysis. Linguistics may have been a seminal force, but what is reaped often bears little resemblance to what was sown.

Identifying narrators is one of the primary ways of naturalizing fiction. The convention that in a text the narrator speaks to his readers acts as support to interpretive operations which deal with the odd or apparently insignificant. In so far as the novel is, as George Eliot says, 'a faithful account of men and things as they have mirrored themselves in my mind', the reader may treat anything anomalous as the effect of the narrator's vision or cast of mind. In the case of first-person narration, choices for which the reader can find no other explanation may be read as excesses which display the narrator's individuality and as symptoms of his obsessions. But even when there is no narrator who describes himself we can explain almost any aspect of a text by postulating a narrator whose character the elements in question are designed to reflect or reveal. Thus, Robbe-Grillet's *La Jalousie* may be recuperated, as Bruce Morrissette has done, by postulating an obsessed narrator with paranoiac suspicions so as to explain certain fixations of description; *Dans le labyrinthe* can be naturalized by reading it as the speech of a narrator suffering from amnesia.[5] The most incoherent text could be explained by assuming that it is the speech of a delirious narrator. Such operations can, of course, be applied to a wide range of modern texts, but the most radical works set out to make this kind of recuperation an arbitrary imposition of sense and to show the reader how dependent his reading is on models of intelligibility. As Stephen Heath has admirably demonstrated, such novels act by becoming thoroughly banal when naturalized and showing the reader at what cost he has purchased intelligibility (*The Nouveau Roman*, pp. 137–45). In Barthes's words, writing becomes truly writing only when it prevents one from answering the question 'who is speaking?'

However, we have developed powerful strategies to prevent texts from becoming writing, and in cases where we should find it difficult to postulate a single narrator we can appeal to that modern literary convention, made explicit by Henry James and the many critics who have followed his lead, of limited point of view. If we cannot compose the text by attributing everything to a single narrator we can break it down into scenes or episodes and give meaning to details by treating them as what was noticed by a character who was present at the time. This convention may be seen as a last-ditch strategy for humanizing writing and making personality the focal point of the text; and indeed it is noteworthy that the authors who are most frequently read in this way are those like Flaubert who attain an impersonality which makes it difficult to attribute the text to a characterizable narrator.

R. J. Sherrington, who is one of the more extreme advocates of this type of recuperation, tells us for instance that the passages in *Madame Bovary* which describe Charles's visits to the farm where he first meets Emma employ a limited point of view in that 'only details which force themselves upon Charles's awareness are mentioned.' Entering the kitchen, he notices that the shutters are closed; 'naturally, this fact draws attention to the patterns of light filtering through the shutters and coming down the chimney to strike ashes in the fireplace'. Since Emma is standing near the fireplace, 'then he sees Emma and notices only one thing about her: "little drops of perspiration on her bare shoulders" '. How characteristic of Charles! Full of admiration for Flaubert's artistry in recounting just what Charles noticed, Sherrington neglects to explain what we are to deduce about Charles's character from the fact that between the sentences describing the patterns of light and Emma there occurs one which displays considerable interest in the behaviour and death of flies: 'Flies, on the table, crawled up and down the sides of glasses which had been used and buzzed as they drowned themselves at the bottom, in the dregs of cider.'[6] If we try to attribute this notation to Charles, we are engaged in recuperating details by a circular argument: flies are described because they are what Charles noticed; we know that they are what Charles noticed because they are what is described.

This is, in fact, simply another version of the representational justification which few sophisticated readers of novels would now allow themselves to employ: that a particular passage is justified or explained by the fact that it describes the world. This is so weak a determination – everything *vraisemblable* is by this criterion equally justified – that it has fallen out of serious use; and the concept of limited point of view offers a determination which is almost equally weak. The proof of its insufficiency is that when discussing novels like *What Maisie Knew* which derive from the explicit project of 'giving it *all*, the whole situation surrounding her, but of giving it only through the occasions and connexions of her proximity and her attention', we are not content to argue that sentences are justified because they tell us what Maisie knew but require that they contribute to patterns of knowledge and form a drama of innocence. The identification of narrators is an important interpretive strategy, but it cannot itself take one very far.

Codes

In his 'Introduction à l'analyse structurale des récits' Barthes identifies, in addition to narration, two other levels of the novel: that of character and that of functions. The latter is the most hetero-geneous but also the most fundamental, because it represents the basic elements of the novel abstracted from their narrative presenta-tion and prior to their reorganization by the synthesizing operations of reading. It is also badly named, since 'function' is used for a particular type of unit found at this level, and we should do better to refer to it by the term used in *S/Z* and call it the level of *lexies*. A lexie is a minimal unit of reading, a stretch of text which is isolated as having a specific effect or function different from that of neighbouring stretches of text. It could thus be anything from a single word to a brief series of sentences. The level of lexies would, then, be the level of one's primary contact with the text, at which items are separated and sorted out so as to be given various functions at higher levels of organization.

In discussing the basic units and their modes of combination one has a variety of proposals to draw upon, and it is necessary to select and order somewhat ruthlessly so as to give shape to the account which follows. In what is the most detailed consideration of the organization of lexies, Barthes distinguishes five 'codes' which are applied in the reading of a text, each of which is a 'perspective of citations' or a general semantic model which enables one to pick out items as belonging to the functional space which the code designates. That is to say, the codes enable one to identify elements and class them together under particular functions. Each code is 'one of the voices of which the text is woven'. To identify an element as a unit of the code is to treat it as 'le jalon d'une digression virtuelle vers le reste d'un catalogue (l'*Enlèvement* renvoie à tous les enlèvements déjà écrits)'; the units are 'autant d'éclats de ce quelque chose qui a toujours été *déjà* lu, vu, fait, vécu: le code est le sillon de ce *déjà*' (the marks of an implied movement towards the other members of a catalogue (a kidnapping refers one to all the kidnappings already written); the units are so many flashes of that something which always has been *already* read, seen, done, lived: the code is the wake of this *already*) (*S/Z*, pp. 27–8). To sort out lexies is to give them a place in the groupings established by one's experience of other texts and of discourse about the world.

For Barthes, as for Lévi-Strauss, codes are determined by their homogeneity – they group together items of a single kind – and by their explanatory function. The number of codes identified can therefore vary according to the perspective chosen and the nature of the texts one is analysing. And indeed, the five codes isolated in *S/Z* do not seem exhaustive or sufficient. The *proairetic code* governs the reader's construction of plot. The *hermeneutic code* involves a logic of question and answer, enigma and solution, suspense and peripeteia. These are undoubted components of the novel and can both be located in the realm of plot structure. The *semic code* provides models which enable the reader to collect semantic features that relate to persons and to develop characters, and the *symbolic code* guides extrapolation from text to symbolic and thematic readings. These codes can be assigned to the realm of character and theme respectively, although an adequate account of thematic interpretation would have to do more than specify our models for symbolic reading. Finally, there is what Barthes calls the *referential code*, constituted by the cultural background to which the text refers. This is perhaps the most unsatisfactory of all the codes, for while it is possible to go through the text, as Barthes does, picking out all specific references to cultural objects (she was like a Greek statue) and stereotyped knowledge (e.g. proverbs), these are far from the only manifestations of 'an anonymous, collective voice, whose origin is human wisdom' and their primary function is to bring into play models of the *vraisemblable* and to substantiate the fictional contract. Since the various levels of *vraisemblance* have already been discussed, we can leave aside this code and proceed to the problems of differentiating the other four, although we should note in passing that the absence of any code relating to narration (the reader's ability to collect items which help to characterize a narrator and to place the text in a kind of communicative circuit) is a major flaw in Barthes's analysis.

In discussing the ways in which items are isolated and given a function Barthes draws upon Benveniste's distinction between distributional and integrative relations in order to distinguish two types of unit: those which are defined by their relationship to other items of the same kind which appear earlier or later in the text, (distributional) and those whose importance derives not from a place in the sequence but from the fact that they are taken up by the reader and grouped with analogous items in paradigm classes which receive a meaning at a higher level of integration (integrative) ('Introduction à l'analyse structurale des récits', pp. 5–8). Thus, if a character in a novel purchases a book, this incident may operate in either of two ways. It may be, as Barthes says, 'an element which will ripen later, at the same level': when reading the book the character learns something crucial and thus the significance of the purchase is its consequence. Alternatively, the event may have no important consequences but may serve as a set of potential semantic features which can be picked up and used, at another level, for the construction of character or of a symbolic reading.

This distinction corresponds to Greimas's separation of dynamic predicates (or functions) and static predicates (or qualifications). And we may say that the proairetic and hermeneutic codes govern the recognition of dynamic predicates, whose sequential distribution in the text is crucial, whereas elements of the semic and symbolic code do not form sequences so much as sets of features (or qualifications) which are combined at higher levels. The distinction has considerable intuitive validity as a representation of the different roles we can give to the lexies of a novel, but relatively little attention has been brought to bear on the basic problem of precisely how we decide, even retrospectively, whether a particular element is to be treated as function or as qualification (or split up into two components, one of which plays each role). Julia Kristeva, who uses the terms *adjoncteur prédicatif* and *adjoncteur qualificatif* instead of function and qualification, notes that the sequence which, in her view, inaugurates the action of *Petit Jéhan de Saintré* 'is no different from the statements which play the role of *adjoncteur qualificatif*'. The properties of the sentences themselves, as isolated sentences, are in no way decisive. How then can we explain the differences in effect? We must, she argues, have recourse to various social models which make certain classes of action stand out. The social discourse of a period will make certain actions significant, notable, worthy of a story, and thus we can say that the role of a dynamic predicate

> will be played by any element which, in the intertextual space
> from which it is taken, corresponds to the dominant
> affirmations of the social discourse to which the text belongs.
> It is not by chance that in *Jéhan de Saintré* the role of
> *predicative adjunct* falls to sequences taken from the discourse of
> duels and war. These are the chief signifiers of the social
> discourse in the period around 1456 . . . In this context any
> other type of discourse (commerce, the fair, old books, the
> court) passes to a secondary position and can only be
> qualificatory . . . it has not the power to form a story.
> (*Le Texte du roman*, pp. 121–3)

There is some measure of truth here; cultural models will deem some actions more significant then others and if such actions appear in a text they are likely to contribute to plot. But if Kristeva's claim were true it would follow that given a knowledge of the culture of the period the reader would be able to recognize the first dynamic predicate or action of the plot as soon as he came upon it, and this does not seem to be the case. We cannot simply list those actions which, in a given period, will belong to plot, for actions will have different functions in different stories. Their role depends on the economy of the narrative more than on any intrinsic or culturally determined properties, and in order to consider how they are given roles in the plot we must turn to the *analyse structurale de récit* or study of plot structure.

Plot

Sequences of actions, Barthes says, constitute the armature of the readable or intelligible text. They provide an order which is both sequential and logical and thus serve as one of the preferred objects of structural analysis (*S/Z*, p. 210). Moreover, it is obvious that in this area there is a kind of literary competence to be studied and explained. Readers can tell that two texts are versions of the same story, that a novel and a film have the same plot. They can summarize plots and discuss the adequacy of plot summaries. And therefore it seems not unreasonable to ask of literary theory that it provide some account of this notion of plot, whose appropriateness seems beyond question and which we use without difficulty. A theory of plot structure ought to provide a representation of readers' abilities to identify plots, to compare them and to grasp their structure.

The first step we must take – one on which all analysts of plot would seem to agree – is to postulate the existence of an autonomous level of plot structure underlying actual linguistic manifestation. A study of plot cannot be a study of the ways in which sentences are combined, for two versions of the same plot need have no sentences in common, nor need they, perhaps, have any linguistic deep-structures in common. But as soon as the matter is stated in these terms the enormity of the task becomes obvious. To explain how sentences combine to form coherent discourse is already a daunting enterprise, but there the units with which one is working are at least given in advance. Difficulties are multiplied in the study of plot structure because the analyst must both determine what shall count as the elementary units of narrative and investigate the ways in which they combine. No wonder Barthes once observed that

faced with the infinitude of plots, the multiplicity of points of
view from which one can talk about them (historical,
psychological, sociological, ethnological, aesthetic, etc.), the

analyst is in nearly the same position as Saussure, confronted by
the diversity of linguistic phenomena and attempting to extract
from this apparent anarchy a principle of classification and a
focal point for description. ('Introduction à l'analyse
structurale des récits', pp. 1–2)

It is none the less apparent that the analysis of plot structure must
be theoretically possible, for if it were not we should have to admit
that plot and our impressions of it were random, idiosyncratic
phenomena. And this is certainly not the case. We can, with some
confidence, discuss whether the summary of a plot is accurate,
whether a particular incident is important for the plot and if so what
function it serves, whether a plot is simple or complex, coherent or
incoherent, whether it follows familiar models or contains unexpected
twists. To be sure, such notions are not explicitly defined. They have,
shall we say, the vagueness appropriate to their function. We may
hesitate to say, in particular cases, whether a sequence plays a
significant role in the plot or whether a plot summary is really
correct, but our ability to recognize borderline cases, to predict when
and where disagreements are likely to occur, shows precisely that we
do know what we are talking about: that we are operating with
concepts whose interpersonal value we understand.

Our ability to discuss and verify statements about plots provides a
strong presumption that plot structure is in principle analysable.
Moreover, plots themselves seem to be ordered rather than random
sequences of actions, and, as Barthes says, 'there is a gulf between the
most complex aleatory process and the most simple combinatory
logic, and no one can combine or produce a plot without referring to
an implicit system of units and rules' (*ibid.*, p. 2).

But when one looks at proposals concerning this implicit system
of units and rules one is likely to be baffled, not simply by their
diversity but by the lack of explicit procedures for evaluating competing approaches. Each theory, constrained to define for itself the units
of plot, becomes a self-contained system in whose terms any plot can
be described, and there has been little attempt to explain how any
particular system could be tested.

This state of affairs is no doubt partly due to structuralists'
interpretation of the linguistic model. The linguists whom structuralists
had read did not devote much time to discussion of the conditions
which a linguistic analysis must meet, and their concentration on
procedures of segmentation and classification and on the development
of abstract units of structure seems to have led structuralists to
assume that if a metalanguage seemed logically coherent, if its
categories were the result of systematic inquiry, whether deductive or

inductive, and if they could be used to describe any plot, then no further justification was required.

But of course there are a great many possible metalanguages which have a certain logical coherence and could be used to describe any text: plots could be analysed in terms of 'successful actions', 'unsuccessful actions' and 'actions which neither succeed nor fail but maintain the story'; or again, in terms of 'actions which destroy equilibrium', 'actions which restore equilibrium', 'actions which seek to destroy equilibrium', and 'actions which seek to restore equilibrium'. Many analogous metalanguages could be invented, and if their categories are sufficiently general it would be difficult to find plots to which they could not be made to apply.

Indeed, the only way to evaluate a theory of plot structure is to determine how far the descriptions which it permits correspond with our intuitive sense of the plots of the stories in question and how far it excludes descriptions which are manifestly wrong. A reader's ability to identify and summarize plots, to group together similar plots, etc., provides a set of facts to be explained; and without this intuitive knowledge, which we display every time we recount or discuss a plot, there is no way of evaluating a theory of plot structure because there is nothing for it to be right or wrong about.

Vladimir Propp, whose pioneering work on the *Morphology of the Folktale* has served as the point of departure for the structuralist study of plot, seems to have grasped the importance of this methodological perspective. The tales he is studying, he argues, have been classed together by investigators because they 'possess a particular construction which is immediately felt and which determines their category, even though we may not be aware of it'. The structure of the tale is 'subconsciously introduced' as the basis of classification and should be made explicit or 'transferred into formal, structural features' (pp. 5–6). He even invokes linguistics to justify his procedure:

> A living language is a concrete fact – grammar is its abstract substratum. These substrata lie at the base of a great many live phenomena; and it is precisely here that science focuses its attention. Not a single concrete fact can be explained without a study of these abstract bases. (p. 14)

The particular analyses suggest that the 'concrete facts' to which he appeals concern the intuitions of readers. Propp's predecessor, Veselovsky, had, in a rudimentary structural analysis, argued that a plot was composed of *motifs*, such as 'a dragon kidnaps the king's daughter'. But, says Propp, this motif can be decomposed into four elements, each of which can be varied without altering the plot. The dragon could be replaced by a witch, a giant, or any other villainous force; the daughter by anything beloved; the king by other fathers or possessors, and kidnapping by any version of disappearance. The claim is that for readers the functional unit of the plot is a paradigm with various members, any of which can be chosen for a particular story, just as the phoneme is a functional unit which can be manifested in various ways in actual utterances. For Propp folktales have two types of component: the first are *roles* which may be filled by a variety of characters, and the second, which constitute the plot, are *functions*.

A function is 'an act of dramatic personae, which is defined from the point of view of its significance for the course of action of the tale as a whole' (p. 20). This definition is the crucial feature of Propp's analysis: he asks what other actions could be substituted for a particular action in a story without altering its role in the tale as a whole, and the general class which subsumes all these actions then serves as the name of the function in question. A function 'cannot be defined apart from its place in the process of narration' because identical actions can have very different roles in two different stories and thus must be subsumed under different functions. The hero could build a huge castle either to fulfil a difficult task that he had been set, or to protect himself from the villain, or to celebrate his marriage with the king's daughter. In each case the action would be commutable with different actions, it would have different relations with those that preceded and followed it, and in short would be an instance of a different function.

Working on a corpus of one hundred tales, Propp isolates thirty-one functions which form an ordered set and whose presence or absence in particular tales may serve as the basis of a classification of plots. Thus, 'four classes are immediately formed': development through struggle and victory, development through the accomplishment of a difficult task, development through both and development through neither (p. 92). But these conclusions bear on the properties of his corpus and are less important for our purposes than the discussions to which his analysis has given rise.

Claude Bremond, in an attack that questions the notion of structure used in Propp's analysis, argues that every function should open a set of alternative consequences. Propp's definition of a function entails 'the impossibility of conceiving that a function can open an alternative: since it is defined by its consequences there is no way in which opposed consequences could result from it' ('Le message narratif', p. 10). When reading a novel we have the impression that at any given moment there are various ways in which the story might continue, and one might suppose that an analysis of plot structure ought to provide a representation of this fact. Moreover, Bremond invokes the linguistic model to support his contention, arguing that Propp is working from the point of view of *parole*, not of *langue*:

> But if we pass from the point of view of speech acts, which use terminal constraints (the end of the sentence determining the choice of the first words), to that of the linguistic system (the beginning of the sentence determining its end), the direction of implication is reversed. We should construct our sequences of functions starting with the *terminus a quo*, which in the general language of plots opens a network of possibilities, and not with the *terminus ad quem*, in respect to which the particular speech acts of Russian tales make their selection from among possibilities. (*ibid.*, p. 15)

Bremond appears to assume that if we think about language as a system then we are aware that the first word of a sentence imposes restrictions on what can follow but leaves open a host of possibilities, whereas if we consider a complete utterance we can say that the first words had to be chosen in order that the particular end might be reached. But whatever truth this view contains, it seems to have little to do with structure. Whether we are speaking of the structure of a sentence or of the structure of a language we will find that relationships of implication among parts of a structure work in both directions. Verbs impose certain restrictions on subjects and objects, objects on verbs, etc. No grammar begins with a list of items which can appear in initial position and then, for each of these, lists all those which may follow it. In fact, far from supporting Bremond's contention, the linguistic analogy indicates that structural analysis bears on reciprocal determination among elements of the sequence as a whole.

The point at issue is a crucial one. For Propp the function of an item is determined by its relation to the rest of the sequence. Functions are not simply actions but the roles actions play in the *récit* as a whole. It is true that if the hero does battle with the villain much of the interest for the reader may depend on the uncertainty of the outcome; but one can say that this is also uncertainty about the function of the struggle. The reader knows its significance and its place in the tale only when he knows the outcome. Bremond argues that this teleological conception of structure is unacceptable; but on the contrary, this is precisely the conception of structure required. 'The essence of every function', says Barthes, 'is, as it were, its seed, what permits it to plant in the tale an element which will ripen later' ('Introduction à l'analyse structurale des récits', p. 7). The plot is subject to teleological determination: certain things happen in order that the *récit* may develop as it does. It is this teleological determination which Genette calls

> that paradoxical logic of fiction which requires one to define
> every element, every unit of the story, by its functional
> qualities, that is to say among other things by its correlation
> with another unit, and to account for the first (in the order of
> narrative time) by the second, and so on. (*Figures II*, p. 94)

The alternative would be an analysis that bore on *actions*, not functions, and tried to specify all the possible consequences of any action. Such a theory would be unable to explain what difference it makes to a story as a whole that an action has one consequence rather than another, for that difference is precisely a change in the function of the first action. One cannot, in short, isolate units of plot without considering the functions they serve. This has been a fundamental feature of the linguistic model and is equally basic to the structural analysis of literature.

Indeed, one could say that the proof of the argument lies in the fact that a theory like Bremond's, which focuses on possible alternatives, would be forced to assign different descriptions to an epic narrative of the adventures of Ulysses, in which the narrator continually mentioned later episodes or the ultimate outcome of the plot, and an account of the same adventures in which there was no narrative anticipation. In the former the range of narrative choice is reduced (if the narrator has announced that Ulysses will reach Ithaca he cannot have Polyphemus kill Ulysses), whereas in the latter there would be many more bifurcations. But by definition the two stories have the same plot. Bremond seems, in fact, to have confused the operations of the hermeneutic code with those of the proairetic code. Elements of the latter must be defined retrospectively, whereas those of the former are recognized prospectively, as a prospect of suspense or mystery. If we say a word about the hermeneutic code we shall be better prepared to return to plot structure proper.

'To make the hermeneutic inventory', Barthes writes, 'will be to distinguish the different formal terms through which an enigma is isolated, posed, formulated, delayed and finally resolved' (*S/Z*, p. 26). Although Barthes concentrates primarily on mysteries, one could bring under this heading anything which, as one goes through the text from beginning to end, seems insufficiently explained, poses problems, arouses a desire to know the truth. This desire acts as a structuring force, leading the reader to look for features which he can organize as partial answers to the questions he has asked, and it is from this point of view that the hermeneutic code is most important. Although a generalized interest or curiosity is thereby excluded – the desire, shall we say, to know what will happen to characters which interest us – this does not seem an unfortunate consequence because in discussing the structure of a story one ought to be able to distinguish the desire to follow the story or to know the end from what we should ordinarily think of as suspense proper, where a specific problem is posed and we read on not simply to learn more but to discover the relevant answer. The desire to see what happens next does not itself act as an important structuring force, whereas the desire to see an enigma or a problem resolved does lead one to organize sequences so as to make them satisfy.

The moments of choice or bifurcation of which Bremond speaks can be thought of as points in the plot when action itself poses a problem of identification and classification. After a severe quarrel hero and heroine may either be reconciled or go their separate ways, and the suspense which the reader might feel at such moments is, structurally, a desire to know whether the quarrel is to be classified as a testing of love or as an end to love. Though the action itself may be presented with all the clarity he could wish, he does not yet know its function in the plot structure. And it is only when the enigma or problem is resolved that he moves from an understanding of action to an understanding or representation of plot.

Barthes does not discuss uncertainties of plot, though they do fall within the scope of the hermeneutic code. He is concerned primarily with mysteries of identity. Titles tend to be enigmas of this kind: it is not until chapter six that we know whether *Middlemarch* is a person, a family, a house, a town or a thematic metaphor. Titles such as *The Wings of the Dove, Intruder in the Dust, Vanity Fair, Tender is the Night* impose a particular kind of attention as we try to determine in what way they apply and to organize the novel in terms of an implied theme. Deictics with unknown references which occur at the beginnings of novels also contribute to a hermeneutic rhythm. Hemingway's 'The Short Happy Life of Francis Macomber' begins with a hermeneutically powerful sentence that poses a number of problems: 'It was now lunch time and they were all sitting under the double green fly of the dining tent pretending that nothing had happened.'

The cases Barthes considers involve for the most part problems to which characters or the narrator draw attention: ' "But who is it? I want to know", she said energetically'; 'No one knew where the Lanty family came from'; or, more subtly, 'Soon the exaggeration natural to people of high society gave birth to and built up the most amusing ideas, the most bizarre statements, the most ridiculous stories about this mysterious character', where the suggestion that such tales need not be taken seriously only heightens the reader's curiosity. The first three constituents of the hermeneutic process are what Barthes calls *la thématisation*, in which the object of the enigma is mentioned, *la position*, an indication that there is indeed a problem or mystery, and *la formulation*, in which it is explicitly stated as an enigma. The third operation may be performed by the text itself or by the reader, but Barthes's suggestion is that to undertake a hermeneutic reading is to bring this model to bear on the text.

The next constituents of the hermeneutic process are more important, for it is here that one follows and is affected by 'the considerable work which discourse must perform if it is to *arrest* the enigma, to keep it open' (*S/Z*, p. 82). Only when a problem is maintained does it become a significant structuring force, making the reader organize the text in relation to it and read sequences in the light of the question which he is attempting to answer. We have, first, the *promesse de réponse*, when the narrator or a character indicates that a reply will be given or that the problem is not insoluble; *le leurre*, a reply which may be strictly true but which is designed to mislead; *l'équivoque*, an ambiguous reply, thickening the mystery and emphasizing its interest; *le blocage*, an admission of defeat, a claim that the mystery is insoluble; *la réponse suspendue*, in which something interrupts a moment of discovery; *la réponse partielle*, in which some truth is learned but mystery remains; and finally *le dévoilement*, which narrator, character or reader accepts as a satisfactory solution (*S/Z*, pp. 91–2 and 215–16).

This is a model of the different roles which readers can give to items in a text once they are involved in a hermeneutic process. It does not go very far towards providing a theory of hermeneutic structures, since it does not specify in detail how items come to be taken as enigmas and thus how the hermeneutic process begins. But Barthes's discussion does at least have the merit of calling our attention to the way in which enigmas lead to a structuring of the text. The dominance of hermeneutic elements gives the detective story its coherence and allows elements of plot, character, description, etc. to be very loosely structured without destroying the unity of the text. Todorov has argued that Henry James's short stories are organized in much the same way: the perpetually deferred reply, the secret which is never revealed, provides a perspective in which the reader can impose an order on heterogeneous elements. Or one might think of the way in which an enigma structures *Oedipus Rex*. 'The Voice of Truth', brought into play by the hermeneutic code, may finally coincide with that of the story itself, but two tales with identical plots could have very different effects if the hermeneutic structures were different.

If Bremond objects to Propp's concentrating on teleologically defined functions instead of empirical actions which could have different consequences, Greimas and Lévi-Strauss argue that Propp is guilty of discovering form 'too close to the level of empirical observation'. Instead of moving from the actions of individual tales to the slightly more abstract names of his thirty-one functions, he should have considered the general structural conditions which a story must fulfil and have stated his functions as manifestations or transformations of more fundamental structures. The class of *récits dramatisés* into which folktales and presumably most novels fall is defined at its most elementary level as a four-term homology in which a temporal opposition (initial situation/final situation) is correlated with a thematic situation (inverted content/resolved content).[7] For a sequence to count as a plot one must be able to isolate not just actions but actions which contribute to a thematic modification. Those aspects of the movement from the initial situation to the final situation which help to produce a contrast between a problem and its resolution are the components of the plot.

All Propp's functions, of course, have a thematic force of this kind, but a set of thirty-one functions cannot but seem an arbitrary array, and it is structurally much more satisfying to the analyst if he can make them transformations of three or four basic elements. In his article 'L'analyse morphologique des contes russes' Lévi-Strauss reduces the number of functions by grouping together those which are logically related ('thus we can treat "violation" as the inverse of "prohibition" and the latter as the negative transformation of "injunction" '), but Greimas, without much explanation, classes together any group of functions for which he can invent a cover term and decides that there are three types of sequences. 'Being unable to undertake exhaustive verifications here, we shall simply say, as a hypothesis, that three types of narrative syntagms can be identified' (*Du Sens*, p. 191). Unfortunately, he does not mention how he would propose to verify this hypothesis nor what claim the hypothesis makes.

The three types of sequence are *les syntagmes performanciels* (relating to the performance of tasks, deeds, etc.), *les syntagmes contractuels*, which direct the situation towards a certain end (one undertakes to do something or refuses to do it), and *les syntagmes disjonctionnels*, which involve movement or displacement of various kinds. The last category is especially fragile and otiose. Although departures and arrivals are of obvious importance, Greimas's theory leads him to produce a homology by opposing 'departure' to 'incognito arrival' and 'arrival' to 'return'. And when he analyses the structure of a particular myth further confusion results: six 'disjunctions' are described as 'departure + movement' (either 'horizontal', 'swift horizontal', 'ascending' or 'descending'), one as a 'negative return' and one as a 'positive return' (*ibid.*, pp. 200–9). It is not clear what such analysis is supposed to achieve. If it represents a claim that direction and speed of movement are more important in determining the function of an incident than the reasons for this movement, then one can only say that the movement of his own thought offers no evidence. If a hero flees the villain horizontally and rapidly, that is rather different from competing in a foot-race, but functionally it is similar to climbing a tree, slowly and vertically, in order to hide and escape.

The *syntagmes performanciels* include the majority of elements which would ordinarily be classified as components of the plot, but there is no attempt to justify either the category itself or its sub-divisions (battles and tests). Yet as Greimas himself is quick to point out, an analysis which transcribes the text according to his meta-language extracts 'only what is *expected* by virtue of knowledge of the formal properties of the narrative model' (*ibid.*, pp. 198–9). The fact that the transcription is much more formal than what we should ourselves offer as a plot summary is not in itself a decisive considera-tion, but it does force us to ask why the model itself should be thought valid.

The only possible answer would be that its categories imply significant hypotheses about narrative structure, but this claim would be difficult to maintain, especially for the first and third category. The second (*syntagmes contractuels*) is more promising: it implies that situations in themselves are not central to the plot but that what we look for are situations which contain an implicit contract or violation of a contract. Most stories, in Greimas's view, move either from a negative to a positive contract (alienation from society to reintegra-tion into society) or from a positive contract to a breaking of that contract. Although this distinction is not easy to make – most novels involve a resolution of some kind, even if it results from the breaking of an implicit contract – it does draw our attention to an important aspect of plot structure which is already adumbrated in the model of narrative as a move from inverted content to resolved content.

In his early work on *Les Liaisons dangereuses* Todorov attempted to use Lévi-Strauss's homological model to describe plot: 'it is postulated that the story represents the syntagmatic projection of a network of paradigmatic relations' and that one must reconstruct this network in the form of a homology of four classes. Although it proved possible to arrange events in four columns such that each column would form a class in the homological structure – after the manner of Lévi-Strauss's analysis of the Oedipus myth – Todorov concluded that 'there was a dangerous margin of arbitrariness' in the process of choosing or describing actions so that they would fit into the structure (*Littérature et signification*, pp. 56–7). This difficulty arises, presumably, because the homological structure, as Lévi-Strauss had then formulated it, took no account of the linear development of the story but assumed that various relationships would be repeated throughout the tale. The plot as a whole would have the same structure as a series of four actions or episodes, or at least the homology representing its structure would have to be so abstract that it could be found repeated in different parts of the story.

In order to retain both the specificity of individual sequences and the forward movement of the plot as a whole, Todorov attempted in his *Grammaire du Décaméron* to develop a metalanguage which could be applied at all levels of generality but which would not compel one to force actions into a particular semantic mould. He isolates three 'primary categories' which he calls 'proper name', 'adjective' and 'verb'. The first represent characters and from the point of view of plot structure are simply subjects of propositions without any internal properties. Adjectives, analogous to Greimas's 'qualifications' and Kristeva's 'qualifying adjuncts', are divided into states (variants of the opposition happy/unhappy), properties (virtues/faults) and conditions (male/female, Jewish/Christian, of high/low birth). There are three types of 'verbs': to modify the situation, to commit a misdeed of some kind and to punish. In addition, any proposition will be in one of five modes: the indicative (actions which really took place), the 'obligatory' ('a codified, collective will which constitutes the law of a society'), the optative (what characters would like to have happen), the conditional (if you do X I shall do Y) and the predictive (in certain circumstances X will occur) (pp. 27–49).

The reasons for choosing such categories are presumably that Todorov wishes to take his linguistic model seriously in writing a 'grammar of narrative' and that categories based on the canonical sentence can be used to rewrite both sentences of the text itself and sentences of the plot summary. He observes that 'the structures remain the same whatever the level of abstraction' (p. 19), but this is true only because descriptions at every level involve sentences and hence predicates. There are no indications of how the reader moves from sentences containing adjectives and verbs to plot summaries in which whole sequences are represented by adjectives or verbs. The fact that the same categories are used at both levels makes a connection between them without elucidating the process of synthesis.

What claims can be made for such a metalanguage? Todorov suggests that by connecting narrative structure with linguistic structure his categories can help us to understand the nature of narration: 'on comprendra mieux le récit si l'on sait que le personnage est un nom, l'action un verbe' (we shall understand narrative better if we know that a character is a proper name and action a verb) (p. 84). But the similarity between verb and action is quite obvious and cannot constitute the justification for a metalanguage; nor can Todorov's half-hearted attempts to argue that his categories must be valid because they are drawn from 'universal grammar' (pp. 14–17).

If his metalanguage is to be justified it will be by the intuitive validity of the distinctions which its categories imply and of the groupings of plot which they establish. First of all, the division of verbs into three classes suggests that there are two types of plot: those which involve modification of the situation and those in which there is transgression and punishment (or lack of punishment); but one fails to see why the latter should be singled out as a special case. Why not allow as separate types sequences involving a quest or a decision which must be made? In view of this anomaly John Rutherford has proposed that transgression and punishment be omitted and that guilt resulting from transgression be treated as an adjectival predicate (to commit a crime is to modify a situation and change the adjectives which describe one's state).[8] This is no doubt an improvement but it reduces the claims which the theory makes. The constitutive feature of a plot is now the modification of a situation – a claim that has not been seriously questioned since Aristotle first enunciated it – and the attributes or qualities involved in the plot are those which are modified by the central action. This seems a valid, if modest, claim: when reading a novel or short story we can produce a series of adjectives which apply to main characters, but until something takes place which signals the actual or prospective modification of one of these attributes we do not know which are pertinent to the plot.

A stronger and more questionable claim made by the system of categories bears on the changes that would be required for a story to pass from one plot structure to another. In one of Boccaccio's tales Peronella hears her husband returning and has her lover hide in a barrel. She tells her husband that he is a prospective buyer who is inspecting the barrel, and while the husband cleans the barrel they continue their dalliance. Todorov's transcription of this plot can be translated as follows: 'X commits a misdeed and the socially required consequence is that Y should punish X; but X desires to avoid punishment and therefore acts to modify the situation, with the result that Y believes her not to have committed a crime and consequently does not punish her though she continues her original action' (p. 63). By Todorov's theory the plot structure is not affected by the way in which Peronella acts to modify the situation. The story would have the same structure if she had used no ruse and had simply told her lover to go away and come back later. If this seems unsatisfactory it is because our cultural models make 'ruse' or 'deception' a basic structural device in narration (stories which involve ruses are thought to differ from those that do not) and we should like to see this fact represented. Note, however, that by Todorov's theory the structure of the story would be altered if Peronella had predicted to her lover when hiding him in the barrel that she could make her husband believe that he was a customer. If the reader feels that this change alters the plot structure less than the change involved in sending the lover away and employing no ruse, he is implicitly questioning the theory carried by Todorov's metalanguage.

Similarly, Todorov is obliged to assign the same structural description to a story in which X finds his friend Y dilatory and upbraids him so tellingly that he reforms and to another story in which X falls in love with Y's wife and seduces her. In the first case X acts to modify an attribute and succeeds; in the second case, 'the attribute in question is the state of sexual relationship in which they find themselves' (he desires that she change the attribute of not being his lover and succeeds in bringing about this modification). Once again we have the curious situation in which the second tale is given the same structure as the first and distinguished from a third tale in which X falls in love with Y's wife, predicts to a friend that he can seduce her and does seduce her. These results are due to the ubiquity of the type A verb: anything which modifies a situation will receive the same structural description, so that the main differences in plot structure which the theory identifies are those due to changes in mode. As Claude Bremond observes, 'we should like to think that the so-called semantic contents of the verb A are only the provisional substitutes for syntactic functions that must be identified', and that further work will enable one to differentiate plots in which situations are modified in radically different ways.[9]

The basic problem seems to be that Todorov has not considered what facts his theory is supposed to account for and so has not considered the adequacy of the implicit groupings which it establishes. He thinks of his grammar as the result of careful study of a corpus and hence as a description of that corpus but has not endeavoured to show why this description should be preferable to others. His neglect of the reading process in which plots are recognized and synthesized leaves him with nothing to explain. But at least his categories are sufficiently well defined that one can actually apply them and see what consequences they have, which is something that cannot be said of many other theories.

Kristeva's approach to the description of plot in *Le Texte du roman* begins in a similar way by taking its basic categories from linguistics. Narrative sequences, she argues, are analogous to nominal and verbal syntagms in the canonical sentence, and therefore the primary categories are verb (predicative adjunct), adjective (qualifying adjunct), 'identifier' (a spatial, temporal or modal indicator attached to a predicate) and subject or 'actant'. With these categories she constructs what she calls 'the applicational model for the generation of classes of narrative complexes in the sequential structure of the novel' (le modèle applicatif de la génération des complexes narratifs en classes narratives dans la structure phrastique du roman) (pp. 129–30). The model generates structural descriptions through recursive operations of combination. There must be at least one verb, but otherwise the grammar combines terms with complete freedom: any number of verbs may occur; any number of adjectives, with or without identifiers, may occur at any point in the sequence; and identifiers may, without restriction on number, be attached to verbs and adjectives. Needless to say, the model does not constitute a strong hypothesis about the structure of the novel.

Kristeva argues that her model establishes a typology of eight different structures, but in fact almost all *récits* will belong to her first type: a series of actions and qualifications with some spatial, temporal and modal identifiers. One might conceivably find instances of her third type (containing only a character and actions), her fourth type (which contains but a single action in addition to qualifications and identifiers), or her sixth type (which consists only of actions performed by various characters), though these would be oddities and exceptions rather than major forms of narrative prose. But the other four types seem impossible rather than simply odd. In types two and five adjectives have no identifiers, but of course even the most neutral presentation ('the tall man . . .') provides modal identification (he *is* tall). In types seven and eight there are no characters, just actions with or without identifiers, and this would seem to take us out of the realm of narrative fiction altogether (p. 132). It is, in fact, extremely difficult to draw any significant hypotheses from Kristeva's model. The categories do not themselves establish pertinent groupings of plots and there is no attempt to justify them except by reference to a linguistic model. And of course Kristeva has replaced the syntactic constraints and structures of language with free combination of elements. Her assumption appears to have been that if all sequences can be described in a metalanguage drawn from linguistics, then perforce the descriptions and the metalanguage must be of some interest and value, but her example alone would suffice to show that this is not the case.

If both Greimas's and Lévi-Strauss's attempts to work downwards from a four-term homology and Todorov's and Kristeva's attempts to work upwards from constituents of the sentence seem inadequate as models of plot structure, what kind of approach should be favoured? If it is to achieve even rudimentary adequacy it must take account of the process of reading so that, rather than leaving the gaps found in Greimas's and Todorov's approaches, it provides some explanation of the way in which plots are built up from the actions and incidents that the reader encounters. It must, that is to say, consider what kind of facts it is attempting to explain. For example, in Joyce's 'Eveline', a story from *Dubliners* which Seymour Chatman has tried to analyse in structuralist terms, we can give a hierarchy of appropriate plot-summaries:

(1) Eveline is supposed to elope and begin a new life but at the last minute refuses.
(2) Having decided to elope with Frank and begin a new life, Eveline muses on her past and present, wondering whether she should go through with it. She decides to go but at the last moment changes her mind.
(3) Eveline has agreed to elope to Argentina with Frank and start a new life, but on the afternoon of her departure she sits by the window looking out on the street where she has always lived, weighing her happy memories of childhood, her sense of attachment and her duty to her family against her father's present brutality, her attraction to Frank and the new life he will give her. She decides that she must escape and will elope, but when she is about to board the ship with him she has a violent, almost physical, reaction and refuses to go.

One could obviously quarrel with details in these summaries, but they would be generally acceptable as accounts of the plot. To reach these summaries we exclude a great many things, and there would be considerable agreement about what should be excluded. For example, in the second paragraph we are told 'The man out of the last house passed on his way home.' This is an action but it would be excluded from any account of the plot. And the reason is simply that it has no consequences. When we read the story for the first time we do not know what role to assign this phrase, but when in the next few sentences no further mention is made of the man we decide that it is not itself an element of the plot but only an illustration of Eveline's desultory observation which will become part of the plot under some heading such as 'musing'.

In his 'Introduction à l'analyse structurale des récits' Barthes distinguishes between 'kernels' which link up with one another to form plot and 'catalysts' or 'satellites' which are attached to kernels but do not themselves establish sequences. This distinction will serve as a representation of part of the reading process if we qualify it in two ways. First of all, kernels and satellites are not necessarily separate phrases in the text. The kernel may well be an abstraction manifested by a series of phrases which may be considered its satellites. Seymour Chatman takes the phrase 'One time there used to be a field there in which' as the second kernel of 'Eveline', but this phrase does not itself belong in the sequence of action; it is simply a manifestation of the kernel 'musing'.[10] Second, kernel and satellite are purely relational terms: what is a kernel at one level of plot structure will become a satellite at another, and a sequence of kernels may itself be taken up by a thematic unit. When Eveline remembers what she and Frank did when they were courting, these actions, though they can be organized as kernels and satellites, are manifestations of a larger unit which we can call something like 'happy courtship' and which, at another level, becomes part of the thematic unit, 'positive qualities of life with Frank'.

What governs this process of identifying kernels and satellites? In *S/Z* Barthes looks to cultural models for an answer:

> Whoever reads the text collects bits of information under the generic names of actions (Walk, Assassination, Rendez-vous), and it is this name which creates the sequence. The sequence comes to exist only at the moment when and because one can name it; it develops according to the rhythm of this naming process, which seeks and confirms. (p. 26)

At the lowest level we can say that when Balzac's narrator brings Sarrasine to an 'orgy', he alerts the reader to the fact that the following sequence is to be read in terms of a model of the orgy, whose moments or elements will be illustrated metonymically by a series of actions: a girl spills wine, a man falls asleep, jokes, blasphemies, curses are uttered; and the syntagmatic operations which produce the series are taken up by a paradigmatic process which gives constituents meaning at the level of the cultural model (*S/Z*, p. 163).

Propp seems to have recognized the importance of such cultural stereotypes in giving so many of his functions names which already figured in the experience of readers (Struggle with the villain, Rescue of the hero, Punishment of the villain, Difficult task, etc.). Though Bremond claims that 'the task, the contract, the error, the trap, etc., are universal categories' used to identify plots in narrative, one could also say that novels themselves have contributed substantially to our sense of the significant events in people's lives – the events powerful enough to constitute a story. And thus the opening sequence of 'Eveline', 'She sat at the window watching the evening invade the avenue. Her head was leaned against the window curtains, and in her nostrils was the odour of dusty cretonne', forces us to wait for something that will give us a clue as to the appropriate name. Is she 'waiting' for something in particular? Is she 'refusing' to do something? Is she 'thinking' or 'making a decision'? Our cultural models are there waiting, but we do not yet know which aspects to draw upon.

'What do we know of proairetic sequences?' asks Barthes at the end of *S/Z*:

> that they are born of a certain power of reading, which seeks to name with a sufficiently transcendent term a sequence of actions, which have themselves issued from a patrimony of human experience; that the typology of these proairetic units seems uncertain, or at least that we can give them no other logic than that of the probable, of the organized world, of the *already-done* or *already-written*; for the number and order of terms are variable, some deriving from a practical store of trivial and ordinary behaviour (to knock at a door, to arrange a meeting), and others taken from a written corpus of novelistic models. (p. 209)

But one need not abdicate so soon and leave the model in this atomistic state, for in choosing which names to apply the reader is guided by structural goals which give him a sense of what he is moving towards. In the case of 'Eveline', for example, after identifying the first kernel, 'musing', we await a structurally more important kernel, for we know that musing itself will not found a story but must be related to a central problem, decision or action on which the character is musing. And when we encounter the sequence, 'She had consented to go away, to leave home. Was that wise?', we can allow this question to serve as the major structuring device. The musings and reminiscences which precede and follow are organized according to their bearing on the question, and our sense of what might serve as a completed structure makes us await both an answer to the question and an act which carries out the decision. Once we have identified the dominant structure of the *récit*, we know how to deal with whatever kernels and satellites we then postulate. They illustrate what Greimas would call the movement from inverted content to resolved content, from one contract to another: Eveline's agreement to elope with Frank, which negates her contract with her mother, is affirmed by a decision but broken by the final action which restores the former contract.

The goals towards which one moves in synthesizing a plot are, of course, notions of thematic structures. If we say that the hierarchy of kernels is governed by the reader's desire to reach a level of organization at which the plot as a whole is grasped in a satisfying form, and if we take that form to be what Greimas and Lévi-Strauss call the four-term homology, Todorov the modification of a situation, and Kristeva the transformation, we have at least a general principle whose effects at lower levels can be traced. The reader must organize the plot as a passage from one state to another and this passage or movement must be such that it serves as a representation of theme. The end must be made a transformation of the beginning so that meaning can be drawn from the perception of resemblance and difference. And this imposes constraints on the way in which one names beginning and end. One can attempt to establish a coherent causal series, in which disparate incidents are read as stages towards a goal, or a dialectical movement in which incidents are related as contraries whose opposition carries the problem that must be resolved. And these same constraints apply at lower levels of structure. In composing an initial and a final state the reader will draw on a series of actions which he can organize in a causal sequence, so that what is named as the state which the larger thematic structure requires is itself a logical development, or he may read a series of incidents as illustrations of a common condition which serves as initial or final state in the overall structure.

In attempting to specify the thematic forms which govern the organization of plots at their most abstract levels one would be able to draw upon a theory of archetypal or canonical plots, such as Northrop Frye's. His four *mythoi* – of Spring, Summer, Autumn and Winter – are simultaneously stereotyped plots and thematic structures or visions of the world. To the *mythos* of spring corresponds the comic plot of love triumphant: a restrictive society poses obstacles but these are overcome and one passes into a new and integrated state of society. The tragic plots of autumn involve a negative alteration of contract: obstacles triumph, opponents (whether human, natural or divine) gain their revenge, and if there is reconciliation or reintegration it is in a sacrificial mode or in another world. The *mythos* of summer has as its favoured plot the romance of the quest, with its perilous journey, the crucial struggle and the exaltation of the hero; and the *mythos* of winter reverses in an ironic mode the plot of romance: quests prove unsuccessful, society is not transformed and the hero must learn that there is no escape from the world except through death or madness (*Anatomy of Criticism*, pp. 158–239). Forms of this kind serve as models which help readers to identify and organize plots: the sense of what will constitute a tragedy or a comedy enables one to name kernels so as to make them thematically relevant.

If structuralists were to undertake investigations of these problems they would find a distinguished predecessor in the Russian formalist

Victor Shklovsky, who is one of the few to have realized that study of 'La construction de la nouvelle et du roman' should be an attempt to explicate the structural intuitions of readers by studying their formal expectations. What do we require, he asks, in order to feel that a story is completed? In some cases we feel that a story has not really ended; what is responsible for this impression? What kind of structure satisfies our formal expectations? (pp. 170–1). Shklovsky investigates some of the types of parallelism which seem to produce structurally satisfying plots: the move from one relationship between characters to its opposite, from a prediction or fear to a realization of that prediction, from a problem to its solution, from a false accusation or misrepresentation of the situation to a rectification. But his most interesting conclusions bear on the episodic novel and its possible endings. Generally what is required is an epilogue which, by differentiating itself from the series, closes the series and shows us how to read it. A description of the hero's situation ten years later will show us whether the series is to be read as steps in his decline, in his loss of illusion, in his coming to terms with his mediocrity, etc. But there is also what Shklovsky calls the 'illusory ending' – an extreme case which nicely illustrates the power of readers' formal expectations and the ingenuity that will be used to produce a sense of completion. 'Usually it is descriptions of nature or of the weather that furnish material for these illusory endings. . . . This new motif is inscribed as a parallel to the preceding story, thanks to which the tale seems completed' (pp. 176–7).

A description of the weather can provide a satisfactory conclusion because the reader gives it a metaphoric or synecdochic interpretation and then reads this thematic statement against the actions themselves. By way of example, Shklovsky cites a brief passage from *Le Diable boiteux* in which a passer-by, stopping to help a man mortally wounded in a fight, is himself arrested. 'I ask the reader to invent even a description of the night in Seville or of the indifferent sky and to add it on' (p. 177). And certainly he is right; such a description would give the story a satisfactory structure because the indifferent sky presents a thematic image which can be read as identifying and confirming the role of the preceding event in the plot. By confirming the irony of the story, it isolates, as the dominant structure of the plot, the ironic movement of the action.

Shklovsky seems to have realized that the analysis of plot structure ought to be a study of the structuring process by which plots take shape, and he knew that one of the best ways of discovering what norms are at work was to alter the text and consider how its effect is changed. The analyst of narrative, Barthes has observed, must be able to imagine 'counter-texts', possible aberrations of the text, whatever would be scandalous in the narration ('L'analyse structurale du récit', p. 23). This would help him to identify the functional norms. The analyst's task, then, is not to develop a taxonomy of plots or new metalanguages for their transcription, for there are an infinite number of such taxonomies and metalanguages. He must attempt, as Barthes says, to explicate 'the metalanguage within the reader himself', 'the language of plot which is within us' ('Introduction à l'analyse structurale des récits', p. 14).

Theme and symbol

Structuralists have not made theme a separate object of investigation. The reason may be quite simply that theme is not the result of a specific set of elements but rather the name we give to the forms of unity which we can discern in the text or to the ways we succeed in making various codes come together and cohere. The ultimate structures of the proairetic code, as Greimas and Lévi-Strauss's model makes clear, are thematic, and we could say that plot is but the temporal projection of thematic structures. Men are born, live and die *in mediis rebus*; 'to make sense of their span they need fictive concords with origins and ends' (Kermode, *The Sense of an Ending*, p. 7). To work something out one makes it into a story so that its parts may be disposed in orderly sequence. This temporal structure brings into play a kind of intelligibility which is essential to the workings of the novel: by theme we do not usually mean a general law which the novel proposes or the kind of knowledge which would permit us to predict what will happen in situations like those presented. To grasp the theme of a novel is, as W. B. Gallie stresses in another context, to have followed the story. Following a story is not like following an argument: successful following does not entail the ability to predict the deductive conclusion but only a sense of its rightness and acceptability, a sense of 'the main bond of logical continuity' which makes its elements intelligible.[11]

But producing unity, resolution, continuity is a matter of extrapolating from elements of the text, assigning them a general function. What does it mean for Louisa in *Hard Times* to be caught peering through a knothole at the horse-riding? That depends on what we take the latter to represent and how we characterize the ethos of the Gradgrinds: she is clearly deviating from her father's law, but is she guilty simply of curiosity or of curiosity about particular objects? What does Fanny Assingham's smashing of the golden bowl – one of the rare events in *The Golden Bowl* – signify? Again it is a matter of generalizing the function of the bowl so that we can apply to the event some of the names which Maggie, Fanny and the Prince refrain from employing. The problem of thematic extrapolation is very closely related to that of symbolic reading: by what logic can we generalize from object or event and make it signify?

The conventions of novel-reading provide two basic operations which might be called *empirical* and *symbolic recuperation*. The former is based on causal extrapolation: if a character's elegant dress is described we may call upon stereotyped models of personality and say that if he is so dressed it is *because* he is a fop or a dandy and establish a sign relation between the description and this latter meaning. Though such extrapolation works better in novels than in other modes of experience because we approach the text with the assumption than anything noted is probably notable and significant, meanings derived from causal connections are less obviously conventional and more difficult to study than those produced by symbolic recuperation. This process operates where causal connections are absent or where those which could be called upon seem insufficient to account for the stress which an object or event receives in the text, or even when we do not know what else to do with a detail. We would presumably be unwilling to assume a causal connection between a perfect or blemished complexion and a perfect or blemished moral character, but the symbolic code permits such associations and enables us to take the former as sign of the latter. Or again, there is no causal connection between moustaches and villainy but the symbolic code permits us to establish a sign relation.

Such extrapolations are extremely curious, especially since symbolic reading is not free association but a rule-governed process whose limits are extremely difficult to establish. Awkwardness in dealing with symbols is one of the clearest marks of the weak undergraduate essay, but few have made much progress in explaining what the reader must learn if he is to accede to grace. Structuralists have not succeeded in accounting for the distinction between acceptable and unacceptable symbolic readings, but Barthes's work on the symbolic code does offer some suggestions about the basic mechanisms of this kind of recuperation.

The formal device on which the symbolic code is based is antithesis. If the text presents two items – characters, situations, objects, actions – in a way which suggests opposition, then 'a whole space of substitution and variation' is opened to the reader (Barthes, *S/Z*, p. 24). The presentation of two heroines, one dark and the other fair, sets in motion an experiment in extrapolation in which the reader correlates this opposition with thematic oppositions that it might manifest: evil/good, forbidden/permitted, active/passive, Latin/Nordic, sexuality/purity. The reader can pass from one opposition to another, trying them out, even inverting them, and determining which are pertinent to larger thematic structures which encompass other antitheses presented in the text. Thus, the first manifestation of the symbolic code in *Sarrasine* finds the narrator seated in a window with an elegant party on his one hand and a garden on the other. The opposition, as so often in Balzac, is explicitly developed in various ways, as the narrator traces possible symbolic readings: dance of death/dance of life, nature/man, cold/hot, silence/noise. The narrator himself becomes the focal point of the antithesis, and his position in the window is read as one of fundamental ambiguity, dangerous detachment: 'Indeed my leg was chilled by one of those draughts which freeze half your body while the other feels the damp heat of the salon' (*ibid.*, p. 33).

The oppositions suggested in this passage are retained and put to use in the next major instance of the symbolic code, the contrast between a withered old man and a beautiful young woman: 'related to the antithesis of interior and exterior, of hot and cold, of life and death, the old man and young woman are by right separated by the most inflexible of barriers: that of meaning' (*ibid.*, p. 71). Seated beside one another, they present a symbolic condensation ('it was indeed life and death'), but when the young woman reaches out and touches the old man this is 'the paroxysm of transgression'. Her fascination and repulsion, her excessive reaction when she touches him, indicates a 'barrier of meaning', underlines the importance of exclusive opposition, and requires the reader to undertake a symbolic reading which exploits the opposition and gives it a place in a larger symbolic structure.

To interpret an opposition is, of course, to produce what Greimas calls the elementary structure of meaning: a four-term homology. But the process need not stop there, as the second pair of terms can serve as the point of departure for further extrapolation. It is striking how little of the original content need be preserved in these semantic transformations. Lévi-Strauss has argued from his vast corpus of myths that although sun and moon cannot by themselves be used to signify anything whatsoever, so long as they are placed in opposition there no limits to the other contrasts which they may express (though of course the range of possible meanings in a given text will be severely restricted) ('Le sexe des astres', p. 1168). In novels most symbolic operations follow the models of metonymy or synecdoche – extrapolation by contiguity or by association is the form of symbolic recuperation that is most closely related to empirical recuperation – but one also finds instances of the peculiar symbolic transference which Lévi-Strauss has studied, in which two terms brought together by some quality which they share are then opposed and made to signify the presence and absence of that quality. Roasting and boiling are both forms of cooking and hence cultural, but the opposition between them (direct exposure to the fire versus exposure mediated by a cultural object, the pot) can be used to manifest, within the cultural system itself, the contrast between culture and nature.[12] The young woman and the old man in *Sarrasine* are both living human beings, but this semantic feature which brings them together, may, perhaps because it is already 'in the air', become one side of the contrast when they are opposed: life and death. Two men, if opposed to one another, may carry the contrast between masculine and feminine or between the human and the animal. Such semantic operations are extremely curious and would no doubt repay further study.

Lévi-Strauss's study of codes suggests that symbolic interpretation is a matter of moving from the antitheses in the text to the more basic oppositions of other social, psychological or cosmic codes. The crucial question would then become, what is meant by 'more basic'? Towards what does symbolic interpretation proceed? What are the constraints on the kind of meaning one is willing to attribute to symbols? Barthes speaks of meaning as

> a force which tries to subjugate other forces, other meanings, other languages. The force of meaning depends on its degree of systematization: the most powerful meaning is that whose system takes in the greatest number of elements, to the point where it seems to encompass everything notable in the semantic universe. (*S/Z*, p. 160)

Weaker meanings must give way to stronger, more abstract meanings which cover more of the experience captured in the text. Barthes suggests that the source of this power – that towards which symbolic interpretation moves – is the human body: 'the symbolic field is occupied by a single object, from which it derives its unity (and from which we derive the ability to name . . .). This object is the human body' (*S/Z*, p. 220). The body is the locus of desire, and to make it the main occupant of the symbolic field would be to privilege certain psychoanalytic interpretations. But in fact, in *S/Z*, as in *Le Plaisir du texte*, Barthes uses the body and sexuality as metaphors for a variety of symbolic forces. The text is erotic in that it involves and tantalizes. Its ultimate appeal is that of an object which draws and escapes my desire. And to make the body the centre of the symbolic field is only to say it is an image of the force which ultimately subjugates other meanings. Even in *Sarrasine*, where castration is an explicit theme, Barthes does not allow the body as such to dominate the thematic structure but makes it one of a number of codes in which is represented the danger of destroying distinctions on which the functioning of various economies (linguistic, sexual, monetary) depends (*S/Z*, pp. 221–2).

But if we cannot say that symbolic interpretation always moves towards the body, there are none the less intuitive constraints on the kind of meaning one is willing to attribute to symbols. If someone were to interpret the contrast between ball and garden in the opening lines of *Sarrasine* as an opposition between hot and cold, this would be unsatisfying: not, of course, because the correlation is invalid but because such an interpretation is not rich enough to count as a proper configuration of the *champ symbolique*. We should want to say 'why *hot* and *cold*?' and to go on from there to something like human passion and its absence, life and death, man and nature, in order to meet the demands of symbolic force. A temerarious critic who wished to try to state these demands might adapt the conclusions which Todorov reaches in his *Introduction à la littérature fantastique*, where, grouping together the themes he has observed, he distinguishes 'themes of the *I*', which concern 'the relation between man and the world, the system of perception and knowledge', and 'themes of the *you*', which concern 'man's relation to his desire, and thus to his unconscious' (p. 146). The significance of these categories lies in the assumptions which must underlie them: that at their most basic level literary themes can always be stated in these terms, as notions of the individual's relation to the world and to himself. And the corresponding assumption would be that our sense of when to stop in generalizing from symbols is determined by our knowledge of structures and elements which fall within this general paradigm and which therefore are worthy to play the role of *symbolisés* to symbols. This might explain why Greimas speaks of symbolic interpretation as a process of constructing 'axiological sememes . . . such as *euphoria of heights* and *dysphoria of depths*', for the most general thematic relation between consciousness and its objects is one of attraction or rejection and the primary evaluative experiences, which fall also within the domain of the body, are those of happiness and unhappiness. Barbara Smith has shown how 'allusions to any of the "natural" stopping places of our lives and experiences – sleep, death, winter, and so forth – tend to give closural force when they appear as terminal features in a poem' (*Poetic Closure*, p. 102). It seems likely that an analogous set of primary human experiences serve as conventional stopping points for the process of symbolic or thematic interpretation.

Barthes puts it the other way around: once the process of extrapolation and naming stops, a level of definitive commentary is created, the work is closed or rounded off, and the language in which semantic transformations terminate becomes 'natural': the truth or the secret of the work (*S/Z*, p. 100). We have discovered, as the unfortunate critical parlance has it, what the work is 'really about'. Sometimes, of course, the work itself tells us where to stop, closes itself by offering a definitive commentary on its theme, but even then we need not accept that stopping place and may go on to reach others which our conventions of reading provide. It may well be that we stop when we feel we have reached the truth or the place of maximum force and not, as Barthes suggests, that wherever we stop becomes the place of truth; though of course the alternatives are not mutually exclusive.

Many works challenge this process of naturalization, prevent us from feeling that the pursuit of symbolic readings is eminently natural. Although such works are of two very different kinds, both might be called allegorical rather than symbolic. Allegory is generally thought of as a form which demands commentary and goes some way toward providing its own, but as Coleridge recognized in his famous definition, it also stresses the artificiality of commentary, the difference between apparent and ultimate meaning:[13]

> We may thus safely define allegoric writing as the employment
> of one set of agents and images with actions and
> accompaniments correspondent, so as to convey, while in
> disguise, either moral qualities or conceptions of the mind that
> are not in themselves objects of the senses, or other images,
> agents, actions, fortunes, and circumstances, so that the
> difference is everywhere presented to the eye or imagination
> while the likeness is suggested to the mind.

In the symbolic text the process of interpretation is made to seem natural. The general, as Goethe said in distinguishing between the symbolic and the allegorical, is made to inhere in the particular so that we appreciate its force and significance without leaving the plane of particulars and thus experience through literature, as apologists for the symbol do not tire of telling us, an organic unity or harmony seldom found in the world: a fusion of the concrete and the abstract, of the appearance and the reality, of form and meaning. The symbol is supposed to contain in itself all the meaning we produce in our semantic transformations. It is a natural sign in which *signifiant* and *signifié* are indissolubly fused, not an arbitrary or conventional sign in which they are linked by human authority or habit. Allegory, on the other hand, stresses the difference between levels, flaunts the gap we must leap to produce meaning, and thus displays the activity of interpretation in all its conventionality. Either it presents an empirical story which does not itself seem a worthy object of attention and implies that we must, in order to produce types of significance that tradition leads us to desire, translate the story into another mode, or else it presents an enigmatic face while posing obstacles even to this kind of translation and forces us to read it as an allegory of the interpretive process. The first type runs from the parable, its simplest version, to the complex extended allegories of Dante, Spenser, Blake, but in each case the proper level of interpretation is identified and justified by an external authority: our knowledge of Christian themes or of Blake's vision enables us to identify satisfying allegorical meanings. The second type occurs when external authorities are weak or when we do not know which should apply. If the work makes sense it will be as an allegory, but we cannot discover a level at which interpretation may rest and thus are left with a work which, like *Finnegans Wake*, *Locus Solus* or even Flaubert's *Salammbô*, flaunts the difference between signifier and signified and seems to take as its implicit theme the difficulties or the factitiousness of interpretation.[14] Allegory, one might say, is the mode which recognizes the impossibility of fusing the empirical and the eternal and thus demystifies the symbolic relation by stressing the separateness of the two levels, the impossibility of bringing them together except momentarily and against a background of disassociation, and the importance of protecting each level and the potential link between them by making it arbitrary. Only allegory can make the connection in a self-conscious and demystified way.

Character

Character is the major aspect of the novel to which structuralism has paid least attention and has been least successful in treating. Although for many readers character serves as the major totalizing force in fiction – everything in the novel exists in order to illustrate character and its development – a structuralist approach has tended to explain this as an ideological prejudice rather than to study it as a fact of reading.

The reasons are not far to seek. On the one hand, the general ethos of structuralism runs counter to the notions of individuality and rich psychological coherence which are often applied to the novel. Stress on the interpersonal and conventional systems which traverse the individual, which make him a space in which forces and events meet rather than an individuated essence, leads to a rejection of a prevalent conception of character in the novel: that the most successful and 'living' characters are richly delineated autonomous wholes, clearly distinguished from others by physical and psychological characteristics. This notion of character, structuralists would say, is a myth.

On the other hand, that argument is often conflated with a

historical distinction. If, as Foucault says, man is simply a fold in our knowledge who will disappear in his present form as soon as the configuration of knowledge changes, it is scarcely surprising that a movement which claims to have participated in this change should view the notion of the rich and autonomous character as the recuperative strategy of another age. Characters in Virginia Woolf, in Faulkner, in Nathalie Sarraute and Robbe-Grillet, cannot be treated according to nineteenth-century models; they are nodes in the verbal structure of the work, whose identity is relatively precarious.

Each of these arguments makes a valid point, but it is perhaps important to keep them separate lest this validity be obscured. There has been a change in novels, with which both the theory and practice of reading must come to terms. The expectations and procedures of assimilation appropriate to nineteenth-century novels with their individuated psychological essences fail before the faceless protagonists of modern fiction or the picaresque heroes of earlier novels. But as is shown by the polemic against the 'Balzacian' novel, carried out with such spirit by Sarraute and Robbe-Grillet, the effect of these modern texts with their relatively anonymous heroes depends on the traditional expectations concerning character which the novel exposes and undermines. What one might call the 'pronominal heroes' of Sarraute's *Les Fruits d'or* or Sollers's *Nombres* function not as portraits but as labels which, in their refusal to become full characters, imply a critique of conceptions of personality. In Sarraute's *Martereau*, for example, the eponymous hero begins as a solid presence, but as the novel progresses 'the firm outline of his character begins to blur until he too flows into the same sea of anonymity as the others . . . The dissolution of Martereau is the essence of the novel: the arabesque of individuality is discarded before the very eyes of the reader to make way for, on Nathalie Sarraute's terms, the more profoundly realistic study of the impersonal life' (Heath, *The Nouveau Roman*, p. 52).

Once equipped with this historical distinction between ways of treating character, we can read many earlier novels in a different way. Although it is possible to treat *L'Education sentimentale* as a study in character, to place Frédéric Moreau at the centre and to infer from the rest of the novel a rich psychological portrait, we are now at least in a position to ask whether this is the best way to proceed. When we approach the novel in this way, we find, as Henry James complained, an absence or emptiness at the centre. The novel does not simply portray a banal personality but shows a marked lack of interest in what we might expect to be the most important questions: what is the precise quality and value of Frédéric's love for Mme Arnoux? for Rosanette? for Mme Dambreuse? What is learned and what is missed in his sentimental education? We can, as readers and critics, supply answers to these questions, and this is certainly what traditional models of character enjoin us to do. But if we do so we commit ourselves to naturalizing the text and to ignoring or reducing the strangeness of its gaps and silences.[15]

If structuralism's historical distinction is valuable, its general critique of the notion of character also has the virtue of making us rethink the notion of rich and 'life-like' characters which has played so important a role in criticism. By arguing that the most fully drawn and individuated characters are not in fact the most realistic, the structuralist challenges that defence of the traditional novel which relies on notions of truthfulness and empirical distinctiveness. Once we doubt that the most vivid and detailed portraits are the most life-like, we must consider other possible justifications and are in a better position to study the inevitable artifice in the construction of characters. 'The character we admire as the result of loving attention is something constructed by conventions as arbitrary as any other, and we can only hope to recover an art by recognizing it as art' (Price, 'The Other Self', p. 293).

A discussion of the conventional basis of characterization would focus on the fact that 'the dimensions of character the novelist presents are determined by something more than his love for the reality of other persons' (*ibid.*, p. 297). What we are told about characters differs greatly from one novelist to another, and though it is no doubt crucial to the impression of *vraisemblance* that we feel other details could have been supplied, we must read a novel on the assumption that we have been told all that we need to know: that significance inheres at precisely those levels where the novelist concentrates. When we go beyond the notion of verisimilitude, we are in a position to take as a major source of interest the production of characters. What system of conventions determines the notions of fullness and completeness operative in a given novel or type of novel and governs the selection and organization of details?

Structuralists have not done much work on the conventional models of character used in different novels. They have been more concerned to develop and refine Propp's theory of the roles or functions that characters may assume. 'Anxious not to define character in terms of psychological essences, structural analysis has so far attempted, through various hypotheses, to define the character as a "participant" rather than as a "being".'[16] But this may well be a case of moving too readily from one extreme to another, for the roles proposed are so reductive and so directly dependent on plot that they leave us with an immense residue, whose organization structural analysis should attempt to explain rather than ignore.

Propp isolated seven roles assumed by characters in the folktale: the villain, the helper, the donor (provider of magical agents), the sought-for-person and her father, the dispatcher (who sends the hero forth on his adventures), the hero and the false hero. He made no claims for the universality of this set of roles, but Greimas has taken his hypothesis as evidence that 'a small number of actantial terms suffices to account for the organization of a micro-universe'. Undertaking to provide a set of universal roles or *actants*, Greimas extrapolates from his account of sentence structure to produce an actantial model which, he claims, forms the basis of any semantic 'spectacle', be it sentence or story. Nothing can be a signifying whole unless it can be grasped as an actantial structure (*Sémantique structurale*, pp. 173–6).

Greimas's model consists of six categories set in syntactic and thematic relation to one another:

destinateur → objet → destinataire

adjuvant → sujet ← opposant

It focuses on the object which is desired by the subject and which is situated between the *destinateur* (sender) and *destinataire* (receiver). The subject himself has as his projections the *adjuvant* (helper) and *opposant* (opponent) (*ibid.*, p. 180). When Propp's roles are cast in this form we have the following diagram:

Dispatcher → Sought-for-person → Hero

Donor and → Hero ← Villain and
Helper   False Hero

An initial objection might be that the relationship between sender and receiver does not, intuitively, seem to be of the same primary nature as the other relations. It is not difficult to grant that all *récits* involve a character seeking something and encountering internal or external help and opposition. But the claim that the relationship between a sender and a receiver is of the same basic nature requires some justification. Greimas offers none.

Moreover, it is striking that precisely on this point he is unable to draw any empirical support from Propp, whose analysis he takes as confirming his own. None of Propp's seven roles corresponds with that of the receiver, and Greimas is forced to argue that the folktale is peculiar in that the hero is both subject and receiver. But this would seem to contradict the claim that the dispatcher is the sender, for the dispatcher generally does not give the hero anything – that is the role of the helper or of the sought-for-person's father, who may finally grant the hero the object of his quest. In view of this problem it seems likely that anyone using the model to study a variety of stories will need to exercise considerable ingenuity in discovering appropriate senders and receivers.

Greimas claims that his model will enable one to establish a typology of stories by grouping together those stories in which the same two roles are fused in a single character. But such a typology would not take one very far. For example, Greimas argues that in the folktale subject and receiver are fused, but this will be true of any tale in which the hero desires something and eventually receives it or fails to receive it. Thus all folktales and most novels would be classed together and distinguished from any story in which the hero desired something for someone else. The other distinction which seems possible is between stories in which helper and opponent are separate characters and those in which they are fused in one or more ambivalent characters. But this would seem a delicate matter, a distinction of degree rather than kind.

These speculations are all very tentative, but since Greimas offers little evidence of how his model would work in practice one can only hope that the examples one devises illustrate difficulties of the model rather than incompetence in applying it. The principle would seem to be that if uncertainty about representatives of each role in a particular novel represents a thematic problem or decision, then the difficulty of applying the model counts as evidence in its favour rather than against it (the model correctly locates a thematic problem). If, however, theme is relatively clear but difficult to state in terms of the model, then these difficulties count against Greimas's hypothesis. For *Madame Bovary* one might propose: Subject – Emma, Object – Happiness, Sender – Romantic literature, Receiver – Emma, Helper – Léon, Rodolphe, Opponent – Charles, Yonville, Rodolphe. Here the difficulty in deciding whether Rodolphe (and perhaps Léon) should count as helpers only or as helpers and opponents does not seem to correspond to a thematic problem in the novel. We can say quite simply that Emma tries to find happiness with each of them and fails, but this is difficult to state in terms of Greimas's model. For *Hard Times* one might propose: Subject – Louisa, Object – Proper existence, Sender – Gradgrind?, Receiver – Louisa, Helper – Sissy Jupes, Fancy?, Opponent – Bounderby, Coketown, Utilitarianism. One might say that unextinguished Fancy is a helper, but one might also say that it rather than Gradgrind is the sender and that Gradgrind is an opponent, despite his love for his daughter. Once again, this indecision does not seem to represent a thematic problem; it is only when the notion of 'sender' is introduced that difficulties arise; and that would seem to count against the model.

In reading a novel we do, presumably, make use of some general hypotheses concerning possible roles. We attempt to decide early in the novel which are the characters to whom we should pay most attention and, having identified a main character, to place others in relation to him. But if the claim is that we attempt subconsciously to fill these six roles, apportioning characters among them, one can only regret that no evidence has been adduced to show that this is the case.

In his analysis of *Les Liaisons dangereuses* Todorov attempted to use Greimas's model by taking desire, communication and participation – the three axes of the actantial model – as the basic relations between characters. He went on to formulate certain 'rules of action' which govern these relations in this novel: e.g. if A love B he attempts to make B love him; if A discovers that he loves B then he will endeavour to deny or conceal that love.[17] In his *Grammaire du Décaméron*, however, he explicitly rejects Greimas's typology of *actants*. Taking the sentence as his model (as of course Greimas does also) he argues that 'the grammatical subject is always without internal properties; these can come only from its momentary conjunction with a predicate' (p. 28). He proposes, then, to treat characters as proper names to which certain qualities are attached during the course of the narrative. Characters are not heroes, villains or helpers; they are simply subjects of a group of predicates which the reader adds up as he goes along.

Todorov offers no evidence to support this view, and one must conclude that the central question is still left open: do we, in reading, simply add together the actions and attributes of an individual character, drawing from them a conception of personality and role, or are we guided in this process by formal expectations about the roles that need to be filled? Do we simply note what a character does or do we try to fit him into one of a limited number of slots? The inadequacy of Greimas's model might dispose us to choose the former reply, but it would no doubt be preferable to hope that a better model of functional roles could be produced and might enable us to choose the latter. As Northrop Frye argues,

> All lifelike characters, whether in drama or fiction, owe their consistency to the appropriateness of the stock type which belongs to their dramatic function. That stock type is not the character but it is as necessary to the character as a skeleton is to the actor who plays it. (*Anatomy of Criticism*, p. 172)

Frye's categories, which seem much more promising than Greimas's, are worked out with respect to the four generic *mythoi* of spring, summer, autumn and winter. In comedy, for example, we have the contrast between the *eiron* or self-deprecator and the *alazon* or impostor, which forms the basis of comic action, and that between the buffoon and the churl which polarizes the comic mood. For each of these categories we can identify various stock figures, of which our cultural codes contain models: for the *alazon* the *senex iratus* or heavy father, the *miles gloriosus* or braggart, the fop or coxcomb, the pedant. The claim is not, as Frye makes clear, that each character in a play or novel precisely fits one of these categories, but rather that these models guide the perception and creation of characters, enabling us to compose the comic situation and attribute to each an intelligible role.

Although Barthes does not work out a comprehensive typology like Frye's, his discussion of character and the semic code in *S/Z* bears on the processes by which, during the activity of reading, various details are combined and interpreted so as to form characters. In his analysis of Balzac's text he picks out from each sentence or passage the elements which can be taken as contributing to character by virtue of the fact that our cultural codes enable us to derive appropriate connotations from them. When we are told that Sarrasine as a youth 'put an extraordinary ardour into his play' and in scuffles with his comrades 'if he was the weaker he bit', we can assimilate directly this 'ardour' and the excess of 'extraordinary' as marks of his character; but biting requires some interpretation: it can be treated as 'excess' in terms of the rules of fair combat, or as 'femininity' in terms of other cultural and psychological stereotypes (p. 98). This process of naming connotations – of casting them into a form in which they can be used later – is crucial to the process of reading.

> To say that Sarrasine is 'alternatively active and passive' is to commit the reader to finding in his character something 'which does not take', to commit him to naming this something.
> Thus begins a process of naming: to read is to struggle to name; it is to make sentences of the text undergo a semantic transformation. (pp. 98–9)

Such naming is always approximate and uncertain. One slides from name to name as the text throws up more semantic features and invites one to group and compose them. 'Reculer de nom en nom à partir de la butée signifiante' (to retreat from name to name, driven by the thrust of signification) – this is the process of totalization that reading involves (p. 100). When one succeeds in naming a series of semes a pattern is established and a character formed. Sarrasine, for example, is the meeting place of turbulence, artistic ability, independence, violence, excess, femininity, etc. (p. 197). The proper name provides a kind of cover; an assurance that these qualities, gathered from throughout the text, can be related to one another and form a whole that is greater than the sum of its parts: 'the proper name permits the character to exist outside of semantic features, whose sum nevertheless wholly constitutes him' (p. 197). The proper name enables the reader to postulate this existence.

The process of selecting and organizing semes is governed by an ideology of character, implicit models of psychological coherence which indicate what sorts of things are possible as character traits, how these traits can coexist and form wholes, or at least which traits coexist without difficulty and which are necessarily opposed in ways that produce tension and ambiguity. To a certain extent, of course, these notions are drawn from non-literary experience, but one should not underestimate the extent to which they are literary conventions. The models which Frye cites, for example, depend for their coherence and efficacy on the fact that they result from literary rather than empirical experience; they are thus more ordered and more ready to participate in the production of meaning. If one of the functions of the novel is to convince us of the existence of other minds, then it must serve as a source of our notions of character; and one could argue with Sollers that *le discours romanesque* has become our anonymous social wisdom, the instrument of our perception of others, the models by which we make them into persons (*Logiques*, p. 228). Whatever their role outside the novel, our models of the braggart, the young lover, the scheming subordinate, the wise man, the villain – polyvalent models with scope for variation, to be sure – are literary constructs which facilitate the process of selecting semantic features to fill up or give content to a proper name. We can extract new features as we read and go on to infer others because a character is not, *pace* Todorov, simply a conglomeration of features but a 'directed or teleological set' based on cultural models.[18]

If we are to understand the operation of the semic code we need a fuller sketch of the literary stereotypes which provide its elementary modes of coherence, but even then the code would remain very much open-ended. As soon as the basic outline of a character begins to emerge in the process of reading, one can call upon any of the languages developed for study of human behaviour and begin to structure the text in those terms. As Barthes emphasizes, the seme is only a point of departure, an avenue of meaning; one cannot say what lies at the end of the road – 'everything depends on the level at which one halts the process of naming' (*S/Z*, pp. 196–7). But it should at least be possible to outline the directions in which meaning can go and its general modes of progression.

Here, as elsewhere, structuralism does not offer a full-fledged model of a literary system, but by the problems it has posed and the formulations it has attempted it does at least provide a framework within which thought about the novel as a semiotic form can take place. By focusing on the ways in which it complies with and resists our expectations, its moments of order and disorder, its interplay of recognition and dislocation, it opens the way for a theory of the novel which would be an account of the pleasures and difficulties of reading. In place of the novel as mimesis we have the novel as a structure which plays with different modes of ordering and enables the reader to understand how he makes sense of the world.

PART THREE

Perspectives

CHAPTER 10

'Beyond' Structuralism: Tel Quel

Un système est une espèce de damnation
qui nous pousse à une abjuration perpétuelle;
il en faut toujours inventer
un autre, et cette fatigue est un cruel
châtiment.*
BAUDELAIRE

Although structuralists of all persuasions would argue that reading is
a structuring activity and that one should study the processes by
which meaning is produced, many would challenge the view of
structuralism presented in Part Two of this book. They might
particularly wish to oppose the notion that reading should be studied
as a rule-governed process or as the expression of a kind of 'literary
competence'. For the theorists associated with the review *Tel Quel*,
the programme which I have presented might seem an ideological
emasculation of all that was vital and radical in structuralism: an
attempt to make it an analytical discipline which studies and describes
the *status quo* instead of an active force which frees semiotic practices
from the ideology that holds them in check. Their argument might
run as follows:

> The aspect of Chomsky's theory of language which you invoke
> in your account of structuralism is precisely that which we have
> rejected. His notion of 'linguistic competence' and his use of the
> 'intuitions' of the native speaker make the individual subject the
> point of reference, the source of meaning, the seat of creativity,
> and give a privileged status to a particular set of rules which
> govern the sentences that he takes to be well formed. The
> concept of literary competence is a way of granting
> pre-eminence to certain arbitrary conventions and excluding
> from the realm of language all the truly creative and productive
> violations of these rules.

* A system is a kind of damnation which drives us to perpetual abjuration.
We are always forced to invent another, and this strain is a cruel
punishment.

We are not likely, therefore, to accept the notion of literary competence, which would be even more prescriptive and repressive. The ideology of our culture promotes a particular way of reading literature, and instead of challenging it you make it an absolute and translate it into a system of rules and operations which you treat as the norms of rationality and acceptability. It is true that in its early stages structuralism envisaged the possibility of a 'literary system' which would assign a structural description to each text; but this, which is the only proposal that would justify talk of literary competence, is now recognized as an error. Texts can be read in many ways; each text contains within itself the possibility of an infinite set of structures, and to privilege some by setting up a system of rules to generate them is a blatantly prescriptive and ideological move.

The claim would be that the kind of poetics which Barthes proposed in *Critique et vérité* – an analysis of the intelligibility of works, of the logic by which acceptable meanings are produced – has been rejected or transcended in favour of a more 'open' approach which stresses the creative freedom of both writer and reader. Speaking of a change in structuralism, which in his own work corresponds to the passage from 'Introduction à l'analyse structurale des récits' (1966) to *S/Z* (1970), Barthes notes that

> in the former text I appealed to a general structure from which would be derived analyses of contingent texts . . . In *S/Z* I reversed this perspective: there I refused the idea of a model transcendent to several texts (and thus, all the more so, of a model transcendent to every text) in order to postulate that each text is in some sort its own model, that each text, in other words, must be treated in its difference, 'difference' being understood here precisely in a Nietzschean or a Derridean sense. Let me put it another way: the text is ceaselessly and through and through traversed by codes, but it is not the accomplishment of a code (of, for example, the narrative code), it is not the *parole* of a narrative *langue*. ('A Conversation with Roland Barthes', p. 44)

The argument is a curious one because it so closely resembles, given a difference in terminology, the attacks on structuralism from more traditional quarters. Those who oppose the idea of poetics do so in the name of the uniqueness of every literary work and the critical impoverishment that results from thinking of it as an instance of the literary system: the heterogeneity of readers and works, the possibilities of literary innovation, prevent one from encompassing in a single theory the forms of literature and the meanings it can produce. No science can exhaust the modalities of creative genius.

This is not, in fact, very far from Barthes's suggestion that each text is its own model, a system unto itself. It does not have a single structure, assigned to it by a literary system, nor does it contain an encoded meaning which a knowledge of literary codes would enable one to decipher. Reading must focus on the differences between texts, the relations of proximity and distance, of citation, negation, irony and parody. Such relations are infinite and work to defer any final meaning.

However, Barthes's argument seems fundamentally ambiguous. Not only does he preserve the notion of code, which entails collective knowledge and shared norms; it is in *S/Z* that the concept reaches its fullest development: the codes refer to all that has already been written, read, seen, done. The text is ceaselessly traversed by codes, which are the source of its meanings. The text may not have *a* structure assigned to it by a grammar of narrative, but that is because the operations of reading enable it to be structured in various ways. If the text has a plurality of meanings it is because it does not itself contain a meaning but involves the reader in the process of producing meaning according to a variety of appropriate procedures. To reject the concept of a system on the grounds that the interpretive codes which enable one to read the text produce a plurality of meanings is a curious *non sequitur*, for the fact that a variety of meanings and structures are possible is the strongest evidence we have of the complexity and importance of the practice of reading. If each text had a single meaning, then it might be possible to argue that this meaning was inherent to it and depended upon no general system, but the fact that there is an open set of possible meanings indicates that we are dealing with interpretive processes of considerable power which require study. It is difficult to avoid the conclusion that the theories of the *Tel Quel* group and the arguments which they might bring to bear against the notions of a literary system and literary competence do, in fact, presuppose these notions which they claim to have rejected.

To show that this is so and that it is extremely difficult to go beyond the kind of structuralism which has been sketched in earlier chapters we shall have to consider in some detail *Tel Quel's* attempts at self-transcendence. The reasons for trying to go beyond structuralism are perhaps best set forth by Jacques Derrida in *L'Ecriture et la différence*.

First of all, in the study of literature the notion of structure has a teleological character: the structure is determined by a particular end; it is recognized as a configuration which contributes to this end.

'How can one perceive an organized whole except by starting with its end or purpose?' (p. 44). Unless one has postulated some transcendent 'final cause' or ultimate meaning for the work, one cannot discover its structure, for the structure is that by which the end is made present throughout the work. The analyst of structure has the task of displaying the work as a spatial configuration in which time past and time future point to one end, which is always present. Derrida writes:

> On nous accordera qu'il s'agit ici de la métaphysique implicite de tout structuralisme ou de tout geste structuraliste. En particulier, une lecture structurale présuppose toujours, fait toujours appel, dans son moment propre, à cette simultanéité théologique du livre.

> (It will be readily granted that we have here the implicit metaphysics of structuralism or of any structuralist procedure. In particular, a structuralist reading, though it takes place in time, always presupposes and appeals to this simultaneity of the book as seen by God.) (p. 41)

The study of structure is in this sense governed by 'a move which consists of giving it a centre, of referring it to a moment of "presence" or a definite origin'. This centre founds and organizes the structure, permitting certain combinations of elements and excluding others: 'the centre closes the play which it inaugurates and makes possible . . . The concept of a centred structure is in fact that of limited or founded play' (pp. 409–10). This closure, it would be argued, testifies to the presence of an ideology.

This notion is not difficult to illustrate. When one speaks of the structure of a literary work, one does so from a certain vantage point: one starts with notions of the meaning or effects of a poem and tries to identify the structures responsible for those effects. Possible configurations or patterns which make no contribution are rejected as irrelevant. That is to say, an intuitive understanding of the poem functions as the 'centre', governing the play of forms: it is both a starting point – what enables one to identify structures – and a limiting principle.

But to grant any principle this privileged status, to make it the prime mover itself unmoved, is a patently ideological step. Notions of the meaning or effects of a particular poem are determined by the contingent facts of readers' history and by the various critical and ideological concepts current at the time. Why should these particular cultural products – what readers have been taught about literature – be allowed to remain outside the play of structure, limiting it but not limited by it in turn? To make any postulated effect the fixed point of one's analysis cannot but seem a dogmatic and prescriptive move which reflects a desire for absolute truths and transcendent meanings.

The status of such centres came to be seriously questioned, Derrida writes, 'at the moment when theory began to consider the structured nature of structures' (la structuralité de la structure) (p. 411). The notion of a *système décentré* came to seem very attractive. Could one not alter and displace the centre during the analysis of the system itself? Though one would still require a point of departure, could not the movement of analysis include a critique of that centre which displaced it from the role of unexamined postulate? Structuralism or semiology thus came to be defined as an activity whose value lay in the avidity with which it scrutinized its postulates:

> Semiotics cannot develop except as a critique of semiotics . . .
> Research in semiotics remains an investigation which discovers
> nothing at the end of its quest but its own ideological moves,
> so as to take cognizance of them, to deny them, and to start out
> anew (Kristeva, *Semiotikè*, pp. 30–1)

Although it is not clear how this programme of Kristeva's would affect an actual semiological analysis, one can at least imagine how language might be treated as a *système décentré*. Linguists have long taken as their point of departure certain 'normal' uses of language: the expression in grammatically well-formed sentences of determinate communicative intentions. Thought about language has thus, Derrida argues, taken place within a metaphysics of the *logos* which grants primacy to the *signifié* and sees the *signifiant* as a notation through which one passes in order to attain the thought. The special ways in which literature produces meaning were left aside as techniques of connotation. If we consider these seriously, structuralists might argue, we find a host of cases in which the signifier does not manifest a signified but exceeds it, offering itself as a surplus which engenders a play of signification. In order to perceive this excess we must take normal uses of language as the 'centre', but once we have grasped the phenomena which this centre excludes we must displace the centre from its role as that which founds and governs the play of linguistic structure and this can be done by taking seriously Saussure's theory of the diacritical nature of meaning and his contention that in the linguistic system 'there are only differences with no positive terms.' If meaning is a function of differences between terms and every term is but a node of differential relations, then each term refers us to other terms from which it differs and to which it is in some kind of relation. These relations are infinite and all have the potential of producing meaning.

One cannot then, the argument would run, begin by identifying the meanings which language produces and use this as a normative concept to govern one's analysis, for the salient fact about language is that its modes of producing meaning are unbounded and the poet exceeds any normative limits. However broad the spectrum of possibilities on which one bases an analysis, it is always possible to go beyond them; the organization of words in configurations which resist received methods of reading forces one to experiment and to bring into play new types of relations from language's infinite set of possibilities. As Mallarmé says,[1]

> les mots, d'eux-mêmes, s'exaltent à mainte facette reconnue la
> plus rare ou valant pour l'esprit, centre de suspens vibratoire;
> qui les perçoit indépendamment de la suite ordinaire, projetés,
> en parois de grotte, tant que dure leur mobilité ou principe,
> étant ce qui ne se dit pas du discours: prompts tous, avant
> extinction, à une réciprocité de feux distante ou présentée de
> biais comme contingence.

> (The words of their own accord become exalted jewels, their
> many facets recognized as of infinite rarity and value to the
> mind, that centre where they hesitate and vibrate. The mind
> sees the words not in their usual order but projected around it,
> like the walls of a grotto, for so long as their mobility, that
> principle which makes them exceed whatever is said in
> discourse, is not exhausted. All are quick, before they fade
> away, to glitter, reflecting against one another, with distant,
> oblique and contingent flashes.)

Thus, with the 'réciprocité de feux distante ou présentée de biais comme contingence', the phrase 'Un coup de dés' gives us, in a mobile contingent sparkle, the differences that set off *coup* from *cou*, *coût*, *coupe*, *couper*; the series *un*, *deux*, *des*; the metathesis *des coups*; or, exploiting the English pun, the blows of the day or the cup of its radiance. The line can open in what Julia Kristeva calls the 'mémoire infinie de la signifiance' the play of all the things which it is not but which stand to it as distant, oblique mirrors. We can read in the phrase the *traces* of other sequences from which it differentiates itself and against which it asks to be set.

This text of infinite possibilities which serves as substratum to any actual text she calls the 'geno-text':

> the geno-text can be thought of as a device containing the
> whole historical evolution of language and the various
> signifying practices it can bear. The possibilities of all language

of the past, present and future are given there, before being masked or repressed in the pheno-text. (*Semiotikè*, p. 284)

This is, in her view, the only kind of concept that can serve as centre to the analysis of poetic language, for it alone includes (by definition) all the possible varieties of signification that poets and readers can invent. Any other notion on which one attempted to found one's analysis would be undermined as soon as new procedures which it excluded were developed.

But it follows, as a direct corollary of its definition, that 'geno-text' is an empty concept, an absence at the centre. One cannot use it to any purpose since one can never know what it contains, and its effect is to prevent one from ever rejecting any proposal about the verbal structure of a text. Every combination or relation is already present in the geno-text and hence a possible source of meaning. There is no standpoint from which a proposal could be rejected. In the absence of any primitive notion of the meanings or effects of a text (any judgment of this kind would represent, in her view, an insidious foreclosure which tried to establish a norm), there is nothing to limit the play of meaning. As Derrida says, 'the absence of an ultimate meaning opens an unbounded space for the play of signification' (*L'Ecriture et la différence*, p. 411). The fear that concepts which govern the analysis of meaning might be attacked as ideological premises has led the *Tel Quel* theorists to attempt, at least in principle, to dispense with them.

The primary practical effect of this reorientation is to stress the active, productive nature of reading and writing and to eliminate notions of the literary work as 'representation' and 'expression'. Interpretation is not a matter of recovering some meaning which lies behind the work and serves as a centre governing its structure; it is rather an attempt to participate in and observe the play of possible meanings to which the text gives access. In other words, the critique of language has the function of freeing one from any nostalgic longing for an original or transcendent meaning and preparing one to accept 'l'affirmation nietzschéenne, l'affirmation joyeuse du jeu du monde et de l'innocence du devenir, l'affirmation d'un monde de signes sans faute, sans vérité, sans origine, offert à une interprétation active' (the joyful Nietzschean affirmation of the play of the world and the innocence of becoming, the affirmation of a world of signs which has no truth, no origin, no nostalgic guilt, and is proffered for active interpretation). There are, Derrida continues, two kinds of interpretation: 'the one tries to decipher, dreams of deciphering a truth or an origin which lies outside the realm of signs and their play, and it experiences the need to interpret as a kind of exile', an exclusion from the original plenitude that it seeks; the other accepts its active, creative function and joyfully proceeds without looking back (*ibid.*, p. 427).

At one level it is not difficult to see the attractions of this approach, which tries to replace the anguish of infinite regress by the pleasure of infinite creation. Given that there is no ultimate and absolute justification for any system or for the interpretations flowing from it, one tries to value the activity of interpretation itself, or the activity of theoretical elaboration, rather than any results which might be obtained. There is nothing to which results ought to correspond; and so, rather than think of interpretation as a game *in* the world, whose results might be of interest if they approximate some truth outside the game, one must recognize that the activity of writing, in its widest Derridean sense of 'production of meaning', is the game or play *of* the world.

> Nous sommes donc d'entrée de jeu dans le devenir-immotivé du symbole . . . L'immotivation de la trace doit être maintenant entendue comme une opération et non comme un état, comme un mouvement actif, une dé-motivation, non comme une structure donnée.
>
> (We are thus from the very outset caught up in the unmotivated play of developing symbols . . . The lack of motivation of the traces which connect them should now be understood as an operation rather than a state, as an active movement, a process of de-motivating, rather than a structure given once and for all.) (*De la grammatologie*, p. 74)

That is to say, we must rid ourselves of that logocentric or theological fiction which, while recognizing the arbitrary nature of the sign, thinks of signs as having been established once and for all, by fiat, and henceforth governed by strict conventions. The fact that form is not a necessary and sufficient determinant of meaning is a continuing condition of the production of meaning. The sign has a life of its own which is not governed by any *archè* or *telos*, origin or final cause, and the conventions which govern its use in particular types of discourse are epiphenomena: they are themselves transitory cultural products. 'Can I say "bububu" and mean "If it doesn't rain I shall go for a walk"?' asks Wittgenstein. 'It is only in a language that I can mean something by something.'[2] This is true, in that I cannot use 'bububu' to express or communicate that meaning. However, I can establish, as Wittgenstein himself has done, a relationship between the two, and now, ironically enough, there is a language in which 'bububu' is traversed by 'If it doesn't rain I shall go for a walk.' It is not so much that 'bububu' has been given a meaning as that in the 'devenir-immotivé du symbole' it has come to bear the trace of a possible meaning. The problem of language, in short, is not only a problem of expression and communication – models ill-suited to the most complex and interesting linguistic phenomena we encounter. It is, as Derrida would say, a problem of inscription and production, of the 'traces' borne by verbal sequences and the developments to which they can give rise. The verbal form does not simply refer us to a meaning but opens a space in which we can relate it to other sequences whose traces it bears.

But whatever the theoretical attractions of this view, it has its practical difficulties. The analysis of cultural phenomena must always take place in some context, and at any one time the production of meaning in a culture is governed by conventions. In the days when Wittgenstein was discussing the problem of meaning and intention one could not say 'bububu' and mean 'If it doesn't rain I shall go for a walk', whatever may be the case today. The semiologist can study the implicit rules which enable readers to make sense of texts – which define the range of acceptable interpretations – and he can try to change those rules, but these are different enterprises which the facts of cultural history alone would enjoin one to separate.

A single example will illustrate the problem: the adoption by the *Tel Quel* theorists of Saussure's theory of anagrams. Saussure was convinced that Latin poets regularly concealed key proper names in their verses, and he devoted considerable time to the discovery of such anagrams. But he thought the question of intention crucial, and his doubts on this score – he could find no references to the practice and the statistical advice he obtained was inconclusive – made him leave his speculations unpublished.[3] Kristeva and others, who are not concerned with intentions, have seen in Saussure's work a theory which emphasized the materiality of the text (the *signifiant* as a combination of letters) and postulated 'the expansion of a particular signifying function, which dispenses with the word and the sign as the basic units of meaning, throughout the whole signifying material of a given text' (*Semiotikè*, p. 293). The text is a space in which letters, contingently arranged in one way, can be grouped differently to bring out a variety of latent patterns.

Clearly this is a possible interpretive technique: if we allow the analyst to find anagrams of key words which enrich his reading of the text we give him a powerful procedure for producing meaning. But it is also clear that at the moment 'ideological' constraints prevent one from reading in this way. If one attempts to remove these constraints one can only do so by making use of other principles which in their way are equally ideological. For example, Kristeva argues that Saussure was 'wrong' to look only for anagrams of proper names.[4]

If she means that one can find other anagrams in texts, that is certainly true, but on those grounds one could say that she is wrong to look only for anagrams of French words, and thus 'arbitrarily' to exclude the anagrams of German words which can be found in French texts or the anagrams of nonsense strings which can be found in any text (*Un coup de dés* as an anagram of *deepnudocus*).

Moreover, and this is the important point, anagrams can be used to produce meaning only if one relies on current interpretive techniques for dealing with whatever this mode of reading discovers. On finding an anagram of *rire* in Mallarmé's title *Brise marine* one can make something of it because one knows what one might do if the word itself appeared in the poem. There must be particular ways of relating anagram to text if any meaning is to result from the operation.

When Kristeva actually analyses part of a text she does in fact seem to be employing principles of relevance drawn from common procedures of reading. Thus, in discussing the sentence 'Un coup de dés jamais n'abolira le hasard', despite her claim that 'this sentence must be read in the register of resonances which make each word a point where an infinite number of meanings can be read', she does not make much use of these infinite possibilities. The nearest she comes to an anagram is the extraction of *bol, lira, ira,* and *lyra* from *abolira,* and she scarcely draws upon 'all the languages of the past and future' supposedly contained in the geno-text. Although she uses images from other poems to show how the word *coup,* 'by a series of retreats, extensions, escapes, could bring to the process of reading a whole thematic corpus that dwells in the text', she neglects such obvious associations as *cou, coût, coupe,* etc., which could lead in a variety of directions ('Sémanalyse et production de sens', pp. 229–31). In order to carry out something resembling an analysis she is forced to deploy quite restrictive conventions of reading. Without them interpretation would be impossible.

Indeed, precisely because of the unlimited freedom that her theory secures, it is the more important for her to apply some principles of relevance, if only in order to decide which of the infinite set of possible relations she is going to use. And she requires some way of integrating what has been selected. The attempt to 'free' the process of reading from constraints imposed by a particular theory of culture requires one to reintroduce some rather powerful rules to apply to the combinations or contrasts produced by random extraction and association. Anything can be related to anything else, certainly: a cow is like the third law of thermodynamics in that neither is a waste-paper basket, but little can be done with that fact. Other relations, however, do have thematic potential, and the crucial question is what governs their selection and development. Even if 'emptied' by a radical theory, the centre will inevitably fill itself in as the analyst makes choices and offers conclusions. There will always be some kind of semiotic or literary competence at work, and the need for it will be greater if the range of relations with which it must deal is enlarged.

This Kristeva might not deny; she might say simply that the centre is never fixed, always constructed and deconstructed with a freedom which the theory seeks as an end in itself.

> At every moment in its development semiotics must theorize its object, its own method and the relationship between them; it therefore theorizes itself and becomes, by thus turning back on itself, the theory of its own scientific practice . . . As the place of interaction between various sciences and a theoretical process always in the course of development, semiotics cannot reify itself as a science, much less as *the* science. It is rather a direction for research, always open, a theoretical enterprise which turns back upon itself, a perpetual self-criticism.
> (*Semiotikè*, p. 30)

This claim invokes quite unashamedly what one might call the myth of the innocence of becoming: that continual change, as an end in itself, is freedom, and that it liberates one from the demands that could be made of any particular state of the system. If as Barthes and Foucault have shown, the argument might run, our social and cultural world is the product of various symbolic systems, should we not refuse any privileged status to the conventions erected by the oppressive institutions of the moment and joyfully claim for ourselves the right to produce meaning *ad libitum*, thus securing by the process of perpetual self-transcendence invulnerability to any criticism based on positivistic criteria and levelled at us from outside?

This vision has its flaws. First of all, though it is true that the study of any set of semiotic conventions will be partially invalidated by the knowledge which results from that study (the more aware we are of conventions the easier it is to attempt to change them), one cannot escape this fact by appeal to self-transcendence. Even if semiology refuse to reify itself as a science it does not, for that, escape criticism. Whatever the past and future of the discipline, any particular analysis takes place at a particular stage, is an object with premises and results; and the possibility of denying these premises at the next moment does not make evaluation impossible or inappropriate.

Second, the notion of freedom in the creation of meaning seems illusory. As Foucault himself is quick to point out, the rules and concepts which underlie the production of meaning – 'so many infinite resources for the creation of discourse' – are simultaneously and necessarily 'principles of constraint, and it is probable that one cannot account for their positive and productive role without taking into account their restrictive and constraining function' (*L'Ordre du discours*, p. 38). Something can have meaning only if there are other meanings it cannot have. One can speak of ways of reading a poem only if there are other imaginable ways that are inappropriate. Without restrictive rules there would be no meaning whatsoever.

Indeed, Derrida himself, never hasty to offer positive proposals, is acutely aware of the impossibility of escape, of the restrictions imposed by the very language and concepts in which escape can be bruited:

> De ce langage, il faut donc tenter de s'affranchir. Non pas *tenter* de s'en affranchir, car c'est impossible sans oublier *notre* histoire. Mais en rêver. Non pas de s'en *affranchir*, ce qui n'aurait aucun sens et nous priverait de la lumière du sens. Mais de lui résister le plus loin possible.

> (We must therefore try to free ourselves from this language. Not actually *attempt* to free ourselves from it, for that is impossible without denying our own historical situation. But rather, to imagine doing so. Not actually *free* ourselves from it, for that would make no sense and would deprive us of the light that meaning can provide. But rather, resist it as far as possible.) (*L'Ecriture et la différence*, p. 46)

Freeing ourselves from our most pervasive ideology, our conventions of meaning, 'makes no sense' because we are born into a world of meaning and cannot even shun its demands without thereby recognizing them. And even if we could we should find ourselves amidst a meaningless babble, deprived of 'la lumière du sens' which makes discussion possible. What we must do is to *imagine* freeing ourselves from the operative conventions so as to see more clearly the conventions themselves.

Whatever type of freedom the members of the *Tel Quel* group secure for themselves will be based on convention and will consist of a set of interpretive procedures. There is a crucial difference between the production of meaning and arbitrary assignment of meaning, between plausible development and random association. They seek the former rather than the latter – they would not want to claim that their analyses are no better than any other – and to that extent are committed to working within conventions. Indeed, the notion that one can, as Sollers attempts to do, 'show' the revolutionary character of Dante's *écriture* or identify Lautréamont's true place in the history of French literature means that one accepts certain standards of argument and plausibility.

What *Tel Quel* is in fact proposing is a change in semiotic competence rather than a move beyond it, the introduction of some new and creative procedures of reading. Such an enterprise is perfectly legitimate, and the interplay between their own theoretical and literary work may give them some chance of success. But by the very nature of things they can proceed only step by step, relying on the procedures which readers actually use, frustrating some of these so that some new ways of producing meaning are developed, and only then dispensing with others. They are very much in the position of Von Neurath's mariners, trying to rebuild their ship in mid-ocean, but instead of realizing that this must be done plank by plank they argue that the whole ship can be scrapped; the difference being that on a real ocean one sinks.

What I should like to argue, then, is that while structuralism cannot escape from ideology and provide its own foundations, this is of little importance because the critiques of structuralism, and particularly of structuralist poetics, cannot do so either and through their strategies of evasion lead to untenable positions. Or perhaps one should say, more modestly, that any attack on structuralist poetics based on the claim that it cannot grasp the varied modes of signification of literature will itself fail to provide a coherent alternative. In fact, both the naïve traditionalist critique, which asserts the uniqueness of the work of art and the inadmissibility of general theories, and the sophisticated *sémanalyse* of *Tel Quel*, which attempts to theorize a perpetual self-transcendence, fail in analogous ways. They both imply that the process of interpretation is random and haphazard: the former by omission (in its refusal to countenance general semiotic theories) and the latter by explicit glorification of the aleatory.

One must assert, on the contrary, that the range of meanings which a line of verse can bear depends on the fact that numerous other meanings are manifestly impossible, and that to ask by what *right* other meanings are excluded and to seek in answer more than a restatement of the operative conventions is to break out of culture into an area where there are no meanings at all. The reader is, as Barthes says, 'guidé par les contraintes formelles du sens; on ne fait pas le sens n'importe comment (si vous en doutez, essayez)' (guided by the formal constraints of meaning; one can't make sense in just any way whatsoever (if you don't believe me, try it) (*Critique et vérité*, p. 65). A simple point, perhaps, but one that has of late been unjustly neglected. One must reply also that the possibility of change depends on some concept of identity, that there must now be operative conventions for the production of meaning if they are to change tomorrow, and that even our sense of the possibility of change therefore indicates that there are interpersonal symbolic systems to be studied. Rather than try to get outside ideology we must remain resolutely within it, for both the conventions to be analysed and the notions of understanding lie within. If circle there be, it is the circle of culture itself.

CHAPTER 11

Conclusion: Structuralism and the Qualities of Literature

L'endroit le plus érotique d'un corps
n'est-il pas *là où le vêtement bâille*?*
BARTHES

'I think that the name of structuralism should today be reserved for a methodological movement which specifically avows its direct link with linguistics', observes Barthes. 'This would be to my mind the most precise criterion of definition' ('Une problématique du sens', p. 10). The definition is apt, but as preceding chapters will have shown, it is scarcely precise. The approaches which it might include are extremely varied, both in their conception of criticism and in their use of linguistics. In fact, there seem three distinct ways in which linguistics has affected French criticism. First of all, as the example of a 'scientific' discipline, it suggested to critics that the desire to be rigorous and systematic did not necessarily entail attempts at causal explanation. An element could be explained by its place in a network of relations rather than in a chain of cause and effect. The linguistic model, therefore, helped to justify the desire to abandon literary history and biographical criticism; and if the notion that one was being scientific led on occasion to a misplaced arrogance, still the conclusion that literature could be studied as 'un système qui ne connaît que son ordre propre'[1] – a system with its own order – has been eminently salutary, securing for the French some of the benefits of Anglo-American 'New Criticism' without leading to the error of making the individual text an autonomous object that should be approached with a *tabula rasa*.

Second, linguistics provided a number of concepts which could be used eclectically or metaphorically in discussing literary works: signifier and signified, *langue* and *parole*, syntagmatic and paradigmatic relations, the levels of a hierarchical system, distributional and integrative relations, the diacritical or differential nature of meaning,

* Is not the body's most erotic zone there where the garment leaves gaps?

and other subsidiary notions such as shifters or performative utterances. These concepts can, of course, be employed either skilfully or ineptly; they do not in themselves, by virtue of their linguistic origin, produce insights. But the use of such terms may help one to identify relations of various kinds, both actual and virtual, within a single level or between levels, which are responsible for the production of meaning.

If these concepts are not used eclectically but taken as constituents of a linguistic model one has a third way in which linguistics may affect literary criticism: by supplying a set of general instructions for semiotic investigation. Linguistics indicates how one should go about studying systems of signs. This is a stronger claim about the relevance of linguistics than is made in the other two cases, and it is the orientation which has here been taken as characterizing structuralism proper.

But within this general perspective there are different ways of interpreting the linguistic model and of applying it to the study of literature. First there is the problem of whether linguistic methods should be applied directly or indirectly. Since literature is itself language it is at least plausible that linguistic techniques, when applied directly to the texts of poems, novels, etc., could help to explain their structure and meaning. Is this in fact a task which linguistics can perform, or must one apply its methods indirectly by developing another discipline, analogous to linguistics, to deal with literary form and meaning? Second, there is the question of whether linguistics, applied directly or indirectly, provides a 'discovery procedure' or precise method of analysis which leads to correct structural descriptions, or whether it offers only a general framework for semiotic investigation which specifies the nature of its objects, the status of its hypotheses, and its modes of evaluation.

If these two sets of alternatives are combined they provide a schematic résumé of four different positions. The first claims that linguistics provides a discovery procedure which can be applied directly to the language of literature and which will bring to light poetic structures. Jakobson's distributional analyses fall under this heading, and I have attempted to show that their inadequacies demonstrate the need to reject this particular use of linguistics. Rather than assume that linguistic description will reveal literary effects, one must start with the effects themselves and then seek an explanation in linguistic structure.

Greimas starts from the assumption that linguistics, and particularly semantics, ought to be able to account for meaning of all kinds, including literary meaning. But as his attempts to develop this semantics show only too clearly, linguistics does not provide an algorithm for the discovery of semantic effects. Indeed, the main conclusions that emerge from a study of his theory are that meaning in literature cannot be explained by a method which works up from smaller units to larger ones; though the ultimate semantic organization of a text may be specifiable in linguistic terms, the process by which these effects are reached involves some complex expectations and semantic operations. Greimas's work, then, can be placed in the second category. It illustrates that, although linguistics does not provide a procedure for the discovery of literary structure, some of the complex operations of reading may at least be partially identified by an attempt to apply linguistic techniques directly to the language of literature.

Moving from the direct to the indirect application of linguistic models, we find two positions analogous to those of Jakobson and Greimas. The first assumes that linguistics provides discovery procedures which can be applied, by analogy, to any corpus of semiotic data. The problems encountered by Barthes's *Système de la mode* indicate that this kind of reliance on linguistic models may lead to a failure to determine what one is attempting to explain. In the study of literature this attitude characterizes Todorov's *Grammaire du Décaméron* and other critical works which assume that if one applies linguistic categories metaphorically to a corpus of texts one will produce results which are as valid as an account of a linguistic system, or that operations of segmentation and classification, applied to a corpus of stories, will yield a 'grammar' of narrative or of plot structure. When used in this way the linguistic model makes possible a wide variety of structural descriptions, and structuralists have occasionally sought to defend their use of the model by arguing that the results of methodological indeterminacy are in fact properties of literary works themselves: if a great many structures can be discovered it is because the work has a variety of structures. This orientation can lead, of course, to a rigorous irrelevance. Any principle or set of categories drawn from linguistics can be used as a discovery procedure, on the assumption that its use is justified by the linguistic analogy; and the problem of evaluation is thus rejected, evaded or ignored.

This problem can be solved only if one proceeds to the fourth position and uses linguistics not as a method of analysis but as the general model for semiological investigation. It indicates how one should go about constructing a poetics which stands to literature as linguistics stands to language. This is the most appropriate and effective use of the linguistic model, and it has the particular advantage of making linguistics a source of methodological clarity rather than of metaphorical vocabulary. The role of linguistics is to emphasize that one must construct a model to explain how sequences have form and meaning for experienced readers, that one must start by isolating a set of facts to be explained, and that hypotheses must be tested by their ability to account for these effects.

The proposal that literary competence be the object of poetics will encounter some resistance on the grounds that anything resembling competence which one might identify would be too indeterminate, changeable, and subjective to serve as the basis for a coherent discipline. There is some justice to such objections, and it will undoubtedly be difficult to steer a middle course, avoiding on the one hand the dangers of an experimental or socio-psychological approach which would take too seriously the actual and doubtless idiosyncratic performance of individual readers, while still avoiding on the other hand the dangers of a purely theoretical approach, whose postulated norms might bear little relation to what readers actually do. But despite this difficulty, the fact remains that unless we reject the activities of teaching and criticism some conception of interpersonal norms and procedures of reading is unavoidable. The notion of literary training or of critical argument makes sense only if reading is not an idiosyncratic and haphazard process. Bringing someone to understand a text or to see an interpretation requires shared points of departure and common mental operations. Disagreement about a text is of interest only because we assume that agreement is possible and that any disagreement will have grounds that can be recognized. Indeed, we notice differences of interpretation precisely because we take agreement for granted as the natural result of a communicative process based on shared conventions.

It should be clear, then, that the notion of competence does not lead, as some structuralists might fear, to a reinstatement of the individual subject as source of meaning. The only subject in question is an abstract and interpersonal construct: 'Ce n'est plus "je" qui lit: le temps impersonnel de la régularité, de la grille, de l'harmonie s'empare de ce "je" dispersé d'avoir lu: alors *on* lit' (It is no longer 'I' who reads; the impersonal time of regularity, of the grid, of harmony, takes up this 'I' which is in fragments from having read; *one* reads) (Kristeva, 'Comment parler à la littérature', p. 48). The subject who reads is constituted by a series of conventions, the grids of regularity and intersubjectivity. The empirical 'I' is dispersed among these conventions which take over from him in the act of reading. Indeed, it is precisely because competence is not coextensive with the individual subject that the notion is required.

What is the role of a structuralist poetics? In one sense its task is a humble one: to make as explicit as possible what is implicitly known by all those sufficiently concerned with literature to be interested in poetics. Viewed in this way it is not hermeneutic; it does not propose startling interpretations or resolve literary debates; it is the theory of the practice of reading.

But it is obvious that structuralism and even structuralist poetics also offer a theory of literature and a mode of interpretation, if only by focusing attention on certain aspects of literary works and particular qualities of literature. The attempt to understand how we make sense of a text leads one to think of literature not as representation or communication but as a series of forms which comply with and resist the production of meaning. Structural analysis does not move towards a meaning or discover the secret of a text. The work, as Barthes says, is like an onion,

a construction of layers (or levels, or systems) whose body contains, finally no heart, no kernel, no secret, no irreducible principle, nothing except the infinity of its own envelopes – which envelop nothing other than the unity of its own surfaces. ('Style and its Image', p. 10)

To read is to participate in the play of the text, to locate zones of resistance and transparency, to isolate forms and determine their content and then to treat that content in turn as a form with its own content, to follow, in short, the interplay of surface and envelope.

There is no structuralist method such that by applying it to a text one automatically discovers its structure. But there is a kind of attention which one might call structuralist: a desire to isolate codes, to name the various languages with and among which the text plays, to go beyond manifest content to a series of forms and then to make these forms, or oppositions or modes of signification, the burden of the text. 'One cannot begin the analysis of a text', Barthes says in an article entitled 'Par où commencer?',

without first taking a semantic view (of content), be it thematic, symbolic or ideological. The (immense) work which remains to be done consists of following these first codes, identifying their terms, sketching their sequences, but also of postulating other codes which are glimpsed in the perspective of the first. In short, if one demands the right to begin with a certain condensation of meaning it is because the movement of analysis, in its endless spinning out, consists of shattering the text, the first cloud of meaning, the first image of content. What is at stake in structural analysis is not the truth of the text but its plurality; the labour does not consist of starting from forms in order to perceive, clarify or formulate content (there would be no need, in that case, for a structural method), but on the contrary of scattering, of postponing, of gearing down, of discharging meaning through the action of a formal discipline. (*Le Degré zéro de l'écriture*, p. 155)

In Balzac's *Sarrasine*, for example, the initial content consists of the narrator's amorous contract with a beautiful woman (she grants him an evening in order to hear the story), the explanation of the Lanty's fortune which the story offers, and the adventure of the young sculptor who falls in love with an opera singer, not knowing that she/he is a eunuch. This content is 'deconstructed', decomposed into the various codes which run through the text, and then the action of those codes becomes the main subject of analysis. How is meaning produced? What resistance does it encounter? What meaning can we find in the process of signification itself? What do the forms of the story tell us about the adventures of meaning?

> il est mortel, dit le texte, de lever le trait séparateur, la barre paradigmatique qui permet au sens de fonctionner (c'est le mur de l'antithèse), à la vie de se reproduire (c'est l'opposition des sexes), aux biens de se protéger (c'est la règle de contrat). En somme la nouvelle *représente* (nous sommes dans un art du lisible) un effondrement généralisé des économies. . . . Cette métonymie, en abolissant les barres paradigmatiques, abolit le pouvoir de *substituer légalement*, qui fonde le sens. . . .
> *Sarrasine* représente le trouble même de la représentation, la circulation déréglée (pandémique) des signes, des sexes, des fortunes.

> (it is deadly, the text says, to remove the distinguishing trait, the paradigmatic opposition which permits meaning to function (this is the barrier of antithesis), life to reproduce (this is the opposition of the sexes), and wealth to be protected (this is the rule of contract). In short, the tale represents (we are in an art of the readable) a general collapse of economies. . . . This metonymy, in transgressing paradigmatic separation, abolishes the possibility of substituting according to rule, on which meaning is based. . . . *Sarrasine* represents the problems of representation, the wild (pandemic) circulation of signs, sex and wealth.) (*S/Z*, pp. 221–2)

This is the type of ultimate recuperation towards which a structuralist criticism moves: to read the text as an exploration of writing, of the problems of articulating a world. The critic comes to focus, therefore, on the play of the legible and illegible, on the role of gaps, silence, opacity. Although this approach may be thought of as a version of formalism, the attempt to turn content into form and then to read the significance of the play of forms reflects not a desire to fix the text and reduce it to a structure but an attempt to capture its *force*. The force, the power of any text, even the most unabashedly mimetic, lies in those moments which exceed our ability to categorize, which collide with our interpretive codes but nevertheless seem right. Lear's 'Pray you, undo this button; thank you, sir' is a gap, a shift in mode which leaves us with two edges and an abyss between them; Milly Theale's 'pink dawn of an apotheosis' before the Bronzino portrait – 'Milly recognized her exactly in words that had nothing to do with her. "I shall never be better than this." ' – is one of those interstices where there is a crossing of languages and a sense that the text is escaping us in several directions at once. To define such moments, to speak of their force, would be to identify the codes that encounter resistance there and to delineate the gaps left by a shift in languages.

Fiction can hold together within a single space a variety of languages, levels of focus, points of view, which would be contradictory in other kinds of discourse organized towards a particular empirical end. The reader learns to cope with these contradictions and becomes, as Barthes says, the hero in the adventures of culture; his pleasure comes from 'the cohabitation of languages, which work side by side' (*Le Plaisir du texte*, p. 10). And the critic, whose job is to display and explain this pleasure, comes to view the text as the happy side of Babel, a set of voices, identifiable or unidentifiable, rubbing against one another and producing both delight and uncertainty. In section 7 of Crane's 'The Open Boat', for example, after being told that nature was 'indifferent, flatly indifferent', we find one of those curious passages which entices and escapes:

It is, perhaps, plausible that a man in this situation, impressed with the unconcern of the universe, should see the innumerable flaws in his life, and have them taste wickedly in his mind, and wish for another chance. A distinction between right and wrong seems absurdly clear to him, then, in this new ignorance of the grave-edge, and he understands that if he were given another opportunity he would mend his conduct and his words, and be better and brighter during an introduction or at tea.

Virulent irony? or an attempt to let irony have its say and then to salvage whatever remains? Who says 'plausible', 'absurdly', 'ignorance'? Why 'understands' rather than 'believes'? Does anything else belong with 'understands'? And above all, where does the last phrase come from? One can try to sort out the various moments of language, or one can elect to read in the passage the difficulty of going beyond what Barthes calls the '*fading* of voices': they jostle one another but offer few holds to the process of naturalization.

Enigmas, gaps, shifts, thus become a source of pleasure and value. 'Neither culture nor its destruction is erotic', says Barthes, but only the gap between them, the space where their edges rub:

> ce n'est pas la violence qui impressionne le plaisir; la destruction ne l'intéresse pas; ce qu'il veut, c'est le lieu d'une perte, c'est la faille, la coupure, la déflation, le *fading* qui saisit le sujet au cœur de la jouissance.

> (it is not violence which impresses pleasure; destruction does not interest it; what it desires is a place of loss, a fault, a break, a moment of deflation, the fading which seizes the reader at the moment of ecstasy.) (*ibid.*, p. 15)

It is not surprising, therefore, that despite their expressed admiration for the most modern and radical texts, structuralists have been more successful in their discussion of works which contain large portions of 'shadow' ('a little ideology, a little mimesis, some subject'), works which make considerable use of traditional codes, and in which, therefore, they can locate the moments of indeterminacy, uncertainty, excess. It is precisely the traditional work, the work that could not be written today, that may most benefit from criticism, and the criticism which encounters the greatest success is one which attends to its strangeness, awakening in it a drama whose actors are all those assumptions and operations which make the text the work of another period. We do not save Balzac by making him relevant – by reading him, for example, as a critic of capitalist society – but by emphasizing his strangeness: the immense pedagogic confidence, the faith in intelligibility, the pre-individualistic conception of character, the conviction that rhetoric may become the instrument of truth; in short, the difference of his approach to the problems of meaning and order.

A criticism which focuses on the adventures of meaning is perhaps better suited than any other to what ought to be the major task of criticism: that of making the text interesting, of combating the boredom which lurks behind every work, waiting to move in if reading goes astray or founders. 'Il n'y a pas d'ennui *sincère*', says Barthes. One cannot, finally, be bored in good faith because boredom draws attention to certain aspects of the work (to particular modes of failure) and enables one to make the text interesting by inquiring how and why it bores. 'L'ennui n'est pas loin de la jouissance: il est la jouissance vue des rives du plaisir' (Boredom is not far from ecstasy; it is ecstasy seen from the shores of pleasure) (*ibid.*, p. 43). A boring text fails to be what one desires; if one were able to make it a challenge to one's desire, to locate an angle from which it could be viewed as refusal or dislocation, then it would be *un texte de jouissance*; but when one views it from the shores of pleasure and refuses to accept its challenge, it becomes simply an absence of pleasure. A semiological criticism should succeed in reducing the possibilities of boredom by teaching one to find challenges and peculiarities in works which the perspective of pleasure alone would make boring.

Criticism usually ignores boredom. A model which enables one to speak of it or which makes it the background against which reading takes place strikes a realistic and salutary note. For one thing, the different rhythms of reading, which affect the structuring of the text, appear to result from that most compelling of imperatives: the desire to escape boredom. 'If you read slowly, read *every word* of a novel by Zola, the book will fall from your hands' (*ibid.*, p. 23). When reading a nineteenth-century novel we speed up and slow down, and the rhythm of our reading is a recognition of structure: we can pass quickly through those descriptions and conversations whose functions identify; we wait for something more important, at which point we slow down. If we reversed this rhythm we would no doubt become bored. With a modern text that we cannot organize as the adventures of a character, we cannot skip and modulate our speed in the same way without encountering opacity and boredom; we must read more slowly, savouring the drama of the sentence, exploring local indeterminacies, and working out the general project which they promote or resist: 'ne pas dévorer, ne pas avaler, mais brouter, tondre avec minutie' (*ibid.*, pp. 23–4). We cannot devour or gobble up but must graze, carefully nibbling each piece of grass. A criticism based on a theory of reading ought at least to have the virtue of being ready to ask, for whatever works it is studying, which operations of reading will be most appropriate to minimize boredom and to awaken the drama latent in every text.

Indeed, one might suppose that structuralism would attempt, as Barthes suggests, to develop an esthetics based on the pleasure of the reader ('the consequences would be enormous').[2] Whatever its other results, it would no doubt lead to the destruction of various myths of literature. We would no longer need to make organic unity a standard of value but might allow it to function simply as a hypothesis of reading, for we would be more aware that our pleasure often comes from the fragment, the incongruous detail, the charming excess of certain descriptions and elaborations, the well-constructed sentence whose elegance exceeds its function, or the flaws in a grand design. We might no longer need to assume that because an author selected all the words and sentences of his text they all deserve to be read with equal care but could recognize that our pleasure and admiration may depend on a variable rhythm of reading. If we did not revere the literary work quite so much we might enjoy it rather more, and there is no surer road to enjoyment of this kind than a criticism which attempts to make explicit the conventions of reading and the costs and benefits of applying them to various works.

But pleasure is not the only value that a structuralist study of literature might serve. It is a concept that made its appearance rather late in structuralist discussions, as though it could only be offered as a value once one had defended the position in other terms. The basic claim would be that a criticism which studies the production of meaning casts light on one of the most fundamental human activities, which takes place in the text itself and in the reader's encounter with the text. Man is not just *homo sapiens* but *homo significans*: a creature who gives sense to things. Literature offers an example or image of the creation of meaning, but that is only half of its function. As fiction it stands in a peculiar relation to the world; its signs must be completed, reordered, brought into the realm of experience by the reader. It thus exhibits all the unhappiness and uncertainties of the sign and invites the reader to participate in the production of meaning so as to overcome or at least take cognizance of them. The opening sentence of a novel, for example, is a very bizarre thing: 'Emma Woodhouse, handsome, clever, and rich, with a comfortable home and happy disposition, seemed to unite some of the best blessings of existence; and had lived nearly twenty-one years in the world with very little to distress or vex her.' The sentence offers an image of confidence, of fullness of meaning and organization; but at the same time it is incomplete; the reader must do something with it, must recognize the insufficiency of language on its own, and must try to bring it within an order of signs so that it may satisfy. Literature offers the best of occasions for exploring the complexities of order and meaning.

The structuralist or semiological project is ruled by a double imperative, intellectual and moral. 'Nous ne sommes rien d'autre, en dernière analyse, que notre système écriture/lecture', writes Sollers (*Logiques*, p. 248). In the final analysis we are nothing other than our system of reading and writing. We read and understand ourselves as we follow the operations of our understanding and, more important, as we experience the limits of that understanding. To know oneself is to study the intersubjective processes of articulation and interpretation by which we emerge as part of a world. He who does not write, Sollers would say – he who does not actively take up and work upon this system – is himself 'written' by the system. He becomes the product of a culture which eludes him. And thus, as Barthes says, 'the fundamental ethical problem is to recognize signs wherever they are; that is to say, not to mistake signs for natural phenomena and to proclaim them rather than conceal them' ('Une problématique du sens', p. 20). Structuralism has succeeded in unmasking many signs; its task must now be to organize itself more coherently so as to explain how these signs work. It must try to formulate the rules of particular systems of convention rather than simply affirm their existence. The linguistic model, properly applied, may indicate how to proceed, but it can do little more than that. It has helped to provide a perspective, but as yet we understand very little about how we read.

Notes

Chapter 1   The linguistic foundation

1 C. Lévi-Strauss, *Anthropologie structurale*. The article was first published in *Word* in 1945.
2 Cf. N. C. W. Spence, 'A hardy perennial: the problem of *la langue* and *la parole*'.
3 See Lévi-Strauss, *op. cit.*, p. 306; and Dan Sperber, 'Le structuralisme en anthropologie', pp. 222–3.
4 C. Hockett, *A Manual of Phonology*, p. 17. Cf. N. Chomsky, *Language and Mind*, p. 61; and M. Halle, 'The strategy of phonemics', p. 198.
5 C. Lévi-Strauss, *Le Totémisme aujourd'hui*, p. 130. Cf. A. J. Greimas, *Sémantique structurale*, pp. 18–25.
6 See R. Barthes, *Mythologies*, pp. 193–247.
7 See M. Foucault, *Naissance de la clinique*.
8 Ludwig Wittgenstein, *Philosophical Investigations* (Oxford, 1963), p. 59.
9 C. Hockett, 'A formal statement of morphemic analysis', p. 27. Cf. B. Bloch and G. L. Trager, *Outline of Linguistic Analysis*, p. 68; and N. Chomsky, 'A Transformational Approach to Syntax', p. 212.
10 See N. Chomsky, *ibid.*, p. 221; C. Hockett, 'Two models of grammatical description', pp. 223–4; and, for a general discussion of the problem, Chomsky, *Current Issues in Linguistic Theory*, pp. 75–95.
11 M. Joos, *The English Verb* (Madison, Wisc., 1964), p. 3.
12 J. Kristeva, *Semiotikè*, p. 281; cf. p. 174.
13 Carl Hempel, 'Fundamentals of Taxonomy', in *Aspects of Scientific Explanation* (New York, 1965), pp. 137–54.
14 See J. Culler, 'Phenomenology and structuralism'.
15 See E. Donato, 'Of structuralism and literature', p. 558; and J.-M. Benoist, 'The end of structuralism', pp. 40–53.
16 M. Heidegger, *Der Satz vom Grund* (Pfullingen, 1957), p. 161.
17 See J. Lacan, *Ecrits*, pp. 93–100.

Chapter 2   The development of a method: two examples ʼ

1 T. Todorov, 'De la sémiologie à la rhétorique', p. 1323. Cf. J. Kristeva, *Semiotikè*, pp. 60–89.
2 Vol. 1: *Le Cru et le cuit*; vol. 2: *Du Miel aux cendres*; vol. 3: *L'Origine des manières de table*; vol. 4: *L'Homme nu.*
3 R. Poole, 'Structures and materials', p. 21. Cf. Todorov, *op. cit.*
4 J. Viet, *Les Méthodes structuralistes dans les sciences sociales*, p. 78. He was referring to Lévi-Strauss's first method.
5 J. A. Boon, *From Symbolism to Structuralism*, p. 97. For discussion see my review, *The Human Context* 5 : 1 (1973).
6 C. Lévi-Strauss, *L'Origine des manières de table*, p. 160, and 'Le sexe des astres', p. 1168.
7 See G. Genette, *Figures II*, pp. 101–22.

Chapter 3   Jakobson's poetic analyses

1 P. Valéry, *Œuvres*, ed. Jean Hytier (Paris, 1957) I, p. 1440.
2 J. Mukarovsky, 'Standard Language and Poetic Language', p. 19. The concept derives from Russian Formalism.
3 For examples see *Questions de poétique*, pp. 285–483; N. Ruwet, *Langage, musique, poésie*, pp. 151–247; J. Geninasca, *Analyse structurale des 'Chimères' de Nerval*. The example discussed here is 'Une microscopie du dernier "Spleen" dans les *Fleurs du Mal*', from *Questions de poétique*.
4 See M. Grevisse, *Le Bon Usage*, 8th edition (Paris, 1964), p. 378.
5 J. Culler, 'Jakobson and the linguistic analysis of literary texts', p. 56. Jakobson's reply is in *Questions de poétique*, pp. 496–7.
6 L. Cellier, *Où en sont les recherches sur Gérard de Nerval*, Archives des lettres modernes 3 (May 1957), p. 24. Cf. Cellier, 'Sur un vers des *Chimères*', *Cahiers du Sud* 311 (1952).

Chapter 4   Greimas and structural semantics

1 J. Katz and J. Fodor, 'The Structure of a Semantic Theory'. Cf. Katz, 'Semi-Sentences'.
2 The best discussion, though it does not touch on literary problems, is by E. U. Grosse, 'Zur Neuorientierung der Semantik bei Greimas'. J.-C. Coquet's review, 'Questions de sémantique structurale', is un-critical. See also Stephen Ullmann's review in *Lingua* 18 (1967).
3 But see C. Zilberberg, 'Un essai de lecture de Rimbaud'; J.-C. Coquet, 'Combinaison et transformation en poésie', and 'Problèmes de l'analyse structurale du récit: *L'Etranger* d'Albert Camus'.
4 See C. J. Fillmore, 'The Case for Case'; J. M. Anderson, 'Ergative and nominative in English', *Journal of Linguistics* 4 (1968); and M. A. K. Halliday, 'Notes on transitivity and theme in English', *ibid.* 3 (1967) and 4 (1968).
5 See T. A. van Dijk, 'Some problems of generative poetics'; I. Bellert,

'On a condition of the coherence of texts'; L. Lonzi, 'Anaphore et récit'; and W. Kummer, 'Outlines of a model for a grammar of discourse', *Poetics* 3 (1972).

6 See J.-P. Richard, *L'Univers imaginaire de Mallarmé* (Paris, 1961); and *Paysage de Chateaubriand* (Paris, 1967).

7 F. Rastier, 'Systématique des isotopies', p. 96. He correctly identifies the goal but does not achieve it.

8 T. A. van Dijk, 'Sémantique structurale et analyse thématique', p. 41. Cf. P. Madsen, 'Poétiques de contradiction'.

9 A. J. Greimas, *Essais des sémiotique poétique*, p. 19. Unfortunately, Greimas does not discuss this problem.

Chapter 5   Linguistic metaphors in criticism

1 J.-P. Richard, *Poésie et profondeur* (Paris, 1955), p. 9; J. Starobinski, 'Remarques sur le structuralisme', p. 277.

2 See his contribution to *Structuralism: Ah Introduction*, ed. Robey.

3 M. Proust, *A la recherche du temps perdu*, ed. Clarac and Ferré (Paris, 1954), I, p. 855.

4 J. L. Austin, 'Performative-Constative', in *Philosophy and Ordinary Language*, ed. C. Caton (Urbana, Ill., 1963). Cf. E. Benveniste, *Problèmes de linguistique générale*, pp. 269–76.

Chapter 6   Literary competence

1 Harold Bloom, *The Visionary Company* (New York, 1961), p. 42.

2 *ibid.*

3 P. Valéry, *Œuvres*, II, pp. 629 and I, pp. 1439–41.

4 Ludwig Wittgenstein, *Philosophical Investigations*, p. 59.

5 See N. Chomsky, *Aspects of the Theory of Syntax*, p. 19.

6 L. Wittgenstein, *op. cit.*, p. 144.

Chapter 7   Convention and naturalization

1 A. Thibaudet, *Physiologie de la critique* (Paris, 1930), p. 141.

2 J. Derrida, *De la grammatologie*, p. 23. Cf. *La Voix et le phénomène*, *passim*.

3 Plato, *Phaedrus*. Cf. J. Derrida, 'La pharmacie de Platon', in *La Dissémination*.

4 Mme de Lafayette, 'La Comtesse de Tende' in *Romans et nouvelles*, ed. E. Magne (Paris, 1961), p. 410.

5 Domairon, *Rhétorique française*, quoted by G. Genette, *Figures*, p. 206.

6 See Genette, *op. cit.*, pp. 205–21; M. Foucault, *Les Mots et les choses*, pp. 57–136; and J. Culler, 'Paradox and the language of morals in La Rochefoucauld'.

7 G. Genot, 'L'écriture libératrice', p. 52. Cf. J. Kristeva, *Semiotikè*, pp. 211–16.

8 Ludwig Wittgenstein, *Tractatus Logico-Philosophicus* (London, 1961), p. 7.
9 S. Heath, 'Structuration of the Novel-Text', p. 74. Cf. *The Nouveau Roman*, p. 21.
10 M. Proust, *A la recherche du temps perdu*, II, p. 406.
11 J. P. Stern, *On Realism* (London, 1973), p. 121.
12 Cf. F. Jameson, 'La Cousine Bette and allegorical realism', p. 244.
13 See J. Culler, *Flaubert: The Uses of Uncertainty*, chapter II, section e.
14 See T. Kavanagh, *The Vacant Mirror*, *passim*.
15 Agatha Christie, *The Body in the Library*, ch. I.
16 W. Empson, *Some Versions of Pastoral* (Harmondsworth, 1966), p. 52.
17 See S. Heath, *The Nouveau Roman*, *passim*; and Kristeva, *op. cit.*, pp. 174–371.
18 *Parodies*, ed. D. Macdonald (London, 1964), p. 218.
19 See B. Tomashevsky, 'Thematics', pp. 78–92.

Chapter 8   Poetics of the lyric

1 See G. Genette, *Figures II*, pp. 150–1.
2 Ludwig Wittgenstein, *Zettel* (Oxford, 1967), p. 28.
3 Robert Graves, *The Common Asphodel* (London, 1949), p. 8.
4 See R. Jakobson, 'Shifters, Verbal Categories, and the Russian Verb', in *Selected Writings*, II, pp. 130–47; E. Benveniste, *Problèmes de linguistique générale*, pp. 225–66; and J. Lyons, *Introduction to Theoretical Linguistics*, pp. 275–81.
5 See M. A. K. Halliday, 'Descriptive Linguistics in Literary Studies', pp. 57–9.
6 John Ashbery, *The Tennis Court Oath* (Middletown, Conn., 1962), p. 13.
7 John Ashbery, *Rivers and Mountains* (New York, 1967), p. 39.
8 J. C. Ransom, 'Art worries the naturalists', *Kenyon Review* 7 (1945), pp. 294–5.
9 Kurt Koffka, *Principles of Gestalt Psychology* (New York, 1935), p. 110.
10 E. H. Gombrich, *Art and Illusion* (London, 1959).
11 See William Carlos Williams, *Collected Earlier Poems* (Norfolk, Conn., 1951), p. 354.
12 J. Cohen, *Structure du langage poétique*, pp. 165–82. The same, of course, applies to other types of poetic parallelism.
13 See P. de Man, *Blindness and Insight*, p. 185.
14 See W. K. Wimsatt, *The Verbal Icon* (Lexington, Ky, 1954), pp. 98–100.
15 See J. Culler, 'Paradox and the language of morals in La Rochefoucauld'.
16 See C. Brooke-Rose, *A Grammar of Metaphor*, pp. 146–205.
17 R. Barthes, *Le Degré zéro de l'écriture*, p. 37. Cf. the passage from Mallarmé's 'Quant au livre' quoted in chapter 10.
18 Gabriel Pearson, 'Lowell's Marble Meanings', in *The Survival of Poetry*, ed. M. Dodsworth (London, 1970), p. 74. See V. Forrest-Thomson, 'Levels in poetic convention'.

19 The best discussion of convention and naturalization in poetry is V. Forrest-Thomson, *Poetic Artifice*.
20 Donald Davie, 'Syntax as Music in Paradise Lost', in *The Living Milton*, ed. F. Kermode (London, 1960), p. 73. Cf. Christopher Ricks, *Milton's Grand Style* (Oxford, 1963).
21 I. Fónagy, *Die Metaphern in der Phonetik* (The Hague, 1963). Cf. T. Todorov, 'Le sens des sons'.
22 G. Hartman, *The Unmediated Vision* (New York, 1966), p. 103.
23 See H. Kenner, 'Some Post-Symbolist Structures', p. 392.
24 D. Davie, *Purity of Diction in English Verse* (London, 1967), p. 137.
25 Tristan Tzara, *40 Chansons et déchansons* (Montpellier, 1972), number 5.

Chapter 9 Poetics of the novel

1 See S. Heath, *The Nouveau Roman*, pp. 187–8.
2 J. Ricardou, *Problèmes du nouveau roman*, p. 25. Cf. Heath, *op. cit.*, pp. 146–9.
3 R. Barthes, 'Ce qu'il advient au signifiant', preface to Pierre Guyotat, *Eden, Eden, Eden* (Paris, 1970), p. 9.
4 R. Barthes, 'Introduction à l'analyse structurale des récits', p. 19. Cf. G. Prince, 'Introduction à l'étude du narrataire'.
5 B. Morrissette, *Les Romans de Robbe-Grillet* (Paris, 1963). Cf. Heath, *op. cit.*, pp. 118–21.
6 R. J. Sherrington, *Three Novels by Flaubert* (Oxford, 1970), p. 83. Cf. J. Culler, *Flaubert*, II, section c.
7 C. Lévi-Strauss, 'L'analyse morphologique des contes russes', p. 142; and A. J. Greimas, *Du Sens*, p. 187.
8 J. Rutherford, 'The Structure of Narrative' (unpublished manuscript), Queen's College, Oxford.
9 C. Bremond, 'Observations sur la *Grammaire du Décaméron*', p. 207. Todorov accepts this point.
10 S. Chatman, 'New ways of analysing narrative structure', p. 6. Chatman does distinguish between 'implicit kernels' and 'explicit kernels'. For further discussion see J. Culler, 'Defining Narrative Units'.
11 W. B. Gallie, *Philosophy and Historical Understanding* (London, 1964), p. 26, and pp. 22–50 *passim*.
12 C. Lévi-Strauss, 'Le triangle culinaire'; *Le Cru et le cuit*, p. 344; and *L'Origine des manières de table*, p. 249.
13 Coleridge, *Miscellaneous Criticism*, ed. T. Raysor (London, 1936), p. 30.
14 See J. Culler, *Flaubert*, ch. III, section c; and P. de Man, 'The Rhetoric of Temporality', in *Interpretation: Theory and Practice*, ed. C. Singleton (Baltimore, 1969), pp. 173–209.
15 Cf. J. Culler, *Flaubert*, ch. II, sections d and e.
16 Barthes, 'Introduction à l'analyse structurale des récits', p. 16. Cf. T. Todorov, *Grammaire du Décaméron*, pp. 27–30.
17 T. Todorov, *Littérature et signification*, pp. 58–64. Cf. S. Chatman, 'On the formalist-structuralist theory of character'.
18 S. Chatman, 'The structure of fiction', p. 212. Cf. C. Bremond, *Logique du récit, passim*.

Chapter 10   'Beyond' structuralism: *Tel Quel*

1 S. Mallarmé, 'Quant au livre', *Œuvres complètes*, ed. Mondor and Jean-Aubry (Paris, 1945), p. 386.
2 Ludwig Wittgenstein, *Philosophical Investigations*, p. 18.
3 See J. Starobinski, *Les Mots sous les mots: les anagrammes de Ferdinand de Saussure*.
4 J. Kristeva, *Semiotikè*, p. 293. Cf. 'Linguistique et littérature' (Colloque de Cluny), pp. 69–71.

Chapter 11   Conclusion: structuralism and the qualities of literature

1 See F. de Saussure, *Cours*, p. 43.
2 R. Barthes, *Le Plaisir du texte*, p. 94. For a sketch of the varieties (neuroses) of reading, see pp. 99–100.

Bibliography

When an author has published a collection of his articles I cite only the collection, unless I have quoted from an article in its original place of publication.

Where English translations of French texts are available I cite titles, publishers and dates.

'Analyse structurale du récit', *Communications* 8 (1966).

ANDREYEV, N., 'Models as a tool in the development of linguistic theory', *Word* 18 (1962), pp. 186–97.

ARON, THOMAS, 'Une seconde révolution saussurienne?', *Langue française* 7 (1970), pp. 56–62.

ARRIVÉ, MICHEL, *Les Langages de Jarry*, Klincksieck, Paris, 1972.

— 'Postulats pour la description linguistique des textes littéraires', *Langue française* 3 (1969), pp. 3–13.

AUZIAS, JEAN-MARIE, *Clefs pour le structuralisme*, Seghers, Paris, 1968.

AVALLE, D'ARCO SILVIO, *L'Analisi letteraria in Italia: Formalismo strutturalismo, semiologia*, Ricciardi, Milan, 1970.

— 'Systems and structures in the folktale', *Twentieth Century Studies* 3 (1970), pp. 67–75.

— 'La sémiologie de la narrativité chez Saussure', *Essais de la théorie du texte*, ed. C. Bouazis, Galilée, Paris, 1973, pp. 17–50.

BADIOU, ALAIN, *Le Concept de modèle*, Maspero, Paris, 1969.

BARBUT, MARC, 'Sur le sens du mot "structure" en mathématiques', *Les Temps modernes* 246 (1966), pp. 791–814.

BARTHES, ROLAND (for a bibliography containing most of the items listed below and others, see *Tel Quel* 47 (1971), pp. 126–32).

— 'Action Sequence', *Patterns of Literary Style*, ed. J. Strelka, Pennsylvania State University Press, 1971, pp. 5–14.

— 'L'analyse rhétorique', in *Littérature et société*, Institut de Sociologie

de l'Université libre de Bruxelles, 1967, pp. 31–45 (Tr. in E. and T. Burns, *Sociology of Literature and Drama*).
— 'L'analyse structurale du récit: à propos d'Actes 10–11', *Recherches des sciences religieuses* 58 (1970), pp. 17–38.
— 'L'ancienne rhétorique: aide mémoire', *Communications* 16 (1970), pp. 172–229.
— 'A Conversation with Roland Barthes', *Signs of the Times*, Granta, Cambridge, 1971, pp. 41–55.
— *Critique et vérité*, Seuil, Paris, 1966.
— *Le Degré zéro de l'écriture, suivi de nouveaux essais critiques* (1st ed. 1953), Seuil, Paris, 1972 (Tr. *Writing Degree Zero*, Cape 1967, Beacon 1970).
— 'Digressions' (interview), *Promesse* 29 (1971), pp. 15–32.
— 'Le discours de l'histoire', *Social Science Information* 6:4 (1967), pp. 65–75 (Tr. in M. Lane (ed.), *Structuralism: A Reader*).
— 'Drame, poème, roman', *Théorie d'ensemble*, Seuil, Paris, 1968, pp. 25–40.
— 'Du nouveau en critique', *Esprit* 23 (1955), pp. 1778–81.
— 'Ecrivains, intellectuels, professeurs', *Tel Quel* 47 (1971), pp. 3–18.
— 'L'effet de réel', *Communications* 11 (1968), pp. 84–9.
— 'Eléments de sémiologie', *Communications* 4 (1964), pp. 91–135 (Tr. *Elements of Semiology*, Cape 1967, Hill & Wang 1968, Beacon 1970).
— *L'Empire des signes*, Skira, Geneva, 1970.
— 'Entretien avec Roland Barthes', *Aletheia* 4 (1966), pp. 213–18.
— *Essais critiques*, Seuil, Paris, 1964 (Tr. *Critical Essays*, Northwestern University Press 1972).
— 'Introduction à l'analyse structurale des récits', *Communications* 8 (1966), pp. 1–27.
— 'Langage et vêtement', *Critique* 142 (1959), pp. 242–52.
— 'Leçon d'écriture', *Tel Quel* 34 (1968), pp. 28–33.
— 'La linguistique du discours', in *Sign, Language, Culture*, ed. A. J. Greimas, Mouton, The Hague, 1970, pp. 580–4.
— 'Linguistique et littérature', *Langages* 12 (1968), pp. 3–8.
— 'Masculin, féminin, neutre', in *Échanges et communications: Mélanges offerts à Claude Lévi-Strauss*, ed. J. Pouillon, Mouton, The Hague, 1970, pp. 893–907.
— *Michelet par lui-même*, Seuil, Paris, 1954.
— 'La mode est au bleu cette année', *Revue française de sociologie* 1 (1960), pp. 147–62.
— *Mythologies* (1st ed. 1957), Seuil, Paris, 1970 (Tr. *Mythologies*, Cape, Hill & Wang 1972).
— *Le Plaisir du texte*, Seuil, Paris, 1973.
— 'Une problématique du sens', *Cahiers Média*, Service d'édition et de vente des productions de l'éducation nationale, 1 (1967–8), pp. 9–22.
— 'Réponses', *Tel Quel* 47 (1971), pp. 89–107.
— 'Rhétorique de l'image', *Communications* 4 (1964), pp. 40–51.
— *S/Z*, Seuil, Paris, 1970.
— *Sade, Fourier, Loyola*, Seuil, Paris, 1971.

— 'Science versus literature', *The Times Literary Supplement* (28 September 1967), pp. 897–8.
— 'Sociologie et sociologique', *Social Science Information* 1:4 (1962), pp. 114–22.
— 'Style and its Image', in *Literary Style: A Symposium*, ed. S. Chatman, Oxford, New York, 1971, pp. 3–10.
— *Sur Racine*, Seuil, Paris, 1963 (Tr. *On Racine*, Hill & Wang 1964).
— *Système de la mode*, Seuil, Paris, 1967.
— 'To Write: an Intransitive Verb', in *The Languages of Criticism and the Sciences of Man*, ed. R. Macksey and E. Donato, Johns Hopkins Press, Baltimore, 1970, pp. 134–45.
BASTIDE, R. (ed.), *Sens et usages du terme 'structure' dans les sciences humaines et sociales*, Mouton, The Hague, 1962.
BEAUJOUR, MICHEL, 'The game of poetics', *Yale French Studies* 41 (1968), pp. 58–67.
BELLERT, IRENA, 'On a condition of the coherence of texts', *Semiotica* 2 (1970), pp. 335–63.
BENOIST, JEAN-MARIE, 'The end of structuralism', *Twentieth Century Studies* 3 (1970), pp. 31–54.
— 'The fictional subject', *Twentieth Century Studies* 6 (1971), pp. 88–97.
— 'Structuralism: a new frontier', *Cambridge Review* 93 (22 October 1971), pp. 10–17.
BENVENISTE, EMILE, *Problèmes de linguistique générale*, Gallimard, Paris, 1966 (Tr. *Problems in General Linguistics*, University of Miami 1970).
— 'Sémiologie de la langue', *Semiotica* 1 (1969), pp. 1–12 and 127–35.
— 'Structure de la langue et structure de la société', *Linguaggi nella società e nella tecnica*, Comunità, Milan, 1970, pp. 96–115.
BIERWISCH, MANFRED, 'Poetics and Linguistics', in *Linguistics and Literary Style*, ed. D. Freeman, Holt Rinehart, New York, 1970, pp. 96–115.
— 'Strukturalismus: Geschichte, Probleme und Methoden', *Kursbuch* 5 (1966), pp. 77–152.
BLOCH, B. (with G. L. TRAGER), *Outline of Linguistic Analysis*, Waverly, Baltimore, 1942.
BLOOMFIELD, MORTON, 'Allegory as interpretation', *New Literary History* 3 (1972), pp. 301–17.
— 'Generative Grammar and the Theory of Literature', *Actes du Xe congrès des linguistes* (1967), Rumanian Academy, Bucharest, 1969, vol. III, pp. 57–65.
BOON, JAMES A., *From Symbolism to Structuralism: Lévi-Strauss in a Literary Tradition*, Blackwell, Oxford, 1972.
BOOTH, STEPHEN, 'On the Value of *Hamlet*', *Reinterpretations of Elizabethan Drama* (English Institute Essays), ed. Rabkin, Columbia, New York, 1969, pp. 137–76.
BOOTH, WAYNE, *The Rhetoric of Fiction*, University of Chicago Press, 1961.
BOUAZIS, CHARLES (ed.), *Essais de la théorie du texte*, Galilée, Paris, 1973.

BOUDON, RAYMOND, *A quoi sert la notion de 'structure'?*, Gallimard, Paris, 1968 (Tr. *Uses of Structuralism*, Heinemann 1971).

— 'Le structuralisme', *Contemporary Philosophy*, ed. Klibansky, Nuova Italia, Florence, 1969, vol. III, pp. 296–302.

BRANDT, PER AAGE, 'Dom Juan ou la force de la parole', *Poétique* 12 (1972), pp. 584–95.

— 'La pensée du texte (de la littéralité de la littérarité)', *Essais de la théorie du texte*, ed. C. Bouazis, Galilee, Paris, 1973, pp. 183–215.

BREMOND, CLAUDE, 'La logique des possibles narratifs', *Communications* 8 (1966), pp. 60–76.

— *Logique du récit*, Seuil, Paris, 1973.

— 'Le message narratif', *Communications* 4 (1964), pp. 4–32.

— 'Observations sur la *Grammaire du Décaméron*', *Poétique* 6 (1971), pp. 200–22.

BRØNDAL, VIGGO, *Essais de linguistique générale*, Munksgaard, Copenhagen, 1943.

BROOKE-ROSE, CHRISTINE, *A Grammar of Metaphor*, Secker & Warburg, London, 1958.

BROOKS, CLEANTH, *The Well-Wrought Urn*, Harcourt & Brace, New York, 1947.

BROWNE, R. M., 'Typologie des signes littéraires', *Poétique* 7 (1971), pp. 334–53.

BURNS, ELIZABETH and TOM (eds), *Sociology of Literature and Drama*, Penguin, Harmondsworth, 1973.

BURRIDGE, K. O. L., 'Lévi-Strauss and Myth', in *The Structural Study of Myth and Totemism*, ed. E. Leach, Tavistock, London, 1967, pp. 91–118.

BUYSSENS, ERIC, *Les Langages et le discours*, Office de publicité, Brussels, 1943.

CALVINO, ITALO, 'Notes towards a definition of the narrative form as a combinative process', *Twentieth Century Studies* 3 (1970), pp. 93–101.

CASSIRER, ERNST, 'Structuralism in modern linguistics', *Word* 1 (1945), pp. 99–120.

CAWS, PETER, 'Structuralism', *Partisan Review*, 35:1 (1968), pp. 75–91.

CHARBONNIER, GEORGES, *Entretiens avec Claude Lévi-Strauss*, Plon, Paris, 1961 (Tr. *Conversations with Claude Lévi-Strauss*, Cape, Grossman 1969).

CHATMAN, SEYMOUR (ed.), *Essays on the Language of Literature*, Houghton Mifflin, Boston, 1967.

— (ed.), *Literary Style: A Symposium*, Oxford University Press, New York, 1971.

— 'New ways of analysing narrative structure', *Language and Style* 2 (1969), pp. 3–36.

— 'On the formalist-structuralist theory of character', *Journal of Literary Semantics* 1 (1972), pp. 57–79.

— 'The structure of fiction', *University Review*, Kansas City (spring 1971), pp. 199–214.

CHOMSKY, NOAM, *Aspects of the Theory of Syntax*, MIT, Cambridge, Mass., 1965.
— *Current Issues in Linguistic Theory*, Mouton, The Hague, 1964.
— 'Degrees of Grammaticalness', in *The Structure of Language*, ed. J. Fodor and J. Katz, Prentice-Hall, Englewood Cliffs, N.J., 1964, pp. 384–9.
— *Language and Mind*, Harcourt Brace, New York, 1968.
— Review of B. F. Skinner's *Verbal Behaviour*, *The Structure of Language*, ed. J. Fodor and J. Katz, Prentice-Hall, Englewood Cliffs, N.J., 1964, pp. 547–78.
— 'Some Empirical Issues in the Theory of Transformational Grammar', *Goals of Linguistic Theory*, ed. S. Peters, Prentice-Hall, Englewood Cliffs, N.J., 1972, pp. 63–130.
— 'Some methodological remarks on generative grammar', *Word* 17 (1961), pp. 219–39.
— *Syntactic Structures*, Mouton, The Hague, 1957.
— 'A Transformational Approach to Syntax', in *The Structure of Language*, ed. J. Fodor and J. Katz, Prentice-Hall, Englewood Cliffs, N.J., 1964, pp. 211–45.
— (with M. HALLE), 'Some controversial questions in phonological theory', *Journal of Linguistics* 1 (1965), pp. 97–138.
COHEN, JEAN, 'La comparaison poétique: essai de systématique', *Langages* 12 (1968), pp. 43–51.
— 'Poésie et motivation', *Poétique* 11 (1972), pp. 432–45.
— *Structure du langage poétique*, Flammarion, Paris, 1966.
— 'Théorie de la figure', *Communications* 16 (1970), pp. 3–25.
COQUET, JEAN-CLAUDE, 'Combinaison et transformation en poésie', *L'Homme* 9 (1969), pp. 23–41.
— 'L'objet stylistique', *Le Français moderne* 35 (1967), pp. 53–67.
— 'Poétique et linguistique', in *Essais de sémiotique poétique*, ed. A. J. Greimas, Larousse, Paris, 1971, pp. 26–44.
— 'Problèmes de l'analyse structurale du récit: *L'Etranger* d'Albert Camus', *Langue française* 3 (1969), pp. 61–72.
— 'Questions de sémantique structurale', *Critique* 248 (1968), pp. 70–85.
CORVEZ, MAURICE, *Les Structuralistes*, Aubier-Montaigne, Paris, 1969.
COSERIU, EUGENIO, 'Sistema, norma, e "parole" ', *Studi Linguistici in onore di Vittore Pisani*, Paideia, Brescia, 1969, pp. 235–53.
CRANE, R. S., *The Languages of Criticism and the Structure of Poetry*, University of Toronto Press, 1953.
CUISENIER, JEAN, 'Le structuralisme du mot, de l'idée, et des outils', *Esprit* 35 (1967), pp. 825–42.
CULLER, JONATHAN, 'Defining Narrative Units', in *Style and Structure in Literature*, ed. R. Fowler, Blackwell, Oxford, 1974.
— *Flaubert: The Uses of Uncertainty*, Elek, London, 1974.
— 'Jakobson and the linguistic analysis of literary texts', *Language and Style* 5:1 (1971), pp. 53–66.
— 'The Linguistic Basis of Structuralism', in *Structuralism: An Introduction*, ed. D. Robey, Oxford University Press, 1973, pp. 20–36.

— 'Paradox and the language of morals in La Rochefoucauld', *Modern Language Review* 68 (1973), pp. 28–39.
— 'Phenomenology and structuralism', *The Human Context* 5 (1973), pp. 35–42.
— 'Structure of ideology and ideology of structure', *New Literary History* 4 (1973), pp. 471–82.
— 'Structural semantics and poetics', *Centrum* 1 (1973), pp. 5–22.
DAVIE, DONALD (ed.), *Poetics*, Proceedings of the International Congress of Work in Progress, Polish Scientific Publishers, Warsaw, 1961.
DEBRAY-GENETTE, RAYMONDE, 'Les figures du récit dans "Un Cœur simple" ', *Poétique* 3 (1970), pp. 348–64.
DE GEORGE, RICHARD and FERNANDE (ed.), *The Structuralists*, Doubleday, New York, 1972.
DEGUY, MICHEL, 'La folie de Saussure', *Critique* 260 (1969), pp. 20–6.
DELEUZE, GILLES, *Différence et répétition*, PUF, Paris, 1968.
— *Logique du sens*, Minuit, Paris, 1969.
— *Proust et les signes*, rev. ed., PUF, Paris, 1970 (Tr. *Proust and Signs*, Braziller, Allen Lane, 1972).
DERRIDA, JACQUES, *De la grammatologie*, Minuit, Paris, 1967.
— *La Dissémination*, Seuil, Paris, 1972.
— *L'Ecriture et la différence*, Seuil, Paris, 1967.
— *Marges de la philosophie*, Minuit, Paris, 1972.
— *Positions*, Minuit, Paris, 1972.
— 'Sémiologie et grammatologie', *Social Science Information* 7:3 (1968), pp. 135–48 (also in *Positions*).
— *La Voix et le phénomène*, PUF, Paris, 1967.
DIJK, TEUN A. VAN, 'Aspects d'une théorie générative du texte poétique', in *Essais de sémiotique poétique*, ed. A. J. Greimas, Larousse, Paris, 1971, pp. 180–206.
— 'Foundation for a typology of texts', *Semiotica* 4 (1972), pp. 298–324.
— 'Modèles génératifs en théorie littéraire', in *Essais de la théorie du texte*, ed. C. Bouazis, Galilée, Paris, 1973, pp. 79–99.
— 'Neuere Entwicklungen in der literarischen Semantik', in *Text, Bedeutung, Ästhetik*, ed. S. Schmidt, Bayerischer Schulbuch Verlag, Munich, 1970, pp. 106–35.
— 'On the foundations of poetics', *Poetics* 5 (1972), pp. 89–123.
— 'Sémantique générative et théorie des textes', *Linguistics* 62 (1970), pp. 66–95.
— 'Sémantique structurale et analyse thématique', *Lingua* 23 (1969), pp. 28–54.
— *Some Aspects of Text Grammars*, Mouton, The Hague, 1972.
— 'Some problems of generative poetics', *Poetics* 2 (1971), pp. 5–35.
DOLEŽEL, LUBOMÍR, 'Toward a Structural Theory of Content in Prose Fiction', in *Literary Style: A Symposium*, ed. S. Chatman, Oxford University Press, New York, 1971, pp. 95–110.
— 'Vers la stylistique structurale', *Travaux linguistiques de Prague* (new series) 1 (1966), pp. 257–66.

DONATO, EUGENIO, 'Of structuralism and literature', *Modern Language Notes* 82 (1967), pp. 549–74.

DORFLES, GILLO, 'Pour ou contre une esthétique structuraliste?', *Revue internationale de philosophie* 73–4 (1965), pp. 409–41.

DOUBROVSKY, SERGE, *Pourquoi la nouvelle critique*, Mercure, Paris, 1966.

DOUGLAS, MARY, 'The Meaning of Myth, with special reference to "La geste d'Asdiwal" ', in *The Structural Study of Myth and Totemism*, ed. E. Leach, Tavistock, London, 1967, pp. 49–70.

— *Purity and Danger*, Routledge & Kegan Paul, London, 1966.

DUBOIS, JACQUES, *et al.*, *Rhétorique générale*, Larousse, Paris, 1970.

DUCROT, OSWALD, 'La commutation en glossématique et en phonologie', *Word* 23 (1967), pp. 101–21.

— 'Le structuralisme en linguistique', in *Qu'est-ce que le structuralisme?*, ed. F. Wahl, Seuil, Paris, 1968, pp. 15–96.

DUPRIEZ, BERNARD, *L'Étude des styles, ou la commutation en littérature*, Didier, Paris, 1969.

DUVERNOIS, PIERRE, 'L'emportement de l'écriture', *Critique* 302 (1972), pp. 595–609.

ECO, UMBERTO, *Apocalittici e integrati*, Bompiani, Milan, 1964.

— 'Codice e ideologie', *Linguaggi nella società e nella tecnica*, Comunità, Milan, 1970, pp. 129–42.

— 'La critica semiologica', in *I metodi attuali della critica in Italia*, ed. M. Corte and C. Segre, ERI, Turin, 1970, pp. 369–87.

— *Le forme del contenuto*, Bompiani, Milan, 1971.

— 'James Bond: une combinatoire narrative', *Communications* 8 (1966), pp. 77–93.

— *L'opera aperta*, Bompiani, Milan, 1962.

— *La struttura assente: Introduzione alla ricerca semiologica*, Bompiani, Milan, 1968.

EHRMANN, JACQUES, 'L'homme en jeu', *Critique* 266 (1969), pp. 579–607.

— 'Structures of exchange in *Cinna*', *Yale French Studies* 36–7 (1966), pp. 169–99.

EICHENBAUM, BORIS, 'The Theory of the "Formal Method" ', in *Russian Formalist Criticism*, ed. L. T. Lemon and M. J. Reis, University of Nebraska Press, Lincoln, 1965, pp. 99–139.

EMPSON, WILLIAM, *Seven Types of Ambiguity* (1st ed., 1930), Penguin, Harmondsworth, 1961.

ERLICH, VICTOR, *Russian Formalism: History-Doctrine*, Mouton, The Hague, 1955.

FAYE, JEAN-PIERRE, *Le Récit hunique*, Seuil, Paris, 1967.

FILLMORE, C. J., 'The Case for Case', in *Universals in Lingui Theosticry* ed. E. Bach and R. Harms, Holt Rinehart, New York, 1968, pp. 1–88.

— 'On Generativity', in *Goals of Linguistic Theory*, ed. S. Peters, Prentice-Hall, Englewood Cliffs, N.J., 1972, pp. 1–19.

FODOR, J. (with J. KATZ) (ed.), *The Structure of Language*, Prentice-Hall, Englewood Cliffs, N.J., 1964.

FONTANIER, PIERRE, *Les Figures du discours* (1821), Flammarion, Paris, 1968.

FORREST-THOMSON, VERONICA, 'Irrationality and artifice: a problem in recent poetics', *British Journal of Aesthetics* 11 (1971), pp. 123–33.

— 'Levels in poetic convention', *Journal of European Studies* 2 (1971), pp. 35–51.

— *Poetic Artifice: A Theory of Twentieth Century Poetry*, Blackwell, Oxford, 1974.

FOUCAULT, MICHEL, *L'Archéologie du savoir*, Gallimard, Paris, 1969 (Tr. *The Archeology of Knowledge*, Pantheon, Tavistock 1972).

— 'La bibliothèque fantastique', in *Flaubert*, ed. R. Debray-Genette, Miroir de la critique, Paris, 1970, pp. 170–90.

— 'Distance, aspect, origine', in *Théorie d'ensemble*, Seuil, Paris, 1968, pp. 11–24.

— *Folie et déraison: Histoire de la folie à l'âge classique*, Plon, Paris, 1961 (Tr. *Madness and Civilization*, Pantheon 1965, Tavistock 1967).

— 'Le langage à l'infini', *Tel Quel* 15 (1963), pp. 44–53.

— *Les Mots et les choses*, Gallimard, Paris, 1966 (Tr. *The Order of Things*, Tavistock 1970, Pantheon 1971).

— *Naissance de la clinique*, PUF, Paris, 1963.

— *L'Ordre du discours*, Gallimard, Paris, 1971 (Tr. in *The Archeology of Knowledge*, Pantheon, Tavistock 1972).

— *Raymond Roussel*, Gallimard, Paris, 1963.

— 'Réponses au cercle d'épistémologie', *Cahiers pour l'analyse* 9 (1968), pp. 9–40.

— 'Un si cruel savoir', *Critique* 182 (1962), pp. 597–611.

— 'Theatrum philosophicum', *Critique* 282 (1970), pp. 885–908.

— (*et al.*), 'Débat sur le roman', *Tel Quel* 17 (1964), pp. 12–54.

FREEMAN, DONALD (ed.), *Linguistics and Literary Style*, Holt Rinehart, New York, 1970.

FRIEDRICH, HUGO, 'Structuralismus und Struktur in literaturwissenschaftlicher Hinsicht', in *Europäische Aufklärung: Herbert Dieckmann zum 60 Geburtstag*, Fink, Munich, 1967, pp. 77–86.

FRYE, NORTHROP, *Anatomy of Criticism* (1st ed. 1957), Atheneum, New York, 1965.

GANDILLAC, M., *et al.* (ed.), *Entretiens sur les notions de genèse et de structure*, Mouton, The Hague, 1965.

GARDIN, J.-C., 'Semantic analysis procedures in the sciences of man', *Social Science Information* 8:1 (1969), pp. 17–42.

GARDINER, A. M., 'De Saussure's analysis of the *signe linguistique*', *Acta Linguistica* 4:3 (1944), pp. 107–10.

GARVIN, PAUL, *On Linguistic Method*, Mouton, The Hague, 1964.

— (ed.), *A Prague School Reader on Esthetics, Literary Structure and Style*, Georgetown University Press, Washington, 1964.

GENETTE, GÉRARD, 'Avatars du Cratylisme', *Poétique* 11 (1972), pp. 367–94, 13 (1973), pp. 111–33, and 15 (1973) 265–91.

— *Figures*, Seuil, Paris, 1966; *Figures II*, 1969; *Figures III*, 1972.

GENINASCA, JACQUES, *Analyse structurale des Chimères de Gérard de Nerval*, La Baconnière, Neuchâtel, 1971.

GENOT, GÉRARD, 'L'écriture libératrice', *Communications* 11 (1968), pp. 34–58.

GODEL, ROBERT, *Les Sources manuscrites du Cours de linguistique générale de F. de Saussure*, Droz & Minard, Geneva, 1957.

GOLDMANN, LUCIEN, *Le Dieu caché*, Gallimard, Paris, 1959 (Tr. *The Hidden God*, Routledge & Kegan Paul, 1964).

— 'Ideology and writing', *The Times Literary Supplement* (28 September 1967), pp. 903–5.

— *Pour une sociologie du roman*, Gallimard, Paris, 1964.

GOODMAN, NELSON, *The Languages of Art*, Oxford University Press, London, 1969.

GOUX, J.-J., 'Numismatiques', *Tel Quel* 35 (1968), pp. 64–89 and 36 (1969), pp. 54–74.

GRANGER, GILLES, *Essai d'une philosophie du style*, Armand Colin, Paris, 1968.

— *Pensée formelle et sciences de l'homme*, Aubier-Montaigne, Paris, 1960.

GREIMAS, A. J., 'Le conte populaire russe (analyse fonctionnelle)', *International Journal of Slavic Linguistics and Poetics* 9 (1965), pp. 152–75.

— *Du Sens*, Seuil, Paris, 1970.

— (ed.), *Essais de sémiotique poétique*, Larousse, Paris, 1971.

— 'La linguistique statistique et la linguistique structurale', *Le Français moderne* 30 (1962), pp. 241–52 and 31 (1963), pp. 55–68.

— *Sémantique structurale*, Larousse, Paris, 1966.

— (ed.), *Sign, Language, Culture*, Mouton, The Hague, 1970.

GRITTI, JULES (pseudonym 'J.-B. FAGES'), *Comprendre le structuralisme*, Privat, Toulouse, 1967.

— (same pseudonym), *Le Structuralisme en procès*, Privat, Toulouse, 1968.

GROSSE, E. U., 'Zur Neuorientierung der Semantik bei Greimas: Grundgedanken, Probleme und Vorschläge', *Zeitschrift für Romanische Philologie* 57 (1971), pp. 359–93.

GUENOUN, DENIS, 'A propos de l'analyse structurale des récits', *La Nouvelle Critique* (special issue, Colloque de Cluny,) (1968), pp. 65–70.

— 'Le Récit clandestin', *La Nouvelle Critique* 39 bis, second Colloque de Cluny (1971), pp. 61–8.

— 'Sur les tâches de la critique', *La Pensée* 139 (1968), pp. 61–75.

GUILLÉN, CLAUDIO, *Literature as System*, Princeton University Press, 1971.

GUIRAUD, PIERRE, *La Sémiologie*, PUF, 1971.

HALLE, MORRIS, 'In Defence of the Number Two,' in *Studies Presented to Joshua Whatmough*, Mouton, The Hague, 1957, pp. 65–72.

— 'The strategy of phonemics', *Word* 10 (1954), pp. 197–209.

HALLIDAY, M. A. K., 'Categories of the theory of grammar', *Word* 17 (1961), pp. 241–92.

— 'Descriptive Linguistics in Literary Studies', in *Patterns of Language* (with A. MCINTOSH), Longmans, London, 1966, pp. 56–69.

— 'Language Structure and Language Function', in *New Horizons in Linguistics*, ed. J. Lyons, Penguin, Harmondsworth, 1970, pp. 140–65.

— 'Linguistic Function and Literary Style', in *Literary Style: A Symposium*, ed. S. Chatman, Oxford University Press, New York, 1971, pp. 330–65.

HAMMOND, MAC, 'Poetic Syntax', in *Poetics*, ed. D. Davie, Proceedings of the International Congress of Work in Progress, Polish Scientific Publishers, Warsaw, 1961, pp. 475–82.

HAMON, PHILIPPE, 'Pour un statut sémiologique du personnage', *Littérature* 6 (1972), pp. 86–110.

— 'Qu'est-ce qu'une description?' *Poétique* 12 (1972), pp. 465–85.

HARARI, JOSUÉ, *Structuralists and Structuralisms* (a bibliography), Diacritics, Ithaca, 1971.

HARRIS, ZELLIG, *Methods in Structural Linguistics*, University of Chicago Press, 1951.

HARTMAN, GEOFFREY, *Beyond Formalism*, Yale University Press, New Haven, 1970.

HAUDRICOURT, A. G., 'Méthode scientifique et linguistique structurale', *L'Année sociologique* (1959), pp. 31–48.

HEATH, STEPHEN, 'Ambiviolences', *Tel Quel* 50 (1972), pp. 22–43 and 51 (1972), pp. 64–76.

— *The Nouveau Roman: A Study in the Practice of Writing*, Elek, London, 1972.

— (pseudonym, 'Cleanth Peters'), 'Structuration of the Novel-Text', *Signs of the Times*, Granta, Cambridge, 1971, pp. 52–78.

— 'Towards textual semiotics', *Signs of the Times*, Granta, Cambridge, 1971, pp. 16–40.

— 'Trames de lecture', *Tel Quel* 54 (1973), pp. 4–15.

HENDRICKS, W. O., 'Folklore and the structural analysis of literary texts', *Language and Style* 3 (1970), pp. 83–121.

— 'The structural study of narration: sample analyses', *Poetics* 3 (1972), pp. 100–23.

HJELMSLEV, LOUIS, *Essais linguistiques*, Travaux du cercle linguistique de Copenhague 12 (1959).

— *Prolegomena to a Theory of Language*, rev. ed., University of Wisconsin Press, Madison, 1961.

HOCKETT, C., *A Course in Modern Linguistics*, Macmillan, New York, 1958.

— 'A formal statement of morphemic analysis', *Studies in Linguistics* 10:2 (1952), pp. 27–39.

— *A Manual of Phonology*, Indiana University Press, Bloomington, 1955.

— *The State of the Art*, Mouton, The Hague, 1967.

— 'Two models of grammatical description', *Word* 10 (1954), pp. 210–33.

HOLLANDER, JOHN, ' "Sense Variously Drawn Out": Some Observations on English Enjambment', in *Literary Theory and Structure*, ed. F. Brady *et al.*, Yale University Press, New Haven, 1973, pp. 201–26.

HOUDEBINE, J.-L., 'Lecture(s) d'une refonte', *Critique* 287 (1971), pp. 318–50.

HOUSEHOLDER, FRED, *Linguistic Speculations*, Cambridge University Press, 1971.

IHWE, JENS, 'Kompetenz und Performanz in der Literaturtheorie', in *Text, Bedeutung, Ästhetik*, ed. S. Schmidt, Bayerischer Schulbuch Verlag, Munich, 1970, pp. 136–52.

— 'On the foundations of a general theory of narrative structure', *Poetics* 3 (1972), pp. 5–14.

ISER, WOLFGANG, 'The reading process: a phenomenological approach', *New Literary History* 3 (1972), pp. 279–99.

JAKOBSON, ROMAN (for a bibliography see *Janua Linguarum* series minor, no. 134, Mouton, The Hague, 1971).

— 'The Grammatical Texture of a Sonnet from Sir Philip Sidney's "Arcadia" ', in *Studies in Language and Literature in Honour of M. Schlauch*, Polish Scientific Publishers, Warsaw, 1966, pp. 165–73.

— 'Linguistics and Poetics', in *Style in Language*, ed. T. Sebeok, MIT Press, Cambridge, 1960, pp. 350–77.

— 'Linguistics in its Relations to Other Sciences', in *Actes du Xe congrès international des linguistes*, Rumanian Academy, Bucharest, 1969, vol. I, pp. 75–111.

— 'On the verbal art of William Blake and other poet-painters', *Linguistic Enquiry* 1 (1970), pp. 3–23 (Tr. in *Questions de poétique*).

— 'Poetry of grammar and grammar of poetry', *Lingua* 21 (1968), pp. 597–609 (Tr. in *Questions de poétique*).

— *Questions de poétique*, Seuil, Paris, 1973.

— *Selected Writings*, Mouton, The Hague, vol. I: *Phonological Studies*, 1962; vol. II: *Word and Language*, 1971; vol. III: *Poetry of Grammar and Grammar of Poetry*, forthcoming; vol. IV: Slavic Epic Studies, 1966.

— (with P. COLACLIDES), 'Grammatical Imagery in Cavafy's Poem "Remember Body" ', *Linguistics* 20 (1966), pp. 51–9.

— (with M. HALLE), *Fundamentals of Language*, Mouton, The Hague, 1956.

— (with LAWRENCE JONES), *Shakespeare's Verbal Art in 'Th'Expence of Spirit'*, Mouton, The Hague, 1970 (Tr. in *Questions de poétique*).

— (with PAULO VALESIO), 'Vocabulorum constructio in Dante's Sonnet "Se vedi li occhi miei" ', *Studi Danteschi* 43 (1966), pp. 7–33 (Tr. in *Questions de poétique*).

JAMESON, FREDRIC, 'La Cousine Bette and allegorical realism', *PMLA* 86 (1971), pp. 241–54.

— *Marxism and Form*, Princeton University Press, 1971.

— 'Metacommentary', *PMLA* 86 (1971), pp. 9–18.

— *The Prison House of Language: A Critical Account of Structuralism and Russian Formalism*, Princeton University Press, 1972.

JOHANSEN, SVEND, 'La notion de signe dans la glossématique et dans l'esthétique', *Travaux du cercle linguistique de Copenhague* 5 (1949), pp. 288–303.

JONES, ROBERT, *Panorama de la nouvelle critique en France*, SEDES, Paris, 1968.

JOSIPOVICI, GABRIEL, 'Structures of truth: the premises of the French new criticism', *Critical Quarterly* 10 (1968), pp. 72–88.

JUILLAND, ALPHONSE, *Outline of a General Theory of Structural Relations*, Mouton, The Hague, 1964.

KATZ, JERROLD, 'Semi-Sentences', in *The Structure of Language*, ed. J. Fodor and J. Katz, Prentice-Hall, Englewood Cliffs, N.J., 1964, pp. 400–16.

— (with J. FODOR), 'The Structure of a Semantic Theory', *ibid.*, pp. 479–518.

KAVANAGH, THOMAS, *The Vacant Mirror: A Study of Mimesis through Diderot's 'Jacques le fataliste'*, Studies on Voltaire and the Eighteenth Century 104 (1973).

KENNER, HUGH, 'Some Post-Symbolist Structures', in *Literary Theory and Structure*, ed. F. Brady *et al.*, Yale University Press, New Haven, 1973, pp. 379–94.

KOCH, WALTER, *Recurrence and a Three Modal Approach to Poetry*, Mouton, The Hague, 1966.

KRISTEVA, JULIA, 'Comment parler à la littérature', *Tel Quel* 47 (1971), pp. 27–49.

— 'Distance et anti-représentation', *Tel Quel* 32 (1968), pp. 49–53.

— 'Du sujet en linguistique', *Langages* 24 (1971), pp. 107–26.

— (signed J. Joyeaux), *Le Langage, cet inconnu*, SGPP & Planète, Paris, 1969.

— 'Matière, sens, dialectique', *Tel Quel* 44 (1971), pp. 17–34.

— 'La mutation sémiotique', *Annales* 25 (1970), pp. 1497–522.

— 'Narration et transformation', *Semiotica* 1 (1969), pp. 422–48.

— 'Objet, complément, dialectique', *Critique* 285 (1971), pp. 99–131.

— 'Problèmes de la structuration du texte', in *Théorie d'ensemble*, Seuil, Paris, 1968, pp. 298–317.

— 'Sémanalyse et production de sens', *Essais de sémiotique poétique*, ed. A. J. Greimas, Larousse, Paris, 1971, pp. 207–34.

— 'La sémiologie comme science des idéologies', *Semiotica* 1 (1969), pp. 196–204.

— 'The semiotic activity', *Signs of the Times*, Granta, Cambridge, 1971, pp. 1–10.

— *Semiotikè: Recherches pour une sémanalyse*, Seuil, Paris, 1969.

— 'Le sujet en procès', *Tel Quel* 52 (1972), pp. 12–30 and 53 (1973), pp. 17–38.

— *Le Texte du roman: Approche sémiologique d'une structure discursive transformationnelle*, Mouton, The Hague, 1970.

LACAN, JACQUES, *Écrits*, Seuil, Paris, 1966.

— 'Lituraterre', *Littérature* 3 (1971), pp. 3–10.

— 'Of Structure as an Inmixing of an Otherness Prerequisite to any Subject Whatever', in *The Languages of Criticism and the Sciences of Man*, ed. R. Macksey and E. Donato, Johns Hopkins Press, Baltimore, 1970, pp. 186–95.

LANE, MICHAEL (ed.), *Structuralism: A Reader*, Cape, London, 1970.

LAPORTE, ROGER, 'L'empire des signifiants', *Critique* 302 (1972), pp. 583–94.

LAVERS, ANNETTE, 'En traduisant Barthes', *Tel Quel* 47 (1971), pp. 115–25.

— 'Some Aspects of Language in the Work of Jacques Lacan', *Semiotica* 3 (1971), pp. 269–79.

LEACH, EDMUND, *Genesis as Myth and Other Essays*, Cape, London, 1969.

— 'Language and Anthropology', in *Linguistics at Large*, ed. Minnis, Gollancz, London, 1971, pp. 137–58.

— *Lévi-Strauss*, Fontana, London, 1970.

— 'Lévi-Strauss in the Garden of Eden: an examination of some recent developments in the analysis of myth', *Transactions of the N.Y. Academy of Science*, series II, 23 (1961), pp. 386–96.

— (ed.), *The Structural Study of Myth and Totemism*, Tavistock, London, 1967.

— 'Telstar et les aborigènes, ou *La Pensée sauvage*', *Annales* 19 (1964), pp. 1100–15.

LEECH, G. N., *A Linguistic Guide to English Poetry*, Longmans, London, 1969.

LEFEBVE, MAURICE-JEAN, 'Rhétorique du récit', *Poetics* 2 (1971), pp. 119–34.

LEFEBVRE, HENRI, *Au-delà du structuralisme*, Anthropos, Paris, 1971.

LEPSCHY, G. C., *A Survey of Structural Linguistics*, Faber & Faber, London, 1970 (new ed. 1973).

LEVI, JIRI, 'Generative Poetics', in *Sign, Language, Culture*, ed. A. J. Greimas, Mouton, The Hague, 1970, pp. 548–57.

LEVIN, SAMUEL, 'The Conventions of Poetry', in *Literary Style: A Symposium*, ed. S. Chatman, Oxford University Press, New York, 1971, pp. 177–93.

— *Linguistic Structures in Poetry*, Mouton, The Hague, 1962.

LÉVI-STRAUSS, CLAUDE, 'L'analyse morphologique de contes russes', *International Journal of Slavic Linguistics and Poetics* 3 (1960), pp. 122–49.

— *Anthropologie structurale*, Plon, Paris, 1958 (Tr. *Structural Anthropology*, Basic Books 1963, Allen Lane 1968).

— 'The Bear and the Barber', *The Journal of the Royal Anthropological Institute* 93 (1963), pp. 1–11.

— 'Comment ils meurent', *Esprit* 39 (1971), pp. 694–706.

— 'Critères scientifiques dans les disciplines sociales et humaines', *Aletheia* 4 (1966), pp. 189–212.

— *Le Cru et le cuit*, Plon, Paris, 1964 (Tr. *The Raw and the Cooked*, Harper Row 1969, Cape 1970).

— *Du Miel aux cendres*, Plon, Paris, 1966 (Tr. *From Honey to Ashes*, Cape, 1973).

— 'Four Winnebago Myths: A Structural Sketch', in *Culture in History*, ed. S. Diamond, Columbia, New York, 1960, pp. 351–62.

— 'La geste d'Asdiwal', *Annuaire de l'Ecole pratique des Hautes Etudes* (Section des sciences religieuses), 1958–9, pp. 3–43 (Tr. in *The Structural Study of Myth and Totemism*, ed. E. Leach, Tavistock, London, 1967).

— *L'Homme nu*, Plon, Paris, 1971.

— 'Introduction à l'œuvre de Marcel Mauss', in Mauss, *Sociologie et anthropologie*, PUF, Paris, 1950, pp. ix–lii.
— *Leçon inaugurale* (5 January 1960) Collège de France, Gallimard, Paris, 1960 (Tr. *The Scope of Anthropology*, Cape 1967).
— *L'Origine des manières de table*, Plon, Paris, 1968.
— *La Pensée sauvage*, Plon, Paris, 1962 (Tr. *The Savage Mind*, University of Chicago Press, Weidenfeld 1966).
— 'Réponses à quelques questions', *Esprit* 31 (1963), pp. 628–53.
— 'Le sexe des astres', in *To Honour Roman Jakobson*, Mouton, The Hague, 1967, vol. II, pp. 1163–70 (Tr. in M. Lane, *Structuralism: A Reader*).
— 'Le temps du mythe', *Annales* 26 (1971), pp. 533–40.
— *Le Totémisme aujourd'hui*, PUF, Paris, 1962 (Tr. *Totemism*, Beacon 1963, Merlin 1964, Penguin 1969).
— 'Le triangle culinaire', *L'Arc* 26 (1965), pp. 19–29.
— *Tristes tropiques*, Plon, Paris, 1955 (Tr. Atheneum 1964).
'Linguistique et littérature', *La Nouvelle Critique* (special issue, Colloque de Cluny, 1968).
'Linguistique et littérature', *Langages* 12 (1968).
'Le linguistique et le sémiologique', *Le Français moderne* 40:3 (1972).
LONGACRE, ROBERT, *Grammar Discovery Procedures*, Mouton, The Hague, 1964.
LONZI, LIDIA, 'Anaphore et récit', *Communications* 16 (1970), pp. 133–42.
LOTRINGER, SYLVÈRE, 'Vice de forme', *Critique* 286 (1971), pp. 195–209.
LYONS, JOHN, *Introduction to Theoretical Linguistics*, Cambridge University Press, 1968.
— (ed.), *New Horizons in Linguistics*, Penguin, Harmondsworth, 1970.
— *Structural Semantics*, Blackwell, Oxford, 1963.
MACHEREY, PIERRE, *Pour une théorie de la production littéraire*, Maspero, Paris, 1966.
MACKSEY, RICHARD (with E. DONATO) (ed.), *The Languages of Criticism and the Sciences of Man*, Johns Hopkins Press, Baltimore, 1970.
MADSEN, PETER, 'Poétiques de contradiction', in *Essais de la théorie du texte*, ed. C. Bouazis, Galilée, Paris, 1973, pp. 100–41.
MALLAC, GUY DE (with M. EBERNACH), *Barthes*, Éditions Universitaires, Paris, 1971.
MAN, PAUL DE, *Blindness and Insight: Essays in the Rhetoric of Contemporary Criticism*, Oxford University Press, New York, 1971.
MARC-LIPIANSKY, MIREILLE, *Le Structuralisme de Lévi-Strauss*, Payot, Paris, 1973.
MARTINET, ANDRÉ, *Eléments de linguistique générale*, Armand Colin, Paris, 1960 (Tr. *Elements of General Linguistics*, Faber, University of Chicago 1964).
MÉLÉTINSKI, E., 'L'étude structurale et typologie du conte', in V. Propp, *Morphologie du conte*, Seuil, Paris, 1970, pp. 201–54.
MELEUC, SERGE, 'Structure de la maxime', *Langages* 13 (1969), pp. 69–99.
MERLEAU-PONTY, MAURICE, *Signes*, Gallimard, Paris, 1960 (Tr. *Signs*, Northwestern University Press 1964).

— *Le Visible et l'invisible*, Gallimard, Paris, 1964 (Tr. *The Visible and the Invisible*, Northwestern University Press 1969).

MESCHONNIC, HENRI, *Pour la poétique*, Gallimard, Paris, 1970; vols II and III, 1973.

MESSING, GORDON, 'The Impact of Transformational Grammar upon Stylistic and Literary Analysis', *Linguistics* 66 (1971), pp. 56–73.

METZ, CHRISTIAN, *Essai sur la signification au cinéma*, Klincksieck, Paris, 1968; vol. II, 1972.

— *Langage et cinéma*, Larousse, Paris, 1971 (Tr. *The Language of Film*, Praeger 1973).

MILLER, JACQUES-ALAIN, 'Action de la structure', *Cahiers pour l'analyse* 9 (1968), pp. 91–103.

MILLET, LOUISE (with M. D'AINVELLE), *Le Structuralisme*, Editions Universitaires, Paris, 1970.

MITCHELL, T. F., 'Linguistic "goings on": collocations and other lexical matters arising on the syntagmatic record', *Archivum Linguisticum* (new series) 2 (1971), pp. 35–70.

MOLES, ABRAHAM, 'La linguistique: méthode de découverte interdisciplinaire', *Revue philosophique* 3 (1966), pp. 375–89.

MOLINO, JEAN, 'La connotation', *La Linguistique* 7 (1971), pp. 5–30.

MOORE, TIM, *Lévi-Strauss and the Cultural Sciences* (Centre for Contemporary Cultural Studies, Occasional Pamphlet no. 4), Birmingham (no date).

MORAVCSIK, J. M. E., 'Linguistic theory and the philosophy of language', *Foundations of Language* 3 (1967), pp. 209–33.

MOULOUD, NOEL, *Langage et structures: Essai de logique et de séméiologie*, Payot, Paris, 1969.

MOUNIN, GEORGES, *Introduction à la sémiologie*, Minuit, Paris, 1970.

MUKAROVSKY, J., 'L'art comme fait sémiologique', *Poétique* 3 (1970), pp. 387–92.

— 'La dénomination poétique et la fonction esthétique', *Poétique* 3 (1970), pp. 392–8.

— 'The Esthetics of Language', in *A Prague School Reader*, ed. P. Garvin, Georgetown University Press, Washington, 1964, pp. 31–69.

— 'Standard Language and Poetic Language', in *A Prague School Reader*, ed. Garvin, Georgetown University Press, Washington, 1964, pp. 17–30.

NICOLAS, ANNE, 'Écriture et/ou linguistique', *Langue française* 7 (1970) pp. 63–75.

— 'R. Jakobson et la critique formelle', *Langue française* 3 (1969), pp. 97–101.

PAGNINI, MARCELLO, *Struttura letteraria e metodo crit'ca*, D'Anna, Messina, 1967.

PARAIN-VIAL, JEANNE, *Analyses structurales et idéologies structuralistes*, Privat, Toulouse, 1969.

PAZ, OCTAVIO, *Claude Lévi-Strauss: An Introduction*, Cape, London, 1970.

PEIRCE, CHARLES SANDERS, *Collected Papers*, 8 vols, Harvard University Press, Cambridge, 1931–58.

PETÖFI, JÁNOS, 'The syntactico-semantic organization of text-structures', *Poetics* 3 (1972), pp. 56–99.

PETTIT, PHILIP, 'Wittgenstein and the case for structuralism', *Journal of the British Society for Phenomenology* 3:1 (1972), pp. 46–57.

PIAGET, JEAN, *Le Structuralisme*, PUF, Paris, 1968 (Tr. *Structuralism*, Routledge & Kegan Paul, Basic Books 1970).

PICARD, RAYMOND, *Nouvelle critique ou nouvelle imposture*, Pauvert, Paris, 1965.

PIKE, KENNETH, *Language in Relation to a Unified Theory of Human Behaviour*, Mouton, The Hague, 1967.

PLEYNET, MARCELIN, 'La poésie doit avoir pour but . . .', *Théorie d'ensemble*, Seuil, Paris, 1968, pp. 94–126.

POOLE, ROGER, 'Introduction', in C. Lévi-Strauss, *Totemism*, Penguin, Harmondsworth, 1966, pp. 9–63.

— 'Lévi-Strauss: myth's magician', *New Blackfriars* 51 (1969), pp. 432–40.

— 'Structuralism and phenomenology: a literary approach', *Journal of the British Society for Phenomenology* 2:2 (1970), pp. 3–16.

— 'Structuralism side-tracked', *New Blackfriars* 52 (1969), pp. 533–44.

— 'Structures and materials', *Twentieth Century Studies* 3 (1970), pp. 6–30.

POP, MIHAI, 'La poétique du conte populaire', *Semiotica* 2 (1970), pp. 117–27.

POTTIER, BERNARD, 'Pensée structurée et sémiologie', *Bulletin hispanique* 60 (1958), pp. 101–12.

— *Systématique des éléments de relation*, Bibliothèque française et romane, series A, II, Geneva and Paris, 1962.

POUILLON, JEAN, 'L'analyse des mythes', *L'Homme* 6 (1966), pp. 100–5.

— 'Présentation: un essai de définition', *Les Temps modernes* 246 (1966), 769–90.

— (with P. MARANDA) (ed.), *Echanges et communications: Mélanges offerts à Claude Lévi-Strauss*, Mouton, The Hague, 1970.

PRICE, MARTIN, 'The Fictional Contract', in *Literary Theory and Structure*, ed. F. Brady *et al.*, Yale University Press, New Haven, 1973, pp. 151–78.

— 'The Other Self: Thoughts about Character in the Novel', in *Imagined Worlds: Essays . . . in Honour of John Butt*, ed. M. Mack, Methuen, London, 1968, pp. 279–99.

PRINCE, GERALD, 'Introduction à l'étude du narrataire', *Poétique* 14 (1973), pp. 178–96.

'Problèmes du structuralisme', *Les Temps modernes* 246 (1966 du).

PROPP, VLADIMIR, 'Fairy Tale Transformations', *Readings in Russian Poetics*, ed. L. Matejka and K. Pomorska, MIT Press, Cambridge, 1971, pp. 94–114.

— *Morphology of the Folktale*, Indiana Research Centre in Anthropology, Bloomington, 1958.

RASTIER, FRANÇOIS, 'Systématique des isotopies', in *Essais de sémiotique poétique*, ed. A. J. Greimas, Larousse, Paris, 1971, pp. 80–106.

'Recherches rhétoriques', *Communications* 16 (1970).

'Recherches sémiologiques', *Communications* 4 (1964).

REY-DEBOVE, JOSETTE, 'L'orgie langagière', *Poétique* 12 (1972), pp. 572–83.

RICARDOU, JEAN, *Pour une théorie du nouveau roman*, Seuil, Paris, 1971.

— *Problèmes du nouveau roman*, Seuil, Paris, 1967.

RICHARD, PHILIPPE, 'Analyse des *Mythologiques* de Claude Lévi-Strauss', *L'Homme et la société* 4 (1967), pp. 109–33.

RICHARDS, I. A., 'Jakobson's Shakespeare: the subliminal structures of a sonnet', *The Times Literary Supplement* (28 May 1970), pp. 589–90.

RICŒUR, PAUL, *Le Conflit des interprétations*, Seuil, Paris, 1969.

RIFFATERRE, MICHAEL, 'Describing poetic structures: two approaches to Baudelaire's "Les Chats" ', *Yale French Studies* 36–7 (1966), pp. 200–42 (Tr. in *Essais de stylistique structurale*).

— *Essais de stylistique structurale*, Flammarion, Paris, 1971.

— 'Le poème comme représentation', *Poétique* 4 (1970), pp. 401–18.

— 'Système d'un genre descriptif', *Poétique* 9 (1972), pp. 15–30.

ROBBE-GRILLET, ALAIN, *Pour un nouveau roman*, Minuit, Paris, 1963 (Tr. *Towards a New Novel*, Calder & Boyars 1970, Grove Press 1965).

ROBEY, DAVID (ed.), *Structuralism: An Introduction*, Oxford University Press, London, 1973.

ROSSI, ALDO, 'Strutturalismo e analisi letteraria', *Paragone* 180 (1964), pp. 24–78.

ROUSSET, JEAN, *Forme et signification*, Corti, Paris, 1964.

RUWET, NICOLAS, *Langage, musique, poésie*, Seuil, Paris, 1972.

SAID, EDWARD W., 'Abecedarium Culturae: Structuralism, Absence, Writing', in *Modern French Criticism*, ed. J. Simon, University of Chicago Press, 1972, pp. 341–92.

SARTRE, JEAN-PAUL, *Qu'est-ce que la littérature?*, Gallimard, Paris, 1948 (Tr. *What is Literature?*, Methuen 1950).

SAUMJAN, S. K., 'Semiotics and the Theory of Generative Grammar', in *Sign, Language, Culture*, ed. A. J. Greimas, Mouton, The Hague, 1970, pp. 244–55.

SAUSSURE, FERDINAND DE, *Cours de linguistique générale*, 3rd ed., Payot, Paris, 1967 (Tr. *Course in General Linguistics*, Peter Owen 1960, Philosophical Library 1959, Fontana 1974).

SCHOLTE, BOB, 'Lévi-Strauss's Penelopean effort: the analysis of myths', *Semiotica* 1 (1969), pp. 99–124.

— 'Lévi-Strauss's Unfinished Symphony: the analysis of myth', in *Claude Lévi-Strauss: The Anthropologist as Hero*, ed. Hayes, MIT Press, Cambridge, 1970, pp. 145–9.

SEARLE, JOHN, *Speech Acts*, Cambridge University Press, 1969.

SEBAG, LUCIEN, *Marxisme et structuralisme*, Payot, Paris, 1964.

SEBEOK, THOMAS (ed.), *Approaches to Semiotics*, Mouton, The Hague, 1964.

— (ed.), *Style in Language*, MIT Press, Cambridge, 1960.

SEGRE, CESARE, 'La critica strutturalistica', in *I Metodi attuali della critica in Italia*, ed. M. Corte and C. Segre, ERI, Turin, 1970, pp. 323–41.
— *I Segni e la critica*, Einaudi, Turin, 1969.
— 'Structuralism in Italy', *Semiotica* 4 (1971), pp. 215–39.
— 'Strutturalismo e critica', in *Catalogo generale de 'Il Saggiatore'*, Saggiatore, Milan, 1965.
SERRES, MICHEL, *Hermès ou la communication*, Minuit, Paris, 1968.
— *L'Interférence (Hermès II)*, Minuit, Paris, 1972.
SHKLOVSKY, VICTOR, 'Art as Technique', in *Russian Formalist Criticism*, ed. L. T. Lemon and M. J. Reis, University of Nebraska Press, Lincoln, 1965, pp. 3–24.
— 'The connection between devices of *Syuzhet* construction and general stylistic devices', *Twentieth Century Studies* 7–8 (1972), pp. 48–72.
— 'La construction de la nouvelle et du roman', in *Théorie de la littérature*, ed. T. Todorov, Seuil, Paris, 1965, pp. 170–96.
— 'The Mystery Novel: Dickens' *Little Dorrit*', in *Readings in Russian Poetics*, ed. L. Matejka and K. Pomorska, MIT Press, Cambridge, 1971, pp. 220–6.
— 'Sterne's *Tristram Shandy:* Stylistic Commentary', in *Russian Formalist Criticism*, ed. L. T. Lemon and M. J. Reis, University of Nebraska Press, Lincoln, 1965, pp. 25–57.
SIMONIS, YVAN, *Lévi-Strauss ou la 'Passion de l'inceste'*, Aubier Montaigne, Paris, 1968.
SMITH, BARBARA H., *Poetic Closure: A Study of How Poems End*, University of Chicago Press, 1968.
SOLLERS, PHILIPPE, *Logiques*, Seuil, Paris, 1968.
— 'R.B.', *Tel Quel* 47 (1971), pp. 19–26.
SOURIAU, ETIENNE, *Les Deux Cent Mille Situations dramatiques*, Flammarion, Paris, 1950.
SPENCE, N. C. W., 'A hardy perennial: the problem of *la langue* and *la parole*', *Archivum Linguisticum* 9 (1957), pp. 1–27.
SPERBER, DAN, 'Le structuralisme en anthropologie', in *Qu'est-ce que le structuralisme?*, Seuil, Paris, 1968, pp. 167–238.
STAROBINSKI, JEAN, 'Considérations sur l'état présent de la critique littéraire', *Diogène* 74 (1971), pp. 62–95.
— *Les Mots sous les mots: Les anagrammes de Ferdinand de Saussure*, Gallimard, Paris, 1971.
— *La Relation critique*, Gallimard, Paris, 1970.
— 'Remarques sur le structuralisme', in *Ideen und Formen: Festschrift für Hugo Friedrich*, Klostermann, Frankfurt, 1965, pp. 275–8.
STENDER-PETERSEN, A.,'Esquisse d'une théorie structurale de la littérature', *Travaux du cercle linguistique de Copenhague* 5 (1949), pp. 277–87.
'Structuralism', *Twentieth Century Studies* 3 (1970).
'Structuralism', *Yale French Studies* 36–7 (1966).
'Le structuralisme', *Aletheia* 4 (1966).
'Structuralismes: Idéologie et méthode', *Esprit* 35:5 (1967).

SUMPF, J., *Introduction à la stylistique du français*, Larousse, Paris, 1971.
TESNIÈRE, LUCIEN, *Eléments de syntaxe structurale*, Klincksieck, Paris, 1959.
Théorie d'ensemble, Seuil, Paris, 1968.
TODOROV, TZVETAN, 'Les anomalies sémantiques', *Langages* 1 (1966), pp. 100–23.
— 'Les catégories du récit littéraire', *Communications* 8 (1966), pp. 125–51.
— 'Connaissance de la parole', *Word* 23 (1967), pp. 500–17.
— 'De la sémiologie à la rhétorique', *Annales* 22 (1967), pp. 1322–7.
— 'La description de la signification en littérature', *Communications* 4 (1964), pp. 33–9.
— 'Les deux logiques du récit', *Lingua e stile* 6 (1971), pp. 365–78.
— 'The discovery of language: *Les Liaisons dangereuses* and *Adolphe*', *Yale French Studies* 45 (1970), pp. 113–26.
— 'Les études du style', *Poétique* 2 (1970), pp. 224–32.
— 'Formalistes et futuristes', *Tel Quel* 35 (1968), pp. 42–6.
— *Grammaire du Décaméron*, Mouton, The Hague, 1969.
— 'Histoire de la littérature', *Langue française* 7 (1970), pp. 14–19.
— 'Introduction', *Le Vraisemblable, Communications* 11 (1968), pp. 1–4.
— *Introduction à la littérature fantastique*, Seuil, Paris, 1970.
— 'Introduction à la symbolique', *Poétique* 11 (1972), pp. 273–308.
— *Littérature et signification*, Larousse, Paris, 1967.
— 'Meaning in literature', *Poetics* 1 (1971), pp. 8–15.
— 'Note sur le langage poétique', *Semiotica* 1 (1969), pp. 322–8.
— 'Perspectives sémiologiques', *Communications* 7 (1966), pp. 139–45.
— 'The Place of Style in the Structure of the Text', in *Literary Style: A Symposium*, ed. S. Chatman, Oxford University Press, New York, 1971, pp. 29–39.
— 'Poétique', in *Qu'est-ce que le structuralisme?*, Seuil, Paris, 1968, pp. 97–166.
— *Poétique de la prose*, Seuil, Paris, 1971.
— 'Roman Jakobson, poéticien', *Poétique* 7 (1971), pp. 275–86.
— 'Le sens des sons', *Poétique* 11 (1972), pp. 446–62.
— 'Synecdoques', *Communications* 16 (1970), pp. 26–35.
— (ed.), *Théorie de la littérature*, Seuil, Paris, 1965.
— 'Valéry's poetics', *Yale French Studies* 44 (1970), pp. 65–71.
TOGEBY, KNUD, 'Littérature et linguistique', *Orbis Litterarum* 22 (1967), pp. 45–8.
TOMASHEVSKY, BORIS, 'Thematics', *Russian Formalist Criticism*, ed. L. T. Lemon and M. J. Reis, University of Nebraska Press, Lincoln, 1965, pp. 61–95.
TRUBETZKOY, N., *Principes de phonologie*, Klincksieck, Paris, 1949 (Tr. *Principles of Phonology*, University of California Press 1969).
UITTI, KARL, *Linguistics and Literary Theory*, Prentice-Hall, Englewood Cliffs, N.J., 1969.
ULLMANN, STEPHEN, *Language and Style*, Blackwell, Oxford, 1964.
— *Principles of Semantics*, Blackwell, Oxford, 1963.

VACHEK, JOSEPH, *The Linguistic School of Prague*, Indiana University Press, Bloomington, 1966.

VAN LAERE, François, 'The problem of literary structuralism', *Twentieth Century Studies* 3 (1970), pp. 55–66.

VAN ROSSOM-GUYON, Françoise *Critique du roman*, Gallimard, Paris, 1970.

VELAN, YVES, 'Barthes', in *Modern French Criticism*, ed. Simon, University of Chicago Press, 1972, pp. 311–40.

VERNIER, FRANCE, *Une Science de la littérature est-elle possible?*, Editions de la nouvelle critique, Paris, 1972.

VERSTRAETEN, PIERRE, 'Esquisse pour une critique de la raison structuraliste', Unpublished doctoral dissertation (microfiches), Université libre de Bruxelles, 1964.

— 'Lévi-Strauss ou la tentation du néant', *Les Temps modernes* 206 and 207–8 (1963), pp. 66–109 and pp. 507–52.

VIET, JEAN, *Les Méthodes structuralistes dans les sciences sociales*, Mouton, The Hague, 1965.

'Le vraisemblable', *Communications* 11 (1968).

WAHL, FRANÇOIS, 'La philosophie entre l'avant et l'après du structuralisme', *Qu'est-ce que le structuralisme?*, Seuil, Paris, 1968.

WEINREICH, URIEL, 'Explorations in Semantic Theory', in *Current Trends in Linguistics*, vol. III, ed. T. Sebeok, Mouton, The Hague, 1966, pp. 395–477.

WEINRICH, HARALD, 'Structures narratives du mythe', *Poétique* 1 (1970), pp. 25–34.

— 'Tense and time', *Archivum linguisticum* (new series) 1 (1970), pp. 31–41.

WELLEK, RENÉ (with AUSTIN WARREN), *Theory of Literature*, 3rd ed., Cape, London, 1966.

— *Discriminations*, Yale University Press, New Haven, 1970.

WELLS, RULON, 'De Saussure's system of linguistics', *Word* 3 (1947), pp. 1–31.

— 'Distinctively human semiotic', *Social Science Information* 6:6 (1967), pp. 103–23.

WILDEN, ANTHONY, *The Language of the Self*, Johns Hopkins Press, Baltimore, 1968.

— *System and Structure: Essays on Communication and Exchange*, Tavistock, London, 1972.

YALMAN, NUR, 'The Raw: the Cooked: Nature: Culture – Observations on *Le Cru et le cuit*', in *The Structural Study of Myth and Totemism*, ed. E. Leach, Tavistock, London, 1967, pp. 71–90.

ZÉRAFFA, MICHEL, 'La poétique de l'écriture', *Revue d'esthétique* 24 (1971), pp. 384–401.

— *Roman et société*, PUF, Paris, 1971.

ZILBERBERG, CLAUDE, 'Un essai de lecture de Rimbaud', in *Essais de sémiotique poétique*, ed. A. J. Greimas, Larousse, Paris, 1971, pp. 140–54.

ZÓLKIEWSKI, STEFAN, 'Contribution au problème de l'analyse structurale', in *To Honour Roman Jakobson*, Mouton, The Hague, 1967, vol. III, pp. 2389–426.

— 'De l'intégration des études littéraires', in *Poetics*, ed. D. Davie, Proceedings of the International Congress of Work in Progress, Polish Scientific Publishers, Warsaw, 1961, pp. 763–94.

— 'Deux structuralismes', in *Sign, Language, Culture*, ed. A. J. Greimas, Mouton, The Hague, 1970, pp. 3–12.

ZUMTHOR, PAUL, *Essai de poétique médiévale*, Seuil, Paris, 1972.

Index

The most important discussions of a topic are indicated by page numbers in bold type. Works are indexed under their authors. Technical terms are defined on the first page listed in the entry.